RECUEIL DES COURS

435 (2024)

L'Académie de droit international de La Haye
honorée du prix Wateler de la Paix (1936, 1950), du prix Félix Houphouët-Boigny pour la recherche de la paix (1992), de l'ordre du Rio Branco, Brésil (1999), et de la médaille de l'Institut royal d'études européennes, Espagne (2000)

The Hague Academy of International Law
awarded the Wateler Peace Prize (1936, 1950), the Félix Houphouët-Boigny Peace Prize (1992), the Order of Rio Branco, Brazil (1999), and the Medal of the Royal Institute of European Studies, Spain (2000)

© Académie de droit international de La Haye, 2024
The Hague Academy of International Law, 2024

| Tous droits réservés | All rights reserved |

ISBN 978-90-04-69432-3

Printed by/Imprimé par Triangle Bleu, 59600 Maubeuge, France

ACADÉMIE DE DROIT INTERNATIONAL

FONDÉE EN 1923 AVEC LE CONCOURS DE LA
DOTATION CARNEGIE POUR LA PAIX INTERNATIONALE

RECUEIL DES COURS

COLLECTED COURSES OF THE HAGUE
ACADEMY OF INTERNATIONAL LAW

2024

Tome 435 de la collection

BRILL | NIJHOFF

Leiden/Boston

COMPOSITION DU CURATORIUM
DE L'ACADÉMIE DE DROIT INTERNATIONAL DE LA HAYE

PRÉSIDENT

Y. DAUDET, professeur émérite de l'Université Paris I (Panthéon-Sorbonne)

MEMBRES

M. BENNOUNA, juge à la Cour internationale de Justice

K. BOELE-WOELKI, doyenne de la faculté de droit de Bucerius, Hambourg ; présidente de l'Académie internationale de droit comparé

H. BUXBAUM, professeure à l'Université de l'Indiana

H. CHARLESWORTH, juge à la Cour internationale de Justice

G. CORDERO-MOSS, professeure à l'Université d'Oslo

D. P. FERNANDEZ ARROYO, professeur à l'école de droit de Sciences Po, Paris

M. T. INFANTE CAFFI, juge au Tribunal international du droit de la mer

B. B. JIA, professeur à l'Université de Tsinghua, Pékin

M. KAMTO, professeur à l'Université de Yaoundé II

M. M. MBENGUE, professeur à l'Université de Genève

D. MOMTAZ, professeur à l'Université de Téhéran

Y. NISHITANI, professeure à l'Université de Kyoto

N. J. SCHRIJVER, professeur émérite de l'Université de Leiden ; Conseiller d'Etat au Conseil d'Etat des Pays-Bas

L.-A. SICILIANOS, doyen de la faculté de droit de l'Université d'Athènes ; ancien président de la Cour européennne des droits de l'homme

P. TOMKA, juge et ancien président de la Cour internationale de Justice

T. TREVES, professeur émérite de l'Université de Milan ; ancien juge au Tribunal international du droit de la mer

SECRÉTAIRE GÉNÉRAL
DE L'ACADÉMIE DE DROIT INTERNATIONAL DE LA HAYE

J.-M. THOUVENIN, professeur à l'Université Paris-Nanterre

COMPOSITION OF THE CURATORIUM OF THE HAGUE ACADEMY OF INTERNATIONAL LAW

PRESIDENT

Y. DAUDET, Emeritus Professor at Paris I University (Panthéon-Sorbonne)

MEMBERS

M. BENNOUNA, Judge at the International Court of Justice

K. BOELE-WOELKI, Dean of Bucerius Law School, Hamburg; President of the International Academy of Comparative Law

H. BUXBAUM, Professor at Indiana University

H. CHARLESWORTH, Judge at the International Court of Justice

G. CORDERO-MOSS, Professor at the University of Oslo

D. P. FERNANDEZ ARROYO, Professor at the Sciences Po Law School, Paris

M. T. INFANTE CAFFI, Judge at the International Tribunal for the Law of the Sea

B. B. JIA, Professor at Tsinghua University, Beijing

M. KAMTO, Professor at the University of Yaoundé II

M. M. MBENGUE, Professor at the University of Geneva

D. MOMTAZ, Professor at the University of Tehran

Y. NISHITANI, Professor at Kyoto University

N. J. SCHRIJVER, Emeritus Professor at Leiden University; State Councillor at the Netherlands Council of State

L.-A. SICILIANOS, Dean of the Law Faculty of the University of Athens; former President of the European Court of Human Rights

P. TOMKA, Judge and former President of the International Court of Justice

T. TREVES, Emeritus Professor at the University of Milan; former Judge at the International Tribunal for the Law of the Sea

SECRETARY-GENERAL OF THE HAGUE ACADEMY OF INTERNATIONAL LAW

J.-M. THOUVENIN, Professor at the University Paris-Nanterre

ACADÉMIE DE DROIT INTERNATIONAL DE LA HAYE
— FONDÉE EN 1923 AVEC LE CONCOURS DE LA DOTATION CARNEGIE —
HONORÉE DU PRIX WATELER DE LA PAIX (1936, 1950), DU PRIX FÉLIX HOUPHOUËT-BOIGNY POUR LA RECHERCHE DE LA PAIX (1992), DE L'ORDRE DU RIO BRANCO, BRÉSIL (1999), ET DE LA MÉDAILLE DE L'INSTITUT ROYAL D'ÉTUDES EUROPÉENNES, ESPAGNE (2000)

L'Académie constitue un centre d'études et d'enseignement du droit international public et privé, et des sciences connexes. Son but est de faciliter l'examen approfondi et impartial des problèmes se rattachant aux rapports juridiques internationaux.

L'enseignement de l'Académie est principalement donné au Palais de la Paix, à La Haye, par des personnalités de différents États. Il porte sur le droit international, sous ses aspects théoriques et pratiques, et sur la jurisprudence internationale. La durée de ses deux principales sessions est en été de six semaines s'étendant sur les mois de juillet et d'août, et partagée en deux périodes, consacrées l'une au droit international public, l'autre aux relations privées internationales, et, en hiver, de trois semaines, consacrée en janvier au droit international. L'enseignement est dispensé en français ou en anglais, avec traduction simultanée dans l'autre langue. Les sessions de l'Académie se déroulent sous l'autorité du Secrétaire général.

L'enseignement de l'Académie est conçu dans un esprit à la fois pratique et hautement scientifique. Nettement différencié des enseignements similaires des universités et écoles nationales, il s'adresse à tous ceux qui possèdent déjà des notions de droit international et ont, par intérêt professionnel ou curiosité d'esprit, le désir de se perfectionner dans cette science.

Il n'existe pas de cadre permanent de professeurs à l'Académie. Le Curatorium, qui est le corps chargé de la direction scientifique de l'institution, et qui se compose de dix-huit membres appartenant statutairement à des nationalités différentes, adresse chaque année, en toute liberté, ses invitations aux personnes qu'il estime qualifiées pour donner un cours ou une conférence à l'Académie. Les personnes ayant donné des cours à l'Académie ne sont donc aucunement fondées à s'intituler professeur de ou à l'Académie de droit international de La Haye.

L'Académie décerne un diplôme à ceux des auditeurs qui, réunissant les qualifications spéciales exigées par le règlement en vigueur, auront subi avec succès des épreuves d'examen devant le jury de la session à laquelle ils se sont inscrits. Elle délivre en outre aux auditeurs un certificat attestant l'assiduité aux cours de l'Académie à la fin de la session suivie.

Toute personne désirant suivre l'enseignement de l'Académie doit faire parvenir par voie électronique au secrétariat de l'Académie, au Palais de la Paix, à La Haye, un formulaire d'inscription dûment rempli. L'Académie perçoit des droits d'inscription fixés par le Conseil d'administration de l'Académie.

Un programme de bourses d'études permettant d'assister aux cours d'été ou d'hiver est institué auprès de l'Académie. Le mode d'attribution de ces bourses fait l'objet d'un règlement disponible sur le site Internet de l'Académie.

Tous les cours professés à l'Académie durant les sessions d'été et d'hiver font, en principe, l'objet d'une publication dans le *Recueil des cours de l'Académie de droit international de La Haye*, ainsi que sur une plateforme Internet, dans la langue dans laquelle ils ont été professés. Certains cours sont également publiés ou réédités dans des collections spéciales.

THE HAGUE ACADEMY OF INTERNATIONAL LAW
— Founded in 1923 with the Support of the Carnegie Endowment —
Awarded the Wateler Peace Prize (1936, 1950), the Félix Houphouët-Boigny Peace Prize (1992), the Order of Rio Branco, Brazil (1999), and the Medal of the Royal Institute of European Studies, Spain (2000)

The Academy is an institution devoted to the study and teaching of Public and Private International Law and related fields. Its mission is to further the thorough and impartial examination of issues arising from international legal relations.

The courses of the Academy are dispensed principally at the Peace Palace in The Hague by personalities from different States. They deal with the theoretical and practical aspects of international law, including international jurisprudence. The duration of its two main sessions is, in Summer, of six weeks in July and August, divided into two periods of three weeks each, one devoted to Public International Law and the other to Private International Law, and, in Winter, of three weeks, in January, devoted to international law. They are taught in either English or in French, with simultaneous interpretation into the other language. The Secretary-General is responsible for managing the sessions of the Academy.

The education offered by the Academy is designed to be both practical and highly academically advanced. Clearly distinct from the teachings provided in national universities and law schools, it is intended for those who already possess some notion of international law and who, out of professional interest or intellectual curiosity, desire to deepen their knowledge in this field.

There is no permanent teaching staff at the Academy. The Curatorium, which is the body entrusted with the scientific management of the institution, and which consists of eighteen members of different nationalities, invites each year, in its unfettered discretion, whomsoever it deems best qualified to dispense a course or give a lecture at the Academy. It follows that no one who has lectured at the Academy is entitled to style himself or herself Professor of or at The Hague Academy of International Law.

The Academy awards a Diploma to those attendees who possess special qualifications as set out in the regulations, after having successfully passed examinations before the Jury of the session in which they are registered. It also delivers a certificate of attendance to registered attendees at the end of the session.

Anyone wishing to attend the courses at the Academy must send a completed electronic registration form to the Secretariat of the Academy at the Peace Palace in The Hague. The registration fee for each session of courses is fixed by the Administrative Board of the Academy.

The Academy manages a programme of scholarships to allocate at its discretion to attendees at the Summer and Winter Courses. The regulations governing scholarships are published on the website of the Academy.

All courses taught at the Academy during the Summer and Winter Courses are, in principle, published in the *Collected Courses of The Hague Academy of International Law*, which also exist in electronic format, in the language in which they were delivered. Some courses are also published or reissued in special collections.

GENERAL TABLE OF CONTENTS
TABLE GÉNÉRALE DES MATIÈRES

Rethinking the United Nations: 75 and Beyond, by Nawaf SALAM, Judge at the International Court of Justice...............	9-32
Le rôle du droit international dans le contrôle des sentences arbitrales, par Dominique HASCHER, Juge international à la Cour suprême de Singapour..	33-72
Legal Facets of the Practice of International Organizations, by Niels BLOKKER, Professor at Leiden University................	73-324

RETHINKING THE UNITED NATIONS:
75 AND BEYOND

by

NAWAF SALAM

N. SALAM

TABLE OF CONTENTS

Rethinking the United Nations: 75 and Beyond   17

BIOGRAPHICAL NOTE

Nawaf Salam, born 15 December 1953, in Beirut.

Since February 2018, served as Judge at the International Court of Justice. Previously, he served as Ambassador of Lebanon to the United Nations in New York (July 2007-Dec 2017) and represented Lebanon in the Security Council in 2010 and 2011, for its two-year term as non-permanent member. He assumed the Presidency of said Council for the months of May 2010 and September 2011. He also taught Political Science and International Law at the American University of Beirut and served as Chair of the Political Studies and Public Administration Department (2005-2007). Judge Salam was also Attorney at Law and counseled and represented various international and domestic, public and private entities in Beirut, Lebanon (1984-1989 and 1992-2007) and in Boston, USA (1989-1992). He holds a Doctorat d'Etat, from the Institut d'Etudes Politiques (Sciences Po), Paris, an LLM (Master of Laws) from Harvard Law School and a Doctorat in History from the Sorbonne University, Paris.

PRINCIPAL PUBLICATIONS

Author of numerous books, essays and articles in the fields of international, constitutional, electoral and Islamic law, as well as on contemporary Arab affairs, his works include:

- –, *Le Liban d'hier à demain*, Sindbad-Actes Sud/L'Orient des livres, Paris, 2021. (Arabic version *Lubnan bayna al-'ams wal-ghad* published by Charq al-Kitab, Beirut 2021; English version *Lebanon Between Past and Future* published by Orient books, Beirut 2022.)
- –, "Reflections on International Law in Changing Times", in *Harvard International Law Journal*, Summer 2019, Vol. 60, No. 2, pp. 201-217.
- –, Editor: *Lebanon in the Security Council 2010-2011* (in Arabic), Dar Al Saqi, Beirut, 2012; and Contributor "Introduction", pp. 9-18.
- –, Editor: *Le Moyen-Orient à l'Epreuve de l'Irak*, Actes-Sud/Sindbad, Paris, 2005; and Contributor: "La crise de la Ligue Arabe", pp. 55-77.
- –, Editor: *Options for Lebanon*, I. B. Tauris, London and New York, 2004; and Contributor "Reforming the Electoral System. A Comparative Perspective", pp. 1-21. (Arabic version *Khiyarat li-Lubnan* published by Dar An-Nahar, Beirut 2004.)
- –, Co-editor with Theodor Hanf *Lebanon in Limbo*, Nomos, Baden-Baden, 2003; and Contributor "Taif Revisited", pp. 39-51.
- –, *Civil Society in the Arab World*, Islamic Legal Studies Program, Harvard Law School, Occasional Publications, Cambridge, 2002.

Mr President,
Mr Secretary-General,
Dear colleagues and friends,
Ladies and gentlemen.

We obviously live in a rapidly changing world which is very different from what it was when the United Nations was created in 1945. Since then, the United Nations has witnessed major crises in the international system and survived historic challenges to the world order such as the Cold War, decolonization, the emergence of new powers and the increased number, role and influence of non-State actors.

Yet the fundamental question that arises today is whether this organization, born in the aftermath of World War II, can still meet the different and complex challenges of our new global order.

Although it has become a cliché to say that we now live in an interconnected and interdependent world as never before, it may still be warranted to stress that, as a result, we are increasingly facing global problems that are beyond the capability of any single nation to tackle alone, however big, powerful or rich it might be.

From the unprecedented numbers of migrants and refugees, to increasing inequalities, environmental degradation and pollution, pandemics and climate change, the eroding nuclear disarmament regime and rise of terrorist acts as well as the spread of cybercrimes and uncertainties of Artificial Intelligence, all such challenges cannot find real solutions in the simplistic fixes of narrow nationalist agendas or in populist slogans and conspiracy theories. Rather, they require effective international cooperation and real action.

In other words, in our world today, multilateralism can no longer be seen as an ethical ambition or an idealistic goal; it has become an existential imperative in many respects inasmuch as a practical necessity more than any other time in history.

Notwithstanding its past shortcomings, owing to its universal membership, its general purpose, the legitimacy it brings, its neutrality and impartiality and its norm-setting advantages, the United Nations remains at the center of such efforts, both as a forum and a tool. However, it is only a reinvigorated – or better, a reformed – United Nations that can live up to the new challenges of our times.

Let me now illustrate this point with three examples of global challenges that can only be addressed through multilateral action: pandemics, climate change and Artificial Intelligence

Borrowing from Gabriel García Márquez's book title "Chronicle of a Death Foretold", one could say that Covid-19 was a crisis foretold. Scientists have been warning against pandemics for decades long. And after the Ebola outbreak in West Africa, Bill Gates wasn't alone with other philanthropists to ring the alarm bell seeking better preparedness for pandemics. In fact, the President of the United States, Barack Obama, had himself declared in December 2014:

> "There may and likely will come a time in which we have an airborne disease that is deadly. And in order to deal with that effectively, we have to put in place an infrastructure – not just here at home, but globally – that allows us to see it quickly, isolate it quickly, respond to it quickly . . . So that if and when a new strain of flu, like the Spanish flu, crops up five years from now or a decade from now, we've made the investment, and we are further along to be able to catch it. . . . It is not just insurance; it is knowing that down the road we are going to continue to have problems like this – particularly in a globalized world where you move from one side of the world to the other in a day." [1]

However, five years later, when Covid-19 broke out, the world's initial response failed to rise to the global challenge posed by the virus. This moment is well captured by Ian Bremmer who writes:

> "Covid has deepened our geopolitical recession. A truly global crisis with both a public health and economic dimension produced far more finger-pointing than cooperation. There was little sharing information or emergency supplies across international borders. Leaders of the world's two most powerful countries [The USA and China] resisted cooperation with the World Health Organization . . . There is so much blame to go around that we must recognize this failure for what it was: the inevitable breakdown in international governance created by a fragmented world order." [2]

In fact, while it had been repeated time and again during the pandemic that "if the virus is active anywhere, it is potentially active

---

1. https://obamawhitehouse.archives.gov/the-press-office/2014/12/02/remarks-president-research-potential-ebola-vaccines.

2. I. Bremer, *The Power of Crisis. How the Three Threats – and Our Response – Will Change the World*, New York, Simon & Schuster, 2022, p. 68.

everywhere", the first responses to the virus went paradoxically in the opposite direction. Most States wrongly thought that they could better protect themselves by opting for a policy of isolation from the rest of the world. They turned inward, closing their borders, implementing export controls and holding back information.

But since by its very nature the virus wasn't going to stop at any national boundary, no national strategy could fight it successfully. The only effective response to Covid-19 had to be international, one seeking greater cooperation and coordination.

However, some of the criticism addressed to the World Health Organization (WHO), the United Nations' specialized agency responsible for international public health, on its initial handling of the crisis might be justified. But one has to also admit that the budget of this organization is too small and its autonomy from Member States too limited to act swiftly and effectively.

Hence, to better prepare for future pandemics, scapegoating the WHO is indeed no proper response. Rather, the lesson to draw from this crisis is the need to strengthen multilateralism through a WHO that has an enhanced mandate, greater funds and more effective preventive policies.

And let us keep in mind that, according to the International Institute for Sustainable Development, up to 827,000 viruses that could infect humans exist today in mammals and birds. Moreover, while Covid-19 was highly infectious, it wasn't the deadliest virus that scientists have identified in the past twenty-five years.

Turning to "climate change" now, let me first underline that what we are here concerned with is not a threat of a "change" that may (or even will) happen in the "future" if we do not change course. Climate change is happening now.

Indeed, climate deniers exist and will most probably continue to exist. However, as the former Executive Secretary of the UN Framework Convention on Climate Change (UNFCCC), Christiana Figueres and Tom Rivett-Carnac put it so well: "Denying climate change is tantamount to saying you don't believe in gravity. The science of climate change is not a belief, a religion, or a political ideology. It presents facts that are measurable and verifiable. Just as gravity exerts its force on all of us whether we believe in it or not, climate change is already affecting us all, no matter where we were born or where we live"[3].

---

3. Christiana Figueres and Tom Rivett-Carnac, *The Future We Choose: Surviving the Climate Crisis*, Manilla Press, London, 2020, p. 4.

It is sufficient to recall that the last decade has been the hottest ever recorded on our blue planet. But climate change is not only a matter of figures attesting the rise of temperature on Earth.

The effects of climate change can be observed all over the planet, from the very existential threat to island States in the Pacific to wild fires in Australia, Europe and California; and from ice melting in the Arctic to locust swarms in East Africa, floods in Jakarta and water shortages and droughts.

Similarly, the costs of climate change are also tangible and not speculative; they range from economic disruptions, political conflicts and the human suffering resulting from the displacement of tens of millions of people to the physical damages caused by extreme weather conditions. One example is the estimated cost of thirteen billion US dollars in the case of Super Cyclone Amphan that hit Eastern India and Bangladesh in 2020.

More importantly, the most far-reaching consequence of climate change is not that it affects our "quality of life" on Earth as some have said, but rather that it is putting in danger the "very existence" on Earth of human life itself due to our own destruction of the ecosystems that support it. This is why climate change is increasingly being considered as the "mother of all issues".

There are two positives, however: first, we know what ought to be done; second, although the hour is late, it is not too late – provided that we act fast, or rather very fast. It is worth repeating here, though it may have become yet another cliché, "that while we are the first generation to realize that we are destroying the Earth, we are also the last one that can do anything about it".

Scientists say that in order to curb climate change we must limit warming to no more than 1.5 degrees Celsius. The main driver of climate change being greenhouse gas emissions, not to ignore deforestation and other factors, they have been very clear that we must halve global emissions by 2030 and reach net-zero by 2050.

However, this goal is only attainable if we all commit and work together to achieve it. The United Nations has played a critical role in raising awareness on climate change. It must now redouble its efforts to enhance State cooperation, based on the Paris Agreement on climate change, and see that States live up to their pledges in that respect.

Finally, let us not lose sight of the fact that alongside climate change, our planet is also facing an irreversible biodiversity loss and a major pollution crisis. They are best illustrated by the estimate that about one million species are on the verge of extinction and that unless we act fast, there would be more plastic than fish in the sea by 2050, according to the United Nations Environmental Program (UNEP).

The third global challenge that I shall address is Artificial Intelligence (AI). Last month, thousands of leading figures in this field of Artificial Intelligence signed a one-sentence open letter which reads:

> "Mitigating the risks of extinction from AI should be a global priority alongside other societal-scale risks, such as pandemics and nuclear war." [4]

According to Anthony Aguirre, the founder of the Future of Life Institute – the organization behind an earlier open letter published in March of this year and which had called for a six-month pause in the training of all advanced AI systems in order to develop and implement joint safety protocols – the risks stem from the fact that "AI will steadily be delegated, and could – as it becomes more autonomous – usurp decision making and thinking from current humans and human-run institutions" [5].

The biggest risk indeed is that AI systems may one day gain autonomy to the extent that if humans tried to shut them down, they could resist or even replicate themselves in order to keep operating. Such danger is obviously not imminent; yet the problem is that it has become a possibility and is no longer a matter confined to the realm of science fiction as in Stanley Kubrick's famous 1968 movie, "2001: A Space Odyssey".

Moreover, because these systems learn from more data than even their creators can understand, they can also exhibit "unexpected behaviour" as observes Cade Metz, the author of "Genius Makers: The Mavericks Who Brought AI to Google, Facebook, and the World", mentioning the staggering fact that "researchers recently showed that one system was able to hire a human online to defeat a Captcha test. When the human asked if it was 'a robot', the system lied and said it was a person with a visual impairment" [6]! And once AI becomes able to improve itself without human intervention, we will have no way of knowing what the AI will do or how to control it. As Tamlyn Hunt writes in the 25 May 2023 issue of Scientific American: "We won't be able to control [AI

---

4. See https://www.safe.ai/statement-on-ai-risk.
5. See https://www.nytimes.com/2023/06/10/technology/ai-humanity.html.
6. *Idem.*

systems] because anything we think of, they will have already thought of, a million times faster than us."[7]

With the rapid development of AI, we are facing urgent policy, ethical and social issues, ranging from the content of (dis)information, control, goal alignment with human values to privacy rights and effects on employment and society. Moreover, neither the issue of the concentration of power in a handful of tech companies whose priority is profit and not the public good, nor the dangers of widening the global digital divide should be ignored.

Obviously, national regulations cannot be sufficient to address such a global challenge involving the need to define global standards, set safety measures, outline principles regarding the collection, use and ownership of data etc. It goes without saying that such guardrails must at the same time not inhibit innovation and ensure that AI is used in ways consistent with international law and human rights treaties.

In its recognized role as a "convener", and as a platform for dialogue and collective action, the United Nations remains uniquely placed to help develop the norms and frameworks to regulate AI. Alongside the idea of a compact on Artificial Intelligence proposed by United Nations Secretary-General António Guterres, establishing an international regulatory body in the form of an International Agency for Artificial Intelligence may also be considered. Here, it has been suggested that the model of the International Atomic Energy Agency could serve as a source of inspiration.

Since global challenges requiring cooperation across borders not only persist but are on the rise, multilateral action has become more needed than ever as I tried to show in the three examples discussed above; and I have also tried to highlight why the United Nations remains at the center of multilateralism.

However, to better address these global challenges, multilateralism ought to become more inclusive today. In fact, while acknowledging that States remain central in our action to meet global challenges, we must also recognize that solutions to the problems they pose may depend on non-State actors. Hence, in addition to its traditional role of fostering intergovernmental efforts, the United Nations should increasingly include in its "collective action" actors from civil society, academia, media, businesses and other relevant non-State actors.

---

7. https://www.scientificamerican.com/article/heres-why-ai-may-be-extremely-dangerous-whether-its-conscious-or-not/.

Could anyone, for example, imagine that States alone may have succeeded in addressing the Covid-19 crisis without the mobilization of researchers and private sector companies involved in the production of vaccines? And can anyone ignore the critical role that scientists, civil society and the media have been playing in raising awareness on the dangers of climate change? Furthermore, wouldn't the United Nations, and multilateral efforts in general, gain in addressing the complex ethical, legal, social and security issues associated with the development of AI by engaging with governments, scientists, tech companies, developers and NGOs, let alone researchers in the humanities and social sciences? Turning now to the Sustainable Development Goals (SDGs) of the UN 2030 landmark Agenda, would their implementation be realistically possible without partnerships with non-State actors and investments from businesses and financial institutions?

Finally, on this point, it should go without saying that a more inclusive and participatory multilateralism is also a more legitimate and effective one. In evolving in that direction, the United Nations will undoubtedly enhance both its credibility and relevance.

Notwithstanding the importance of inclusive multilateralism, while assessing the credibility and relevance of the United Nations today, one should not lose sight of the fact that peace remains the central promise of its Charter whose preamble affirms the determination "to save succeeding generations from the scourge of war which twice in a lifetime has brought untold sorrow to mankind".

Indeed, after 1945, the world has seen no wars in any measure comparable to WWI and WWII. However, the threat of interstate wars has endured, and intrastate wars (or civil wars) have been on the rise in the past twenty-five years. Let me just mention here that more than 238,000 people died in global conflicts last year, according to the Global Peace Index released last month by the Institute for Economics and Peace. This index also revealed that the average level of global peacefulness has deteriorated for the ninth consecutive year with seventy-nine countries witnessing increased levels of conflict.

The Tigrayan conflict in Ethiopia, which has displaced more than two million people and claimed the most lives in 2022, formally came to an end last November after two long years of fighting. However, with 82,000 deaths registered in 2022, the war still goes on in Ukraine as we all know; and this year has already seen another new war – in fact, a civil war – in Sudan that began in April, and which has already caused over 3,500 deaths.

Clearly, peace and security are under threat in many parts of the globe. Trust among major powers is eroding. Pacts on nuclear arms and other weapons of mass destruction are increasingly fragile. No agreements have yet been reached on lethal autonomous weapons systems, and new technologies are placing the capacity to disrupt security in the hands of terrorists and other criminal actors as in cyberspace.

Let us also recall that the United Nations, paralyzed as it was during the Cold War by the US-Soviet rivalry, had failed to respond decisively to major crises and wars whether in Vietnam, Cambodia and Laos or in Hungary and Czechoslovakia, let alone failing to meaningfully address the Arab-Israeli conflict, the oldest "permanent item" (!) on the Security Council agenda. However, nothing has damaged the UN's image and credibility more than the inability of this Council, though after the end of the Cold War, to stop genocide and mass crimes in Bosnia, Rwanda and Kosovo, and later in Syria and Myanmar. Moreover, the UN image and credibility have been further undermined by unilateral military actions taken by permanent members of the Security Council without the authorization of the latter as in Serbia, Iraq and Ukraine. Today, the Security Council is again paralyzed by the return of great power rivalry and looks often marginal to international crisis management with part of its role on political matters now played by groups like the G7 (formerly G8) and the G20.

Notwithstanding such major failures on the "peace and security" front, let us recall that Dag Hammarskjöld, a celebrated Secretary-General, used to repeat that the United Nations "was not created to take mankind to heaven, but to save humanity from hell".

From this perspective, the UN glass could also be seen as half full with the organization helping avert a Third World War, while such a specter kept looming over decades. And in almost all corners of the globe, the United Nations also helped mitigate dozens of conflicts and save hundreds of thousands of lives through the humanitarian action of UN relief agencies, especially in conflict zones, such as recently with UNHCR in Syria and the UN World food program in Ethiopia and Afghanistan. The United Nations has also deployed peacekeeping operations to reduce tensions, keep opposing forces apart and stabilize the situation in many conflict zones. Today, some 88,000 people from 120 countries serve in twelve missions, which range from ceasefire monitoring as in the Middle East to large, complex operations such as those in the Central African Republic, Congo and Mali.

The truth, however, is that in a number of these areas there was no real peace to keep and only a truce. Therefore, the UN peacekeepers ended up paradoxically participating in freezing many conflicts instead of fostering their resolution. Indeed, such endeavors might not have brought about peace, but they definitely did make the resumption of hostilities less likely and more limited. In a number of cases, the UN has also been the only mediator available in situations ranging from the decades-long division of Cyprus to a disintegrated central power in Libya.

The UN also gets credit for the facilitating role it played in the negotiation of several critical disarmament and arms control treaties such as the Treaty on the Non-Proliferation of Nuclear Weapons (NPT), the Comprehensive Nuclear-Test-Ban Treaty (CTBT), the Treaty on the Prohibition of Nuclear Weapons (TPNW), the Biological and Chemical Weapons Convention and the Arms Trade Treaty (ATT).

It remains, however, that the Security Council – the organ with primary responsibility, under the United Nations Charter, for the maintenance of international peace and security – has been increasingly criticized for both its composition and decision-making process as still reflecting the outdated power dynamics of 1945, instead of adapting to the new global geopolitical realities of our changing times.

As a matter of fact, the seats of the five permanent members with veto power were then allocated as follows: three for the Western Europe and Other Group (WEOG), France, the United Kingdom and the US; one for the Eastern European Group, Russia; and one for the Asia-Pacific Group, China. Obviously, no seat is left for Africa or Latin America, let alone rising European or Asian powers like Germany, Japan and India, when the latter is believed to have become the most populous country on Earth as of April of this year.

For over three decades now, the question of enlarging the Security Council and revisiting the attribution of veto and its use has been endlessly debated in the UN General Assembly without reaching an agreement on whether and how the Council might take in more States. Should they be permanent with a veto, or non-permanent without one, or a combination of both, and how? In 2007, the General Assembly adopted a resolution aiming at rationalizing the debate by focusing it on five issues: categories of membership, the veto, regional representation, the size and working methods of the Council and its relationship with the General Assembly. However, despite tens of meetings since the issue was introduced in 1993, no real progress has been achieved.

The reality is that the question of the Security Council reform continues to face four obstacles:

First, is how to reconcile the bid of Germany, Japan, Brazil and India (known as the G4 nations) for a permanent seat with the "Uniting for Consensus" (or UFC) group seeking only an expansion of non-permanent seats. Noteworthy is that the UFC leaders are the regional rivals and economic competitors of the G4. The group is led by Italy and Spain (opposing Germany), Pakistan (opposing India), Mexico and Argentina (opposing Brazil) and South Korea (opposing Japan). As to the African group, it sticks to the consensus it reached in Ezulwini for two permanent seats with veto powers plus five non-permanent seats for African States. Stopping short of specifying how the two permanent seats will be allocated is obviously due to competition within the group, while its overall maximalist position seems to indicate that the time for real bargaining hasn't come yet.

Second, is the yet unresolved question of balance *between the need for a larger membership and doing so without jeopardizing the effectiveness of the Council.*

Third, is that any change in the number or structure of membership would require an amendment of the Charter, which would in turn need the votes of two-thirds of the General Assembly and more importantly the approval of the current five permanent members, a very problematic issue to say the least.

Fourth, is the question of veto. Here, proposals have ranged from limiting its use to vital national security issues, or requiring agreement from multiple States before exercising it, to abolishing it entirely. However, any such reform of the veto will require that all five permanent members agree to it as the Charter grants them veto over any amendment of its provisions, that is, including over the veto power that they themselves hold, thereby rendering it quite impossible to happen.

Unfortunate as this may be, a radical Security Council reform – as one may wish to see – seems to have no prospect for a breakthrough today. But this does not mean that the status quo is condemned to continue if a more pragmatic and incremental approach is followed.

For example, as long as the expansion of the permanent membership of the Council remains highly improbable in the near future, shouldn't the idea of the creation of a new category of non-permanent members, with a longer (four years) and renewable term, be worth reconsidering by those who initially opposed it fearing to forfeit their bid for a permanent seat? The latter concern could also be addressed by linking the establishment of such a new class of membership on an agreement to convene a special "charter review conference" pursuant to Article 109 of the Charter, in ten years, for example.

Likewise, what could represent a step towards revisiting the whole veto institution is the idea of self-regulation by the five permanent members of the Security Council to voluntarily and collectively commit to refrain from using the veto where mass atrocities are ascertained, such as genocide, crimes against humanity and large-scale war crimes. This idea has the merit of being pragmatic and not seeking to fully abolish the veto, nor requiring an amendment of the Charter. Proposed in 2013 by France, the other permanent members have not yet come to agreement on such self-regulation. Still, the idea is gaining momentum. Taking now the form of a joint French-Mexican initiative, it has received the support of 106 States, as at January 2023.

In the same vein, in July 2015, the "Accountability, Coherence and Transparency Group" of States (known as ACT) proposed a "Code of Conduct regarding Security Council action against genocide, crimes against humanity and war crimes". It calls upon all members of the Security Council (both permanent and elected) to not vote against any credible draft resolution intended to prevent or halt mass atrocities. As at 1 May 2023 the "Code" was signed by 129 Member States, including two Security Council permanent members, France and the UK.

In turn, in May 2016, "The Elders", an independent group of global leaders founded by Nelson Mandela in 2007, joined the call on members of the Security Council to exercise veto restraint to prevent mass atrocities.

Let me also mention that on 26 April 2022, the General Assembly adopted a resolution mandating a debate when a veto is cast in the Security Council. It goes without saying that such a referral to the General Assembly may not deter a permanent member from casting a veto, it nonetheless increases the political costs that this permanent member will have to take into account.

The veto institution has been rightfully criticized as anachronistic, unjust and undemocratic. It is the main cause of Security Council paralysis, preventing the United Nations from effectively responding to major threats to international peace and security, including wars and situations of genocide and massive violations of human rights. Here, the numbers speak loud enough, for until last year, Russia (and the former USSR) had used its veto 121 times, the US 82 times, the UK 29 times, China 17 times and France 16 times. Moreover, even the mere threat of a veto (the so-called "pocket veto") may inhibit any Security Council action.

However, short of abolishing the veto, which remains at least as highly improbable as the expansion of the permanent membership of the Council, it seems warranted to ask if world "peace and security" won't be better served if the use of the veto now requires justification before the General Assembly, and even better if the five permanent members (P5) agree to refrain from using it where mass atrocities are established.

In my opinion, given the sovereignty prerogatives of States and the national interests which are at stake, especially those of great powers, UN reform will have to be gradual. Hence, an imperfect reform today seems definitely better than no reform at all; and any step, whatever small and partial, would be better than the perpetuation of the present immobilism.

Finally, let me conclude on "peace and security" by mentioning a much needed "measure" – and not a "reform" as the matter relates only to implementing still unimplemented provisions of the Charter. The "measure" in question here is to activate Articles 43-47 of the Charter in view of the fact that the UN lacks the means to intervene swiftly when action ought to be taken urgently. The idea of a standing UN force was first floated by the first Secretary-General, Trygve Lie, and later endorsed by almost all succeeding Secretary-Generals. The inability to halt genocidal violence, particularly in Rwanda, brought renewed attention to the idea of such a force, now labelled "rapid reaction force". Moreover, had such a force existed, it might have prevented the intervention in Libya "to protect civilians" from tuning into a NATO operation, with all its controversial consequences. And although a standing military staff committee was originally envisioned under Article 47 of the Charter, it never became a reality, largely due to P5 opposition during the Cold War. Such a standing force could consist of military units from Security Council members and other UN Member States. Until ordered to deploy by the Security Council, they would remain stationed in their home countries (no need for barracks in New York!), but will have the same equipment, procedures and training. Such a force will undoubtedly enhance the UN image, credibility and efficiency.

True that peace, as I already mentioned, was the central promise of the UN. However, the Charter preamble also stressed the organization's determination to "reaffirm faith in fundamental human rights, in the dignity and worth of the human person, [and] in the equal rights of men and women" as well as "the promotion of the economic and social advancement of all peoples".

Let me therefore address both issues now.

I would like first to stress that while Article 2 of the Charter reaffirmed the "principle" of sovereignty, the organization has also been a staunch promoter of human rights since its creation in 1945 through the adoption of landmark instruments such as the Universal Declaration of Human Rights, the Genocide Convention and the Covenants on Civil and Political Rights and on Economic, Social and Cultural Rights, leading to the establishment of the Human Rights Council and the redefinition of "sovereignty as responsibility" in the R2P (Responsibility to Protect) doctrine, which was endorsed in the 2005 World Summit declaration.

Under this doctrine, if a State proves to be unable or unwilling to protect its own citizens, the international community will be entitled to intervene through a Security Council resolution. In other words, invoking "sovereignty" could no longer serve as a protection for mass murder and crimes against humanity, or better as a "license to kill" as goes the expression.

Though progressive in content, this doctrine did not fare well in practice. It was referred to by the Security Council to justify the "use of all necessary means" – a euphemism for the use of force – to protect the civilians in Libya in 2011. However, the ensuing military intervention of Western countries ended up transforming the "protection of civilians" goal into a regime change venture (or better – adventure!), thus raising serious doubts and suspicions about the implications of the R2P doctrine among several countries mainly from the South, let alone Russia and China.

Notwithstanding the ill-fated first implementation of this doctrine, let us not lose sight of the important successes achieved by the United Nations in advancing the centrality of human rights, especially by increasingly stressing that they must be fully considered in all decision-making and operations whether in the field of peace and security, development or humanitarian action.

As this year marks the commemoration of the 75th anniversary of the Universal Declaration of Human Rights, it should be an occasion on the one hand to pay tribute to the UN role in promoting the culture of human rights, ending apartheid, fighting discrimination, seeking to end impunity and accelerating gender equality in its organs and agencies. On the other hand, it should also be stressed on this occasion that a lot still ought to be done especially with the increase in inequalities and the rise of hate speech, racism and xenophobia in many corners of the globe, as well as of violations of international humanitarian law.

Let me turn now to the 2030 Agenda for Sustainable Development, adopted by all United Nations Member States in 2015. At its heart are seventeen Sustainable Development Goals and 169 targets. While they build on the Millennium Development Goals which were launched in 2000, they seek to emphasize the interconnected environmental, social and economic aspects of sustainable development by putting sustainability at their center.

The goals cover a wide range of areas, including eradicating poverty, fighting hunger, reducing inequalities, providing clean energy, quality education, good health, empowering women and girls, promoting economic growth and good governance – all while tackling climate change and working to preserve our oceans and forests.

With such an ambitious list of goals, the "Agenda" is more of a call for action which requires a revitalized global partnership that includes the mobilization of financial resources as well as capacity-building and the transfer of technologies to developing countries on concessional and preferential terms.

However, halfway to the 2030 deadline, UN Secretary-General, António Guterres, warned in his remarks last month at the Paris Summit on a New Global Financing Pact that the Sustainable Development Goals are drifting further away by the day.

> "Even the most fundamental goals on hunger and poverty have gone into reverse after decades of progress [noting that] in 2023, more than 750 million people do not have enough to eat [and stressing that] developing countries are grappling today with exorbitant borrowing costs – up to eight times higher than those of developed countries, with 52 countries being in default or dangerously close to it." [8]

As rightly pointed out by Guterres, the problem lies in the fact that the global financial architecture which was built in the aftermath of World War II has become outdated, dysfunctional and unjust. Worse, the global financial system perpetuates and even exacerbates inequalities.

---

8. See https://www.un.org/sg/en/content/sg/speeches/2023-06-22/secretary-general-remarks-the-paris-summit-new-global-financing-pact.

To illustrate his point, the Secretary-General noted that while in 2021, the International Monetary Fund allocated over 650 billion US dollars in Special Drawing Rights, European Union countries received 160 billion US dollars and African countries 34 billion US dollars.

In other words, European citizens received on average nearly thirteen times more than African citizens.

Clearly, without serious reforms of the global financial architecture, neither the deadline nor the goals of the SDGs will be met.

However, it is not only the international financial institutions that need to reform in order to meet the needs of our twenty-first century and serve as a safety net for all countries, but all multilateral institutions must also not remain static and should adapt to the unprecedented scope and pace of change in our times.

The fundamental values and core principles of the UN as enshrined in its Charter are enduring. Moreover, in view of the global challenges humanity is facing today, the UN, as I have argued, is even more relevant than it was in 1945. Yet it is only a more representative, inclusive, dynamic and future-oriented UN that can effectively live up to these complex challenges.

On 23 January 2023, the famous astrophysicist Neil deGrasse Tyson, tweeted: "Visiting space aliens, upon seeing humans oppress – or kill – one another over who they worship, who they sleep with, what side of an arbitrary line they are born on, or how absorptive their skin is to sunlight, would surely race home and report no sign of intelligent life on Earth." [9]

Observing also how these same humans have neither been responsive enough to the global challenges that could put the very existence of their species in jeopardy from climate change to unregulated AI, nor have they demonstrated enough collective action to upgrade and reform the universal tool which they founded over seventy-five years ago to save them from "the scourge of war" and promote their "economic and social advancement" (as per the words of the Charter), all this would only confirm to our "visiting space aliens" the dire truth of their finding.

Yet it might be that "it takes something more than intelligence to act intelligently", as wrote Dostoïevsky in *Crime and Punishment* [10].

Thank you.

---

9. See https://twitter.com/neiltyson/status/1617606347234897922.
10. Raskolnikov, about Pyotr Petrovich; Part 3, Chapter 3.

LE RÔLE DU DROIT INTERNATIONAL DANS LE CONTRÔLE DES SENTENCES ARBITRALES

par

DOMINIQUE HASCHER

D. HASCHER

TABLE DES MATIÈRES

Introduction	41
Chapitre 1. L'attraction du droit international	43
A. Le droit international régit la sentence	43
B. La force du droit international	47
Chapitre 2. Le droit international, élément modérateur du contrôle	52
A. S'introduire dans le fond?	52
B. Les limites	58
Chapitre 3. Un contrôle nourri de principes universellement reconnus, élevés au rang de principes de droit international, à titre de langage commun	61
Conclusion	69

NOTICE BIOGRAPHIQUE

Dominique Hascher, né le 22 mai 1956 à Neuilly sur Seine (France).
Etudes secondaires au Lycée Henri IV (Paris), études de droit aux Universités de Paris II et Harvard (boursier *Fulbright*).
Entré en 1978 dans les services judiciaires français (concours étudiant), détaché à la Cour internationale d'arbitrage de la Chambre de commerce internationale en qualité de *General Counsel* et secrétaire général-adjoint (1990-1998), conseiller à la Cour de cassation en 2012, aujourd'hui juge international à la Cour suprême de Singapour.
Président ou membre de comités *ad hoc* constitués au titre de la Convention de Washington du 18 mars 1965 (CIRDI).
Président d'un tribunal arbitral international à Bruxelles (nommé par les coarbitres, juge à la Cour internationale de Justice et professeur de droit).
Autorité de nomination nommé par la Cour permanente d'arbitrage dans l'affaire *Pey Casado c. Chili*.
Professeur associé, Université de Paris I (2001-2015); professeur invité, *University College London* (2005) *University of Texas School of Law*, Austin (2007).
Président de la Société de législation comparée (2015-2019), membre de l'*American Law Institute*, du *Governing Board (Advisory Member)* de l'*International Council Commercial Arbitration* (ICCA), de *l'International Arbitration Institute*, des comités français de l'arbitrage et de droit international privé; secrétaire général de la branche française de l'*International Law Association* (1998-2006); membre du comité scientifique de la Revue de l'arbitrage, conseiller à la rédaction de la Revue camerounaise de l'arbitrage.
Chevalier dans l'Ordre National de la Légion d'honneur (2005) l'Ordre National du Mérite (1998), *Hon. Bencher* de *Gray's Inn*, Londres (2004).

PRINCIPALES PUBLICATIONS

Les grandes décisions du droit de l'arbitrage commercial, Dalloz, 2019 (avec I. Fadlallah).

Les représentations de l'arbitrage à travers la jurisprudence, Les Conférences de l'Académie sur l'héritage scientifique d'Emmanuel Gaillard, Brill, Nijhoff, 2023, p. 109.

«Principes et pratique de procédure dans l'arbitrage commercial international», *Recueil des cours*, tome 279 (2000), p.50.

Articles, notes de jurisprudence et notices bibliographiques au *Journal du droit International, Revue de l'arbitrage, Revue critique de droit international privé, Travaux du comité français de droit international privé, Bulletin de la Cour internationale d'arbitrage de la CCI, Revue de règlement des différends de McGill, Bulletin ASA, Arbitration International, Yearbook Commercial Arbitration, Journal of Arab Arbitration, American Review of International Arbitration, Maritime and Commercial Law Quarterly*; chapitres dans des ouvrages collectifs et divers Mélanges.

INTRODUCTION

1. Les organes nationaux ou internationaux de contrôle [1] ont pour mission de stabiliser la justice arbitrale en s'assurant de l'intégrité des sentences qui leur sont présentées et, au-delà, de préserver l'intégrité du système d'arbitrage dans lequel la sentence a été rendue. L'importance des enjeux confiés aux tribunaux arbitraux, dont les décisions ont des répercussions excédant les seuls litiges qui leur sont confiés [2], permet de mieux évaluer la gravité de cette mission.

2. Principalement exposés dans la Convention de New York du 10 juin 1958 pour la reconnaissance et l'exécution des sentences arbitrales étrangères, la Convention de Washington du 18 mars 1965 pour le règlement des différends relatifs aux investissements entre Etats et ressortissants d'autres Etats (CIRDI), ou encore la loi-type de la Commission des Nations Unies pour le droit commercial international (CNUDCI) sur l'arbitrage commercial international, les cas qui se prêtent à la discussion de la sentence sont bien connus. Aucun en particulier ne favorise l'intervention du droit international.

3. Le mouvement du texte de cette conférence inaugurale vous convie à une réflexion sur la régulation d'un système universel de justice arbitrale. Comment les organes de contrôle établissent-ils des connexions entre les ordres juridiques nationaux et internationaux pour contrôler les sentences en les faisant passer d'un ordre juridique à l'autre? Leur aptitude à mobiliser des principes issus d'une pluralité d'ordres juridiques est révélateur de leurs forces et de leurs faiblesses dans l'accomplissement de leur mission. Dans l'ordre international, il y a beaucoup de sous-ordres qui sont en réseau : ordre juridique international interétatique, ordre juridique transnational qui transcende les ordres juridiques des Etats (*lex mercatoria* ou ordre juridique propre

---

[1]. Cette conférence ne porte pas sur la Cour internationale de Justice, sur laquelle on consultera W. M Reisman, « The Supervisory Jurisdiction of the International Court of Justice: International Arbitration and International Adjudication », *Recueil des cours*, tome 258 (1996), p. 9. Le thème de la conférence s'est dégagé des discussions tenues avec M. le Professeur I. Fadlallah lors de la rédaction de l'ouvrage *Les grandes décisions du droit de l'arbitrage commercial international*, Dalloz, 2019.

[2]. Alain Plantey, « L'arbitrage dans les échanges internationaux », *Rev. Sciences morales et pol.*, 1995, p. 323. B. Oppetit, « Théorie de l'arbitrage », PUF, 1998; G. Aguilar-Alvarez et W. M. Reisman, « The Reasons Requirement in International Investment Arbitration », Martinus Nijhoff, 2008, p. 2.

au commerce international[3], droit international des contrats[4], *lex sportiva*[5]) ou ordre juridique arbitral dans lequel on réunit ensemble les règles de l'arbitrage auxquelles on attribue une valeur internationale, dégagées d'après le consensus étatique ou puisées dans le droit international[6]. Quelle que soit la composition de ces ordres juridiques, variable selon les constructions doctrinales[7], on est en présence de plurivers qui coexistent et se traversent, et non d'univers isolés et hiérarchiquement disposés[8]. S'enfermer dans une catégorie ou donner une définition du droit international empêcherait de raisonner sur le caractère composite de ce droit tel qu'il est produit par les instances de contrôle qui essayent d'élaborer les règles et dont ce serait casser la dynamique.

4. La soumission des sentences au droit international est un facteur d'attraction du droit international (chap. 1) lequel joue un rôle modérateur (chap. 2) dans un contrôle nourri de principes universellement reconnus, élevés au rang de principes de droit international, à titre de langage commun (chap. 3).

---

3. A. Pellet, « La *lex mercatoria*, tiers ordre juridique ? », dans Mélanges Kahn, Litec, 2000, p. 53. M. Virally, « Un tiers droit ? », Réflexions théoriques, études Goldman, Litec, 1982, p. 373.
4. Sentence *Texaco c. Libye* du 19 janvier 1977, *JDI*, 1977, p. 350, ILM, vol. 17 (1978), p. 1, *International Law Reports*, vol. 53, p. 389, par. 32, 44.
5. M. Maisonneuve, « L'arbitrage des litiges sportifs », LGDJ, 2011 ; A. Rigozzi, « L'arbitrage international en matière de sport », Bruylant, LGDJ, Helbing & Lichtenhahn, 2005, n° 1222.
6. La représentation de l'ordre juridique arbitral n'exclut en aucune manière les normes étatiques, mais le positivisme étatique de cette vision prend en considération les Etats dans leur ensemble, E. Gaillard, « Aspects philosophiques du droit de l'arbitrage international », Adi-poche, Martinus Nijhoff, 2008, par. 50 ; E. Gaillard, « Transcending National Legal Orders », dans *International Arbitration : The Coming of a New Age*, ICCA Congress Series, n° 17, Wolters Kluwer, 2013, p. 371. Les Conférences de l'Académie sur l'héritage scientifique d'Emmanuel Gaillard, Brill Nijhoff, 2023.
7. E. Loquin, « L'ordre juridique arbitral », JDI, 2022, p. 1157 ; J.-B. Racine, « Réflexions sur l'autonomie de l'arbitrage commercial international », *Rev. arb.* 2005, p. 305. «
8. F. Ost et M. de Kerchove, « De la pyramide au réseau ? », *Publications des Facultés universitaires Saint Louis*, n° 94, 2002.

CHAPITRE 1

L'ATTRACTION DU DROIT INTERNATIONAL

A. Le droit international régit la sentence

5. La soumission des sentences au droit international est un facteur d'attraction du droit international dans le contrôle. Bien que régie par le droit international, la procédure arbitrale n'est pas le lieu où il se manifeste plus spécifiquement. Beaucoup de règles de procédure sont de source internationale, sans que cela n'exprime une emprise du droit international sur la sentence. Une typologie fondée sur les règles applicables au litige rend mieux compte du fondement international des sentences. Le choix permissif des règles de fond fait place à l'application des règles du droit international, dans les contrats du commerce international avec la *lex mercatoria*, dans les différends sportifs avec la *lex sportiva* [9], ou encore en matière d'investissement [10]. Leur application est marquée par le décloisonnement et l'extension. Ainsi la sentence *El Paso c. Argentine* s'appuie sur les Principes UNIDROIT pour conforter l'identification d'un principe général du droit international sur l'exonération de responsabilité [11]. Plus largement, rien n'interdit le choix du droit international comme droit du contrat ou concurremment avec un droit national, remarque Grossen :

> « [l]'élection d'un système juridique déterminé emporte la désignation concurrente du droit international dans la mesure où le

---

[9]. F. Latty, « La *lex sportiva* », Martinus Nijhoff, 2007 ; sentence TAS n° 98/200 du 20 août 1999, par. 156 : « sports law has developed and consolidated along the years, particularly through the arbitral settlement of disputes, a set of unwritten legal principles – a sort of *lex mercatoria* for sports or, so to speak, a *lex ludica* » (*Recueil des sentences du TAS*, tome II (1998-2000), M. Reeb (dir. publ.), Kluwer Law International, 2002, p. 38) ; sentence TAS n° 2014/A/3505 du 3 décembre 2014, par. 85-87.

[10]. A. Carlevaris, « General Principles of Commercial Law and International Investment Law », dans General Principles and the Coherence of International Law, Queen Mary Studies in International Law, M. Andenas, M. Fitzmaurice, A. Tanzi et J. Wouters (dir. publ.), vol. 37, Brill Nijhoff, 2019, p. 205. Résolution de l'Institut de droit international sur la loi du contrat dans les accords entre un Etat et une personne privée étrangère, session d'Athènes 1979, S. Karger, vol. 58, tome II, p. 192. P. Juillard, « L'évolution des sources du droit des investissements », *Recueil des cours*, tome 250 (1994), p. 9.

[11]. *El Paso c. Argentine*, sentence CIRDI du 31 octobre 2011, ARB/03/15, par. 621-624.

droit international est censé faire partie de ce système ou y est intégré par des dispositions de droit interne » [12].

Plantey explique :

« [i]lest souvent opportun d'élever la contestation au-dessus du système juridique d'un des Etats intéressés afin de la soumettre à des grands principes de caractère international » [13].

6. L'application du droit national n'est pas exclusive des principes généraux du droit international énonce la sentence *Texaco c. Libye* [14]. Les recherches sur l'ordre juridique de base correspondent à des théories construites à des fins déterminées pour internationaliser les contrats et justifier que l'investisseur soit considéré comme un personnage du droit international public.[15] Aujourd'hui, on l'admet et beaucoup de conventions internationales protègent l'investissement par le droit international.

7. Certains traités de protection des investissements stipulent des clauses de droit applicable qui, outre les dispositions du traité et le droit de l'Etat hôte, mentionnent les principes du droit international [16]. Mais dans tous les cas, nous éclaire le tribunal arbitral dans l'affaire *AAPL c. Sri Lanka* :

« the Bilateral Investment Treaty is not a self-contained closed legal system limited to provide for substantive material rules

---

12. J.-M. Grossen, « La prise en compte du droit international public dans l'arbitrage commercial international », Festschrift für Franz Kellerhals, Stämpfli Verlag Bern, 2005, p. 35.

13. Alain Plantey, « Le rôle de l'arbitrage dans le développement de l'économie », IDEF, 29 mars 1996.

14. Sentence *Texaco c. Libye*, JDI, 1977, p. 350, ILM, vol. 17 (1978), p. 1, *International Law Reports*, vol. 53, p. 389 :

« [t]out droit national est porteur des principes généraux de droit tels que ceux-ci sont prévus par l'article 38 du Statut de la Cour internationale de Justice. Sous ce nom générique de principes généraux du droit on désigne, en effet, certains principes communs aux systèmes juridiques des différents Etats du monde. Ils constituent une source du droit international qui trouve son origine dans les divers droits nationaux : par conséquent, l'application du droit national n'exclut pas celle des principes généraux du droit, lesquels font eux-mêmes partie des principes du droit international » (par. 50).

15. Ch. Leben, « Quelques réflexions théoriques à propos des contrats d'Etat », dans Mélanges Kahn, Litec, 2000, p. 119 ; « La théorie des contrats d'Etat et l'évolution du droit international des investissements », *Recueil des cours*, tome 302 (2003), p. 197 ; P. Weil, « Ecrits de droit international », PUF, 2000, p. 351, 379, 409.

16. Y. Banifatemi et E. Gaillard, « The Meaning of "and" in Article 42 (1), Second Sentence, of the Washington Convention : The Role of International Law in the ICSID Choice of Law Process », 18(2) *ICSID Review* (2004), p. 375.

of direct applicability, but it has to be envisaged within a wider juridical context in which rules from other sources are integrated through implied incorporation methods, or by direct reference to certain supplementary rules, whether of international law character or of domestic law nature »[17].

Il est d'ailleurs constant depuis la sentence Georges Pinson que tout traité est réglé par le droit international[18].

8. La Convention CIRDI jette les bases d'un système d'arbitrage organisé conduisant à l'application du droit international qu'il s'agisse de la compétence[19] ou du fond. En dirigeant les arbitres vers « les principes de droit international applicables en la matière » pour statuer sur le différend, la Convention renvoie aux sources du droit international identifiées à l'article 38 (1) du Statut de la Cour internationale de Justice (CIJ)[20].

9. Tout le droit international ne peut pas servir à contrôler les sentences. Toutes les violations du droit international ne sont pas des violations de l'ordre public substantiel nous rappelle le Tribunal fédéral suisse à propos d'un arbitrage de la Charte européenne sur l'énergie :

> « Sans doute la primauté du droit international sur le droit interne est-elle un principe généralement admis, y compris par la Suisse ... Il ne s'ensuit pas pour autant qu'il faille nécessairement taxer d'incompatible avec la définition restrictive de l'ordre public matériel ... une sentence imposant à une partie l'obligation de dédommager de façon équitable la partie adverse, quand

---

17. Sentence CIRDI du 27 juin 1990, *Asian Agricultural Products Ltd* v. *Sri Lanka*, ARB/87/3, par. 21.
18. Commission des réclamations franco-mexicaine, décision n° 1 du 19 octobre 1928 *(Georges Pinson)*, RSA, p. 422, n° 50 (4), « [t]oute convention internationale doit être réputée s'en référer tacitement au droit international commun, pour toutes les questions qu'elle ne résout pas elle-même en termes exprès et d'une façon différente ».
19. Sentence CIRDI du 15 avril 2009, n° ARB/06/5 *Phoenix Action c. Rép. Tchèque*, par. 74-75 ; Decision of the Tribunal on Objections to Jurisdiction du 24 mai 1999, *CSOB c. Slovaquie*, CIRDI n° ARB/97/4, par. 35.
20. Comité *ad hoc*, *Wena c. Egypte*, décision du 28 janvier 2002, CIRDI n° ARB/98/4, par. 37-46. Y. Banifatemi et E. Gaillard, « The Meaning of "and" in Article 42 (1) », Second Sentence, of the Washington Convention : The Role of International Law in the ICSID Choice of Law Process, 18 (2) *ICSID Review* (2004), p. 375. W. M. Reisman, « The Regime for Lacunae in the ICSID Choice of Law Provision and the Question of its Threshold », 15 *ICSID Review* (2000), p. 362. H. Slim, « Host State's liability in Investment Dispute Arbitration : The Role of Domestic Law », dans Mélanges El Kosheri, Wolters Kluwer, 2015, p. 345.

bien même cette injonction contredirait une norme tirée du droit supranational.»[21]

10. L'impérativité de certaines règles n'est pas exclue. Encouragée par la doctrine, telle la résolution de l'Institut de droit international sur l'arbitrage entre Etats et entreprises étrangères[22], la jurisprudence arbitrale établit sans détour la nécessité de respecter les principes du droit international dotés d'impérativité, que ce soit en droit du commerce international[23], sportif[24] ou des investissements[25]. La sécurité des transactions est identifiée comme un principe d'ordre public de la *lex mercatoria*[26], la bonne foi comme un principe d'ordre public transnational reflété dans le *jus cogens* de l'arbitrage international[27]. Dans son cours à l'Académie, Gaillard soulignait combien la méthode des règles transnationales permet de dégager «des règles d'ordre public réellement international, correspondant, en droit international, au *jus cogens*»[28]. Les jurisprudences française ou suisse incluent dans l'ordre public international les principes d'exécution de bonne foi des

---

21. TF 6 octobre 2015, 4A_34/2015, par. 5.31.
22. «En aucun cas un arbitre ne doit méconnaître les principes d'ordre public international sur lesquels un large consensus s'est formé dans la communauté internationale» (art. 2), *Annuaire de l'Institut de droit international*, session de St-Jacques de Compostelle 1989, Pedone, 1990, vol. 63-II, p. 218.
23. Sentence CCI 2730 de 1982 (fond), S. Jarvin et Y. Derains, *Recueil des sentences arbitrales de la CCI*, vol. I, 1974-1985, Kluwer, 1990, p. 490; sentences CCI 7047 de 1994 (fond) et 6474 de 1992 (compétence), J.-J. Arnaldez, Y. Derains et D. Hascher, *Recueil des sentences arbitrales de la CCI*, vol. IV, 1996-2000, Kluwer Law International, 2003, p. 32, 341.
24. Sentence TAS 2002/A/431 du 23 mai 2003, *Recueil des sentences du TAS*, M. Reeb (dir. publ.), tome III, 2001-2003, Kluwer Law International, Staempfli, 2004, p. 410.
25. Sentence NAFTA *Methanex c. United States*, 3 août 2005,

«... as a matter of international constitutional law a tribunal has an independent duty to apply imperative principles of law or jus cogens and not to give effect to parties' choice of law that are inconsistent with such principles» (part. IV, chap. C, p. 11, par. 24); sentence CIRDI du 11 juin 2012, n° ARB/03/23, *EDF, Saur et al. c. Argentine*, «It is common ground that the Tribunal should be sensitive to international jus cogens norms, including basic principles of human rights» (par. 909).

26. Sentence CCI n° 3267 de 1979 et commentaire, S. Jarvin et Y. Derains, *Recueil des sentences arbitrales de la CCI*, vol. I, 1974-1985, Kluwer, 1990, p. 376.
27. Sentence CCI n° 6474 de 1992, par. 36-38, J.-J. Arnaldez, Y. Derains et D. Hascher, *Recueil des sentences arbitrales de la CCI*, vol. IV, 1996-2000, Kluwer Law International, 2003, p. 341. A. Gomez Robledo, «Le *ius cogens* international: sa genèse, sa nature, ses fonctions», *Recueil des cours*, tome 172 (1981), p. 9.
28. E. Gaillard, «Aspects philosophiques du droit de l'arbitrage international», Adi-poche, Martinus Nijhoff, 2008, par. 61.

Le rôle du droit int. dans le contrôle des sentences arbitrales 47

conventions[29] et *pacta sunt servanda*[30]. Il faut donc des règles de droit international qui s'imposent aux arbitres.

B. La force du droit international

11. L'application du droit international n'est pas toujours isolée et n'est pas systématiquement explicite. D'autres sources se joignent, telles les règles matérielles transnationales[31], sur lesquelles il n'y a pas lieu à s'attarder dans la mesure où il suffit de rappeler que la régularité de la sentence est examinée au regard des règles du pays où la reconnaissance et l'exécution sont recherchées.

12. Le fondement contractuel de l'arbitrage n'enlève rien à la force du droit international. On a l'exemple du comité *ad hoc* dans l'affaire *Duke c. Pérou* qui mobilise la volonté des parties et le principe de bonne foi pour interpréter la clause compromissoire d'un contrat soumis à la loi péruvienne :

> « In addressing this question of consent under Article 25 [of the ICSID Convention], a tribunal is not bound to apply host state law, even in a case where the parties' consent derives from or relates to an agreement under host state law. Thus, in *SPP* v. *Egypt*, the source of the state's consent was a provision in its investment law. Egypt submitted that the jurisdictional issues were governed by Egyptian law, and that, pursuant to the Egyptian Civil Code, no effective arbitration agreement had been concluded. This submission was rejected by a Tribunal presided by Jiménez de Aréchaga. It applied instead general principles of interpretation and international law to the question of consent. In *CSOB* v. *Slovakia*, the Tribunal's jurisdiction was derived from a contract. The Tribunal held nevertheless, citing Amco with approval, that: The question of whether the parties have effectively expressed their consent to ICSID jurisdiction is not to be answered by reference to national law. It is governed by international law as set out in Article 25 (1) of the ICSID Convention.
>
> Thus, an ICSID tribunal determining its jurisdiction is not required to interpret the instrument of consent according solely

---

29. CA Paris, 29 mars 1991, Rev. arb. 1991, p. 478, note L. Idot; 12 janvier 1993, Rev. arb. 1994, p. 685 ; 20 juin 1996, Rev. arb. 1996, p. 657, obs. DB.
30. TF 8 avril 2021, 4A_516/2020, par. 4.2.2.
31. Sur lesquelles, E. Gaillard, « Les vertus de la méthode des règles matérielles appliquées à la convention d'arbitrage », *Rev. arb.* 2020, p. 701.

to national law, but rather it is to consider directly whether there is the requisite evidence of consent required by Article 25 (1) of the ICSID Convention, having regard to the common will of the parties on which arbitration is grounded and the general principle (widely applied in municipal law as well as in international law) of good faith. » [32]

13. Si soumettre la compétence à des règles enracinées dans le droit international procède d'une certaine cohérence pour un comité *ad hoc* en raison de son rôle de garant de l'intégrité de la Convention CIRDI [33], l'application du droit international est plus remarquable lorsque les règles de conflit du for sont sollicitées.

14. L'accord d'arbitrer entre l'investisseur et l'Etat fondé sur les dispositions d'un traité de protection des investissements n'est pas un traité, nous rappelle le juge anglais [34]. Pour autant, et indépendamment de toute ratification d'un tel traité par le Royaume-Uni, cet accord obéit au droit international :

«The question may then arise: under what law is that agreement to arbitrate to be regarded as subject, applying the principles of private international law of the English forum? ... It is common ground that English private international law recognises an agreement to arbitrate substantive issues such as the present according to international law (cf. *Orion* v. *Belfort* [1962] 2 LlR 257, 264, per Megaw J, Dicey & Morris, The Conflict of Laws, Vol. 1, para. 16-031 and Mustill & Boyd's Commercial Arbitration (2nd ed.), pp. 80-81), and it is also clear that the present is such. (The words "in accordance with the law" in s. 46 (1) *(a)* and "the law determined by the conflict of laws rules which it considers applicable" in s. 46 (3) of the Arbitration Act 1996 are capable of having this broad meaning, and s. 46 (1) *(b)* now adds further to the

---

32. Décision du 1ᵉʳ mars 2011, CIRDI n° ARB/03/28, par. 141-142.
33. Décision du comité *ad hoc* du 5 juin 2007, *Soufraki c. UAE*, ARB/02/7 :

«[T]he object and purpose of an ICSID annulment proceeding may be described as the control of the fundamental integrity of the ICSID arbitral process in all its facets ... Integrity of the dispute settlement mechanism, integrity of the process of dispute settlement and integrity of solution of the dispute are the basic interrelated goals projected in the ICSID annulment mechanism » (par. 23).

34. CA Angleterre et Pays de Galle, 9 septembre 2005, *Occidental* v. *Republic of Ecuador* [2005] EWCA Civ 1116 : « the agreement to arbitrate which results by following the Treaty route is not itself a treaty. It is an agreement between a private investor on the one side and the relevant State on the other » (n° 33). Voir aussi CIJ, arrêt du 22 juillet 1952, *Anglo-Iranian Oil Co.*, *Recueil 1952*, p. 93.

flexibility of arbitration, by permitting an agreement to arbitrate issues in accordance with other, non-legal considerations.) All this being so, we would be minded to accept that, under English private international law principles, the agreement to arbitrate may itself be subject to international law, as it may be subject to foreign law. That possibility also appears to us to have been embraced as long ago as 1962 by Megaw J in *Orion* v. *Belfort* (above). And, if one assumes that this is possible, then that is the view that we would, like the judge, take of this particular arbitration agreement. Although it is a consensual agreement, it is closely connected with the international Treaty which contemplated its making, and which contains the provisions defining the scope of the arbitrators' jurisdiction. Further, the protection of investors at which the whole scheme is aimed is likely to be better served if the agreement to arbitrate is subject to international law, rather than to the law of the State against which an investor is arbitrating.» [35]

15. La même orientation en faveur du droit international se retrouve dans la jurisprudence du Tribunal fédéral suisse :

«Le Tribunal arbitral, dont le siège a été fixé à Zurich, a statué sur sa propre compétence et jugé la cause à la lumière du TCE [Charte européenne sur l'énergie], convention qui fait partie intégrante du droit suisse et qui ne renvoie pas au droit d'un autre Etat pour l'interprétation et l'application de sa clause juridictionnelle. Faute d'une élection de droit se rapportant à ladite clause, le droit suisse constitue donc à la fois la *lex causae* et la *lex fori* en l'occurrence. L'examen de la Cour de céans se limitera donc à la question de savoir si le Tribunal arbitral a méconnu le droit suisse – concrètement, le TCE – en admettant sa compétence.» [36]

16. On voit que la distinction moniste/dualiste n'est plus une ligne claire, tellement il y a de manières d'intégrer le droit international dans le droit interne [37]. Le Tribunal fédéral n'admet pas l'application directe

---

35. CA Angleterre et Pays de Galle, 9 septembre 2005, *Occidental* v. *Republic of Ecuador* [2005] EWCA Civ 1116, n° 33. Résolution de l'Institut de droit international sur la loi du contrat dans les accords entre un Etat et une personne privée étrangère, session d'Athènes 1979, S. Karger, vol. 58, tome II, p. 192.
36. *Supra* note 22, TF, 6 octobre 2015, n° 4A-34/2015, par. 3.4.2.
37. H. Triepel, Les rapports entre le droit interne et le droit international, *Recueil des cours*, tome 1 (1923) p. 73 ; G. A. Walz, «Les rapports du droit international et du droit interne», *Recueil des cours*, tome 61 (1937) p. 375 ; Y. Iwasawa, «Domestic

du droit international alors qu'il s'agit au surplus d'un traité ratifié par la Suisse. Il raisonne à partir de l'article 178 LDIP[38] comme s'il s'agissait d'un conflit de lois pour appliquer la Charte de l'énergie en tant qu'élément du droit suisse. Compliquée, la démonstration n'en est pas moins satisfaisante. L'expression «closely connected with the international Treaty» dans l'arrêt de la cour d'appel d'Angleterre se réfère à la technique du conflit de lois, mais le juge anglais rejette toute approche mécaniste à laquelle il préfère une subtile flexibilité. Chacun a la responsabilité de maintenir l'équilibre du système de la justice internationale[39], il ne faut pas s'enfermer dans un formalisme, fut-il de droit international privé. Une règle donnée par diverses sources, avec la possibilité de nuances et de contenus différents, procure une souplesse à celui qui applique la règle en le distançant d'une application mécanique qui le limiterait à une seule source. Cela se rapproche du raisonnement tenu par les arbitres dans la recherche du droit applicable en s'efforçant de retenir des règles qui correspondent aux attentes légitimes des parties. L'attraction du droit international en tant que source d'inspiration incite à raisonner au-delà de la recherche des sources formelles et de leurs hiérarchies qui ne permettent pas d'appréhender la situation internationale de la sentence dans toutes ses dimensions.

17. L'attraction du droit international doit tout autant se manifester pour le contrôle des sentences rendues dans des arbitrages fondés sur une loi nationale d'investissement. Un raisonnement en termes d'application de loi étrangère, comme le fait une décision anglaise à propos d'une sentence fondée sur la loi kirghize sur les investissements[40], laisse moins de place à une unité d'interprétation des concepts du droit des investissements que lorsqu'il s'agit d'un arbitrage fondé sur un traité.

Application of International Law», *Recueil des cours*, tome 378 (2015) p. 9. Sur l'intégration de la coutume internationale dans la *common law*, voir le jugement du 25 novembre 2015 de la Cour suprême du Royaume Uni, *Keyu* et al. v. *Secretary of State for Foreign and Comonwealth Affairs* [2015] UKSC 69, n° 142-151.

38. L'article 178 LDIP avec ses rattachements alternatifs à la loi choisie par les parties, à la *lex causae* ou au droit suisse valide la clause d'arbitrage aussi bien que le ferait une règle matérielle (E. Gaillard et P. Lalive, «Le nouveau droit de l'arbitrage international en Suisse», *JDI* 1989.905; voir aussi B. Oppetit, «Le développement des règles matérielles», *Trav. Com. fr. DIP*, Journée du cinquantenaire, CNRS, 1988, p. 121).

39. La cour d'appel anglaise le souligne dans le jugement rendu le 9 septembre 2005 dans l'affaire *Occidental* v. *Republic of Ecuador*: «the protection of investors at which the whole scheme is aimed is likely to be better served if the agreement to arbitrate is subject to international law, rather than to the law of the State against which an investor is arbitrating» ([2005] EWCA Civ 1116, n° 33).

40. Jugement du 13 octobre 2017, *The Kyrgyz Republic* v. *Stans Energy and Kutisay Mining* [2017] EWHC 2539 (Comm).

Le rôle du droit int. dans le contrôle des sentences arbitrales 51

Comment favoriser une interprétation harmonisatrice, quand le principe est celui de l'absence de contrôle de l'application et de l'interprétation de la loi étrangère par les juridictions du fond [41] ? Les lois nationales sur les investissements ont un contenu largement uniforme, avec des notions qui recouvrent celles utilisées dans les traités. Il n'est donc pas vrai que l'application des normes internationales dépende seulement de la source nationale ou internationale de la protection. Nonobstant une saisine sur le fondement de la loi égyptienne sur les investissements, la sentence *SPP c. Egypte* est convaincante dans son utilisation du droit international plutôt que du droit égyptien [42]. Lorsqu'une loi nationale assure la protection des investisseurs, elle prend place dans les relations internationales. Si cette loi vient à violer les exigences minimales de la protection, il doit y avoir sanction par le tribunal arbitral. Les organes de contrôle sont aussi encouragés à ranger leurs solutions sous la bannière du droit international.

18. L'attraction du droit international s'explique mieux si l'on accepte que la fonction du droit international dans le contrôle des sentences n'est pas la même que sa fonction dans les relations entre Etats. Si son rôle n'est pas différent de celui de la loi étrangère, l'application du droit international montre que l'on ne peut faire abstraction de l'ordre juridique international qui a donné naissance à la sentence, dont les objectifs et la cohérence sont mieux préservés qu'avec l'application du droit national. Que le droit international n'ait pas tout le temps le même caractère n'est pas gênant.

---

41. The Application of Foreign Law in Civil Matters in the EU Member States and its Perspectives for the Future, Institut Suisse de droit comparé, avis 09-184, 11 juillet 2011.

42. Décision sur la compétence, 14 avril 1988, *SPP c. Egypte*, ARB/84/3, par. 61, E. Gaillard, *La jurisprudence du CIRDI*, Pedone, 2004, vol. 1, p. 347.

CHAPITRE 2

LE DROIT INTERNATIONAL, ÉLÉMENT MODÉRATEUR DU CONTRÔLE

19. Le contrôle à l'aune du droit international n'exige pas que celui-ci régisse la sentence. Le droit international peut s'inviter dans le contrôle d'une sentence qui ne lui était pas soumise ou pour une question qui ne lui était pas soumise. Un droit international plus conquérant ne doit pas être la cause de débordements. Le contrôle doit être nécessaire pour éviter tout ce qui peut causer un trouble dans un ordre juridique international paisible. Pour restaurer l'harmonie, les organes de contrôle disposent d'instruments juridiques globaux, la Convention de New York ou la Convention de Washington, dont aucun ne les autorise à réviser le jugement des arbitres [43]. Il ne faudrait pas que le poids du droit international se transforme en restriction de la liberté des arbitres. D'autant qu'à partir du moment où on a reconnu un ordre juridique arbitral, il faut lui laisser les mains libres dans tous les domaines où il n'y a pas lieu de contrôler.

A. S'introduire dans le fond ?

20. Nous nous intéressons à la Convention de Vienne sur le droit des traités du 23 mai 1969 en tant qu'outil d'interprétation pour équilibrer le contrôle, et à la proportionnalité, en tant qu'outil méthodologique tout particulièrement pour la confrontation des condamnations pécuniaires et de la corruption à l'ordre public.

21. La Convention de Vienne représente une codification de la coutume internationale [44] dont les règles d'interprétation peuvent être appliquées indépendamment de sa ratification par l'Etat hôte signataire du traité de protection des investissements [45]. La Convention de Vienne

---

43. W. M. Reisman, *Systems of Control in International Adjudication & Arbitration*, Duke University Press, 1992.
44. M. Villiger, *Commentary on the 1969 Vienna Convention on the Law of Treaties*, Martinus Nijhoff, 2009, article 31, para. 25, p. 433. Voir aussi G. Berlia, «Contribution à l'interprétation des traités», *Recueil des cours*, tome 114 (1965), p. 287-334; L. Ehrlich, «L'interprétation des traités», *Recueil des cours*, tome 24 (1928), p. 1-146; H. Lauterpacht, «De l'interprétation des traités», *Annuaire de l'Institut de droit international*, Bâle, 1950, tome 1, p. 366.
45. TF, 25 mars 2020, 4A_306/2019, par. 3.4.1.

s'appliquant à l'interprétation de tout traité, la ratification par le for du traité de protection des investissements au regard duquel les arbitres statuent est une donnée non pertinente pour son application.

22. Il ne devrait pas être possible de s'introduire dans le fond au prétexte de contrôler la compétence [46]. La jurisprudence des pays européens qui sont le siège d'arbitrages d'investissement montre que le recours à la Convention de Vienne pour interpréter les clauses du traité maintient le contrôle dans les limites autorisées de la compétence, sans envahir le fond [47]. Les lignes du contrôle ne sont donc pas modifiées avec l'intervention de la Convention de Vienne. Mais en l'absence de mécanisme référendaire, comment éviter différentes interprétations nationales des conventions internationales ? Sans le soutien d'un mécanisme préjudiciel, la recherche d'une interprétation cohérente accentue l'intérêt du raisonnement comparatif. Un consensus n'est pas toujours atteint [48]. Les juges nationaux devraient s'efforcer d'interpréter les traités comme s'ils étaient des juges internationaux [49], particulièrement les juridictions supérieures, qui, par leur action régulatrice, approfondissent le contrôle en l'unifiant.

23. Cette proposition reste valable en cas de non-ratification du traité qui fonde l'arbitrage par le for. Assimiler un traité auquel le for n'est pas Partie à la loi étrangère dont la constatation est laissée au pouvoir souverain des juges du fond, ne rend pas compte que l'on ne peut donner à un traité un sens qui soit contraire au droit international [50]. Seule compte l'application du droit international dont les traités sont une source et auquel ils sont soumis. Il y a une obligation de respecter

---

46. Un délai de prescription, question de recevabilité, ne permet pas au juge de l'annulation, sous le couvert de compétence *ratione temporis*, de parcourir le fond en élaguant les condamnations des arbitres prononcées pour des faits dommageables considérés hors délai, Civ. 1re, 31 mars 2021, *Rusoro Mining c. Venezuela*, n° 19-11.551.

47. « International Investment Law in European Courts », dans *International Investment Law: An Analysis of the Major Decisions*, H. Ruiz Fabri et E. Stoppioni (dir. publ.), Oxford, Hart Publishing, 2022, p. 617.

48. Ainsi dans l'affaire *PAO Taneft c. Ukraine*, l'abus du droit d'agir devant le tribunal d'investissement est considéré comme une question de recevabilité par le juge anglais (jugement du 13 juillet 2018 [2018] EWHC 1797 (Comm), par. 99-100) donc insusceptible de contrôle, mais traité par le juge français comme une question de compétence sujette à contrôle (CA Paris, arrêt du 29 novembre 2016, *PAO Tatneft c. Ukraine*, n° 14/17964).

49. B. Conforti, « L'activité du juge interne et les relations internationales de l'Etat », *Annuaire de l'Institut de droit international*, session de Milan, vol. 65-I, Pedone, 1993, p. 328 ; H. Mosler, « L'application du droit international public par le juge interne », *Recueil des cours*, tome 91 (1957), p. 619.

50. Il ne s'agit pas d'appliquer des règles de droit étranger qui ont leur origine dans un traité non ratifié, Civ. 1re, 1er février 1972, *Rev. crit. DIP* 1973, p. 313, note G. Droz ; D. 1973.59, note P. Lagarde ; JCP 1973 II 17406, note M. G.

le droit international et donc de vérifier si ce qui est prévu par le traité a été observé. La solution inverse traduirait un manque de responsabilité par le refus de s'inscrire dans une application à vocation universelle des principes de bonne gouvernance qui régissent les investissements et façonnent les relations économiques internationales [51].

24. La proportionnalité est un principe de raisonnement de l'ordre juridique international, mais elle n'intervient pas systématiquement dans l'interprétation de tout traité. L'admission de la proportionnalité comme règle de droit dans les grands systèmes juridiques internes [52] ne suffit pas à en faire un principe général du droit international au sens de l'article 38 (1) *(c)* du Statut de la CIJ [53]. Mais la proportionnalité n'est pas qu'un principe commun aux systèmes juridiques nationaux, on peut aussi l'identifier comme un principe formé dans plusieurs sous-ordres juridiques internationaux, l'Organisation mondiale du commerce [54], l'Union européenne [55] et la Convention européenne des droits de l'homme [56], ou encore l'ordre juridique sportif [57]. La jurisprudence arbitrale sur les investissements y recourt également comme méthode d'interprétation des règles de protection [58].

---

51. G. Canivet, «Rôle et responsabilité des juridictions dans la mise en œuvre des principes de la gouvernance mondiale», dans Mélanges E. Zoller, p. 543.
52. A. Barak, *Proportionality*, Cambridge University Press, 2012 («Democracy, the rule of law, principle theory, and constitutional interpretation are all legal sources from which proportionality may be derived as a constitutional concept», p. 240). S. Breyer, *La Cour suprême, le droit américain et le monde*, préf. G. Canivet et O. Jacob, 2015, p. 268.
53. M. Vazquez-Bermudez, *2ᵉ rapport sur les principes généraux du droit*, CDI, 9 avril 2020, A/CN.4/741 (2ᵉ partie, p. 5-37).
54. M. Andenas et S. Zleptnig, «Proportionality and Balancing in WTO Law: a Comparative Law Perspective», 2007, *Texas Intl. Law Journal*, vol. 42.371.
55. CJCE, 13 novembre 1990, Fedesa, affaire C-331-88, par. 13. G. Canivet, «La fonction du principe en droit constitutionnel français et en droit européen», dans M. Delmas-Marty et S. Breyer (dir. publ.), Regards croisés sur l'internationalisation du droit: France-Etats-Unis, SLC, UMR de droit comparé de Paris, vol. 18, 2009, p. 140.
56. S. van Drooghenbroek, «La proportionnalité dans le droit de la Convention européenne des droits de l'homme : prendre l'idée simple au sérieux», *Publications des Facultés universitaires Saint Louis*, n° 90, 2001.
57. Sentence TAS 2018/0/5794 & 5798 du 30 avril 2019, par. 582-586; sentence TAS 2016/A/4745 du 30 août 2016, par. 73-85; sentence TAS 2016/O/4684 du 10 octobre 2016, par. 129-132; sentence TAS n° 2014/A/3665, 3666&3667 du 2 décembre 2014, par. 91-108; sentence TAS JO 00/04 du 18 septembre 2000, par. 11-12.
58. L'expropriation: *Tecmed c. Mexique* sentence du 29 mai 2003, CIRDI n° ARB (AF)/00/2, par. 122; *LG&E c. Argentine*, sentence du 25 juillet 2007, ARB/02/1, par. 195; *El Paso c. Argentine*, sentence du 31 octobre 2011, ARB/03/15, par. 241, 243 (CIRDI); *Azurix c. Argentine*, sentence du 14 juillet 2006, ARB/01/12, par. 311-312; *Siemens c. Argentine*, sentence du 17 janvier 2007, CIRDI n° ARB/02/8, par. 354; *PL Holdings c. Poland*, SCC affaire n° 2014/13, sentence du 28 juin 2017, par. 354-391.

L'obligation de pleine protection et sécurité (FPS) et le traitement juste et équitable (FET): *Occidental c. Equateur*, sentence du 5 octobre 2012, ARB/06/11, par. 402-452;

25. Il est difficile de caractériser une violation de l'ordre public [59] ou un excès de pouvoir [60] à propos d'une interprétation. L'application de la proportionnalité par le tribunal arbitral est difficile à contrôler parce qu'on se heurte rapidement au fond, qui est incontrôlable. Peut-on déraper vers le fond, lors du contrôle de la sentence, en utilisant la proportionnalité? Il y a des exemples [61]. Il ne s'agit pas avec la proportionnalité de renverser les solutions, même les mieux acquises. Mais il ne faut pas méconnaître l'utilité méthodologique de la proportionnalité pour le maniement de l'exception d'ordre public. Nous en avons un exemple avec la jurisprudence du Tribunal fédéral suisse à propos d'une sanction disciplinaire imposée dans un arbitrage sportif dont la proportionalité ne pourrait se poser « sous l'angle restreint de l'incompatibilité à l'ordre public, que si la sentence consacrait une atteinte à la personnalité qui soit extrêmement grave et hors de toute proportion avec le comportement qu'elle sanctionne » [62]. Le refus d'accueillir la sentence est une ingérence dans le droit à l'exécution effective des

---

MTD c. Chili, ARB/01/7, sentence du 25 mai 2004, par. 109; *Marfin c. Chypre*, sentence 26 juillet 2018, ARB/13/27, par. 1211-1213; *Joseph Lemire c. Ukraine*, décision sur la compétence et la responsabilité du 14 janvier 2010, ARB/06/18, par. 285; *Saluka Investments c. République Tchèque*, sentence partielle CNUDCI du 17 mars 2006, par. 306; *Total c. Argentine*, décision sur la responsabilité du 27 décembre 2010, n° ARB/04/01, par. 123, 162, 164; *Belenergia c. Italie*, affaire ARB/15/40, sentence du 6 août 2019, par. 605,606; *Electrabel c. Hongrie*, sentence du 25 novembre 2015, ARB/07/19, par. 179, 219; *Stadtwerke München c. Espagne*, sentence 2 décembre 2019, ARB/15/1, par. 323-355; *RWE Innogy c. Espagne*, décision, 30 décembre 2019, ARB/14/34, par. 550-600; *Antaris & Göde c. Rep. Tchèque*, PCA affaire 2014-01, sentence 2 mai 2018, par. 444-445; *EDF c. Roumanie*, sentence du 8 octobre 2009, ARB/05/13, par. 293. G. Bücheler, Proportionality in Investor-State Arbitration, Oxford University Press, 2015.
Clause d'exclusion (NPM): *Continental Casualty c. Argentine*, sentence du 5 septembre 2008, CIRDI n° ARB/03/9, par. 227.
59. TF 25 août 2020, 4A_248/2019 et 4A_298/2019, par. 9.8.2-9.8.3.
60. Décision du comité *ad hoc* 2 novembre 2015, *Occidental Petroleum Corp. & Occidental Petroleum Cie c. République de l'Equateur*, ARB/06/11, par. 343-351.
61. CA Caire, 3 juin 2020, n° 39/130, par. 22:

> « L'indemnité accordée par la sentence en tant qu'indemnité pour gain manqué, a dépassé les limites raisonnables et a contredit ses objectifs, devenant une indemnité injuste, inéquitable, mal fondée, ne prenant pas en compte les buts juridiques des parties de l'arbitrage. Et ce, car ladite sentence viole les garanties de la sécurité juridique visée par tout législateur. Ce dépassement injuste de toute limite a eu son impact négatif sur la sentence d'arbitrage et la structure de son prononcé. »

62. TF, 31 mars 1999, 5P.83/1999, par. 3 *(c)*, Recueil des sentences du TAS, M. Reeb (dir. publ.), vol. II, 1998-2000, Kluwer Law International, 2002, p. 767. Voir aussi, TF, 25 août 2020, 4A_248_2019 & 4A_398_2019 pour la proportionnalité d'une mesure de traitement hormonal imposée par un règlement sportif avec le principe d'interdiction de discrimination.

décisions de justice [63]. En tant qu'aspect du droit au procès équitable [64], le droit à l'exécution n'est pas absolu [65], mais l'atteinte doit rester proportionnée et légitime.

26. Rappelons pour les condamnations pécuniaires, les plus fréquentes en arbitrage, que la r*estitutio in integrum* [66] est un principe de raisonnement [67]. Si elle est aussi un principe général ayant pour objectif d'éviter la double indemnisation [68], l'obligation de réparation intégrale n'est pas un principe fondamental [69]. Une condamnation à des dommages intérêts punitifs n'est pas en soi contraire à l'ordre public international, sauf « lorsque le montant alloué est disproportionné au regard du préjudice subi et des manquements aux obligations contractuelles du débiteur » a jugé la Cour de cassation française [70]. Ceci n'est pas une invite à revisiter le montant de la condamnation au regard des facultés de paiement du débiteur, mais à vérifier si la condamnation prononcée est mesurée à l'inexécution contractuelle dans les circonstances de

---

63. CEDH, 29 avril 2008, *McDonald c. France*, requête n° 18648/04 ; 3 mai 2011, *Negropontis c. Grèce*, requête n° 56759/08, par. 89-92 ; 18 décembre 2008, *Sacoccia c. Autriche*, requête n° 69917/01, par. 60-62.

64. CEDH, 19 mars 1997, *Hornsby*, requête n° 18357/91, par. 40 ; 31 octobre 2006, *Jelicic c. Bosnie-Herzégovine*, requête n° 41183/02, par. 38 ; 15 janvier 2009, *Bourdov c. Russie*, requête n° 33509/04, par. 65 ; 7 janvier 2014, *Fondation foyer de l'église réformée c. Roumanie*, requête n° 2699/03, par. 55.

65. CEDH, 18 février 1999, *Waite et Kennedy c. Allemagne*, requête n° 26083/94, par. 59.

66. CPIJ, arrêt du 13 septembre 1928, *Usine de Chorzow*, série A, n° 27, 1928, Leyde, Sijthoff.

67. *Texaco c. Libye*, sentence ad hoc du 19 janvier 1977, par. 98.

68. Les articles de la CDI sur la responsabilité de l'Etat, Pedone, 2003, article 36, p. 260.

69. TF 8 avril 2021, 4A_516/2020

« Les principes du droit international ne confèrent d'ailleurs pas un droit absolu à une pleine indemnisation (arrêt précité 4P.200/2001 let. B et consid. 2c). Pour le surplus, la cour de céans n'a pas à sanctionner, au titre de l'ordre public, une interprétation erronée, voire arbitraire d'une clause d'un TBI ; elle ne peut être conduite à examiner si l'indemnité prévue par le TBI inclut ou non le manque à gagner (arrêt précité 4P.200/2001 consid. 2c in fine ; arrêt 4A_157/2017 du 14 décembre 2017 consid. 3.3.4) » (par. 4.2.3)

« ... En l'occurrence, cet ordre n'est pas déjà nécessairement enfreint parce que l'investisseur turc n'obtient pas la réparation intégrale de son dommage, parce qu'il se voit allouer une indemnité ne couvrant pas complètement le préjudice subi - ou ne se trouvant pas dans une proportion raisonnable avec la valeur des investissements perdus. Encore faut-il qu'en tenant compte de toutes les circonstances concrètes, l'indemnité apparaisse hors de toute proportion avec la valeur de l'investissement perdu, qu'il y ait entre les deux une extrême disproportion au point de heurter de manière choquante les principes les plus essentiels de l'ordre juridique. Or, comme cela sera démontré ci-dessous, un tel cas de figure n'est pas réalisé » (par. 4.4).

70. Civ. 1re, 1er décembre 2010, n° 09-13.303 ; Civ. 1re, 7 novembre 2012, n° 1123871.

l'espèce[71]. La non-reconnaissance de la sentence ne viole-t-elle pas le droit au respect des biens de la partie créancière[72]? Le droit au respect des biens est une valeur essentielle protégée par l'ordre public international et les droits de l'homme. La créance indemnitaire dans le patrimoine du bénéficiaire de la sentence est ainsi un bien protégé auquel toute atteinte portée par la non-reconnaissance doit rester proportionnée[73].

27. Un droit international discret, même en cas de critique de la violation de l'ordre public, est-il encore de mise aujourd'hui? L'ordre public a toujours mis en avant la lutte contre la corruption, le trafic d'influence et le blanchiment, comme le démontre la consultation de la jurisprudence arbitrale[74]. La réprobation de ces comportements s'effectue sur le fondement du principe général du caractère illicite de la corruption dans la *lex mercatoria* et dans le droit international, où il est exprimé dans plusieurs conventions internationales[75]. Même si ces dernières ne sont pas d'application directe, les valeurs qu'elles protègent sont assurément essentielles pour l'ordre juridique du for. Le contrôle de la corruption, tel qu'il se présente devant certaines juridictions au regard de leur droit national, est destructif de la distinction entre contrôle de l'ordre public et révision au fond[76]. Le droit international ne commande en rien de s'assurer de la correction de la sentence comme dans un appel. C'est à travers le prisme du recours contre la sentence que le juge doit effectuer toute appréciation de la corruption, et non directement, comme le ferait l'arbitre.

---

71. Civ. 1re, 17 octobre 2018, n° 17-18.995, *Rev. crit. DIP*, 2019, p. 982, note P. de Vareilles-Sommières; Civ. 1re, 12 janvier 2022, n° 2016189; Civ. 1re, 28 janvier 2009, n° 07-11.729.
72. Cette problématique a été remarquablement développée par le professeur P. de Vareilles-Sommières, *Rev. crit. DIP*, 2019, p. 982, n° 19.
73. CEDH, 30 juin 2022, *BTS Holding c. Slovak Republic*, requête n° 55617/17, par. 53; *Raffineries grecques Stran et Stratis Andreadis c. Grèce*, 9 décembre 1994, par. 58-62, série A n° 301-B; également CEDH, 24 septembre 2013, *Pennino c. Italie*, requête n° 42892/04, par. 54-60 (décision de justice).
74. Sentence CIRDI ARB/00/7 du 4 octobre 2006, *Work Duty Free Ltd. c. Republic of Kenya*; Sentence CCI 12290 de 2005, J.-J. Arnaldez, Y. Derains et D. Hascher, *Recueil des sentences arbitrales de la CCI*, vol. VII, 2008-2011, Kluwer, p. 831. E. Gaillard, «La corruption saisie par les arbitres du commerce international», Rev. arb. 2017, p. 805; A. Llamzon, «Corruption in International Investment Arbitration», OUP, 2014.
75. Conventions des Nations Unies de Mérida du 9 décembre 2003 contre la corruption et de Palerme du 15 novembre 2000 contre la criminalité transnationale organisée, Convention OCDE du 17 décembre 1997 sur la lutte contre la corruption d'agents publics étrangers dans les transactions commerciales internationales.
76. I. Fadlallah, «L'ordre public dans les sentences arbitrales», *Recueil des cours*, tome 249 (1994), p. 369; la corruption corrompt l'arbitrage, *Rev. arb.* 2022, 620.

28. Voici les questions pertinentes auxquelles il convient de répondre. La sentence qui ouvre droit à une indemnité compensatrice au profit de la partie à laquelle on reproche un comportement illicite, heurte-t-elle le droit au respect des biens de la partie condamnée à indemniser ? Ou bien cette dernière peut-elle prétendre, sans excéder le droit au respect de ses biens, à une solution confiscatoire consistant à conserver l'investissement sans indemnisation ? Cette question est d'autant plus pressante que les pouvoirs publics de l'Etat hôte de l'investissement sont souvent complices de l'illégalité reprochée à l'investisseur qui a remporté l'arbitrage. En abandonnant à l'Etat l'investissement et le prix d'acquisition versé par l'investisseur attiré par le climat de corruption entretenu par l'Etat hôte qui confisque encore les bénéfices des activités de blanchiment de l'investisseur auxquelles il a activement participé, la jurisprudence Belokon [77] représente un solide encouragement à la corruption institutionnalisée. Dans la réponse à ces questions, il conviendra d'examiner le comportement respectif des parties, pour évaluer si l'atteinte au droit au respect des biens d'une partie est légitime et proportionnée.

29. On réduit l'impérativité des normes avec la proportionnalité pour mieux canaliser la confrontation à l'ordre public en évitant une révision au fond de la sentence [78]. Technique de conciliation entre systèmes juridiques pour résoudre les conflits entre normes, la proportionnalité est un encouragement au dialogue entre les juridictions [79]. Encore faut-il que les juridictions soient accessibles au dialogue, ce qui n'est pas possible si l'on défend une position politique.

B. Les limites

30. La Cour de justice de l'Union européenne (« CJUE ») détruit l'arbitrabilité des litiges fondés sur les traités de protection des investissements considérés comme contraire aux traités européens. Peu importe qu'il ne soit pas sûr que le droit européen joue un rôle

---

77. Cass. civ. 1re, 23 mars 2022, *Belokon c. Kirghizistan*, n° 17-17.981. Pour une solution équilibrée, voir affaire *Spentex c. Ouzbekistan* (sentence CIRDI du 27 décembre 2016, n° ARB/13/26) ; Ch. Jarrosson, La jurisprudence Belokon-Sorelec, ou l'avènement d'un contrôle illimité des sentences, *Rev. arb.* 2022, 1251.

78. K. Lund-Turner, « The Corruption Defense in Investment-Treaty Arbitration : Tempering the Zero-Tolerance Approach », *Pacific McGeorge School of Law*, Spring 2015.

79. S. W. Schill, « Cross-Regime Harmonization through Proportionality Analysis : The Case of International Investment Law, the Law of State Immunity and Human Rights », *ICSID Review*, vol. 27, n° 1 (2012), p. 87.

dans la résolution du litige. Divers motifs sont avancés. On va de l'absence de mécanisme référendaire pour un tribunal arbitral alors que l'interprétation du droit d'un Etat membre est toujours susceptible de soulever une interprétation du droit européen, au caractère obligatoire du droit européen pour les juridictions et les institutions des Etats membres dont il faut garantir la pleine application, en passant par la soustraction dans un accord international, signé ou non par l'Union européenne, au système juridictionnel de l'Union[80]. Tout se passe comme si un traité auquel un Etat membre est partie était, pour ce qui le concerne, comme une loi nationale soumise à l'ordre européen.

31. La jurisprudence de la CJUE modifie les équilibres antérieurs, en retournant à l'époque où l'on avait interdit aux arbitres d'appliquer des règles d'ordre public. Elle nous ramène à une conception du droit international contraire aux origines mêmes de ce droit[81]. Aucun système juridique n'interdit aux autres d'appliquer ses règles, car il n'y a pas de règles plus dignes que d'autres, d'autant que le droit européen pose avant tout des questions de réglementation économique qui se prêtent mal à une reconnaissance universelle[82]. Le droit international commande plutôt la dissidence que le respect par rapport au droit européen.

32. On mesure avec l'affaire *Micula* les répercussions de la politique jurisprudentielle européenne sur le système international d'exécution des sentences. L'exécution de la sentence CIRDI, rendue

---

80. CJUE, Achmea, arrêt du 6 mars 2018, affaire C-284/16, *Rev. crit. DIP*, 2018, p. 616, note E. Gaillard; CJUE 26 octobre 2021, *PL Holdings c. Pologne*, affaire C-109/20; CJUE, 2 septembre 2021, *Moldavie c. Komstroy*, affaire C-741/19. EU Law and International Investment Arbitration, H. Ruiz-Fabri et E. Gaillard (dir. publ.), IAI 2018; G. Cordero-Moss, «Towards the End of Arbitrability? About Achmea, Komstroy», PL Holdings *et al.*, Conférence Brierley, 19 janvier 2022.

81. B. Ancel, «Eléments d'histoire du droit international privé», Panthéon-Assas, 2017.

82. TF 1er février 2002, 128 III 234

«De toute manière, comme le Tribunal fédéral a déjà eu l'occasion de le relever, il paraît douteux que les dispositions du droit – national ou européen – de la concurrence fassent partie des principes juridiques ou moraux fondamentaux reconnus dans tous les Etats civilisés au point que leur violation devrait être considérée comme contraire à l'ordre public (arrêt 4P.119/1998 du 13 novembre 1998, consid. 1b/bb, ...). D'ailleurs, l'auteur cité par la recourante constate, même s'il le déplore, qu'au regard de ce dernier arrêt, l'arbitre siégeant en Suisse est certes obligé d'appliquer le droit communautaire de la concurrence, mais que cette obligation ne peut faire l'objet d'aucune sanction au stade du recours en annulation...».

W. Ganshof van der Meersch, L'ordre juridique des Communautés européennes et le droit international, *Recueil des cours*, tome 148 (1975), p. 1; 50e anniversaire de l'arrêt van Geend en Loos, 1963-2013, Actes du Colloque, Luxembourg, 13 mai 2013, Office des pubs de l'UE, 2013.

sur le fondement du tribunal entre la Suède et la Roumanie revenant, pour la Commission européenne, à accorder une aide d'état en infraction avec le traité sur le fonctionnement de l'Union européenne, la Roumanie avait reçu interdiction de satisfaire l'investisseur[83]. La Roumanie était toutefois débitrice, outre indemniser l'investisseur, d'une autre obligation internationale, celle de donner effet à la sentence en vertu de l'article 53 de la Convention de Washington. Saisi d'une demande d'exécution de la sentence, le juge anglais avait l'obligation de mettre en œuvre l'article 54 (1) de ladite Convention prescrivant aux Etats contractants d'assurer l'exécution des obligations pécuniaires imposées par la sentence. A la Roumanie, qui proposait d'interpréter la Convention du CIRDI selon les visions européennes, la Cour suprême britannique oppose les principes d'interprétation du droit international, mettant ainsi un engagement international du Royaume Uni au-dessus du droit européen :

> « The first step in the analysis should be to ask whether the United Kingdom has relevant obligations arising from the ICSID Convention which, by operation of Article 351 TFEU, preclude the application of the Treaties... on a proper interpretation of the ICSID Convention, the United Kingdom clearly does have such obligations. Therefore, the Treaties do not have any relevant effect and this court is not bound by EU law to interpret the Convention in the manner for which Romania contends. In any event, the proper interpretation of the Convention is given by principles of international law applicable to all Contracting States and it cannot be affected by EU law. »[84]

33. C'est un raisonnement que la Commission européenne ne peut accepter et elle a ouvert une procédure en infraction à l'encontre du Royaume-Uni[85]. On sort donc du droit international pour prohiber l'arbitrage en vertu du droit européen.

---

83. Décision (UE) 2015/470 de la Commission du 30 mars 2015, JO (L 232) 2015, p. 43.
84. [2020] UKSC 5, arrêt du 19 février 2020, par. 87.
85. Communiqué de presse de la Commission européenne du 9 février 2022.

CHAPITRE 3

UN CONTRÔLE NOURRI DE PRINCIPES UNIVERSELLEMENT RECONNUS, ÉLEVÉS AU RANG DE PRINCIPES DE DROIT INTERNATIONAL, À TITRE DE LANGAGE COMMUN

34. Les principes sont une source de droit dans tous les systèmes juridiques. En raison de son postulat universaliste, on a remarqué que «[l]e droit international des droits de l'homme offre un environnement particulièrement fertile au dialogue entre juges»[86]. Le plus démonstratif est, dès lors, de prendre les droits fondamentaux comme guide pour illustrer l'adhésion à des valeurs fédératrices à titre d'exemple d'un langage commun. Les valeurs universelles portées par ces droits expliquent leur intervention dans les relations entre associations sportives et athlètes par le biais des principes généraux du droit[87].

35. Le contrôle des sentences mobilise sans conteste les traités sur les droits de l'homme en vigueur dans le for[88]. Est-il plus difficile pour un comité *ad hoc*, agissant sous l'égide de la Convention de Washington, d'appliquer le droit international des droits de l'homme ? Hormis un comité *ad hoc* qui n'a su qu'en faire, au prétexte que les traités qui n'ont pas pour objet la protection des investissements, sont d'une utilité limitée[89], on relève qu'un premier comité *ad hoc* dans l'affaire *Fraport c. Philippines* convoque les principaux instruments internationaux sur les droits de l'Homme[90] et que, s'appuyant sur cette

---

86. L. Hennebel et A. van Waeyenberge, «Réflexions sur le commerce transnational entre juges», dans I. Hachez, Y. Cartuyvels, H. Dumont, Ph. Gérard, F. Ost et M. van de Kerchove (dir. publ.), *Les sources du droit revisitées, vol. 2, normes internes et infraconstitutionnelles*, Université Saint-Louis, 2012, p. 713.
87. M. Maisonneuve, «Le TAS et les droits fondamentaux», RDLF 2017, chron. 09.
88. CEDH, 2 octobre 2018, *Mutu et Pechstein c. Suisse*, requête n° 40575/10 et 67474/10 ; 20 mai 2021, *BEG c. Italie*, requête n° 5312/11.
89. Décision du comité *ad hoc* du 1 septembre 2009, *Azurix c. Argentine*, CIRDI n° ARB/01/12 (par. 128).
90. *Fraport c. Philippines*, décision du 23 décembre 2010, CIRDI n° ARB/03/25 (Déclaration universelle des droits de l'homme, Pacte international relatif aux droits civils et politiques et Convention de sauvegarde des droits de l'homme et des libertés fondamentale) «The right to present one's case is also accepted as an essential element of the requirement to afford a fair hearing accorded in the principal human rights instruments» (par. 202).

décision, un autre comité *ad hoc* dans l'affaire *Churchill Mining c. Indonésie* fait référence aux traités sur les droits de l'homme comme source du contenu du droit à être entendu :

> « Even if ad hoc committees operate within the ICSID Convention, the reference to the jurisprudence of specialized courts which are an integral part of human rights treaties fosters the consistency of the content of the right to be heard and strengthens the effectiveness of this concept. It also enhances the legitimacy of the interpretation by linking it to the broader body of international law. » [91]

36. Mais c'est le comité *ad hoc* dans l'affaire *Tulip Real Estate and Development Netherlands c. République de Turquie* qui a systématisé l'introduction des droits de l'Homme en recourant à l'article 31 (3) *(c)* de la Convention de Vienne sur le droit des traités :

> « Provisions in human rights instruments dealing with the right to a fair trial and any judicial practice thereto are relevant to the interpretation of the concept of a fundamental rule of procedure as used in Article 52 (1) *(d)* of the ICSID Convention. This is not to add obligations extraneous to the ICSID Convention. Rather, resort to authorities stemming from the field of human rights for this purpose is a legitimate method of treaty interpretation. » [92]

37. Il y a également un comité *ad hoc* qui s'est fondé sur le principe du droit international à un juge indépendant et impartial pour ouvrir, au-delà de la seule constitution du tribunal mentionnée à l'article 52 (1) *(a)* de la Convention de Washington, le contrôle de la sentence à l'indépendance et l'impartialité des arbitres [93].

38. S'il est exact que les droits de l'homme n'ont pas pour objectif la protection des investissements [94], l'investisseur n'est pas, pour autant, exclu de leurs préoccupations [95], au point qu'un auteur a pu

---

91. *Churchill Mining c. Indonésie*, décision du 18 mars 2019, CIRDI n° ARB/12/14 et 12/40, par. 179.
92. Décision du comité *ad hoc* du 30 décembre 2015, CIRDI n° ARB/11/28, par. 87, 92.
93. Décision du comité *ad hoc* du 11 juin 2020 *Eiser c. Spain*, CIRDI n° ARB/13/36, par. 176-178.
94. *Mondev c. USA*, sentence du 11 octobre 2002, ARB(AF)/99/2, par. 144 ; *Veteran Petroleum c. Russia*, sentence CPA du 18 juillet 2014, n° AA228, par. 765.
95. *Human Rights in International Investment Law and Arbitration*, P.-M. Dupuy, F. Francioni et E.-U. Petersmann (dir. publ.), OUP, 2010 ; A. Pellet, « Notes sur la fragmentation du droit international : droit des investissements et droits de l'Homme »,

parler de « bizarre human rights treaty » concentré sur les seuls droits de l'investisseur [96]. Certes, les tribunaux arbitraux ne peuvent statuer qu'au regard du traité de protection des investissements qui leur donne compétence [97], mais il faut distinguer la compétence du droit applicable [98]. Un traité ne peut être considéré isolément du droit international [99]. Les atteintes à la propriété, à la sécurité juridique ou à la prévisibilité du droit, à la réputation et à la vie privée, la discrimination, le déni de justice [100] enfreignent des valeurs communes à une pluralité d'ordres juridiques ainsi qu'au droit de l'investissement [101]. Des sentences soulignent l'importance des droits de l'Homme, en tant que partie

---

écrits en l'honneur de Pierre-Marie Dupuy, Martinus Nijhoff, 2014, p. 757 ; V. Kube et E.-U. Petersmann, « Human Rights Law in International Investment Arbitration », *EUI Working Paper Law* 2016 (2) AJWH, p. 65. G. Puma, « Human Rights Law and Investment Law : Attempts at Harmonization Through a Difficult Dialogue Between Arbitrators and Human Rights Tribunals », dans M. Arcari et L. Balmond (dir. publ.), *Le dialogue des juridictions dans l'ordre juridique international*, Editoriale Scientifica, 2014, p. 193.

96. J. E. Alvarez, « Critical Theory and the North American Free Trade Agreement's Chapter Eleven », 28 *U. Miami Inter-Am Law Rev.* 303 n° 2 (1996).

97. *Pezold c. Zimbabwe*, ordonnance n° 2 du 26 juin 2012, CIRDI n° ARB/10/15, par. 57 ; *Rompetrol c. Roumanie*, sentence du 6 mai 2013, CIRDI n° ARB/06/3, par. 172.

98. C. McLachlan, « The Principle of Systemic Integration and Article 31 (1) *(c)* of the Vienna Convention », ICLQ, vol 54, avril 2005, p. 279-320.

99. *Phoenix c. République Tchèque*, sentence CIRDI ARB/06/5 du 15 avril 2009 :

« It is evident to the Tribunal that the same holds true in international investment law and that the ICSID Convention's jurisdictional requirements – as well as those of the BIT cannot be read and interpreted in isolation from public international law, and its general principles » (par. 78).

100. C. de Visscher, « Le déni de justice en droit international », *Recueil des cours*, tome 52 (1935), p. 365 ; J. Paulsson, « Issues arising from Findings of Denial of Justice », *Recueil des cours*, tome 405 (2019), p. 9.

101. P. Juillard, « Existe-t-il des principes généraux du droit international économique ? », études Alain Plantey, Pedone, 1995, p. 243 ; M. Paparinskis, « The International Minimum Standard and Fair and equitable Treatment », OUP, 2013, p. 171 ; « Convergences et contradictions du droit des investissements et des droits de l'Homme : une approche contentieuse », W. Ben Hamida et F. Coulée (dir. publ.), Pedone, 2017 ; B. Simma, « Foreign Investment Arbitration : A Place for Human Rights ? », ICQL, vol. 60, juillet 2011, p. 573-596 ; C. McLachlan, L. Shore et M. Weiniger, « International Investment Arbitration », OUP, 2010, n° 7.15. Dans la jurisprudence arbitrale, on consultera *Saluka c. République tchèque*, sentence partielle CPA du 17 mars 2006 (CNUDCI), par. 308, 309 ; *Waste Management c. Mexique*, sentence du 30 avril 2004, ARB(AF)/00/3 (Alena), par. 98 ; *Jan de Nul c. Egypte*, sentence du 6 novembre 2008, CIRDI, ARB/04/13, par. 188 ; *Victor Pey Casado c. Chili*, sentence du 8 mai 2008, CIRDI, ARB/98/2, par. 657 ; *Alex Genin c. Estonie*, sentence du 25 juin 2001, CIRDI, n° ARB/99/2, par. 348-373. *Robert Azinian c. Mexique*, sentence du 1ᵉʳ novembre 1999, n° ARB (AF)/97/2, par. 97-103 *EDF & Saur c. Argentine*, sentence du 11 juin 2012, CIRDI, ARB/03/23, par. 909-914 ; *Rumeli Telekom c. Kazakhstan*, sentence du 29 juillet 2008, CIRDI, ARB/05/16, par. 651-654 ; *Loewen c. USA*, sentence du 26 juin 2003, ARB(AF)/98/3, par. 129 ; *Chevron & Texaco c. Ecuador*, sentence partielle CPA, n° 2007-02/AA277 du 30 mars 2010, par. 242-244 ; *Chevron & Texaco c. Ecuador*,

du droit international, pour les préoccupations environnementales [102]. La différence de méthode ou de contenu d'un ordre juridique à l'autre n'est pas ce qui importe, mais l'utilisation croisée des sources [103].

39. La jurisprudence arbitrale dévoile un travail analogique, d'inspiration, de transposition, comme on peut également le voir avec l'utilisation méthodologique de la proportionnalité [104]. Des tribunaux arbitraux se sont refusés à prendre en compte tout autre traité des droits de l'homme que celui ratifié par les Etats concernés par l'arbitrage [105]. L'universalité des valeurs défendues doit conduire, de préférence, à une vision plus large qui, nonobstant l'état des ratifications ou le champ d'application géographique du traité, mène à la prise en compte combinée de plusieurs instruments, au moins à titre de raisonnement par analogie avec les protections des traités sur les investissements [106], sinon en tant qu'expression de principes généraux du droit au sens de

---

sentence CPA n° 2009-23 du 30 août 2018, par. 7.12, 7.13 ; *Lauder c. République tchèque*, sentence CNUDCI du 3 septembre 2001, par. 200.

102. *Urbaser c. Argentine*, sentence CIRDI du 8 décembre 2016, ARB/07/26, par. 1193-1221 ; *Saur International c. Argentine*, décision sur la compétence et la responsabilité du 6 juin 2012, CIRDI n° ARB/04/4, par. 328-332. O. Danic, «Droit international des investissements, droits de l'Homme, droit de l'environnement», dans Ch. Leben (dir. publ.), *Droit international des investissements et de l'arbitrage transnational*, Pedone, 2015, p. 531 ; T. Voon et A. Mitchell, «Community Interests and the Rights to Health in Trade and Investment Law», OUP, 2018, p. 249.

103. *Rompetrol c. Roumanie*, sentence du 6 mai 2013, CIRDI n° ARB/06/3, par. 172.

104. Cl. Reiner et Ch. Schreuer, «Human Rights and International Investment Arbitration», dans P.-M. Dupuy, F. Francioni et E.-U. Petersmann (dir. publ.), *Human Rights in International Investment Law and Arbitration*, OUP, 2010, p. 82 ; B. Simma, «Foreign Investment Arbitration : A Place for Human Rights?», ICQL, vol. 60, juillet 2011, p. 573-596 ; G. Bücheler, *Proportionality in Investor-State Arbitration*, OUP, 2015.

105. Décision sur la compétence du 11 septembre 2009, CIRDI n° ARB/07/12, *Toto Costruzioni c. Liban*, par. 150, 157-158.

106. Déni de justice : *Chevron c. Ecuador*, sentence CPA n° 2009-23 du 30 août 2018, par. 8.57-8.58 (Déclaration universelle des droits de l'homme du 10 décembre 1948, Pacte international relatif aux droits civils et politiques du 16 décembre1966, Convention américaine des droits de l'homme du 22 novembre 1969).
Présomption d'innocence : sentence CNUDCI du 15 décembre 2014, *Hesham Al Warraq c. Indonésie*, par. 556-569 (Pacte international relatif aux droits civils et politiques du 16 décembre1966), par. 572, 577 (Comité des droits de l'homme NU), par. 574 (Cour interaméricaine des droits de l'homme), par. 575 (CEDH, Charte africaine des droits de l'homme et des peuples du 1er juin 1981 et Commission africaine des droits de l'homme et des peuples), par. 576 (Déclaration NU 1948) ; *Non bis in idem* : TAS2007/A/1396&1402, sentence du 31 mai 2010, par. 116, 117 (Pacte 1966, Protocole n° 7 CEDH).
Protection des intérêts essentiels de l'Etat et circonstances excluant l'illicéité : *El Paso c. Argentine*, sentence du 31 octobre 2011, CIRDI n° ARB/03/15, par. 561, 598 (CEDH (art. 15), Convention interaméricaine (art. 27))).

l'article 38 (1) du Statut de la CIJ [107]. La jurisprudence de la Cour européenne des droits de l'Homme [108] occupe une place importante dans ce travail de mise en cohérence [109].

40. La jurisprudence arbitrale nous rappelle que les sentences rendues en application d'un traité d'investissement n'assurent que la protection des investissements et ne peuvent réprimer, en tant que telle, une violation des droits de l'homme [110]. La mission des arbitres n'est pas la réforme judiciaire [111] et on a relevé l'absence d'objectif de transformation sociale dans le droit des investissements qui «n'est pas un instrument de l'ordre public du marché de l'Etat d'accueil» [112]. La Cour européenne des droits de l'homme remplit une mission constitutionnelle au service des objectifs de la société démocratique. Un tribunal arbitral n'exerce pas une mission de nature constitutionnelle, comme une juridiction nationale ou une cour régionale des droits de l'homme. En l'absence d'un mécanisme préjudiciel, les tribunaux arbitraux ont d'ailleurs reconnu les obstacles posés à une action de contrôle de constitutionnalité [113]. Ceci ne doit pas empêcher les arbitres

---

107. M. Virally, «Le rôle des «principes» dans le développement du droit international», dans *Etudes Guggenheim*, Faculté de droit de Genève, 1968, p. 531.
108.
109. *Tecmed c. Mexique*, sentence du 29 mai 2003, CIRDI n° ARB(AF)/00/2, par. 122; *Philip Morris c. Uruguay*, CIRDI, sentence du 8 juillet 2016, ARB/10/7, par. 531; *El Paso c. Argentine*, sentence du 31 octobre 2011, CIRDI, n° ARB/03/15, par. 598; *Total c. Argentine*, décision sur la responsabilité du 27 décembre 2010, n° ARB/04/01, par. 129; *Perenco c. Equateur*, Décision sur les mesures provisoires du 8 mai 2009, ARB/08/6, par. 70; *Victor Pey Casado*, sentence du 8 mai 2008, n° ARB/98/2, par. 662; *Saipem c. Bangladesh*, décision sur la compétence et les mesures provisoires du 21 mars 2007, ARB/05/07, par. 130-132; *ADC c. Hongrie*, sentence du 2 octobre 2006, ARB/03/16, par. 497; *Mondev c. USA*, sentence du 11 octobre 2002, ARB(AF)/99/2, par. 138, 141-144.
110. *Biloune c. Ghana*, sentence (CNUDCI) sur la compétence et la responsabilité du 27 octobre 1989, par. 61; *Loewen c. Etats-Unis*, sentence du 26 juin 2003, ARB(AF)/98/3, par. 242.
111. *Philip Morris c. Uruguay*, sentence CIRDI du 8 juillet 2016, ARB/10/7: «arbitral tribunals should not act as courts of appeal to find a denial of justice, still less as bodies charged with improving the judicial architecture of the State», par. 528.
112. E. Castellarin, «Le principe de non-discrimination», dans W. Ben Hamida et F. Coulée (dir. publ.), *Convergences et contradictions du droit des investissements et des droits de l'Homme: une approche contentieuse*, Pedone, 2017, p. 171, 196.
113. Sentence CCI n° 6320 de 1992:
> «Un tribunal arbitral peut initialement douter de sa compétence en matière d'inconstitutionnalité d'une loi nationale, même s'il est compétent pour se prononcer sur son application. En effet, en déclarant qu'une loi promulguée dans un Etat souverain est inconstitutionnelle et en se refusant à l'appliquer pour ce motif, le tribunal nierait la validité et les effets d'une partie du droit de cet Etat, alors qu'elle est encore en vigueur dans le territoire de cet Etat et qu'elle n'a pas été déclarée inconstitutionnelle par les tribunaux compétents. De l'avis du tribunal, il est tout à fait vraisemblable qu'il ne possède pas et ne peut exercer un

de vérifier si une loi de l'Etat hôte est, pour les raisons qui conduiraient à son inconstitutionnalité, également contraire aux valeurs protégées par le traité de protection des investissements. Non pour faire cesser la violation des droits constitutionnels ou fondamentaux, mais pour tirer les conclusions quant au non-respect des normes du traité. La tendance à respecter les Etats ne saurait l'emporter sur les violations des droits humains qui peuvent constituer, en même temps, une violation des droits de l'investisseur.

41. Plus généralement, il n'est pas interdit de défendre des objectifs et des valeurs pour apprécier la validité des sentences. L'internationalité des organes de contrôle ne les prédispose pas obligatoirement à l'internationalisme dans leurs décisions, mais peut y inciter, pour peu que l'on veuille contribuer à un système de justice universel. Ils doivent donc s'emparer de principes universellement reconnus. Le contrôle ne doit pas faire abstraction de ces règles qui se situent à l'intersection de plusieurs ordres juridiques.

42. Le refus d'application des prescriptions du traité de protection des investissements à des situations qui mettent en cause la bonne gouvernance de l'Etat [114], telles une expropriation au mépris du principe de légalité [115], le détournement d'une loi ou d'une procédure pour servir des fins particulières, ou encore le déni de justice, constitue une violation par l'arbitre de ses devoirs en raison du délaissement des normes qui fondent son autorité. Il ne serait pas aussi interdit de voir dans la violation des normes du *jus cogens* une non-application du droit international [116]. Il n'y aurait pas alors un simple mal jugé par erreur de droit mais une méconnaissance du pouvoir de juger [117]. La sentence serait de plus viciée par l'emploi de motifs elliptiques sur ces questions ou impropres à justifier l'application des dispositions du traité en

---

tel pouvoir extraordinaire, en tout cas quand la loi en question ne contrevient pas à l'ordre public transnational... »

J.-J. Arnaldez, Y. Derains et D. Hascher, « Recueil des sentences arbitrales de la CCI, vol. III, 1991-1995 », *Kluwer Law International*, ICC Publishing, 1997, p. 577. CA Paris, 24 novembre 2011, *EGPC c. NATGAS*, n° 10/16525 (exception d'inconstitutionnalité et mission de l'arbitre). Voir *Contrôle de constitutionnalité et de conventionalité du droit étranger*, G. Cerqueira et N. Nord (dir. publ.), *Société de Législation Comparée*, Collection Colloques, vol. 34, 2017.

114. *Cargill c. Mexique*, sentence du 18 septembre 2009, ARB(AF)/05/2, par. 276 ; CEDH 15 septembre 2009, *Moskal c. Pologne*, requête n° 10373/05, par. 51.

115. Voir CEDH 4 novembre 2014, *Sociedad Anonima Del Ucieza c. Espagne*, requête n° 38963/08, par. 74.

116. Ch. Schreuer (with L. Malintoppi, A. Reinisch et A. Sinclair), « The ICSID Convention », CUP, 2ᵉ éd. 2010, p. 975-976 (n° 263-264).

117. F. Catsberg, « L'excès de pouvoir dans la justice internationale », *Recueil des cours*, tome 35 (1931), p. 353.

raison de l'absence ou de l'insuffisance des recherches effectuées par le tribunal arbitral sur les faits de la cause.

43. On ne peut pas faire abstraction de l'universalité des valeurs protégées par la non-discrimination, l'accès à la justice, le procès équitable et la légalité ou la sécurité juridique. La présence de ces valeurs dans l'ordre public s'explique à de multiples titres et quelle qu'en soit la source: droit constitutionnel, principe général du droit, droit des droits de l'homme ou encore normes du *jus cogens*[118]. Peu importe les déformations qu'une règle subit par son utilisation en dehors de l'ordre juridique qui lui a donné naissance ou l'acception particulière qui lui est donnée dans un ordre juridique ou dans un autre. La force du contenu de la règle tirée de son universalité compte, non la source qui donne la règle.

44. Comme le relevaient Batiffol et le professeur Lagarde, en cas de doute sur l'insertion de règles dans l'ordre public

> «[u]ne approche comparative paraît plus féconde. L'idée serait de soumettre à un test de droit comparé les dispositions du droit étranger qui s'éloignent des dispositions du for et de leur opposer l'ordre public lorsqu'elles s'éloignent de manière essentielle du standard de droit comparé»[119].

La distinction entre ordre public international et transnational, qu'il est arrivé à la jurisprudence d'utiliser[120], n'offre pas un grand intérêt ici, sauf qu'avec une notion universelle, le référentiel n'est plus national. Le contenu est le même, à moins de trouver avec le système national

---

118. Cour interaméricaine des droits de l'homme, arrêt du 23 juin 2005, *Yatama c. Nicaragua*, série C, n° 127, par. 184-186; deuxième rapport de la CDI sur le *jus cogens*, 16 mars 2017 (n° 84, 85) A/CN.4/706 (toutefois: CEDH, 21 juin 2016, requête n° 5809/08, *Al-Dulimi et Montana Management c. Suisse*, par. 136). Bruxelles, Trib. 1re instance, 18 février 2022, n° 19/3390/A, *Rép. de Pologne c. Manchester Securities*; CA Québec, n° 500-09-009391-004, *Air France c. Libyan Arab Airlines*, 31 mars 2003; Ch. Lords, 16 mai 2002, *Kuwait Airways Corporation* v. *Iraqi Airways Company*, [2002] UKHL 19; CA Alger, 20 février 1925, JDI 1926.701. J.-M. Grossen, «La prise en compte du droit international public dans l'arbitrage commercial international», *Festschrift für Franz Kellerhals*, Stämpfli Verlag Bern, 2005, p. 35; M. Forteau, «L'ordre public international face à l'enchevêtrement croissant du droit international public», JDI 2011.3; E. Gaillard, «Dialogue des ordres juridiques: ordre juridique arbitral et ordres juridiques étatiques», *Rev. arb.* 2018, p. 493.

119. H. Batiffol et P. Lagarde, «Traité de droit international privé», tome 1, LGDJ, 8e éd., 1993, n° 363.

120. CA Paris, 25 mai 1990, *Rev crit DIP*, 1990, p. 753, note B. Oppetit; TF 19 avril 1994, Westland, ATF 120 II 155, par. 6; P. Lalive, «Ordre public transnational (ou réellement international) et arbitrage international», Rev. arb. 1986, p. 329; J.-F. Poudret et S. Besson, «Droit comparé de l'arbitrage international», Bruylant, LGDJ, Schulthess, 2002, n° 824-826.

une différence dont l'influence demeurerait marginale, s'agissant de normes impératives à l'intersection d'une majorité d'ordres juridiques. Les décisions des juridictions nationales et internationales servent de preuve à la reconnaissance d'une norme internationale en tant que norme impérative [121]. Les sources formelles du droit ne sont pas une limite. Les codes de conduite peuvent signaler l'émergence de normes juridiques ayant une forte identité commune. De manière générale, la *soft law* accompagne l'universalité des droits fondamentaux et précise le contenu de droits nouveaux, comme ceux sur l'environnement [122].

45. La mobilisation de principes réunissant le consensus le plus large raffermit le contrôle des sentences et contribue en retour au développement des ordres juridiques dont les normes sont concernées. Les principes renforcent non seulement la cohésion des solutions, mais ils sont des éléments de communication. Rechercher une meilleure cohérence ou promouvoir les objectifs de principes communs à une pluralité d'ordres juridiques ne prend sa pleine mesure que si les organes de contrôle ont la volonté et le sentiment de participer à la sécurisation de la justice arbitrale [123]. Mais un langage commun n'a de sens que si l'on se parle.

---

121. Deuxième rapport de la CDI sur le *jus cogens*, 6 mars 2017, A/CN.4/706 (n° 91, projet de conclusion 9) ; M. Andenas et J. R. Leiss, «The Systemic Relevance of "Judicial Decisions" in Article 38 of the ICJ Statute», HJIL, 4/2017, p. 907.
122. B. Frydman et G. Lewkowicz, «Les codes de conduite, source du droit global?», dans I. Hachez, Y. Cartuyvels, H. Dumont, Ph. Gérard, F. Ost et M. van de Kerchove (dir. publ.), *Les sources du droit revisitées* (vol. 3), normativités concurrentes, Anthémis, Université St-Louis, 2012, p. 179 ; *Soft Law* et droits fondamentaux, M. A. Ailincai (dir publ.), Pedone, 2017.
123. A. M. Slaughter, «A Global Community of Courts», (2003) 44 *Harvard International Law Journal*, n° 1, p. 191 : «Common Principles and an awareness of a common enterprise will help make simple participation in transnational litigation into an engine of common identity and community».

CONCLUSION

46. L'intervention du droit international dans le contrôle des sentences contribue à en accroître la légitimité et l'efficacité. L'établissement de connexions entre divers ordres juridiques, conséquence de la pluralité des sources du droit international, requiert, pour mener cette tâche à bien, un contrôleur suffisamment habile ou décidé pour tirer parti de principes qui empruntent à plusieurs ordres juridiques. Dans tous les cas, la démarche suppose un esprit d'ouverture dans l'exercice de la mission juridictionnelle.

47. On a conçu le contrôle des sentences comme le moyen de les insérer dans un ordre juridique national. Faut-il une évolution vers une reconnaissance d'emblée par les ordres juridiques nationaux, le contrôle ne servant plus alors à faire entrer les sentences, mais à écarter celles qu'on ne peut pas accueillir ? Ceci suppose une perspective plus ambitieuse que celle de statuer sur le sort de la sentence attaquée. Il s'agit d'inscrire la décision de l'autorité de contrôle dans le contexte global du système international de règlement des différends par l'arbitrage. Comme la professeure A.-M. Slaughter le relève

> « [t]he emergence of global judicial relations is rooted in the pluralism of multiple legal systems, but driven by the expression of a deeper common identity » [124]

Sans la conscience et la volonté de participer à un objectif commun, les décisions étrangères à l'ordre juridique du for, réduites à n'être que des anecdotes, ne susciteront, au mieux, qu'une curiosité condescendante. Dans les systèmes juridiques qui ne reconnaissent pas la valeur de précédent à leurs propres décisions judiciaires, il est paradoxal de préférer leur accorder une autorité décisionnelle supérieure aux décisions étrangères en niant la dimension internationale des règles à appliquer et des problèmes à résoudre. Si l'on pense à la mobilisation par les juridictions de *common law* des précédents étrangers en vue de rechercher la meilleure solution pour résoudre le litige, il n'y a rien d'impossible [125]. Les principes sont un langage universel, leur utilisation

---

124. A. M. Slaughter, « A Global Community of Courts », (2003) 44 *Harvard International Law Journal*, n° 1, p. 191.
125. R. French, « The Globalisation of Public Law – A Quilting of Legalities », *Cambridge Public Law Conference*, 12 septembre 2016 ; Home Grown Laws in a

doit provoquer une prise en considération des décisions étrangères, sans égard à l'appartenance du juge d'origine à telle ou telle tradition juridique [126]. Il faut donc un certain volontarisme pour entreprendre une motivation qui parle aux autres.

48. Les organes de contrôle ne réunissent pas tous les conditions souhaitables. Seuls ceux qui s'inscrivent dans une approche collaborative avec les arbitres et avec les autres autorités de contrôle peuvent prétendre réguler la justice arbitrale. Développer une jurisprudence cohérente, globale, ouverte à l'influence du droit international est plus aisé lorsque les juridictions de contrôle ne travaillent pas dans un monde clos [127]. Une mission qui demeurera sans objet pour nombre d'entre elles. Deux solutions pour celles-ci. Pallier leurs insuffisances, ce qui suppose une prise de conscience de la part de leurs pouvoirs publics. On pourrait alors préconiser une politique d'externalisation pour déléguer le contentieux aux juridictions les mieux aptes à traiter les questions posées et qui sont disposées à mettre leurs ressources au service de la communauté internationale [128]. Si cette division interna-

---

Global Neighbourhood – Australia, the United States and the Rest, Albritton Lecture, University of Alabama School of Law, 18 janvier 2011.

126. E. Gaillard, «Comparative Law in International Arbitration», *Jus Comparatum* 1 (2020), p. 1-35 (International Academy of Comparative Law: *aidc-iacl.org*). Voir aussi G. Canivet, «L'influence de la comparaison des droits dans l'élaboration de la jurisprudence», Etudes Malinvaud, Litec, 2007, p. 133; «Le juge est-il un comparatiste?», Ecole doctorale de l'Université Lyon III, conférence du 15 décembre 2005; B. Markesinis, «Judicial Mentality: Mental Disposition or Outlook as a Factor Impeding Recourse to Foreign Law», *Tulane Law Review*, 2006, vol. 80, n° 4, p. 1325. J. Allard et L. Van den Eynde, «Le dialogue des jurisprudences comme source du droit», dans I. Hachez, Y. Cartuyvels, H. Dumont, Ph. Gérard, F. Ost et M. van de Kerchove (dir. publ.), *Les sources du droit revisitées*, vol. 3, normativités concurrentes, Anthémis, Université St-Louis, 2012, p. 285; S. Cassese, «La fonction constitutionnelle des juges non nationaux. De l'espace juridique global à l'ordre juridique global», Conférence à la Cour de cassation, 12 juin 2007.

127. G. Canivet, Rôle et responsabilité des juridictions dans la mise en œuvre des principes de la gouvernance mondiale, mélanges E. Zoller, Dalloz, 2018, p. 543:

> «[l]a coopération judiciaire internationale est examinée sous l'angle de la gouvernance, c'est-à-dire d'un processus institutionnel, formel ou informel, générant l'autorité nécessaire à la mise en œuvre d'actions collectives visant non seulement à la réalisation d'objectifs de valeur universelle mais aussi à leur légitimation devant un large public» (n° 22);

M. Delmas-Marty, «Penser un monde juridique poreux», dans V. Grosswald Curran (dir. publ.), *Porosités du droit*, Société de Législation Comparée, coll. Colloques, vol. 45, 2020, p. 15.

128. S. Menon, «International Commercial Courts: Towards a Transnational System of Dispute Resolution», Opening Lecture for the DIFC Courts Lecture Series 2015; L. Reed, «International Dispute Resolution Courts: Retreat or Advance? 10 thJohn E. C. Brierley Memorial Lecture», *La revue de règlement des différends de McGill*, vol. 4 (2017-2018), 129. A. S King et P. K. Bookman, Traveling Judges, *Am J. Intl. Law*, vol. 116, issue 3, juillet 2022, p. 477-533.

tionale du travail ne convient pas, on peut, sans préjudicier à la sécurité de l'ensemble dans la mesure où, s'agissant d'un contentieux volatile, les utilisateurs peuvent opérer, au vu des performances des contrôleurs, les corrections nécessaires en modifiant leurs choix des sièges d'arbitrage ou en concluant des clauses d'élection de for pour le recours en annulation [129], se résoudre à laisser chaque institution sur la route de l'évolution, et pour extrapoler sur une comparaison empruntée à l'historien Yuval Noah Harari sur l'évolution de l'ADN entre espèces, les unes à la vitesse de la charrette tirée par un bœuf, les autres à celle du supersonique [130]*.

---

129. CA Paris, *Le Parmentier, Miss francophonie c. Miss France*, 17 juin 2004, n° 2002/20314.
130. Y. N. Harari et omo Deus, « Une brève histoire du futur », Albin Michel, 2017.
*Mes remerciements vont encore à Mme la professeure S. Poillot-Peruzzetto, conseillère en service extraordinaire à la Cour de cassation (France), pour ses remarques au cours de la préparation de cette conférence et à M. J.-J. Arnaldez, ancien greffier-adjoint de la Cour internationale de Justice, pour son amicale relecture.

LEGAL FACETS OF THE PRACTICE
OF INTERNATIONAL ORGANIZATIONS

by

NIELS BLOKKER

N. BLOKKER

TABLE OF CONTENTS

Introduction 87

Chapter 1. Practice as a rule: "established practice" as part of the law of international organizations 95

1.1. Origin and development. 95
1.2. Some examples of the established practices of international organizations 103
    1.2.1. A wealth of "unknown" established practice 103
    1.2.2. The study by Christopher Peters. 104
    1.2.3. Practice of the United Nations and the specialized agencies. 108
        (i) Examples from the *United Nations Juridical Yearbook* . 108
            (a) UN conferences 109
            (b) UN peacekeeping 110
            (c) The UN Secretariat as a depositary of multilateral treaties 112
            (d) The relations between organizations and their staff . 113
            (e) The conduct of meetings and the daily operation of organs. 114
            (f) Issues of representation, the leadership role of the General Assembly 115
            (g) Privileges and immunities 116
        (ii) A few observations 117
1.3. Some further reflections on the notion of "established practice of the organization" 121
    1.3.1. The most dynamic component of rules of international organizations 121
    1.3.2. To define or not to define? 122
    1.3.3. A wealth of undocumented, little-known practices 123
    1.3.4. When is a practice "established"? 125
    1.3.5. Who decides? 128

Chapter 2. Practice as a power: the power-generating capacity of the practice of international organizations 131

2.1. "Clean theory": The principle of attributed powers 131
2.2. "Messy life": Examples from practice – *intra* or *ultra vires*? 138
    2.2.1. The establishment of *ad hoc* criminal tribunals by the UN Security Council 138
    2.2.2. Was the UN Human Rights Council Libya Inquiry Commission acting *ultra vires* by including NATO operation Unified Protector in its report (2012)? 142
    2.2.3. Julian Assange in the Embassy of Ecuador in London: Voluntary stay or arbitrary deprivation of liberty? Was the UN Working Group on Arbitrary Detention competent to consider the case of Julian Assange? 144
    2.2.4. Was the OPCW acting *ultra vires* by deciding in June 2018 that the OPCW Secretariat may play a role in identifying "those who were the perpetrators, organisers, sponsors or otherwise involved" in the use of chemical weapons? 146
    2.2.5. Does NATO have the power to carry out "out of area operations"? 150

2.2.6. The power of the CTBTO PrepCom to use its verification installations not only for nuclear explosions but also for tsunami warning 153
2.3. Bridging the gap *(i)*: Amending the constituent instrument 157
2.4. Bridging the gap *(ii)*: Implied powers 160
    2.4.1. Implied powers and the principle of attribution 162
    2.4.2. The scope of implied powers 163
    2.4.3. Inherent powers 167
2.5. Bridging the gap *(iii)*: Organizational practice and the conundrum of customary powers 168
2.6. How to read the "open book" of "messy practice" in the light of express, implied and customary powers?................ 177
    2.6.1. The establishment of ad hoc criminal tribunals by the UN Security Council 177
    2.6.2. Was the UN Human Rights Council Libya Inquiry Commission acting *ultra vires* in discussing NATO operation Unified Protector in its report? 178
    2.6.3. Was the UN Working Group on Arbitrary Detention competent to consider the case of Julian Assange? 179
    2.6.4. Was the OPCW acting *ultra vires* by deciding in June 2018 that the OPCW Secretariat may play a role in identifying "those who were the perpetrators, organisers, sponsors or otherwise involved" in the use of chemical weapons? 179
    2.6.5. Does NATO have the power to carry out "out of area operations"?............................. 179
    2.6.6. The power of the CTBTO Prepcom to use its verification installations not only for nuclear explosions but also for tsunami warning 180
2.7. In conclusion: Practice, the attribution principle, and beyond 180

Chapter 3. Practice in interpretation: practice of international organizations as an interpretative device 182

3.1. Introduction 182
3.2. The rules on treaty interpretation in the 1969 and 1986 Vienna Conventions and practice of international organizations 184
    3.2.1. The Vienna rules on treaty interpretation 185
    3.2.2. Treaty interpretation and the practice of international organizations 188
3.3. The role of practice of international organizations in the interpretation of treaties to which they are parties 193
3.4. The role of practice of international organizations in the interpretation of their constituent instruments 195
    3.4.1. A special approach for the interpretation of constituent instruments? 195
    3.4.2. Interpretation of constituent instruments: The 1996 ICJ Advisory Opinion requested by the WHO 199
    3.4.3. Limits to the interpretation of constitutions? The work of the Institut de Droit International 204
3.5. The role of organizational practice in the interpretation of other rules of international organizations 210
3.6. The interpreter I: (Organs of) the organization............ 217
3.7. The interpreter II: The members – membership support for an interpretation by the organization 224
3.8. In conclusion: Practice, interpretation, and beyond 231

Chapter 4. The international court of justice and practice of international organizations 234

4.1. Introduction 234
4.2. The Permanent Court of International Justice 236
    4.2.1. Competence of the ILO in regard to international regulation of the conditions of the labour of persons employed in agriculture (1922) 237
    4.2.2. Competence of the ILO to regulate incidentally the personal work of the employer (1926) 238
    4.2.3. Jurisdiction of the European Commission of the Danube (1927). 239
4.3. The International Court of Justice 240
    4.3.1. Early references to the practice of (organs of) the organization 240
        (i) Conditions of Admission (1948) 240
        (ii) Reparation for Injuries (1949) 241
        (iii) Second Admission Case (1950) 242
        (iv) International Status of South West Africa (1950) 243
        (v) Judgments of the ILO Administrative Tribunal in cases against UNESCO (1956) 244
        (vi) Constitution of the Maritime Safety Committee of IMCO (1960) 245
    4.3.2. Certain Expenses (1962). 246
        (i) Background. 246
        (ii) The Advisory Opinion. 249
        (iii) Separate and Dissenting Opinions: Judge Spender . . . 251
    4.3.3. Namibia (1971). 256
    4.3.4. WHO Nuclear Weapons (1996) 259
    4.3.5. Further references to organizational practice, post *WHO Nuclear Weapons*. 263
        (i) Cumaraswamy (1999). 264
        (ii) Legal consequences of the construction of a wall in the Occupied Palestinian Territory (2004) 264
        (iii) Accordance with international law of the unilateral declaration of independence in respect of Kosovo (2010) 266
        (iv) Chagos (2019). 267
4.4. Concluding observations 268

Chapter 5. The international law commission and practice of international organizations 273

5.1. Introduction 273
5.2. The ILC, customary international law and practice of international organizations. 275
    5.2.1. Introduction. 276
    5.2.2. The work of the ILC on the "identification of customary international law" 279
        (i) Direct relevance of the practice of international organizations, "in certain cases". 280
        (ii) Observation 13 281
        (iii) Observation 14 281
        (iv) Resolutions of international organizations 286
        (v) Other issues and comments. 289

5.3. Subsequent agreements and subsequent practice in relation to interpretation of treaties: What role for the practice of international organizations? 290
    5.3.1. Introduction. 290
    5.3.2. The ILC Study Group on "Treaties over time" (2009-2012). 291
    5.3.3. The ILC work on the topic "Subsequent agreements and subsequent practice in relation to the interpretation of treaties" (2013-2018). 292
    5.3.4. Draft conclusions on subsequent agreements and subsequent practice in relation to the interpretation of treaties (2018) . . 297
5.4. Concluding observations: Does the ILC take the practice of international organizations seriously? 302

Concluding observations 307
    Legal facet one: Practice as a rule 307
    Legal facet two: Practice as a power. 309
    Legal facet three: Practice in interpretation 310
    Legal facet four: The ICJ and the practice of international organizations 312
    Legal facet five: The ILC and the practice of international organizations 313

Bibliography. 318

BIOGRAPHICAL NOTE

Niels Blokker, born in Bussum, the Netherlands, on 18 February 1958.
Educated at Leiden University, where he obtained his doctorate (1989).
Senior legal counsel at the Netherlands Ministry of Foreign Affairs (2000-2007).
Deputy Legal Adviser at the Netherlands Ministry of Foreign Affairs (2007-2013).
In this capacity, he has given legal advice on a wide variety of international law questions, particularly relating to the *ius ad bellum*, privileges and immunities, and the law of international organizations. He represented the Netherlands in the negotiations on the crime of aggression (2000-2010).

Professor of International Institutional Law ("Schermers Chair") at the Law Faculty of Leiden University (Netherlands), part-time since 2003, full-time since 2013. In this capacity, he is co-founder of the journal *International Organizations Law Review*, of which he has been a co-Editor-in-Chief (together with R. Wessel) from the beginning in 2004. He has taught as a guest professor in universities in many countries and has frequently given presentations at international conferences. On an *ad hoc* basis, he has advised international organizations.

PRINCIPAL PUBLICATIONS

International Regulation of World Trade in Textiles, Dordrecht, Martinus Nijhoff, 1989.
Towards More Effective Supervision by International Organizations: Essays in Honour of Henry G. Schermers, Vol. 1, Dordrecht, Martinus Nijhoff Publishers, 1994 [co-edited with S. Muller].
International Institutional Law: Unity within Diversity, 3rd rev. ed., The Hague, Martinus Nijhoff, 1995 [co-authored with H. G. Schermers].
"The European Union: Historical Origins and Institutional Challenges", in T. Heukels, N. Blokker and M. Brus (eds.), *The European Union after Amsterdam: A Legal Analysis*, The Hague, Kluwer Law International, 1998, pp. 9-50 [co-authored with T. Heukels].
"Decisions of International Organizations: The Case of the European Union", *Netherlands Yearbook of International Law*, Vol. 30 (1999), pp. 3-44.
"Is the Authorization Authorized? Powers and Practice of the UN Security Council to Authorize the Use of Force by 'Coalitions of the Able and Willing'", *European Journal of International Law*, Vol. 11 (2000), pp. 541-568.
Proliferation of International Organizations: Legal Issues, The Hague, Kluwer Law International, 2001 [co-edited with H. G. Schermers].
"Beyond 'Dili': On the Powers and Practice of International Organizations", in G. Kreijen *et al.* (eds.), *State, Sovereignty, and International Governance*, Oxford, Oxford University Press, 2002, pp. 299-322.
International Institutional Law: Unity within Diversity, 4th rev. ed., Leiden, Martinus Nijhoff, 2003 [co-authored with H. G. Schermers].
"International Organizations and Their Members", *International Organizations Law Review*, Vol. 1 (2004), pp. 139-161.
The Security Council and the Use of Force, Leiden, Martinus Nijhoff, 2005 [co-edited with N. Schrijver].
"From a Dispute about the Use of Force to a Non-Dispute about Jurisdiction", in N. Blokker, R. Lefeber, L. Lijnzaad and I. Van Bladel (eds.), *The Netherlands in Court: Essays in Honour of Johan G. Lammers*, Leiden, Martinus Nijhoff, 2006, pp. 19-49.
"The Crime of Aggression and the United Nations Security Council", *Leiden Journal of International Law*, Vol. 20 (2007), pp. 867-894.
International Institutional Law: Unity within Diversity, 5th rev. ed., Leiden, Martinus Nijhoff, 2011 [co-authored with H. G. Schermers].
"International Organizations: the Untouchables?", *International Organizations Law Review*, Vol. 10 (2013), pp. 259-275.
Immunity of International Organizations, Leiden, Brill Nijhoff, 2015 [co-edited with N. Schrijver].
"Member State Responsibility for Wrongdoings of International Organizations: Beacon of Hope or Delusion?", *International Organizations Law Review*, Vol. 12 (2015), pp. 319-332.
"Outsourcing the Use of Force: Towards More Security Council Control of Authorized Operations?", in M. Weller (ed.), *The Oxford Handbook of The Use of Force in International Law*, Oxford, Oxford University Press, 2015, pp. 202-226.
"Constituent Instruments: Creating a Genie that May Escape from the Bottle?", in J. Katz Cogan, I. Hurd and I. Johnstone (eds.), *The Oxford Handbook of International Organizations*, Oxford, Oxford University Press, 2016, pp. 943-961.
"Asian and Pacific International Organizations: Mainstream or *Sui Generis*? An International Institutional Law Perspective", in C.-J. Cheng (ed.), *A New International Legal Order: In Commemoration of the Tenth Anniversary of the Xiamen*

Academy of International Law (Collected Courses of the Xiamen Academy of International Law 8), Leiden, Brill, 2016, pp. 188-221.

"The Governance of International Courts and Tribunals: Organizing and Guaranteeing Independence and Accountability", in A. Follesdal and G. Ulfstein (eds.), *The Judicialization of International Law: A Mixed Blessing?*, Oxford, Oxford University Press, 2018, pp. 26-44.

International Institutional Law: Unity within Diversity, 6th rev. ed., Leiden, Brill Nijhoff, 2018 [co-authored with H. G. Schermers].

"Revisiting Questions of Organisationhood, Legal Personality and Membership in the OSCE: The Interplay Between Law, Politics and Practice", in M. Steinbrueck Platise, C. Moser and A. Peters (eds.), *The Legal Framework of the OSCE*, Cambridge, Cambridge University Press, 2019, pp. 135-164 [co-authored with R. Wessel].

Elected Members of the Security Council, Leiden, Brill Nijhoff, 2020 [co-edited with Nico Schrijver].

Saving Future Generations from the Scourge of War: The UN Security Council at 75, Leiden, Brill Nijhoff, 2021.

"Withdrawing from International Organizations", in N. Blokker, D. Dam-de Jong and V. Prislan (eds.), *Furthering the Frontiers of International Law: Sovereignty, Human Rights, Sustainable Development. Liber Amicorum Nico Schrijver*, Leiden, Brill Nijhoff, 2021, pp. 1-20.

ACKNOWLEDGEMENTS

I would like to thank colleagues, friends and students for assisting me in the preparation of this manuscript. In particular, I would like to mention Dr Zsuzsanna Deen-Racsmány for reading the entire draft text and giving incisive comments, Sarah Dent-Cullen for her language corrections, Vanya Kumar for sharing her OPCW expertise, Eva Bajema, Juliana Burgos Sanchez and Juliette Quist for their research assistance, my colleagues in Leiden for discussions on parts of this special course, and last but certainly not least my students in Leiden and at the Hague Academy for their interest, questions and comments.

INTRODUCTION

This special course is devoted to legal facets of the practice of international organizations, a topic that is highly relevant for all of the hundreds of international organizations that exist today. A few more introductory words may be necessary to further explain this topic and sketch the contours of this course. This introduction will first briefly define international organizations and indicate what is understood by "practice" in this course. Subsequently, it will mention the background to the creation of international organizations, the rules for their functioning and the legal relevance of their practice. To conclude, it will outline the overall structure of this special course.

In practice and in doctrine, international organizations are defined in different ways. However, these definitions are more similar than is sometimes suggested. This may explain why it was possible for the United Nations International Law Commission (ILC) to agree on a definition of international organizations in the context of its work on the topic of the responsibility of international organizations[1]. Most of the elements of this definition are also included in the definition used in this special course: international organizations are forms of cooperation that are founded on an international agreement and that have at least one organ with a will of its own; they must be established under international law[2]. International organizations are almost always treaty-based. They normally enjoy legal personality both under international law and under the domestic law of at least their own member states. Their members

---

1. Articles on the Responsibility of International Organizations (ARIO), adopted by the ILC in 2011. In its Resolution 66/100, the UN General Assembly took note of ARIO (the text of which is annexed to this Resolution). According to Art. 2 ARIO: "For the purposes of the present articles: *(a)* 'International organization' means an organization established by a treaty or other instrument governed by international law and possessing its own international legal personality. International organizations may include as members, in addition to States, other entities." A slightly different definition has been suggested in 2023 by Special Rapporteur Reinisch in the context of the ILC work on the topic "settlement of international disputes to which international organizations are parties"; see UN Doc. A/CN.4/756, at p. 35 ("'International organization' refers to an entity established by States and/or other entities on the basis of a treaty or other instrument governed by international law and possessing at least one organ capable of expressing a will distinct from that of its members").
2. See H. G. Schermers and N. M. Blokker, *International Institutional Law*, 6th ed., Leiden, Brill Nijhoff, 2018, at p. 41 *et seq.*, where the three elements of this definition are explained in more detail.

are mostly states, although increasingly international organizations are also members [3].

The word "practice" in the title of this special course has two distinct meanings [4]. On the one hand, in a broad sense, it refers to all activities carried out by international organizations, "in real life", to perform their functions. In this sense, it is the opposite of theory. There is a variety of theories about international organizations, mainly in the field of international relations, aiming to provide explanations for their existence and functioning [5]. In contrast, this special course concerns the practice of international organizations. Its focus is on legal facets of what international organizations actually do. Practice in this broad sense may also be contrasted with the rules of international organizations. While these rules prescribe, for example, how international organizations should take decisions (e.g. unanimously or by majority vote), practice may be different (e.g. by consensus).

On the other hand, in a narrower sense, "practice" refers to doing something normally, routinely, customarily, not occasionally. This is the meaning of "practice" in one of the constituent elements of rules of customary international law, "general practice" [6]. In the life of international organizations, often certain qualifiers are used for "practice" in this sense, such as standard practice, common practice or general practice. A certain practice of an international organization may also develop into what is now generally called "established practice", which is part of the rules of the organization (see Chap. 1).

*

---

3. The best example is the EU, which is a member of an increasing number of international organizations. However, there are also other examples: the African Union, the Andean Community and some other organizations are members of the Common Fund for Commodities. See in more detail Schermers and Blokker, note 2, at pp. 78-82.

4. See further on the notion of "practice" in international law: P. Reuter, "Quelques réflexions sur la notion de 'pratique internationale', spécialement en matière d'organisations internationales", in *Studi in onore di Giuseppe Sperduti*, Milan, Giuffrè, 1984, pp. 189-207; L. Boisson de Chazournes, "Subsequent Practice, Practices, and 'Family-Resemblance': Towards Embedding Subsequent Practice in its Operative Milieu", in G. Nolte (ed.), *Treaties and Subsequent Practice*, Oxford, Oxford University Press, 2013, pp. 53-68.

5. See e.g. L. Hooghe, T. Lenz and G. Marks, *A Theory of International Organization: A Postfunctionalist Theory of Governance*, Vol. 4, Oxford, Oxford University Press, 2019.

6. See the Conclusions on Identification of Customary International Law, adopted by the ILC in 2018 (Conclusion 2: "[t]o determine the existence and content of a rule of customary international law, it is necessary to ascertain whether there is a general practice accepted as law *(opinio juris)*").

The variety of existing international organizations is difficult to overestimate. Both at the global, the regional, and the subregional levels, large and small organizations exist, old and young, well-known and hardly known, in political, socio-economic, financial, cultural, technical or other fields. The acronyms of some organizations need no explanation (UN, WHO, EU); others are only known to insiders. However, what international organizations have in common is also difficult to overestimate, although this may be harder to notice than their diversity. Most fundamentally, all international organizations have been established to perform in practice one or more particular functions that states cannot, or not fully, deal with themselves individually. These functions are usually mentioned in the preamble or in the first article(s) of their constituent instruments and may be rather general (e.g. the maintenance of international peace and security) or very specific (e.g. cooperation in the field of vine and wine). Whatever these functions are, they need to be performed in a future that is by definition uncertain. However, even though it is uncertain, or precisely because it is uncertain, the creators of an international organization anticipate that it is better to face it together than alone. As the former Italian Prime Minister Draghi stated in 2021: "there is no sovereignty in solitude"[7]. As Morgenstern wrote many years earlier: "Absence from international organizations is tantamount to isolation"[8]. In other words: the founders of an international organization perceive it to be in their common interest to cooperate more closely, within a permanent institutional framework, to face the future in a particular area together rather than alone.

Once states have agreed to cooperate more closely by establishing an international organization, these sovereign parents never give *carte blanche* to their brainchild to carry out its functions in practice. The constituent instrument always lays down "rules of the game" for such future cooperation. This may be considered a manifestation of the rule of law. Future cooperation and governance within the framework of an international organization is not to be carried out at random and purely determined by the whims of the most powerful, but in accordance with a minimum of predetermined rules, no matter how general these may be[9]. These are partly institutional, partly substantive rules. Substantive

---

7. In the original text: "Non c'è sovranità nella solitudine", speech before the Italian Senate, see *Corriere della sera / Politico*, 17 February 2021.
8. F. Morgenstern, *Legal Problems of International Organizations*, Cambridge, Grotius, 1986, at p. 1.
9. For example, the constituent instrument of NATO only contains fourteen articles, including only the germ of its institutional structure, that was mostly developed in the organization's practice.

rules are rules of conduct, both for the organization's members and for its organs. Institutional rules govern the organizational framework that is created to implement the new body's functions.

These "rules of the game", the law that governs the functioning in practice of an international organization, are first of all laid down in the organization's constituent instrument, its primary law. Further rules are subsequently agreed in secondary law: decisions, rules, and so forth, adopted by organs of the organization. Furthermore, it has become gradually accepted that an organization's law also comprises its established practice. The acceptance of the latter notion in itself is the ultimate recognition of the legal relevance of the practice of international organizations. Such acceptance is conditioned by the need for this practice to be "established". The notion of established practice, as part of the law of international organizations, will be discussed in Chapter 1.

While these "rules of the game" need to have a minimum rigour, giving some certainty, some predictability, some indication of how the founders of an organization perceived future governance in the area concerned, they also need to be sufficiently flexible, to allow the organization to perform its functions in a world that may sooner rather than later be quite different from the one existing at the time of its creation. This indispensable flexibility is mainly provided by giving powers to organs of the organization, enabling them to both respond to developments in practice and to steer or influence such practice to a greater or lesser extent. Chapter 2 will discuss the relevant rules and practice regarding the powers of international organizations.

If there is too much rigidity in the law governing the functioning of an international organization, it is likely to soon become obsolete and irrelevant [10]. If there is too much flexibility, the organization and its founders may soon experience a lack of institutional stability or normative guidance when facing new questions. At the creation of a new international organization, it is a challenge for its founders to find a proper balance between these key characteristics of its constituent instrument. Given the agreed mix of rigour and flexibility, a newly

---

10. As former IMF General Counsel Joseph Gold has observed in the context of the original IMF rules that constituted the par value system, they "were based on the principle of stability without rigidity but in time they did produce rigidity.... Inflexibility ... led to the withdrawal of respect for the norms so that rigidity became *rigor mortis*". J. Gold, *The Rule of Law in the International Monetary Fund*, Washington, IMF Pamphlet Series No. 32, 1980, at pp. 11-12.

established organization leaves the shipyard and embarks on its governance journey to perform its functions.

The practice of international organizations is a vast and fascinating object for research. There are hundreds of international organizations. Often, their practice covers decades, in some cases even more than a century. Furthermore, their practice is pivotal for their successful functioning, since legal rules guiding such functioning are often lacking and the amendment of their constituent instruments is usually complicated [11]. Einstein's aphorism comes to mind: "[d]ie Welt vor uns, ein geöffnetes Buch. Wenn wir es nur lesen können."[12] Most of the practice of international organizations is visible and accessible, although this is more true for some organizations than for others. The biggest challenge is not to find it but to know how to "read" it, to obtain a fuller understanding of it.

The practice of international organizations is highly diverse. Each organization has its own practice. At the same time, all international organizations face similar questions in their practice. To what extent do constituent instruments provide the necessary powers to perform the functions of the organization effectively, in rapidly changing circumstances? How much room is there for a flexible interpretation of these instruments? To what extent is the practice of the organization taken into account in such interpretation? How much support of the organization's members is required for its practice? When the limits of interpretative flexibility are reached, is it feasible to amend these instruments? In short, there is unity within diversity.

The practice of international organizations has a number of facets, *facettes* in French, like the flat sides of a jewel. Each of these facets merits separate study. Historians, international relations scholars and others may analyse those facets of such practice that are most relevant from the perspective of their own disciplines, and may demonstrate what an organization has been able to achieve, what not, and why and

---

11. As Reuter wrote: "les règles juridiques concernant toutes les organisations internationales sont très limitées et insuffisantes. . . . Comme les organisations vivent néanmoins et même se développent, c'est la 'pratique' qui pourvoit à l'absence de règles expressément formulées ; la 'pratique' est donc pour elles plus importante encore que pour les Etats", Reuter, note 4, at p. 199. See also Second Report on the Question of Treaties Concluded between States and International Organizations or between Two or More International Organizations, prepared in 1972 by Reuter as Special Rapporteur of the ILC, UN Doc. A/CN.4/271, reproduced in the *Yearbook of the International Law Commission 1973* (hereinafter: *Yb. ILC 1973*), Vol. 2, esp. p. 78, para. 17.

12. J. Neffe, *Einstein – Eine Biographie*, 3rd ed., Rowohlt, Reinbek, 2005, at p. 169: "The world before us, an open book. If only we were able to read it."

how this has or has not happened. This may enrich our knowledge and understanding of such practice.

The practice of international organizations is also a vast and fascinating object for legal research. After all, such practice is not *ad hoc*, spontaneous international cooperation, ungoverned by any legal rules. It has been decided, sometimes long ago, that international cooperation in the area concerned should take place within an organizational framework, on the basis of certain predetermined "rules of the game". This framework is not static. It is a living instrument, interacting with the practice that it is mandated to guide. It is this interaction that is the object for legal research and to which this special course is devoted. If the existing organizational frameworks were studied in isolation, without taking into account the relevant practice, this would be like *l'art pour l'art*, focusing exclusively on the intrinsic nature and characteristics of the framework and its rules. Even though this may still be useful, the existing organizational frameworks with their rules have been created for something extrinsic: a part of social reality, which the founders of an international organization can no longer govern only individually. This course is about the interaction between international organizations and the external *milieu* for which they have been created. The aim is to analyse a number of salient legal facets of the practice of international organizations. While there are some publications in this field [13], the topic of this special course has not been extensively researched.

There is a myriad of examples to illustrate the above. Perhaps the *locus classicus* to demonstrate the importance of practice of international organizations is the establishment and development of peacekeeping within the United Nations [14]. Not foreseen in the Charter, UN peacekeeping developed in practice, a key moment being the 1956 Suez crisis. While this was unforeseen in the Charter, it was "on the basis of principles reflected in the constitution of the United Nations" [15]

---

13. Two recent publications are J. Barkholdt, "The Contribution of International Organizations to the Formation, Interpretation and Identification of International Law", *International Organizations Law Review*, Vol. 18 (2021), pp. 1-45; L. Gasbarri, "The Notion of Institutional Practice in United Nations Law", *Max Planck Yearbook of United Nations Law*, Vol. 24 (2021), pp. 1-35.

14. As Christopher Peters has observed, the development of UN peacekeeping is "ein – wenn nicht sogar das – Paradebeispiel für politische und rechtliche Innovation durch die Praxis der Vereinten Nationen", C. Peters, *Praxis Internationaler Organisationen – Vertragswandel und völkerrechtlicher Ordnungsrahmen*, Berlin, Springer, 2016, at p. 332.

15. UN Doc. A/3302, 6 November 1956, at p. 2, para. 4.

Legal Facets of the Practice of International Organizations 93

and "within the limits of the Charter"[16]. Visionary leaders including the Canadian Foreign Minister Lester Pearson and UN Secretary-General Dag Hammerskjöld rose to the occasion and played a decisive role, not only in the establishment by the General Assembly of the UN Emergency Force[17], but also in laying down some general basic principles for the creation and functioning of future UN peacekeeping operations[18]. A less well-known example are the tsunami warning activities performed by an international organization that was created for a completely different purpose: the Preparatory Commission for the Comprehensive Nuclear-Test-Ban Treaty Organization[19].

At the same time, these two examples should not give the impression that this is the regular way in which international organizations perform their functions. Often they do what is more or less prescribed in their constituent instruments, as the following examples illustrate. The International Labour Organization (ILO) has adopted many conventions and recommendations on a wide variety of labour issues[20]. The World Meteorological Organization has taken many decisions to "facilitate worldwide cooperation in the establishment of networks of stations for the making of meteorological observations as well as hydrological and other geophysical observations related to meteorology"[21]. CERN (the European Organization for Nuclear Research) operates the largest particle physics laboratory in the world, as mentioned in its constitution[22]. The East African Community has established a customs union and subsequently a common market, as foreseen in the organization's constituent instrument[23].

*

In the following chapters, a number of legal facets of the practice of international organizations will be discussed. As mentioned, Chapter 1 will analyse the notion of "established practice", which is part of

---

16. UN Doc. A/3943, 9 October 1958, at p. 32, para. 193.
17. GA Res. 1000 (ES-I), adopted 4 November 1956; GA Res. 1001 (ES-I), adopted 7 November 1956. See on this episode of the history of the UN: B. Urquhart, *Hammarskjold*, New York, W. W. Norton and Company, 1972, in particular pp. 159-194.
18. See in particular UN Docs. A/3302 and A/3943.
19. See Sec. 2.2.6 below.
20. ILO Constitution, Art. 19.
21. Convention of the World Meteorological Organization, Art. 2 *(a)*. See e.g. Resolution 1 (Cg-Ext(2021)).
22. CERN Convention, Art. II.2.
23. Treaty for the Establishment of the East African Community, Arts. 75-76.

the law of international organizations. Chapter 2 will examine to what extent an organization's practice can be a source of its legal powers. It is agreed that international organizations do not, unlike states, have general powers, but only have the powers that have been attributed to them. If a certain power has not been attributed to an organization in its constituent instrument, for example the power for the UN to establish a peacekeeping operation, why and how can the UN's practice nevertheless generate such a power? This chapter is about the "power-generating capacity" of practice.

Chapter 3 will analyse the practice of organizations as a means of interpretation of an organization's constituent instrument and of other rules of the organization. How robust should a certain practice be before it can be accepted as a way to "read" this instrument? What organs are relevant for the development of an organization's subsequent practice? Policymaking organs, the secretariat, other organs? Should all members support a certain practice, or is a certain majority of the membership sufficient? Are there any limits to this interpretative device? Chapter 4 will focus on relevant decisions of the Permanent Court of International Justice and the International Court of Justice. To what extent have they taken into account the practice of international organizations when applying and interpreting their rules?

Chapter 5 will discuss relevant work of the UN's ILC. It will concentrate on two topics discussed within the ILC in recent years, the identification of customary international law and subsequent agreements and subsequent practice in relation to the interpretation of treaties. The practice of international organizations is relevant for these two topics: as a constituent element of rules of customary international law and as a means of treaty interpretation. The result of the work on these topics was adopted by the ILC in 2018, with the UN General Assembly subsequently taking note of it. Finally, Chapter 6 will contain a few concluding reflections.

CHAPTER 1

PRACTICE AS A RULE: "ESTABLISHED PRACTICE" AS PART OF THE LAW OF INTERNATIONAL ORGANIZATIONS

As mentioned in the introduction, the law that governs the functioning of an international organization comprises first of all the organization's constituent instrument, its primary law. In addition, this law is subsequently laid down in secondary law, that is, decisions, resolutions, acts, and so forth, adopted by organs of the organization. Furthermore, it has become gradually accepted that an organization's law also includes its established practice, which will be discussed in this chapter. This is the ultimate recognition of the legal relevance of the practice of international organizations. Normally, the practice of international organizations is, not more and not less, essentially of a *factual* nature. It is about the way in which organizations act in their daily functioning. However, if certain conditions are fulfilled, such practice may become "established" and enter the sphere of *normativity*. Then it is no longer merely a matter of political choice, voting majority or personal preferences what course of action an organization should take to perform its functions, against the background of a normative void, but there is the expectation that the organization *should* act in a particular way. Very much like the formation of customary international law, a certain practice of the organization may develop into the law of the organization.

This chapter will first describe the origin and development of the notion of "established practice of the organization" (1.1). Next, Section 1.2 will discuss some examples, mainly in the context of the UN. Section 1.3 will conclude this chapter with some reflections on the current relevance and future prospects for this notion.

1.1. Origin and development

The notion of established practice of the organization was gradually developed over many years before it was first laid down in a treaty in 1975. Building blocks for the emergence of this notion can be found in UN practice (see Sec. 1.2) and in the *travaux préparatoires* of the 1969

Vienna Convention. Article 5 of this Convention contains a reference to the broader concept of "rules of the organization", as follows:

"The present Convention applies to any treaty which is the constituent instrument of an international organization and to any treaty adopted within an international organization without prejudice to any relevant rules of the organization."

This article deals with the relationship between the general rules on treaties as laid down in the 1969 Convention and the specific rules that may exist within the legal order of an international organization. Such specific rules may not always be consistent with the general rules of the Vienna Convention. In its preparations for the 1969 Convention, the ILC drafted several articles with specific reservations concerning the application of "*established rules* of an international organization" [24]. At a later stage of its work, it decided to "generalize" these into one single reservation included in the introductory articles of the Convention, which would apply to the entire Convention and not only to a few specific provisions. This was done to "simplify the drafting of the articles containing specific reservations", and also "in case the possible impact of rules of international organizations in any particular context of the law of treaties should have been inadvertently overlooked" [25]. The final outcome of these preparations, laid down in the above-quoted Article 5, is a compromise between different views as to the appropriate balance between general rules of treaty law and specific rules that may exist within international organizations [26].

---

24. ILC Commentary on the Draft Articles on the Law of Treaties, see *Yb. ILC 1966*, Vol. 2, at p. 191 (italics added). The word "established" was used more often in combination both with "practice" and with "rules" by the ILC in the context of its *travaux* for the 1969 Vienna Convention. See e.g. *Yb. ILC 1962*, Vol. 2, at pp. 173-174 (relating to "acceptance" as a way for states to become a party to a treaty: "[a]cceptance has become *established* in treaty *practice* during the past twenty years as a new procedure for becoming a party to treaties" (italics added)), and at p. 174 ("[b]ut in the absence of such a provision, the *established rule* is that laid down in . . ." (italics added)). In his first report, Special Rapporteur Waldock also uses the expressions "established usage" (*Yb. ILC 1962*, Vol. 2, at p. 60) and "established organizational procedure" (*id.*, at p. 76). The text of what later became Art. 5 is usually attributed to Waldock, but it has also been claimed that the ILO is its *auctor intellectualis*; see A. Trebilcock, "The International Labour Organization", in M. Bowman and D. Kritsiotis (eds.), *Conceptual and Contextual Perspectives on the Law of Treaties*, Cambridge, Cambridge University Press, 2018, pp. 848-880, in particular at pp. 854-855, where Trebilcock writes that "Article 5 is known informally within the institution [the ILO] as 'the ILO clause'".

25. ILC Commentary on the Draft Articles on the Law of Treaties, see *Yb. ILC 1966*, Vol. 2, at p. 191.

26. The final outcome, contained in Art. 5 of the Vienna Convention, uses the words "without prejudice to", whereas the ILC draft used the words "shall be subject to". See

Legal Facets of the Practice of International Organizations 97

The concept of "rules of the organization" was not defined in the Vienna Convention [27]. However, during the diplomatic conference where this Convention was adopted, the Chairman of the Drafting Committee (ILC member Yasseen) indicated that it also covered practice to some extent, when he explained that "the term 'rules' applied to written rules and unwritten customary rules" [28]. This statement reflected the wish of some delegations at the conference to include a reference to "settled practices or agreed interpretations of the constituent instruments" [29].

A few years later, in 1975, the notion "established practice of the organization" was for the first time referred to in a treaty, the Vienna

---

S. Rosenne, *Developments in the Law of Treaties 1945-1986*, Cambridge, Cambridge University Press, 1989, at p. 253 (indicating that the ILC in its preparatory work for the Vienna Convention was careful not to encroach upon the internal law of international organizations). See also p. 256, where Rosenne rightly refers to the balanced nature of this provision, which makes clear that the Convention applies "in principle" to constituent instruments and treaties adopted within an international organization. But "it leaves open the question of how far, or how long, the constituent instrument is to be regarded as an international treaty, and at what point it becomes generically different". At p. 257, Rosenne concludes that this approach "is of long-standing general advantage. . . . The law governing the constituent instruments of international intergovernmental organizations is in process of development along lines peculiar and appropriate to those instruments and their function in the international community, and their resemblance to the multilateral treaty is for the most part a superficial one . . . the application of the constituent instrument is dominated by the institutional element provided by the organization".

27. See on this term C. Brölmann, *The Institutional Veil in Public International Law: International Organisations and the Law of Treaties*, Oxford, Hart Publishing, 2007, at pp. 225-231; C. Ahlborn, "The Rules of International Organizations and the Law of International Responsibility", *International Organizations Law Review*, Vol. 8 (2011), pp. 397-482 (criticizing the ILC for "almost mechanically" using "rules of the organization" where the state responsibility articles refer to "internal law", and for not having characterized the legal nature of the term "rules of the organization" (at p. 399 and p. 402). The ILC indicated that these rules cannot be equated to the internal law of states since, at the very least, the constituent instruments of international organizations are part of international law and other rules of an organization possibly are too (see the ILC Commentary to its draft for the 1986 Vienna Convention, in *Yb. ILC 1982*, Vol. 2, Part 2, at p. 21, para. 25, and the ILC Commentary to Art. 5 of the ARIO, in *Yb. ILC 2011*, Vol. 2, Part 2, at p. 54, para. 2). See, however, Reuter, Special Rapporteur for the ILC preparations for the 1986 Vienna Convention, who observed that the definition of rules of the organization "merely describes the very general components of the 'distinctive law', the 'internal law' of the organization, including constituent instruments, resolutions, decisions and many other instruments ('in particular'), as well as *well-established practice*"; Reuter, Tenth Report, in *Yb. ILC 1981*, Vol. 2, Part 1, at p. 51, para. 30, emphasis in the original.

28. D. Heywood Anderson, in O. Corten and P. Klein (eds.), *The Vienna Conventions on the Law of Treaties: A Commentary*, Vol. 1, Oxford, Oxford University Press, 2011, pp. 88-103, at p. 92, para. 13. The Chairman added that the term did not cover "procedures which had not reached the stage of mandatory legal rules". See also about this episode Rosenne, note 26, at p. 255.

29. Heywood Anderson, note 28, at p. 94, para. 21. As an example, the interpretation of Art. 27.3 of the UN Charter was mentioned, concerning abstentions by permanent members of the Security Council.

Convention on the Representation of States in Their Relations with International Organizations of a Universal Character, as part of the concept of "rules of the organization"[30]. This Convention has not yet entered into force and its relevance is limited because major host states of international organizations have not become parties to it[31]. However, this lack of success is not caused by the introduction of the notion of established practice of the organization, and this notion was subsequently also included in other legal instruments: the 1986 Vienna Convention on the Law of Treaties between States and International Organizations or between International Organizations[32], and the 2011 ILC Articles on Responsibility of International Organizations (ARIO)[33].

In these three legal instruments, established practice is mentioned as part of the definition of the wider concept of "rules of the organization", as follows:

– "Rules of the Organization" means, in particular, the constituent instruments, relevant decisions and resolutions, and established practice of the Organization (1975 Vienna Convention).
– "Rules of the organization" means, in particular, the constituent instruments, decisions and resolutions adopted in accordance with them, and established practice of the organization (1986 Vienna Convention[34]).
– "Rules of the organization" means, in particular, the constituent instruments, decisions, resolutions and other acts of the international organization adopted in accordance with those instruments, and established practice of the organization (2011 ARIO).

---

30. Article 1.1 (34). Here, in contrast to the 1969 Vienna Convention, a definition is given of "rules of the organization". See also E. Roucounas, "Practice as a Relevant Factor for the Responsibility of International Organizations", in M. Ragazzi (ed.), *Responsibility of International Organizations*, Leiden, Nijhoff, 2013, pp. 159-171.
31. See J. G. Fennessy, "The 1975 Vienna Convention on the Representation of States in their Relations with International Organizations of a Universal Character", *American Journal of International Law*, Vol. 70 (1976), pp. 62-72.
32. Article 2.1 *(j)*. This Convention has not entered into force.
33. Art. 2 *(b)*, see UN Doc. A/66/10, at 52. In Res. 66/100 the UN General Assembly "takes note" of the ARIO. See above note 1.
34. Writers support the view that this definition would also apply, fully or largely, to the 1969 Convention. For example, Heywood Anderson, note 28, at p. 94 ("[w]hile there may be some nuances, the definition would probably be equally applicable with regard to the Vienna Convention of 1969"); Peters, note 14, at pp. 168-171; C. Peters, "Subsequent Practice and Established Practice of International Organizations: Two Sides of the Same Coin", *Goettingen Journal of International Law*, Vol. 3 (2011), pp. 617-642, esp. at pp. 626-629.

These three definitions have much in common. All three provide a non-exhaustive list of examples of specific "rules of the organization" ("in particular"), which include constituent instruments, acts, as well as the notion of established practice of the organization. However, there are also differences. While the 1975 definition is limited to "relevant" decisions and resolutions, the qualification "relevant" no longer appears in the 1986 and the 2011 definitions. There was some discussion about this during the *travaux préparatoires* of the 1986 Vienna Convention. ILC Special Rapporteur Reuter proposed to delete the word "relevant". In his view, the restriction to relevant decisions and resolutions in the 1975 Convention "is perfectly justifiable in view of the *limited scope* of this Convention, but becomes out of place in a definition referring to all the rules of the organization" [35]. However, the 1982 ILC draft of the 1986 Vienna Convention retained the restriction to "relevant" decisions and resolutions [36]. As is explained in the Commentary to this draft, "[t]he effect of the adjective 'relevant' is to underline the fact that it is not all 'decisions' or 'resolutions' which give rise to rules, but only those which are of relevance in that respect" [37]. In the end, during the Vienna Conference that adopted the 1986 Convention the word "relevant" was again deleted [38]. It did not reappear in the 2011 ARIO.

Second, there is a more fundamental difference between the definition of "rules of the organization" in the 1975 Convention and how this concept is defined in the 1986 Convention and in the 2011 ARIO. Whereas the 1975 Vienna Convention does not lay down a hierarchy within the list of specific rules, this is different for the 1986 Convention and the 2011 ARIO. According to the 1986 and 2011 legal instruments, only decisions and resolutions (1986) as well as other acts (2011) adopted in accordance with the relevant constituent instruments are "rules of the organization"; whatever their legal status is, if they are adopted "unconstitutionally", they are not rules of the organization. This condition is absent with respect to "established practice of the organization". Therefore, even if such practice would not be in accordance with the constituent instrument of the relevant organization, it would still be a rule of the organization [39]. This raises questions regarding the principle of attributed powers of international organizations, as will

---

35. *Yb. ILC 1981*, Vol. 2, Part 1, at p. 51, para. 29.
36. *Yb. ILC 1982*, Vol. 2, Part 2, at p. 18.
37. *Id.*, at p. 21, para. 25.
38. See Brölmann, note 27, at p. 231, with references.
39. Obviously, this is only the case for *established* practices. See in this context the twelfth preambular paragraph of the 1986 Vienna Convention: "Recognizing that the

be further discussed in Chapter 2. It was criticized at the 1986 Vienna Conference, in particular by eastern European states (socialist at the time) and China [40].

The commentaries to the above-mentioned three legal instruments do not define the notion of established practice, although the commentaries to the 1986 and the 2011 instruments give some indications as to its meaning. The Commentary to the 1975 Convention dates from 1971 and relates to the draft text of this Convention prepared by the ILC. This draft did not yet contain a definition of "rules of the organization" as it was later included in the final text of the Convention. A description of the expression "relevant rules of the Organization" was given in the Commentary to Article 3 of the 1972 draft text, which *inter alia* refers to "a well-established practice prevailing in that organization" [41], without further explanation.

The Commentary to the 1986 Convention offers more guidance [42]:

"It is true that most international organizations have, after a number of years, a body of practice which forms an integral part of their rules. However, the reference in question is in no way intended to suggest that practice has the same standing in all organizations;

---

practice of international organizations in concluding treaties with States or between themselves should be in accordance with their constituent instruments."

40. See e.g. UN Doc. A/CONF.129/16 (Vol. 1), at p. 50 (China, stating that "the central point of subparagraph 1 *(j)* was that the treaty-making capacity of an international organization could come only from the will of its member States as reflected in its constituent instruments; the term 'rules of the organization' therefore meant not only the constituent instruments but also such relevant decisions, resolutions and established practice as were in conformity with the objectives and purposes specified in the constituent instruments. While the wording proposed in document A/CONF. 129/ C. 1/L.2 was an improvement on the original subparagraph, it did not make it sufficiently clear that established practice too must conform to the constituent instruments"), pp. 45-46 (German Democratic Republic, stating that "the practice of an organization could be used as a criterion only in so far as that practice was in accordance with the constituent instruments"), p. 48 (Chile, stating: "The constituent instrument was an internationally binding legal act, and if established practice was not subordinated to it there would be a violation of that act"), p. 48 (Cuba), and p. 49 (Soviet Union).

41. See *Yb. ILC 1971*, Vol. 2, Part 1, at p. 288, para. 5.

42. See *Yb. ILC 1982*, Vol. 2, Part 2, at p. 21, para. 25; footnote omitted (referring to the ICJ's 1971 Namibia Advisory Opinion). See also the Fourth Report prepared by ILC Special Rapporteur Reuter, in which he indicated that "[t]he expression "rules of the organization" is to be understood in a broad sense and includes the constituent instrument of the organization, such written rules as it may have been able to elaborate in the exercise of its powers, and the unwritten rules resulting from the practices established by the organization" (*Yb. ILC 1975*, Vol. 2, at p. 40, para. 4). See further P. Gautier, in Corten and Klein, note 28, pp. 57-65, at pp. 64-65, para. 24, footnote omitted: "This expression may be understood as referring to a form of customary law. To this extent, the term presupposes a well-recognized practice. A practice *in nascendu*, ie at an early stage of its development, would not be sufficient."

on the contrary, each organization has its own characteristics in that respect. Similarly, by referring to 'established' practice, the Commission seeks only to rule out uncertain or disputed practice; it is not its wish to freeze practice at a particular moment in an organization's history."

The Commentary to the ARIO (2011) states that "[o]ne important feature of the definition of 'rules of the organization . . . is that it gives considerable weight to practice', referring to the NATO practice of decision-making by consensus as an example"[43]. In addition, it observes that the definition of rules of the organization "seeks to strike a balance between the rules enshrined in the constituent instruments and formally accepted by the members of the organization, on the one hand, and the need for the organization to develop as an institution, on the other hand"[44].

The Commentary to the ARIO does not include a number of observations made by ILC Special Rapporteur Gaja in his preparatory reports. These observations are worth mentioning as they reflect some of the discussions surrounding the inclusion of the notion of established practice as part of the definition of "rules of the organization" and may further clarify its meaning.

In the preparations for the ARIO, the ILC invited the views of governments on the question of whether "a general rule of attribution of conduct to international organizations should contain a reference to the 'rules of the organization'" and, if so, whether the definition of "rules of the organization", as it appears in the 1986 Vienna Convention "is adequate"[45]. The answers given by a number of governments demonstrate that there was much support for a reference to "rules of the organization" as defined in the 1986 Convention. However, some states indicated in the General Assembly that they were not in favour of using this definition and others suggested that it should be improved[46]. In his second report (2004), Special Rapporteur Gaja emphasizes the importance of the reference to practice in this definition and suggests two improvements to the 1986 definition. The first improvement concerns the reference to "decisions and resolutions" in this definition (which

---

43. *Yb. ILC 2011*, Vol. 2, Part 2, at p. 51, para. 17.
44. *Id.*, at para. 18 (in this context, the Commentary refers to the ICJ *Reparation for Injuries* Advisory Opinion).
45. *Yb. ILC 2003*, Vol. 2, Part 2, at p. 14, para. 27.
46. See the summary of these comments in the Second Report of Special Rapporteur Gaja, UN Doc. A/CN.4/541, at p. 8, para. 21.

finally resulted in the addition of "other acts" in the 2011 definition). The second suggested improvement relates to the term "established practice" itself. Gaja rightly notes that

> "[t]his wording puts stress on the element of time, which is not necessarily relevant, while it expresses less clearly the role of general acceptance, which appears more significant" [47].

Five years later, in his seventh report (2009), Special Rapporteur Gaja reviewed comments by states and international organizations on the slightly amended draft definition of the notion "rules of the organization" (now including a reference to "other acts") [48]. He notes that a few states expressed doubts about the reference to "established practice" but reacted by observing that "[e]ven if this reference may appear vague, it is hardly dispensable when considering functions and instruments of international organizations" [49]. In a footnote, he mentions that the European Commission had suggested to replace the term "established practice" with "generally accepted practice" [50].

It may be concluded that the notion "established practice" has gradually become recognized in several international legal instruments. Even though the two aforementioned Vienna Conventions have not yet entered into force, the preceding discussions within the ILC and in the General Assembly, as well as the inclusion of this notion in the ARIO, demonstrate that it enjoys sufficiently broad support. The broader concept of "rules of the organization" had already found general acceptance in the 1969 Vienna Convention, but at the time it was less clear than it is now that this concept does not only comprise the constituent instruments and the different types of decisions adopted by international organizations but also those parts of their practice that have become "established". However, while this may offer some clarity and certainty, it also raises further questions. For example: what conditions must be fulfilled before a certain practice of a certain organization can be qualified as "established"? Are such conditions unique for each international organization, or even for each organ of an international organization, or is there some unity within diversity in the sense that certain minimum requirements must always be met before a practice can be considered as "established" (and therefore as a

---
47. *Id.*, at p. 9, para. 25; footnote omitted.
48. UN Doc. A/CN.4/610, at p. 77.
49. *Id.*, at para. 16.
50. *Id.*, at footnote 18.

Legal Facets of the Practice of International Organizations 103

rule of the organization)? Before offering some general reflections on questions such as these in Section 1.3, Section 1.2 will first examine some examples of established practice, mainly from the UN context.

1.2. Some examples of the established practices of international organizations

1.2.1. A wealth of "unknown" established practice

For a wide variety of reasons, there is no full overview of cases in which a practice of an international organization has been or should be qualified as an established practice. First, the notion of established practice has only gradually been developed and accepted in recent decades, but it is still not widely and consistently recognized, accepted and used in practice. Second, there is no central "depository" where established practices of international organizations are collected, like treaties are registered with the UN Secretariat. Each organization has its own practice and its own way of archiving it. The UN has its own *Repertory of Practice of United Nations Organs* and its *Repertoire of the Practice of the Security Council*[51], but it is the exception rather than the rule in this regard. The vast majority of international organizations, in particular the smaller ones, do not have such collections that could provide information on their established practices. Third, most international organizations, in particular the smaller ones, do not have their own legal adviser or legal office. Whenever they need legal advice or a legal adviser to perform their functions, this is arranged on an *ad hoc* basis. However, such *ad hoc* legal input normally relates to specific issues, not to systematically keeping record of relevant practice of the organization. It is therefore hardly surprising that it is not easy for the ILC to collect full overviews of the practices of international organizations and to receive timely reactions to questionnaires and observations regarding draft provisions prepared in the context of work on one of the topics on its agenda relevant for international organizations.

This vacuum is only filled to a very limited extent by academic studies. For the purpose of finding examples of established practices of international organizations, one in-depth German study is available, by Christopher Peters[52]. Below, Subsection 1.2.2 will mention a number

---

51. See https://legal.un.org/repertory/; https://www.un.org/securitycouncil/content/repertoire/structure.
52. Peters, note 14.

of important examples of established practices as identified by Peters. Next, Subsection 1.2.3 will give an overview of practices that have been qualified by the UN Secretariat or by the UN Administrative Tribunal as established practices of the UN.

1.2.2. The study by Christopher Peters

Part of Peters' book is about the practice of international organizations. As observed by Peters, "the constitutional character of the founding treaties can either hinder (e.g., the international rule of law can require more legal certainty) or promote practice (i.e., if the treaty is understood as a living constitution)"[53]. The notion of established practice may cover both treaty-extending and treaty-modifying practice; it is the "quasi-customary law of the particular organization"[54]. At the same time, Peters mentions the following limits to how far the constituent instruments of international organizations may be stretched in this way[55]:

> "Informal treaty modifications and extensions are not limitless: they cannot violate the purpose of the organization or alter the basic structure of the international organization concerned. Everything beyond these requires a formal amendment, if not dissolution and a new foundation."

In his study, Peters examines the practice of the UN[56], some specialized agencies and several other international organizations. He concludes that some of this practice can be qualified as "established practice"; in other examples given this is not the case. The most important examples qualified by Peters as established practices (either treaty-extending or treaty-modifying) are the following. A first set of examples relates to the United Nations.

– A well-known example relates to voting in the Security Council. The text of Article 27.3 of the Charter seems to require a positive vote by each of the permanent members. However, since the late 1940s it often happened that permanent members abstained, and the

---

53. *Id.*, at p. 437.
54. *Id.*
55. *Id.*, at p. 438, and, in more detail in German, at pp. 237-239.
56. As indicated on pp. 245-246, the cases selected by Peters are the result of a systematic analysis of the Repertory of the Practice of United Nations Organs and can be considered to a limited extent as representative, "begrenzt repräsentativ".

resolutions concerned were nevertheless considered adopted. This is now generally accepted and qualifies as (modifying) established practice [57].
- Another well-known example is UN peacekeeping. Probably the most visible activity of the UN, not emerging from the minds of the drafters of the Charter but from those of visionary practitioners, this is qualified by Peters as a treaty-extending established practice [58].
- According to Article 9.2 of the Charter, "[e]ach Member shall have not more than five representatives in the General Assembly". However, from the early days of the UN many member states had more than five representatives in the Assembly, and this should now be seen as (modifying) established practice [59].
- A further example is decision-making by consensus in the General Assembly. A large majority of resolutions are now adopted in this way, even though Article 18 of the Charter prescribes (normal or two-thirds) majority voting [60]. This is an extension rather than a modification of the Charter.
- Another example of (treaty-extending) established practice is the creation and development of the status of observer in the UN General Assembly [61].
- Article 23.1 of the Charter mentions criteria for the election by the General Assembly of non-permanent members of the Security Council: "due regard being specially paid, in the first instance to the contribution of Members of the United Nations to the maintenance of international peace and security and to the other purposes of the Organization, and also to equitable geographical distribution". In practice, however, the last-mentioned criterion (equitable geographical distribution) plays a decisive role. According to Peters, this is an example of treaty-modifying established practice [62].
- Article 100 of the Charter provides for strict obligations to guarantee the independence of the UN Secretary-General and the staff of the UN Secretariat. In practice, however, arrangements have been introduced according to which member states make nationals available

---

57. *Id.*, at pp. 249-250. This example is further discussed in Chapter 4.
58. *Id.*, at pp. 332-335.
59. *Id.*, at pp. 247-249.
60. *Id.*, at pp. 250-251. The General Assembly did not amend its rules of procedure to mention decision-making by consensus, unlike the Economic and Social Council (see Rule 59 of the ECOSOC Rules of Procedure).
61. *Id.*, at pp. 261-264.
62. *Id.*, at pp. 320-322.

for the UN Secretariat, but these may raise questions about whether the Charter requirements of independence are respected. One arrangement is "secondment", another one is "gratis personnel". These arrangements are qualified by Peters as examples of (treaty-modifying) established practice [63].

- There are also numerous examples of established practices that relate to the exercise of powers by UN organs. Peters refers to Article 34 of the Charter, which empowers the Security Council to "investigate any dispute, or any situation which might lead to international friction or give rise to a dispute, in order to determine whether the continuance of the dispute or situation is likely to endanger the maintenance of international peace and security". In practice, the Security Council has often decided to investigate a dispute not so much "in order to determine whether the continuance of the dispute or situation is likely to endanger the maintenance of international peace and security", but for wider purposes [64]. Another example is the practice of the Security Council to determine the existence of a threat to the peace (under Article 39 of the Charter) not only in cases of *inter*-state conflicts, but also, in particular since the 1990s, in cases of conflicts *within* states (*intra*-state conflicts) [65]. Further examples of established practices are the exercise of political competences and the conclusion of treaties by the UN Secretary-General [66].

- In addition to these examples from the United Nations, Peters mentions several examples from other international organizations. This selection is more limited than that of the UN since the practice of these other organizations is not documented systematically. A few salient examples discussed by Peters include the following:

- According to Article 19.1 of the Constitution of the ILO, it is for its plenary organ, the International Labour Conference, when it "has decided on the adoption of proposals with regard to an item on the agenda, ... to determine whether these proposals should take the form: *(a)* of an international Convention, or *(b)* of a Recommendation".

---

63. *Id.*, at pp. 327-329.
64. As an example, Peters refers to Security Council Res. 1595, which establishes an international independent investigation commission "to assist the Lebanese authorities in their investigation of all aspects of this terrorist attack [the killing of former Lebanese Prime Minister Rafiq Hariri and others], including to help identify its perpetrators, sponsors, organizers and accomplices" (*id.*, at p. 288).
65. *Id.*, at pp. 290-294.
66. *Id.*, at pp. 312-317.

Legal Facets of the Practice of International Organizations 107

The Conference must therefore make a choice between these two alternatives. However, in practice the Conference often adopts recommendations together with, or subsequently to, a convention. This has become a treaty-modifying established practice of the ILO [67].
- Under Article 22 of the ILO's Constitution, member states are obliged "to make an annual report to the International Labour Office on the measures which it has taken to give effect to the provisions of Conventions to which it is a party". In practice, however, such reporting is often not done annually but less often. This is also an example of treaty-modifying established practice [68].
- Some further examples of established practices can be found within the International Monetary Fund and the World Bank [69].
- The North Atlantic Treaty Organization (NATO) was originally created for the purpose of collective self-defence of its member states. However, in particular since the 1990s it also started to conduct so-called out of area operations (non-Art. 5 operations), for example in Libya and in Afghanistan. This will be further analysed in Chapter 3. This development is qualified by Peters as an example of treaty-extending established practice [70].
- Peters also includes a few regional organizations in his analysis: the European Union, Mercosur and the Arab League. The experience of the EU is of particular interest because of its supranational structure, with far-reaching competences for the institutions to apply, implement and further develop the treaty rules. The role and functioning of the European Court of Justice is of special importance. While the Court, in its case law, has not given much room for a role for the practice of the European Commission and the Council in the interpretation and further development of EU law, it has itself played a major role in this [71]. In a number of cases, the Court has stated that "a mere practice cannot derogate from rules laid down in the Treaty" [72]. In addition, Peters briefly discusses two examples where what is now part of EU law originated in practice: the status of the

---

67. *Id.*, at pp. 351-352.
68. *Id.*, at pp. 352-353.
69. *Id.*, at pp. 354-367.
70. *Id.*, at pp. 368-375.
71. According to Peters, the Court not only interpreted the treaties in a dynamic way but also "betrieb aggressive Rechtsfortbildung", *id.*, at p. 380.
72. E.g. Case 131/86, *ECR 1986*, at p. 933; Case 68/86, *ECR 1988*, at p. 898; Case C-327/91, *ECR 1994*, at p. I-3677; Opinion 1/94, *ECR 1994*, at p. I-5403; Opinion 1/08, *ECR 2009*, at p. I-11186.

EU as an international legal person and the origin and development of the European Council [73]. However, he does not qualify these two as examples of established practice.

On the basis of his in-depth research, Peters concludes that the role and importance of "practice of the organization" (therefore: not only *established* practice of the organization) depends on characteristics of international organizations such as "the complexity of formal amendments, the existence of an explicit power to provide authoritative interpretations, the specificity of regulation by the constituent instrument and the degree of constitutionalization of the organization" [74].

1.2.3. Practice of the United Nations and the specialized agencies

(i) *Examples from the* United Nations Juridical Yearbook

In addition to the findings by Peters, which are based on a theoretical analysis of the concept of practice of the organization that is subsequently used to study the practice of the UN and other international organizations, this subsection will examine when the UN and the specialized agencies themselves have qualified a particular practice as established practice. This is done by systematically researching the *United Nations Juridical Yearbook*. In 1962, the UN General Assembly took the initiative to prepare and publish this *Yearbook* [75], following some years of consultations regarding its form and contents, and the financial implications of its publication [76]. This *Yearbook* was to include, *inter alia*, the text of selected legal opinions of the Secretariat of the UN and the specialized agencies, as well as an index with a brief description of decisions of administrative tribunals [77].

The first *UN Juridical Yearbook* was published in 1962. Currently, there is a backlog in the publication of the *Yearbook*; the most recently published volume covers the year 2016 [78]. These *Yearbooks* from 1962 to 2016 reproduce a selected number of legal opinions of the

---

73. Peters, note 14, at pp. 382-384.
74. *Id.*, at p. 439.
75. GA Res. 1814 (XVII).
76. GA Res. 1506 (XV); also GA Res. 1451 (XIV) and GA Res. 1291 (XIII).
77. GA Res. 1814 (XVII), Annex.
78. See the *United Nations Juridical Yearbook* (*UNJY*) at https://legal.un.org/unjuridicalyearbook/. This website also publishes a special edition of the *UNJY*, mandated by the General Assembly (GA Res. 68/110, as requested by the Secretary-General in his report, UN Doc. A/68/521, para. 42 *(a)*), "to contain select legal opinions that have not been previously published in the *Juridical Yearbook*". This special edition

Legal Facets of the Practice of International Organizations 109

UN Secretariat as well as a selection of decisions of administrative tribunals, relevant treaties and documents. In total, several dozen legal opinions and a number of decisions of administrative tribunals refer to the notion of established practice. The following overview will give an impression of these legal opinions and decisions.

All in all, the *Juridical Yearbooks* include more than 100 instances (legal opinions, judgments of administrative tribunals, treaties, reports of organs of the UN and the specialized agencies, etc.) in which the notion of established practice is used [79]. It would be too much to reproduce or even summarize all these examples. Instead, a number of these cases are selected and grouped in different categories, which should serve the purpose of illustrating the meaning of this notion in the practice of mainly the UN.

(a) *UN conferences*

The first *UN Juridical Yearbook* (1962) reproduces a so-called conference agreement, namely the "Exchange of letters constituting a supplementary agreement to the Agreement of 28 June 1962 between the United Nations and the Federal Republic of Germany regarding arrangements for the United Nations Technical Conference on the International Map of the World on the Millionth Scale to be held in Bonn in August 1962" [80]. According to paragraph 8 of this exchange of letters:

> "The Government undertakes to authorize the entry into and exit from its territory for the duration of the Conference of the

---

contains legal opinions from the period 1948 to 2014. None of these legal opinions mention the notion of established practice.

79. The references are in the following *UNJYs*: 1962, p. 59; 1963, pp. 181-182; 1964, p. 251; 1965, p. 42 and p. 236; 1966, p. 263; 1968, p. 205; 1969, p. 223; 1971, p. 211 and p. 227; 1972, p. 178; 1973, p. 133, p. 143, p. 160 and p. 176; 1974, p. 165, p. 177, p. 191, p. 192; 1975, pp. 166-167; 1976, p. 165, pp. 173-174, pp. 181-183; 1977, p. 162, p. 218, p. 221, pp. 226-227; 1978, p. 141; 1979, p. 134, p. 183; 1980, p. 209; 1981, p. 111; 1982, p. 181, pp. 194-195; 1983, p. 170, p. 180, p. 208; 1984, p. 181; 1985, p. 128, p. 142, p. 164; 1986, p. 157, p. 289, pp. 291-292, p. 324, p. 337; 1987, p. 141, p. 160; 1988, pp. 346-349; 1989, p. 284, p. 292; 1992, p. 89, p. 429, p. 468; 1993, pp. 355-356, p. 418, p. 427, p. 451; 1994, p. 137, p. 346, p. 463, p. 490, p. 504; 1995, p. 132, p. 420 (twice); 1996, p. 400, p. 446, p. 488; 1997, p. 405, p. 439; 1998, p. 446, p. 488, p. 489; 1999, p. 380, p. 410, p. 418, p. 421; 2000, p. 347; 2001, pp. 387-388; 2003, p. 352, p. 533, p. 559 and p. 564; 2005, p. 441, p. 500, p. 501; 2006, p. 465 and p. 469; 2008, p. 434 (footnote 33); 2010, p. 272, p. 449, p. 516, p. 521; 2011, p. 466; 2012, p. 403; 2013, p. 373, p. 379, p. 385; 2014, p. 198; 2016, p. 111, p. 412.
80. *UNJY 1962*, at pp. 58-60.

following categories of persons: . . . *(f)* Representatives of the press, or of radio, television, film, or other information agencies accredited by the United Nations after consultation with the Federal Government in accordance with the established practice of the United Nations at its Headquarters, as well as persons invited to the Conference by the United Nations on official business." [81]

The purpose of this provision is to ensure that representatives of the press (etc.) would have access to the conference to the same extent as would be the case if this conference would take place at the UN headquarters. Conditions of access to UN conferences should be similar wherever such conferences take place, and should therefore not depend on the rules and policies of the host country. The details of the relevant established practice are not mentioned in this exchange of notes, but the paragraph would give guidance to those who implement it in practice.

Another conference agreement, concluded between the UN and the Government of Indonesia, includes a dispute settlement provision stating that disputes will be settled amicably through negotiation and that any outstanding dispute will be settled "in consultation with the Government of Indonesia, in accordance with the established United Nations practices" [82].

Other examples concern invitation policies for UN conferences [83]. Some legal opinions of the UN Secretariat have mentioned the established practice that, when a UN organ has spelled out states and others to be invited to the UN conference concerned, neither that conference nor the Secretariat is competent to depart from this, by inviting others or by excluding those who are invited [84].

(b) *UN peacekeeping*

Numerous established practices concern UN peacekeeping. For example, in 1965 the UN concluded an agreement with Belgium "relating to the settlement of claims filed against the United Nations in the Congo by Belgian nationals" in the context of the United Nations Operation in the Congo (ONUC) peacekeeping force. In this exchange of

---

81. *Id.*, at p. 59.
82. *UNJY 1995*, at p. 132.
83. E.g. *UNJY 2014*, at p. 198 (invitations for the preparatory process of a special session of the General Assembly, "in accordance with the relevant rules of procedure and established practice").
84. *UNJY 1968*, at p. 205; *UNJY 1972*, at p. 178.

letters, the UN Secretary-General agreed to pay the Belgian government "without prejudice to the privileges and immunities enjoyed by the United Nations, . . . one million five hundred thousand United States dollars in lump-sum and final settlement of all claims" arising from the operations of ONUC, particularly those which took place in Katanga. The Soviet Union protested against this claims settlement in a letter of 2 August 1965 [85]. In this letter, the Soviet Union stated, *inter alia*, that "this action by the United Nations Secretariat is unlawful and contrary to decisions taken by the United Nations". In addition, it stated that "Belgium, as is well known, committed aggression against the Republic of the Congo and as an aggressor has no moral or legal basis for making claims against the United Nations either on its own behalf or on behalf of its citizens. Belgium is responsible to the Congo and the United Nations for its aggression against that country, and not vice versa" [86]. In the opinion of the Soviet Union, the Secretariat "has no right in this case to enter into any agreements on behalf of the United Nations concerning the payment of compensation without the authorization of the Security Council" [87]. UN Secretary-General U-Thant replied to this in a letter dated 6 August 1965. In his reply, the Secretary-General stated that he had acted "in his capacity of chief administrative officer of the Organization, consistently with the established practice of the United Nations under which claims addressed to the Organization by private individuals are considered and settled under the authority of the Secretary-General" [88]. The Secretary-General did not further elaborate on the origin or legal basis of this established practice, aside from the reference to his capacity of chief administrative officer of the organization, a status bestowed on him in Article 97 of the Charter.

Another established practice in the field of peacekeeping concerns the payment of compensation for death or injury sustained by military contingent personnel. According to this established practice, claims relating to death, injury, and so forth, of such personnel while performing official peacekeeping duties "are settled, in the first instance, by the respective national authorities of the State concerned on the basis of its national legislation. In such cases, the United Nations reimburses the troop-contributing State for compensation paid on behalf of one of its contingent members provided that the State's claim for reimbursement

---

85. Reproduced in *UNJY 1965*, at pp. 40-41.
86. *Id.*, at p. 40.
87. *Id.*, at p. 41.
88. *Id.*, at p. 42.

has been duly certified by its Auditor-General (or an official of similar rank) as based on payment properly made pursuant to specific provisions of national legislation applicable to service in the armed forces of that State"[89]. A further established practice in UN peacekeeping regards "the requirement that a Government assume financial responsibility for damage caused by the gross negligence or willful misconduct of its personnel to equipment provided by another country"[90].

(c) *The UN Secretariat as a depositary of multilateral treaties*

Many legal opinions that refer to "established practice" concern the role of the UN Secretariat as the depositary of treaties (on the basis of Art. 102 of the Charter). For example, when the Soviet Union found a number of errors in the authentic Russian text of the 1962 International Coffee Agreement, it requested the Secretary-General to rectify these errors. "Following the established practice", the UN Secretariat addressed a circular letter to all governments represented at the 1962 UN International Coffee Conference and to all other governments that had signed the 1962 Coffee Agreement or acceded thereto, informing them of the errors and proposing to correct the text, with ninety days for states to react[91]. Many other examples of legal opinions of the UN Secretariat relating to its depositary functions refer to established practices[92]. This extensive "established depositary practice" is also

---

[89]. *UNJY 1993*, at p. 355.

[90]. *UNJY 2001*, at pp. 387-388.

[91]. *UNJY 1964*, at p. 251. One government informed the Secretariat that it "found the suggested procedure unacceptable" *(id.)*. In response, the Secretary-General indicated that he "was following the long established depositary practice in the matter. The correction procedure suggested in the circular letter concerned has been employed in the past, without any objection, either on the Secretary-General's own initiative or at the request of the interested Governments, when errors or inconsistencies between the authentic texts were discovered in multilateral treaties in respect of which he acts as depositary" (*id.*, at p. 252). In the end, the government concerned withdrew its objections (*id.*, at p. 254, footnote 48).

[92]. For example, *UNJY 1965*, at p. 236; *UNJY 1969*, at p. 223; *UNJY 1973*, at p. 176 ("our Secretariat has a well-established practice for dealing with treaty time-limits that fall on weekends"); *UNJY 1974*, at pp. 191-192 (established practices regarding reservations); *UNJY 1980*, at p. 209 (the established practice that a treaty is presumed to apply to the entire territory of each party unless it appears otherwise from the treaty (this practice was subsequently codified in Art. 29 of the 1969 Vienna Convention)); *UNJY 1984*, at p. 181 ("the established practice under which the Secretary-General accepts depositary functions on the basis of universal or, very exceptionally, regional participation") (*UNJY 1994*, at p. 504 also refers to this established practice); *UNJY 1988*, at p. 346 and p. 349 (memo by the Secretariat of the United Nations Industrial Development Organization, UNIDO); *UNJY 1992*, at p. 469 (permissibility of reservations).

reflected in the publication of a separate UN document of 149 pages, the *Summary of Practice of the Secretary-General as Depositary of Multilateral Treaties* [93].

(d) *The relations between organizations and their staff*

Established practices are also important in the relations between organizations and their staff. Numerous legal opinions of the UN Secretariat refer to established practices in this context. For example, it has indicated that "[s]ickness or ill health does not preclude the non-renewal of an appointment after expiry date; none the less it is established United Nations practice for fixed-term appointments to be extended to permit the exhaustion of sick leave entitlements already accrued if the staff member is on sick leave at the time of expiry of the original appointment" [94]. While the statutes of international administrative tribunals normally do not mention established practice as a source of law [95], it is fully accepted in their case law [95]. Many administrative tribunal judgments reproduced in the *UN Juridical Yearbook* refer to an established practice as a source of law [96]. One judgment of the UN

---

93. See UN Doc. ST/LEG/7/Rev.1 (1999).
94. *UNJY 1979*, at p. 183.
95. See further C. Rohde, "Organizational Practice as a Source of Law", in D. Petrović (ed.), *90 Years of Contribution of the Administrative Tribunal of the International Labour Organization to the Creation of International Civil Service Law*, Geneva, ILO, 2017, pp. 53-73.
96. E.g. *UNJY 1977*, at p. 162 (step increments (in staff grades)); *UNJY 1978*, at p. 141 ("a long-established practice" of holding consultations between the representatives of the Executive Heads and of the staff of the Geneva-based organizations on the revision of salary scales); *UNJY 1979*, at p. 134 (the appointment of a staff member at the P-3 level to a post graded P-4/P-5 "in no way contravened the United Nations Staff Regulations or the established practice"); *UNJY 1981*, at p. 111 (the established practice of the Secretary-General to include in his annual report to the General Assembly on the composition of the Secretariat statistical tables showing "staff in posts subject to geographical distribution"); *UNJY 1998*, at p. 446 (ILOAT, the "established practice to consult an employee on a proposed redeployment"). See also the World Bank Administrative Tribunal in its famous first judgment, *de Merode* (1981, at para. 23): "The practice of the organization may also, in certain circumstances, become part of the conditions of employment. Obviously, the organization would be discouraged from taking measures favorable to its employees on an *ad hoc* basis if each time it did so it had to take the risk of initiating a practice which might become legally binding upon it. The integration of practice into the conditions of employment must therefore be limited to that of which evidence is that it is followed by the organization in the conviction that it reflects a legal obligation, as was recognized by the International Court of Justice in its *Advisory Opinion on Judgments of the Administrative Tribunal of the ILO*, (*ICJ Reports 1956*, p. 91)." For the text of this judgment, see *WBAT Reports* (1981), Decision No. 1, quotation at pp. 11-12. On the reference to practice in this judgment, see C. F. Amerasinghe, *Principles of the Institutional Law of International Organizations*, 2nd ed., Cambridge, Cambridge University Press, 2005, at pp. 290-292.

Dispute Tribunal referred to "well-established practice of the United Nations" to consult a doctor in case a UN official is arrested for driving under the influence of alcohol [97].

(e) *The conduct of meetings and the daily operation of organs*

Numerous legal opinions deal with the conduct of meetings and the daily operation of the General Assembly and other UN organs. For example, there is the established practice that the Secretary-General provides observer facilities to a non-member state which establishes permanent offices at headquarters only if this state is a member of one of the specialized agencies of the UN [98]; the established practice in the General Assembly hall "to seat observers in areas normally reserved for them" [99]; "the established United Nations practice" according to which "observers are given the opportunity to speak after the members of the United Nations body concerned have been given that opportunity" [100]; the established practice when a Main Committee of the Assembly has before it two or more proposals relating to the same question, to vote on the proposals in the order of their submission [101]; the established practice that the right of reply "is regarded to be an absolute right of Member States which is not subject to the discretion of the presiding officer as regards States which are full members of the organ concerned" [102]; the established practice "that, once given the floor, a speaker has every right to state that he is speaking on behalf of whomever he wishes" [103]; the established practice that "the right to participate 'in the deliberations' of meetings does not encompass the right to circulate documents" [104]; the established practice relating to the accreditation of representatives [105]; and "the long-established practice of the General Assembly and its Main Committees to strive for consensus whenever possible" [106]. In addition, there is a "well-established practice, which it

---

97. *UNJY 2010*, at p. 449.
98. *UNJY 1994*, at p. 463.
99. *UNJY 1975*, at p. 166.
100. *UNJY 1992*, at p. 429.
101. *UNJY 1976*, at p. 181.
102. *UNJY 1983*, at p. 170.
103. *UNJY 1993*, at p. 418 (the text continues: "It is not for the Secretariat, nor in fact for any United Nations body, to prevent a speaker from stating for whom he speaks (of course, if the speaker is not in fact authorized to speak on behalf of others as purported, that is a different matter and would no doubt be the source of discussion)").
104. *UNJY 1995*, at p. 420.
105. *UNJY 1993*, at p. 427.
106. *UNJY 2003*, at p. 533.

may be difficult to change", that the formal action taken by the Fifth Committee on its first reading of the budget "is not on the Secretary-General's proposals, but on those proposals as modified by any recommendations of the Advisory Committee on Administrative and Budgetary Questions" [107]. A further example concerns the composition of the Credentials Committee of the General Assembly: "in accordance with a well-established practice", this Committee is composed of nine members, of which three are permanent (China, Russian Federation, United States), two are from the African Group, two from the Latin American Group, one from the Asian Group and one from the Group of Western European and Other States [108]. Another example concerns the established practice of credentials committees of international conferences of a short duration "to approve . . . provisional credentials on the understanding that the formal credentials will be submitted in due course" [109]. A final example is "the established practice of the General Assembly" that representatives of a member state whose credentials have been challenged continue to act in that capacity until the General Assembly, on the recommendation of the Credentials Committee, has decided otherwise [110].

(f) *Issues of representation, the leadership role of the General Assembly*

Resolution 396 (V) of the General Assembly applies to situations in which more than one authority claims to be the government entitled to represent a member state in the UN. In view of the "risk that conflicting decisions may be reached by its various organs", this resolution recommends that the Assembly should consider these situations when they arise, in the light of the Purposes and Principles of the Charter and the circumstances of each case, and that the attitude adopted "should be taken into account in other organs of the United Nations and in the specialized agencies". When the question arose in 1982 of whether the Executive Committee of the Programme of the High Commissioner for Refugees had the competence to expel or suspend a member of the Executive Committee, the Secretariat indicated in a legal opinion that "established practice has applied [this Resolution] by analogy also to

---

107. *UNJY 1982*, at pp. 194-195.
108. *UNJY 1985*, at p. 128.
109. *UNJY 1996*, at p. 446.
110. *UNJY 2003*, at p. 532.

other questions involving the representation of States"[111]. Four years later, a question arose concerning the representation of Western Sahara in the UN's Economic Commission for Africa. In a legal opinion, the UN Secretariat stated that "[i]t is the established practice on the basis of this resolution [Resolution 396] that the attitude adopted by the General Assembly be followed by all organs of the United Nations. Although Western Sahara is not a Member State, its representation is nevertheless a disputed matter and the situation is therefore analogous to that envisaged in General Assembly Resolution 396 (V)"[112].

(g) *Privileges and immunities*

A number of legal opinions concern privileges and immunities of the UN and the specialized agencies, as well as their officials[113]. For example, whenever a case is brought against the UN before a domestic court, it is established practice of the UN

> "to assert the immunity from suit of the United Nations in a written communication to the Ministry of Foreign Affairs of the State concerned. When time permits this communication is sent through the Permanent Representative of the State concerned at United Nations Headquarters. In the written communication the Ministry of Foreign Affairs is requested to take the necessary steps to inform the appropriate office of Government (usually the Ministry of Justice or the Attorney General's Office) to appear or otherwise move the court to dismiss the suit on the grounds of the Organization's immunity"[114].

Some final examples of established practices of the UN are the following. Obviously, whenever it is necessary in UN documents to refer to Taiwan, the precise name given to Taiwan is a delicate issue. Therefore, it is helpful that there is established practice in this regard. Since the adoption of Resolution 2758 (XXVI) of 25 October 1971, "the established practice of the United Nations has been to use the term 'Taiwan, Province of China' when a reference to 'Taiwan' is required in United Nations Secretariat documents"[115]. With respect to contracts concluded by the UN, it is established practice "to reject any

---

111. *UNJY 1982*, at p. 181.
112. *UNJY 1986*, at pp. 291-292.
113. See e.g. *UNJY 2005*, at p. 441 and p. 501; *UNJY 2013*, at p. 373 and p. 375.
114. *UNJY 1976*, at pp. 173-174; *UNJY 2013*, at pp. 379-380; *UNJY 2016*, at p. 111.
115. *UNJY 2010*, at p. 516.

specific reference to municipal laws and to rely on general principles of law in the interpretation of contracts with private parties" [116]. It is also established practice of the UN to submit claims by individuals "to arbitration on the basis of an arbitration clause in a contract or a separate arbitration agreement" [117]. A final example concerns the position of the legal office within the organization; it is "the established practice in the United Nations and the specialized and related agencies" that the legal office is "a separate and independent office reporting directly to the head of the organization" [118]. The legal adviser "provides independent legal advice directly to those who request it and who, in the exercise of his/her mandate, does not receive instructions from another official" [119].

(ii) *A few observations*

The overview above is a selection of examples where the UN, and in some cases a specialized agency [120], takes the view that a certain established practice exists. Even though this overview is incomplete, it illustrates that the UN and the specialized agencies use the notion of established practice extensively. In addition, a few more specific observations include the following.

First, some references are simply to "established practice", for example: "following the established practice. . . ." [121]. Other references are to "the established practice of the United Nations" [122], "the established United Nations practices" [123], "the established practice of the Organization" [124], "well-established practice of the United

---

116. *UNJY 1976*, at p. 165; *UNJY 1986*, at p. 324.
117. *UNJY 2000*, at p. 347.
118. *UNJY 2003*, at pp. 564-565.
119. *Id.*, at p. 565.
120. E.g. *UNJY 1985*, at p. 164 (legal opinion by the UNESCO Secretariat: "in accordance with a well-established practice, many member States have accredited permanent delegations to UNESCO"); *UNJY 1986*, at p. 157 (letter from the Director-General of FAO referring to modes of settlement of disputes arising out of contracts or other disputes of private character, mentioning that "FAO, in accordance with its established practice, has undertaken to set up procedures safeguarding the fundamental principles on which judicial proceedings are based both under national legal systems and under national law"); *UNJY 1987*, at p. 160 (World Bank); *UNJY 1988*, at pp. 346-349 (UNIDO); *UNJY 1989*, at p. 292 (International Civil Aviation Organization, ICAO); *UNJY 1993*, at p. 451 (UNIDO); *UNJY 1996*, at p. 488 (ILO); *UNJY 1999*, at p. 380 (IMF); *UNJY 2005*, at p. 500 and p. 501 (UNIDO); *UNJY 2010*, at p. 272 (ILO); *UNJY 2016*, at p. 111 (FAO); *UNJY 2016*, at p. 412 (UNIDO).
121. E.g. *UNJY 1964*, at p. 251.
122. E.g. *UNJY 1962*, at p. 59; *UNJY 1992*, at p. 429.
123. *UNJY 1995*, at p. 132.
124. E.g. *UNJY 1993*, at p. 418; *UNJY 1994*, at p. 463; *UNJY 2013*, at p. 373 and p. 375.

Nations"[125], "the established practice of the Security Council"[126], "the established practice of the General Assembly"[127], "the established practice of the Secretariat"[128], "a well-established practice of the United Nations Secretariat"[129], and "an established practice of the Secretary-General"[130]. More broadly, reference was even made to "the established practice in the United Nations and the specialized and related agencies"[131], and to "the long-established policies and practice of the United Nations system organizations"[132]. There are also more specific references, to the established practice of the Commission on Human Rights[133], "the established practice under this Convention"[134], "the well-established practice under the Headquarters Agreement and the Convention on the Privileges and Immunities of the United Nations"[135], and to "the established depositary practice"[136]. In the context of the ILO, reference was made to "the long-established constitutional practice of the Organization"[137].

Second, the references to "established practice" do not consistently use the same terminology as a generally used term of art. There are also references to "well-established practice"[138], "the clearly established practice"[139], long-established practice[140], "established administrative practice"[141], and to "long-established administrative practice"[142]. Exceptionally, there is a reference to "established rules and prac-

---

125. *UNJY 2010*, at p. 449.
126. E.g. *UNJY 1983*, at p. 180.
127. *UNJY 1994* (this reference is made in a World Intellectual Property Organization legal instrument). Similarly: *UNJY 1996*, at p. 400; *UNJY 2012*, at p. 403.
128. E.g. *UNJY 1963*, at p. 182.
129. *UNJY 2005*, at p. 500.
130. E.g. *UNJY 1981*, at p. 111.
131. *UNJY 2003*, at p. 564.
132. *UNJY 1999*, at p. 421 (relating to the freedom for World Bank borrowers "to make their own determination of whether it is in their best interest to request the assistance of a United Nations system organization or to obtain the required services commercially from a private company").
133. *UNJY 1999*, at p. 410.
134. *UNJY 1965*, at p. 236 (the convention concerned is the 1947 Convention on the Privileges and Immunities of the Specialized Agencies). Similarly: *UNJY 1973*, at p. 133 ("established practice in applying the Convention", relating to the 1946 Convention on the Privileges and Immunities of the United Nations).
135. *UNJY 1985*, at p. 142.
136. *UNJY 1969*, at p. 223.
137. *UNJY 1996*, at p. 488.
138. E.g. *UNJY 1968*, at p. 205; *UNJY 1995*, at p. 420; *UNJY 2003*, at p. 559.
139. *UNJY 1994*, at p. 490.
140. E.g. *UNJY 1978*, at p. 141; *UNJY 2003*, at p. 533.
141. *UNJY 1989*, at p. 292.
142. *UNJY 1987*, at p. 141.

tice" [143], and to "[t]he established principle and consistent practice of the Organization" [144]. Sometimes slightly different terminology is used, such as "standard practice" [145], "constant practice of the Organization" [146], or: "it is the consistent practice of the United Nations Archives to routinely provide regular copies of documents that are accessible to the general public" [147], or "it has been the practice of the Secretary-General routinely to waive the immunities enjoyed by its officials of the rank of Assistant Secretary-General and above where the acts performed by those officials and in respect of which they are being prosecuted or sued were performed by them otherwise than in their capacity as officials of the United Nations" [148]. It is uncertain whether, in these examples where slightly different terminology is used, the term established practice has deliberately not been used.

Third, in almost all cases in which the UN refers to a certain established practice, this is merely stated as a given. Only exceptionally is the rationale for that practice explained [149].

Fourth, it rarely happens that the UN examines whether or not there is a certain established practice in a particular area and concludes that this is not the case [150]. In a few cases, it has been claimed before an

---

143. *UNJY 1986*, at p. 289 ("States that are full participants in the activities of a United Nations organ are, in accordance with the established rules and practice, assessed contributions for expenses relating to the activities of the organ concerned"). See also *UNJY 1996*, at p. 446 ("the established practices and rules of United Nations bodies" (relating to the issuance of credentials)).
144. *UNJY 2013*, at p. 385. This was in relation to experts on mission: "There is no definition of 'experts on mission' in the General Convention. The established principle and consistent practice of the Organization is to consider as 'experts on mission' persons who are performing missions for the United Nations provided they are serving in an individual capacity and are neither officials of the Organization nor representatives of Member States."
145. *UNJY Special Edition 2009*, at p. 4.
146. *UNJY 1985*, at p. 142.
147. *UNJY Special Edition 2001*, at p. 6.
148. *UNJY Special Edition 2006*, at p. 3.
149. For an example, see *UNJY 1974*, at p. 165.
150. For exceptions, see *UNJY 1983*, at p. 208 ("no practice has been established in this regard"); *UNJY 1986*, at p. 337 (memo prepared by the UNIDO Secretariat about the exclusive authority of the Director-General to appoint staff: "it would be erroneous to maintain that the established practice of the United Nations and of the former UNIDO has been to conclude agreements with Governments requiring the Government's consent to the appointment of 200 series personnel to be stationed in their countries" (at p. 337)); *UNJY 1998*, at p. 489 ("As there are no provisions in the rules of procedure of the General Assembly relating to observer status in the General Assembly, the status and rights of participation of observers rest solely on the practice of the General Assembly"; "the General Assembly does not have an established practice on the participation of non-governmental organizations").

administrative tribunal that a certain established practice exists, and the tribunal has rejected such a claim [151].

Fifth, it may happen that a certain established practice is at variance with a resolution or other act or rule of an organization. What should prevail? In 2006, a legal opinion of the UN's Office of Legal Affairs addressed this issue, when two offices of the UN Secretariat (the Office of Internal Oversight Services (OIOS) and the Office of Programme Planning, Budget and Accounts (OPPBA)) disagreed as to whether a report prepared by OIOS (the Programme Performance Report (PPR) of the United Nations for the biennium 2004-2005)) "is a report of the Secretary-General that should be submitted by him to the General Assembly in accordance with long-standing practice or, rather, is a report of OIOS that, in accordance with resolution 59/272, should be submitted directly to the General Assembly" [152]. OPPBA was in favour of the former procedure (report of the Secretary-General) and referred to this as "established practice" [153]. The Office of Legal Affairs supported this position. In its legal opinion, it examined the existing rules governing PPRs as well as the mandate of OIOS. It concluded that, in this specific case, "unless the General Assembly clearly mandates that PPRs should be subject to the reporting procedures set forth in resolution 59/272, PPRs should continue to be submitted by the Secretary-General to the General Assembly" [154]. The memo itself did not explicitly mention the notion of established practice; it only used the expression "long-standing practice". In another judgment, before the ILO Administrative Tribunal, a complainant contested a decision to appoint a Chief of Cabinet of the Organisation for the Prohibition of Chemical Weapons (OPCW) directly, without holding a competitive process, in violation of the relevant staff regulation. The OPCW Appeals Council decided that this was indeed a breach of this regulation but that this breach was "mitigated by the existence of a well-established practice of filling the post of Chief of Cabinet without holding a competition" [155]. The ILO Administrative Tribunal ruled, however, that "the existence of an established practice of directly appointing a Chief of Cabinet was not

---

151. E.g. *UNJY 1997* (the World Bank Administrative Tribunal "did not find this episode . . . to be conclusive evidence of "established practice" complementing the Applicant's conditions of employment").
152. *UNJY 2006*, at p. 469.
153. *Id.*
154. *Id.*, at p. 471.
155. *UNJY 2011*, at p. 466.

relevant, as a practice which was in violation of a rule could not have the effect of modifying the rule itself" [156].

1.3. Some further reflections on the notion of "established practice of the organization"

Following this overview of examples of established practices of international organizations (mainly the UN and the specialized agencies), this concluding section will offer some further reflections on the notion of "established practice of the organization". These reflections concern the nature of "established practice of the organization" as a component of the rules of international organizations, the question of whether it is necessary to define this notion (and if so, how), the need to know more about current established practices of international organizations, the question of when a practice is established, and who decides.

1.3.1. The most dynamic component of rules of international organizations

The 1969 Vienna Convention applies to treaties generally, including treaties which are the constituent instruments of international organizations, as is indicated in Article 5 of this Convention. But Article 5 also contains the price to be paid for this inclusion, and this is value for money. The rules of the Vienna Convention apply to constituent instruments up to where they conflict with any relevant rules of the organizations concerned. This conflict rule is a recognition of the separate legal order of international organizations. They have their own life, and the performance of their functions may require that they deviate from the Vienna rules. This is true for international organizations generally, but also more for certain organizations than for others. Given their infinite variety, the rules of some of them may conflict with Vienna rules while the rules of others don't.

During the final negotiations of the 1969 Vienna Conference, international organizations were adamant on giving a broad interpretation of the concept of rules of the organization, covering also established practice and "the right to institute new practices", so that they could react in a flexible way to new challenges arising in

---

156. *Id.*

the future [157]. How justified this was. A broad interpretation was subsequently codified in the 1975 Vienna Convention, which defined "rules of the organization" to also include "established practice". This part of the rules of international organizations is their most dynamic component. It reflects certain needs originating in the ever-changing *milieu* in which international organizations perform their functions but that have not (or not yet) been crystallized into written rules of the organization. It is this part of the rules of international organizations that is of growing importance with the ageing of international organizations and the difficulties involved in amending their constituent instruments. It is essential to prevent the organization from becoming obsolete. For good reasons therefore the notion of established practice has also been included in subsequent definitions of "rules of the organization": in the 1986 Vienna II Convention and in the 2011 ARIO. In addition, the latter two instruments have further recognized the flexibility needs of international organizations by not requiring that established practices are in accordance with their constituent instruments.

1.3.2. To define or not to define?

While the concept of "rules of the organization" has therefore become more clearly defined over time, as well as the place of "established practice" within these rules, the notion of "established practice" as such has so far remained ill-defined. While this is true, it may be questioned whether it would be necessary or wise at all to fully define this notion, or whether it would be better to leave its interpretation and implementation to the infinite variety of practices of international organizations, for the benefit of flexibility and optimal performance of their functions. It is indeed necessary to proceed with caution in this area. What Reuter has observed during the preparations for the Vienna II Convention, relating to the codification of general rules for international organizations, is also true for further circumscribing "established practice" of international organizations [158]:

---

157. See P. Reuter, First Report on the Question of Treaties Concluded between States and International Organizations or between Two or More International Organizations, *Yb. ILC 1972*, Vol. 2, quotation at p. 187, para. 51. Reuter observed that international organizations desired "to avoid confining the creative freedom . . . within rules which would not be fully adapted to their needs as those needs became progressively clearer with the development of their activities"; "the dominant feeling was one of fear lest a process of change essential for the future of the organizations be interrupted" *(id.)*.

158. Reuter, ILC Second Report, at p. 78, para. 17.

"Hitherto, international organizations, acting principally through their secretariats and in most cases with no general texts or precedents to use as a basis, have – slowly and unobtrusively, by the development of practice alone – built up a corpus of solutions adjusted to the individual needs and character of each organization. The codification now envisaged may affect this spontaneous process."

At the same time, without defining this notion in detail, "this spontaneous process" may benefit from some guidance. Some further specifications could be helpful, to have some rule of law for international organizations and their members in the twilight zone between mere practice and law. Therefore, even though it is by now generally accepted, the notion of established practice should be given greater consideration, both in practice, at the level of each specific international organization, and more generally, at a conceptual level. While the emphasis should be on the specific way in which it is used by each individual organization, at the same time there is merit in further circumscription, just like the concept of rules of the organization has become defined and further refined over time. Such further specification would meet the twin needs of stability and change. It would lay down certain minimum requirements that would need to be fulfilled before a certain practice – whatever it is – can be considered as "established". How much support by the membership is required? How extensive and consistent should the relevant practice be? Can a certain practice become established only to fill certain unforeseen gaps, or can it also, and if so to what extent, go against existing rules of an organization? Do not only international organizations have their own established practice but also each of their organs?

1.3.3. *A wealth of undocumented, little-known practices*

For the purpose of drafting such specifications, it is obvious that the existing practice must be taken into account. The previous section (1.2) gave some examples of established practices of international organizations. The examples are mainly from the experience of the UN and the specialized agencies. The relevant practice of other international organizations is hardly documented. Only some of this is published in official documents. An example is the OPCW. Its published documents contain several references to established practices, and also to other practices. For example, in connection with the technical assistance offered to the United Kingdom in 2018, following the poisoning a former Russian military officer and his daughter in Salisbury, the OPCW Director-General indicated that

> "[i]n keeping with *its standard practice*, the Secretariat does not disclose the identities of members of teams or mission planning details to State Parties other than the State Party hosting the technical assistance visit" [159].

Furthermore, he indicated that access of other State Parties than the UK to the report of this visit "is subject to the agreement of the United Kingdom, pursuant to the Confidentiality Annex of the Convention, the OPCW Policy on Confidentiality, and *the consistent practice* in relation to other technical assistance visits" [160]. Two weeks later, when the Director-General presented the report of this visit to the Executive Council of the OPCW, he mentioned that "in accordance with *the established practice* the Secretariat does not share the full reports of the analysis of the samples that it receives from the designated Labs with the States Parties. This practice is aimed at protecting the identity of the labs which conduct off-site analysis of samples" [161]. Other examples of OPCW established practices concern its reporting to the UN Security Council [162], its reporting on planned activities [163] and its consultations with member states [164].

The examples mentioned in this chapter are therefore only the tip of the iceberg, but they already show the great variety of practices that have become established. On the one hand, it may be presumed that this variety will only be multiplied if an overview of established practices of many other international organizations would be available. Established practices of international organizations are very specific, tailored to

---

159. OPCW Doc. EC-M-57/DG.1, 4 April 2018, at para. 3 (italics added).
160. *Id.*, at para. 5 (italics added).
161. OPCW Doc. EC-M-59/DG.1, 18 April 2018, at p. 3 (italics added).
162. See https://www.opcw.org/media-centre/news/2015/11/director-general-circulates-opcw-ffm-reports-states-parties, 6 November 2015 ("in accordance with the established practice, the Director-General will attach these FFM reports to his next monthly report to be submitted to the UN Security Council through the Secretary-General").
163. OPCW Doc. EC-98/DG.14, 9 September 2021, at para. 6 ("In accordance with established practice, the factual reporting on the planned activities for the period from 1 September to 31 December 2021 will be provided as an annex to the next Note by the Director-General on the Africa Programme").
164. OPCW Doc. EC-97/DG.13, 22 June 2021, at para. 4 ("Through a note verbale dated 16 April 2021, and in line with the established practice, the Secretariat informed the Syrian Arab Republic that a new outstanding issue would be opened and discussed at the next round of consultations").

the needs of international organizations that are very different from one another. Each organization is unique. Each organization performs its own functions, in – sometimes rapidly – changing circumstances. On the other hand, it may also be presumed that a number of these established practices could be similar because they are based on logic and common experience. For example, why should the right of reply only in the UN be "regarded to be an absolute right of Member States which is not subject to the discretion of the presiding officer as regards States which are full members of the organ concerned"? Is this not so fundamental that it also applies to the exercise of the right of reply in other international organizations? Likewise, as mentioned above, it is an established practice in the UN that "observers are given the opportunity to speak after the members of the United Nations body concerned have been given that opportunity". Why would that be different in other international organizations? However, these are only presumptions since a full overview of established practices of international organizations is lacking. If this were available, it would provide an important source of information when preparing some sufficiently solid minimum requirements that would need to be fulfilled before a certain practice can be considered as "established". It would make it less arbitrary when the UN or any other international organization would claim that a certain practice is established.

1.3.4. When is a practice "established"?

The purpose of the qualifier "established" is to add a legal dimension to a practice of an organization, as a requirement for this practice to qualify as a rule of the organization. In this way, it resembles *opinio iuris* as a requirement for rules of customary international law. "Established practice" has therefore also been referred to as the "quasi-customary law" of the particular organization [165]. But why "quasi"? Is it not "simply" customary law of the organization? The Statute of the International Court of Justice (ICJ) refers to customary law as "international custom, as evidence of a general practice accepted as law" [166]. "Established practice of the organization" could indeed be seen as "customary law of the organization" [167]. As more often is the case,

---
165. See Peters, note 14, at pp. 176-178, 241.
166. ICJ Statute, Art. 38.1 *(b)*.
167. See also ILC Special Rapporteur P. Reuter in the ILC, *Yb. ILC 1974*, Vol. 1, at p. 163 ("established practice, which was to say customary rules"). Reuter, note 4, at

in the context of international organizations law, a term is used that is different from the term used in inter-state relations, even though the two essentially have the same legal meaning [168]. Nevertheless, emphasizing the *opinio iuris* purpose that the qualifier "established" serves as well as the similarity to customary international law could assist in developing criteria that must be fulfilled for practice to be "established".

In developing such criteria, the bar must be high. Other types of rules of international organizations are required to be in accordance with their constituent instruments and therefore there is a link with the consent that the member states once expressed, even though this may have been a long time ago. Such a link is missing in the case of established practice, which is not required to be in accordance with the relevant constituent instrument. The support by the members of a certain organizational practice is therefore of particular importance. This is particularly true for "treaty-modifying" (in contrast to "treaty-extending") established practice, to use Peters' terminology, because such practice is different from what the members originally consented to, and cannot be considered as a further development *(Fortentwicklung)* of the inherently dynamic project in which they decided to participate.

When is an organizational practice "established"? *Prima facie*, "established" seems to require the lapse of a certain period of time, during which a certain conduct has become regular so that those involved may hold a legitimate expectation that this is no longer a coincidence but rather the norm. Perhaps this may be compared to the

---

pp. 204-205 ("Il semblerait d'autre part qu'une 'pratique bien établie', constituant 'une règle de l'organisation', c'est-à-dire présentant un caractère obligatoire sera normalement une règle coutumière . . . [t]out ceci évoque bien l'atmosphère du droit coutumier, bien que le terme de 'coutume' n'ait jamais été employé" (footnote omitted)). In addition, Gautier, note 42, at pp. 64-65 ("This expression [established practice] may be understood as referring to a form of customary law"). See for an early reference Pollux (E. Hambro), "The Interpretation of the Charter", *British Yearbook of International Law*, Vol. 23 (1946), pp. 54-82, at p. 54: "A constitutional customary law will grow up and the Charter itself will merely form the framework of the Organization which will be filled in by the practice of the different organs". It should be noted that the ILC in its commentary to the 1986 Vienna II Convention stated that "by referring to 'established' practice, the Commission seeks only to rule out uncertain or disputed practice; it is not its wish to freeze practice at a particular moment in an organization's history" (*Yb. ILC 1981*, Vol. 2, Part 2, at p. 124, para. (24)).

168. Other examples are the use of the term "juridical personality" (international organizations) rather than "international personality" (states) during the *travaux préparatoires* of the UN Charter (see 13 *UNCIO Doc.* (1945), at pp. 622-623) and the use of the term "act of formal confirmation" (international organizations) rather than "ratification" (states) in the 1986 Vienna Convention on the Law of Treaties between States and International Organizations or between International Organizations (Art. 2.1 *(b)*).

freezing of water. First, a thin sheet of ice will cover the water. When the frost continues, the ice will become thicker and finally strong and reliable enough for people to stand or skate on it. However, there is a downside to this interpretation requiring a lapse of time. The legality of a certain practice is uncertain until it has become established, that is, crystallized into a rule. Gaja mentions the example of "treaties for which there is no provision in the constituent instrument"; these "would have to be considered invalid until practice has developed sufficiently" [169]. As mentioned above, seventeen years later, when Gaja was ILC Special Rapporteur for the topic "Responsibility of International Organizations", he referred to this disadvantage again, noting that "[t]his wording puts stress on the element of time, which is not necessarily relevant, while it expresses less clearly the role of general acceptance, which appears more significant" [170].

Indeed, on second thought, while the time factor is certainly relevant, it seems to be the requirement of general acceptance that is key for the development of a certain practice into a rule, as its "passport for normativity" [171]. This explains the suggestion by the European Commission to replace the term "established practice" with "generally accepted practice" [172]. However, as the overview in Section 1.2 has demonstrated, the term established practice is used regularly, for example in treaties, legal opinions and the judgments of administrative tribunals. Its use is by now sufficiently established to focus on its further development rather than renaming it. Moreover, "accepted" also falls within the ambit of the meaning of "established", and it is this meaning that it generally has in the many instances where it is used in the two Vienna Conventions on the Law of Treaties [173].

An advantage of the use of the somewhat loose term "established" in this context is that it provides some flexibility, which may be helpful. The somewhat imprecise nature of this term is also illustrated by how it is referred to in the other authentic languages of relevant legal

---

169. G. Gaja, "A 'New' Vienna Convention on Treaties between States and International Organizations or Between International Organizations: A Critical Commentary", *British Yearbook of International Law*, Vol. 58 (1987), pp. 253-269, at p. 262.
170. Gaja, ILC Second Report, at p. 9, para. 25; footnote omitted.
171. This expression is from G. Cahin. See his *La coutume international et les organisations internationales – l'incidence de la dimension institutionnelle sur le processus coutumier*, Paris, Pedone, 2001, at p. 474, "son passeport pour la normativité".
172. See UN Doc. A/C.6/59/SR.21, at p. 5, para. 19.
173. For example in the context of the authentication of the text of a treaty (Art. 10) or the expression of a consent to be bound by as treaty (Arts. 12-15).

instruments. For the Vienna II Convention (1986), these are Arabic, Chinese, French, Russian and Spanish [174]. In French, the words used for "established practice" are *la pratique bien établie*. This is more a translation of "*well*-established practice", a term that is also sometimes used in practice (as was illustrated in Sec. 1.2.3) and that suggests a higher standard [175]. In Arabic, the words used are الممارسة المتقررة. These words are similar to "established practice", not to *la pratique bien établie* ("*well*-established practice", which would be translated into Arabic as ممارسة راسخة which indicates a longer and much more established practice) [176]. In Chinese, the words used for "established practice" are 确立的惯例 (Vienna II Convention) and 已确立的惯例 (ARIO). Both mean firmly built or formed conventions that have been followed in the past but not incorporated as written laws [177]. In Russian, the words used for "established practice" are установившаяся практика. This means common, developed or stable practice (put differently, "the behaviour that normally or regularly takes place") [178]. In Spanish, it is *práctica establecida*, which is similar to "established practice".

1.3.5. Who decides?

Who decides whether a certain organizational practice is "established"? Both the organization and its members play a role. The members would certainly want to have an important say in this. When creating a new organization, states may decide to keep this in their own hands as much as possible, by supporting practices to which they agree and by opposing practices that they reject. However, they may also decide to relinquish some direct control and attribute review competences to a judicial organ of the new organization. Using these

---

174. The text of the Vienna II Convention in these other languages can be found in the certified true copy of the Convention, reproduced on the website of the UN Treaty Collection, see https://treaties.un.org/Pages/ViewDetails.aspx?src=IND&mtdsg_no=XXIII-3&chapter=23&clang=_en.

175. See the observation by the delegate from Venezuela during the 1975 UN Conference that adopted the 1975 Vienna Convention: "In so far as established practice was concerned, he considered that it was not necessary to qualify it by the word 'bien' ('well') which appeared in the French and Spanish texts. The delicate difference implied by the word 'bien' might give rise to practical difficulties" (UN Doc. A/CONF.67/18, at p. 337, para. 22). In reply, the French delegate "had no objection to deleting the word 'bien', as the Venezuelan representative had requested", *id.*, at para. 27.

176. With thanks to my colleagues Dr Suliman Ibrahim and Prof. Jan Michiel Otto.
177. With thanks to my students Mei Yee Kang and Lai Xiao Zhang.
178. With thanks to my students Eliza Shyhapova and Valeriya Trubacheva.

competences, the court or tribunal concerned can decide in specific instances whether other organs of the organization have acted *intra* or *ultra vires*.

However, most of the hundreds of existing international organizations do not have a court of justice that, like the EU Court, will act on demand in situations when the time has come to draw the line between a practice that violates the rules of the organization and a practice that should be recognized as a new rule of the organization. Fleshing out when a certain practice should be considered as "established" is less certain and more complex in the absence of judicial guidance. Doubts about the legality of a certain practice may continue to exist for considerable time or may disappear, the controversial practice may stop or it may revive sooner or later. To give an example: in the 1950s and 1960s, there were a few instances where it was decided to split the two-year term of non-permanent members of the Security Council – prescribed by Article 23.2 of the UN Charter – into two terms of one year, for two different UN member states competing for a seat on the Council, as part of a political compromise. Christopher Peters discusses these few early *Teilungskompromisse* and concludes with good arguments, and also in the light of the absence of more recent cases, that these are not examples of an established practice, but a "faktisch-politische Praxis" of "rechtswidriger Natur"[179]. When the ink of his manuscript was barely dry, the old and limited practice of splitting the two-year term revived when Italy and the Netherlands agreed, and the General Assembly accepted, that Italy would become a member of the Security Council during the year 2017, and the Netherlands in 2018. Practice can be capricious. Even though many may have concluded for good reasons that the early practice of splitting the two-year term in a few instances was unlawful rather than (the beginning of) an established practice, vigorous political pressure may sometimes be stronger than the rules of the Charter. Old sins may have long shadows.

* * *

This chapter has discussed "practice as a rule", demonstrating the ultimate recognition of the legal relevance of practice of international organizations. However, while this is an important legal facet in this special course devoted to the practice of international organizations, it

---

179. In English: a factual-political practice of an unlawful nature, see Peters, note 14, at pp. 322-323.

is certainly not the only one. Others will be analysed in the remaining chapters. This will demonstrate that even without being a "rule of the organization", practice may have other significant legal dimensions. First, the next chapter will analyse "practice as a power".

CHAPTER 2

PRACTICE AS A POWER: THE POWER-GENERATING CAPACITY OF THE PRACTICE OF INTERNATIONAL ORGANIZATIONS

2.1. *"Clean theory": The principle of attributed powers*

Julian Barnes wrote in his novel *The Noise of Time*: "Theories were clean and convincing and comprehensible. Life was messy and full of nonsense." [180] To some extent this is also true for the theory and practice of legal powers (hereinafter, more briefly, powers or competences) of international organizations. This important part of international organizations law is governed by a generally accepted, very clear and straightforward basic principle: the principle of attribution (also named: principle of speciality or the principle of conferral) [181], according to which international organizations only have those powers that have been attributed to them (mostly, and originally, in their constituent instruments). However, it seems that some of what international organizations do in practice can hardly, if at all, be based on powers attributed in this way, as will be illustrated below. Does this mean

---

180. J. Barnes, *The Noise of Time*, London, Jonathan Cape, 2016, at p. 53.
181. The term "attribution" has been used in this context from the outset, in particular in French writings (e.g. PCIJ, *Jurisdiction of the European Commission of the Danube*, Advisory Opinion, *PCIJ Reports, Series B, No. 14 (1927)*; ICJ, *Interpretation of the Agreement of 25 March 1951 between the WHO and Egypt*, Advisory Opinion of 20 December 1980, *ICJ Reports 1980*, p. 73 *et seq.*, Separate Opinion of Judge Gros, in particular at pp. 103-104). "Principle of speciality" is the term used by the ICJ in its 1996 *WHO Nuclear Weapons* Advisory Opinion (see note 183). This term most likely originates from French doctrine. See in particular C. M. Chaumont, "La signification du principe de spécialite des organisations internationales", in *Mélanges offerts à Henri Rolin. Problèmes de droit des gens*, Paris, Pedone, 1964, pp. 55-66. The term is normally not used in the English language literature (except when this 1996 ICJ Advisory Opinion is discussed). Before 1996, it was used by ILC Special Rapporteur Diaz Gonzalez: "International organizations, according to their speciality, exercise the powers attributed to them within the framework of their functions, which depend on the purposes assigned to them by their creators. Thus, as has already been seen, their powers are functional." See his Second Report on Relations between States and International Organizations (second part of the topic), *Yb. ILC 1985*, Vol. 2, Part 1, at p. 110; see also his statement in the ILC on 18 July 1985, 1929th meeting (*Yb. ILC 1985*, Vol. 1, at p. 305). The term "principle of conferral" is used in particular in the context of the European Union (e.g. Treaty on the European Union, Art. 5.2; the French version of Art. 5 uses the expression "le principe d'attribution").

that they act *ultra vires* in these cases? The answer to this question is normally in the negative. The key question in this chapter is therefore whether, in such cases, international organizations can generate their own powers, by their own practice, and therefore, whether there is an exception to the attribution principle. Or should this, in some way or another, be considered as part of the attribution principle?

When a new state comes into being, it has its own territory, its own population and a government. Automatically it has a plenitude of powers, limited only by international law. The reverse is true for international organizations. When a new international organization is established, it lacks a territory, a population and a government. It only has those powers that its creators agreed to attribute to it. This principle of attributed powers (in French: *compétences d'attribution*) has long been established. As early as 1927, the Permanent Court of International Justice (PCIJ) observed with respect to one of the oldest international organizations, the European Commission of the Danube [182]:

> "As the European Commission is not a State, but an international institution with a special purpose, it only has the functions bestowed upon it by the Definitive Statute with a view to the fulfilment of that purpose, but it has power to exercise these functions to their full extent, in so far as the Statute does not impose restrictions upon it."

The principle is so fundamental and so generally accepted that the ICJ, sixty-nine years later, referred to it in the following way, in general terms [183]:

> "The Court need hardly point out that international organizations are subjects of international law which do not, unlike States, possess a general competence. International organizations are governed by the 'principle of speciality', that is to say, they are invested by the States which create them with powers, the limits

---

182. PCIJ, *Danube* Advisory Opinion, note 181, at p. 64. The French version of this sentence uses the word "attribution": "Comme la Commission européenne n'est pas un Etat, mais une institution internationale pourvue d'un objet spécial, elle n'a que les attributions que lui confère le Statut définitif, pour lui permettre de remplir cet objet; mais elle a compétence pour exercer ces fonctions dans leur plénitude, pour autant que le Statut ne lui impose pas de restrictions."
183. *Legality of the Use by a State of Nuclear Weapons in Armed Conflict*, Advisory Opinion, *ICJ Reports 1996*, p. 66 *et seq.*, at p. 78, para. 25. See also, earlier, the Separate Opinion of Judge Gros in the ICJ, *WHO and Egypt* Advisory Opinion, note 181, at p. 103.

of which are a function of the common interests whose promotion those States entrust to them."

The primary and clearest way in which powers are attributed to international organizations is by explicitly mentioning them in the organization's constituent instrument, in either a general or a more detailed way. According to the Charter of the Organization of American States (OAS), this is even the *only* way of attributing powers to the organization: "[t]he Organization of American States has no powers other than those expressly conferred upon it by this Charter" [184]. Some examples of provisions attributing powers include the following. Chapter IV of the UN Charter refers to the "Functions and Powers" of the General Assembly. It includes both the power to "discuss any questions or any matters within the scope of the present Charter or relating to the powers and functions of any organs provided for in the present Charter" (Art. 10) and the power to "consider and approve the budget of the Organization" (Art. 17.1). Likewise, the UN Security Council has very broad enforcement powers under Chapter VII of the Charter, in particular under Articles 41 and 42. Article VIII of the constituent instrument of the OPCW includes provisions on the "Powers and Functions" of the Conference of the States Parties. The Conference "shall consider any questions, matters or issues within the scope of this Convention, including those relating to the powers and functions of the Executive Council and the Technical Secretariat" (Art. VIII.B.19). It shall also "Appoint the Director-General of the Technical Secretariat" (Art. VIII.B.21*(d)*).

It is clear from some of these examples, that (organs of) international organizations can have very broad explicit powers. In addition, as the PCIJ stated in 1927, they are entitled to use their powers "to their full extent" [185]. However, this does not mean that their powers are unlimited; they continue to be specific and attributed. As the ICJ stated in 1996, international organizations "do not, unlike States, possess a general competence" [186]. These two key elements are reflected in the statement made by the Australian Minister of Navy Makin, chairing the first meeting of UN Security Council, on 17 January 1946 in London: "Our work must be based on the Charter. We are not permitted to go beyond it, but we shall not fail to exercise to the full the very great powers

---
184. OAS Charter, Art. 1.
185. PCIJ, *Danube* Advisory Opinion, note 181, at p. 64.
186. ICJ, *WHO Nuclear Weapons* Advisory Opinion, note 183, at p. 78, para. 25.

which have been given to this Council."[187] Indeed, the Security Council is "not permitted to go beyond" the Charter, as was also emphasized by the ICJ, two years later: "The political character of an organ cannot release it from the observance of the treaty provisions established by the Charter when they constitute limitations on its powers or criteria for its judgment."[188] In the same spirit, the International Criminal Tribunal for the former Yugoslavia (ICTY), when scrutinizing the power of the Security Council to establish this Tribunal, observed in 1995 that the Council[189]

> "plays a pivotal role and exercises a very wide discretion under this Article. But this does not mean that its powers are unlimited. The Security Council is an organ of an international organization, established by a treaty which serves as a constitutional framework for that organization. The Security Council is thus subjected to certain constitutional limitations, however broad its powers under the constitution may be. Those powers cannot, in any case, go beyond the limits of the jurisdiction of the Organization at large, not to mention other specific limitations or those which may derive from the internal division of power within the Organization. In any case, neither the text nor the spirit of the Charter conceives of the Security Council as *legibus solutus* (unbound by law)".

Quoting Article 24.2 of the Charter, the Tribunal concludes that "[t]he Charter thus speaks the language of specific powers, not of absolute fiat"[190]. What the Tribunal stated with respect to the Security Council is also true generally for organs of international organizations. They only have attributed powers. These may be wide and can also be fully used, but they are not unlimited.

While the founding fathers of an international organization agree on the existence, as such, of powers that they have explicitly laid down in the organization's constituent instrument, they may disagree during the life of the organization what such explicit powers entail and what not. Indeed, disagreements about the interpretation and application

---

187. Security Council Official Records No. 1, at 5 (1946).
188. ICJ, *Admission of a State to the United Nations (Charter, Art. 4)*, Advisory Opinion, *ICJ Reports 1948*, p. 57 *et seq.*, at p. 64.
189. ICTY, Case No. IT-94-1-AR72, decision of 2 October 1995 on the defence motion for interlocutory appeal on jurisdiction, at para. 28.
190. *Id.*

of explicit powers have long since occurred [191]. Already in the early history of international organizations, some of those disagreements resulted in requests for advisory opinions from the PCIJ. For example, not too long after the ILO was established, its member states disagreed as to whether the organization was competent to regulate the conditions of labour of persons employed in agriculture. Did the use of the words *industrie* and *industrielle*, "which originally refer to manufactures", in the French text of some provisions of the ILO Constitution imply that the *entire* Constitution excluded agriculture as a field of labour in which the organization could exercise its competences [192]? It was decided to bring this issue before the PCIJ. In 1922 the Court answered that the competence of the ILO extends to the international regulation of the conditions of labour of persons employed in agriculture [193]. The Court rejected the argument – frequently made during the proceedings – that the establishment of the ILO "involved an abandonment of rights derived from national sovereignty, and that the competence of the Organization therefore should not be extended by interpretation" [194]. It observed that even though "there may be some force in this argument", "the question in every case must resolve itself into what the terms of the Treaty actually mean, and it is from this point of view that the Court proposes to examine the question" [195].

Since international organizations only have attributed powers, and not general powers, it is not necessary to specify which powers they

---

191. It was even observed, with respect to the UN Charter generally: "It is no exaggeration to say that the whole history of the United Nations has been a series of disputes about the correct interpretation of the Charter", P. Malanczuk, *Akehurst's Modern Introduction to International Law*, 7th rev. ed., London, Routledge, 1997, at p. 364.
192. PCIJ, Advisory Opinion No. 2, 12 August 1922, *PCIJ Reports, Series B, No. 2*, quotation at p. 33.
193. *Id.* On the same day, the Court also answered another question, namely whether the "examination of proposals for the organization and development of methods of agricultural production, and of other questions of a like character, fall within the competence of the International Labour Organization"? The Court gave a negative answer to this question: neither in the field of agriculture nor in the case of any other branch of industry "do the functions of the Organization extend to the promotion of improvements in the processes tending to increase the amount of production" (PCIJ, Advisory Opinion No. 3, 12 August 1922, *PCIJ Reports, Series B, No. 3*). A few years later, the Court answered another question about the competence of the ILO. It concluded "that it is within the competence of the International Labour Organization to draw up and to propose labour legislation which, in order to protect certain classes of workers, also regulates incidentally the same work when performed by the employer himself" (PCIJ, Advisory Opinion No. 13, 23 July 1926, *PCIJ Reports, Series B, No. 13*).
194. *Id.*, at p. 23.
195. *Id.*

do *not* have. As a rule, international organizations do not have powers that are not attributed to them. Nevertheless, in some exceptional cases constituent instruments explicitly state that the relevant organization does not have certain powers or is not to exercise its powers in a particular area. For example, the competence of the Central American Court of Justice explicitly excludes "the area of human rights which falls under the exclusive jurisdiction of the Inter-American Court of Human Rights" [196]. A further example is Article 5.1 of the International Agreement on Olive Oil and Table Olives (2015), which provides that the International Olive Council "shall not have the power to borrow money". In addition, the constitutions of some organizations explicitly exclude military or national defence cooperation from their scope of activities [197]. A final example is the constitution of INTERPOL, which contains the following rather broad provision: "It is strictly forbidden for the Organization to undertake any intervention or activities of a political, military, religious or racial character." [198] Presumably such exceptional "non-power provisions" are mentioned so as to emphasize, out of an abundance of caution, that the organization, in exercising its powers, is to stay clear of the areas or activities mentioned in these provisions.

Powers explicitly mentioned in an organization's constituent instrument, no matter how general, may be inadequate in addressing certain issues that present themselves during the life of the organization. Therefore, in addition to specific powers, the constituent instruments of a number of organizations include a rather open-ended more general power for the organization or for one of its organs. A few examples are the following:

– Constitution of the World Health Organization (1946)
Article 2: "In order to achieve its objective, the functions of the Organization shall be: . . . *(v)* generally to take all necessary action to attain the objective of the Organization."
Article 18: "The functions of the Health Assembly shall be: . . . *(m)* to take any other appropriate action to further the objective of the Organization."

---

196. Statute of the Central American Court of Justice, Art. 25.
197. E.g. Statute Council of Europe, Art. 1.*d*: "Matters relating to national defence do not fall within the scope of the Council of Europe"; Convention for the Establishment of a European Organization for Nuclear Research (CERN), Art. II.1: "The Organization shall have no concern with work for military requirements."
198. INTERPOL Constitution (1956), Art. 3.

– Agreement on the Status and Functions of the International Commission on Missing Persons (2014), Article 6 (Powers): "In furtherance of the foregoing purposes and activities, the Commission shall have the following powers: . . . *(e)* to take other lawful action necessary to accomplish the purposes of the Commission."
– Articles of Agreement of the Asian Infrastructure Investment Bank (2015), Article 16 (General Powers), paragraph 9: "The Bank may exercise such other powers and establish such rules and regulations as may be necessary or appropriate in furtherance of its purpose and functions, consistent with the provisions of this Agreement."
– Treaty on the Functioning of the European Union, Article 352, paragraph 1: "If action by the Union should prove necessary, within the framework of the policies defined in the Treaties, to attain one of the objectives set out in the Treaties, and the Treaties have not provided the necessary powers, the Council, acting unanimously on a proposal from the Commission and after obtaining the consent of the European Parliament, shall adopt the appropriate measures. Where the measures in question are adopted by the Council in accordance with a special legislative procedure, it shall also act unanimously on a proposal from the Commission and after obtaining the consent of the European Parliament."

The inclusion of such broad "catch-all clauses", as in the four examples mentioned above, may compensate to a certain extent for the inherent constitutional constraint that not all powers necessary for the performance of the organization's functions can be anticipated or enumerated in detail. To some extent, such clauses make the seemingly absolute distinction between general powers (for states) and attributed powers (for international organizations) more relative [199]. Nevertheless, even if the constituent instrument of an international organization includes a "catch-all clause", it is unavoidable that sometimes situations occur in practice where there is a demand for action by an international organization, but where the necessary constitutional powers are lacking. The next section will mention some examples.

---

199. "To some extent . . ." because such clauses do not nullify this distinction. States keep their general powers; *these* are not attributed to the relevant organization. As Seidl-Hohenveldern and Loibl write with regard to these clauses: "Bestimmungen über Satzungsänderungen durch implied powers sind von den Mitgliedstaaten ja kraft ihres eigenen, im Gründungsvertrag zum Ausdruck gebrachten Willens *so gewollt*", I. Seidl-Hohenveldern and G. Loibl, *Das Recht der Internationalen Organisationen einschließlich der Supranationalen Gemeinschaften*, 7th rev. ed., Cologne, Carl Heymanns, 2000, at p. 233.

2.2. "Messy life": Examples from practice – intra or ultra vires?

International organizations have sometimes acted while there was – sometimes considerable – controversy over whether they actually had the power to do so. The following examples may serve as an illustration.

2.2.1. The establishment of ad hoc criminal tribunals by the UN Security Council [200]

The collapse of the Soviet Union and the end of the Cold War facilitated not only the (re-) emergence of internal conflicts in a number of states (e.g. Yugoslavia, Somalia, Angola, Georgia) but also the ability of the Security Council to actively contribute to their resolution and make better use of its broad Charter powers. Soon after the beginning of the armed conflict in the former Yugoslavia, an increasing number of sources reported about mass killings, ethnic cleansing and other violations of international humanitarian law. In 1992 the Security Council requested the Secretary-General to establish a Committee of Experts to examine and analyse information about such violations [201]. Early in 1993 this Committee presented an interim report in which it not only found extensive evidence of grave violations of international humanitarian law but also, at the very end of its report, "was led to discuss the idea of the establishment of an *ad hoc* international tribunal. In its opinion, it would be for the Security Council or another competent body of the United Nations to establish such a tribunal in relation to events in the territory of the former Yugoslavia" [202].

Subsequently, the Security Council decided to establish the proposed *ad hoc* criminal tribunal in two steps. First, it took the decision that such a tribunal "shall be established" and it asked the Secretary-General to prepare a report "on all aspects of this matter" [203]. In this report the Secretary-General essentially proposed most details of the future tribunal, including its Statute [204]. Next, in a second resolution, the Security Council approved this report, established the tribunal and adopted its Statute [205].

---

200. This section about the establishment of *ad hoc* criminal tribunals is largely taken from my book *Saving Succeeding Generations from the Scourge of War*, Leiden, Brill Nijhoff, 2021, at pp. 126-129.
201. SC Res. 780, 6 October 1992.
202. UN Doc. S/25274, 10 February 1993.
203. SC Res. 808, 22 February 1993.
204. UN Doc. S/25704, 3 May 1993.
205. SC Res. 827, 25 May 1993.

While there was broad agreement in the international community about the need for an *ad hoc* tribunal in this case, there was considerable disagreement about how to establish it. Essentially three options were on the table: the creation of the tribunal by a multilateral treaty, by the General Assembly or by the Security Council. It was generally agreed that the first option was to be preferred. The main question, however, was whether the other options were legitimate and acceptable under the circumstances, as an exceptional measure, because it was widely believed that it would take too long before a treaty could be concluded and enter into force. These discussions about the proper legal basis for the tribunal are reflected in the report by the Secretary-General and in the reports of the two relevant Security Council meetings.

The Secretary-General stated in his report that a Chapter VII decision by the Security Council would be the preferred way of establishing the proposed tribunal. This "would constitute a measure to maintain or restore international peace and security" and "would be legally justified, both in terms of the object and purpose of the decision ... and of past Security Council practice"[206]. The reference to "past Security Council practice" is explained briefly in the report. This practice includes the earlier determination by the Council that the situation in the former Yugoslavia constituted a threat to international peace and security; a Chapter VII decision that, if the parties concerned would not comply with its Resolution 771, it would need to take further measures under the Charter; the affirmation by the Council that persons who commit grave breaches of the Geneva Conventions are individually responsible; and finally, Council Resolution 808 (in which the Council stated that it was convinced "that in the particular circumstances of the former Yugoslavia, the establishment of an international tribunal would bring about the achievement of the aim of putting an end to such crimes and of taking effective measures to bring to justice the persons responsible for them, and would contribute to the restoration and maintenance of peace"[207]). In addition, the Secretary-General referred to "various occasions" on which the Security Council had taken Chapter VII measures involving the establishment of subsidiary organs for a variety of reasons, mentioning, in particular, the creation of the UN Compensation Committee as an example.

---

206. UN Doc. S/25704, at paras. 22 and 24.
207. *Id.*, at para. 26.

It is clear from this explanation of past Security Council practice that the Secretary-General could not refer to any precedent for the establishment of a criminal tribunal by the Security Council since this had never happened before. The practice to which the Secretary-General refers essentially consists of "stepping stones" for the later creation of a tribunal. There could hardly have been any doubt regarding the powers of the Security Council in relation to these earlier steps. However, this was different for the final step that was now proposed, the creation of a tribunal [208]. It was widely agreed that an international criminal tribunal should normally be created by treaty and that the Charter does not explicitly attribute any powers in the field of international criminal justice to the Security Council. The doubts regarding this final step were overcome by emphasizing the exceptional nature of the situation in the former Yugoslavia and the wide powers of the Security Council to maintain and restore international peace and security. There was broad support for this approach in the Security Council.

However, while both above-mentioned Security Council resolutions were adopted unanimously, doubts about the creation of the tribunal by a Security Council resolution were expressed in particular by Brazil, and to some extent by China [209]. Brazil questioned whether it was within the powers of the Security Council to establish an *ad hoc* criminal tribunal. In its statement in the Security Council in February 1993, it concluded [210]:

> "In this rapidly changing world, we consider it increasingly important to promote the rule of law, in international relations by acting to ensure strict respect for the provisions of our Charter and other norms of international law."

More specifically, Brazil explained its "rule of law criticism" in the following way [211]:

> "It is of particular importance that the international tribunal to be established rest on a solid legal foundation, which will ensure the effectiveness of its actions."

---

208. It is therefore too bold for the ICTY Trial Chamber to have stated in 1995: "the fact that the Security Council has not taken a similar step in other, earlier cases cannot in itself be of any relevance in determining the legality of its action in this case" (ICTY, *Prosecutor* v. *Dusko Tadic a/k/a/ "Dule"*, Decision on the Defence Motion on Jurisdiction, 10 August 1995, at para. 25).
209. China stated that its support for the resolution did not "prejudge China's position on future Security Council actions on the subject", UN Doc. S/PV.3175, at p. 7.
210. UN Doc. S/PV.3175, p. 7.
211. *Id.*, at pp. 6-7.

As regards the definition of the best method for the establishment of an *ad hoc* international criminal tribunal, it should be borne in mind that the authority of the Security Council is not self-constituted but originates from a delegation of powers by the whole membership of the Organization. It is never too much to recall that the Security Council, in the exercise of its responsibilities, acts on behalf of the States Members of the United Nations, in accordance with Article 24, paragraph 1, of the Charter.

Just as the authority of the Council does not spring from the Council itself but derives from the fact that certain responsibilities have been conferred upon it by all the Members of the United Nations, the powers of the Council cannot be created, recreated or reinterpreted creatively by decisions of the Council itself but must be based invariably on specific Charter provisions. Especially when the Council is being increasingly called upon to fully exercise the considerable powers entrusted to it, the definition of such powers must be construed strictly on the basis of the text of the relevant Charter provisions. To go beyond that would be legally inconsistent and politically unwise."

Subsequently, Brazil repeated its criticism in a letter to the UN Secretary-General [212] and during the Security Council meeting of 25 May 1993, when the Statute of the tribunal was adopted [213]. China expressed reservations as well: "to adopt by a Security Council resolution the Statute of the International Tribunal which gives the Tribunal both preferential and exclusive jurisdiction is not in compliance with the principle of State judicial sovereignty" [214]. Therefore, this "can only be an ad hoc arrangement suited only to the special circumstances of the former Yugoslavia and shall not constitute any precedent" [215].

In the Security Council, the "rule of law criticism" expressed by Brazil was rejected in particular by Spain, by referring to "rule of law provisions" in the Preamble of the UN Charter [216]:

> "In the final analysis, the Council, by adopting resolution 827 (1993) is seeking to make a reality of the determination contained in the preamble of the Charter to reaffirm faith in fundamental

---

212. UN Doc. A/47/922 – S/25540, 6 April 1993.
213. UN Doc. S/PV.3217. In this meeting, Brazil stated that it "did not favour" the creation of the tribunal by the Security Council (at p. 37).
214. *Id.*, at p. 33.
215. *Id.*, at p. 34.
216. *Id.*, at p. 41.

human rights, in the dignity and worth of the human person, and indeed to establish conditions for the maintenance of justice and respect for international law in so tragic a situation as that unfortunately still being experienced by the peoples of the former Yugoslavia."

The unanimous adoption of the Security Council resolutions establishing the Yugoslavia Tribunal did not silence the criticism voiced in particular by Brazil. Two years later, in the first case before the Tribunal, counsel for the defence of Duško Tadić argued that the Tribunal lacked jurisdiction, *inter alia*, because it was improperly established. The Tribunal rejected this preliminary defence motion. According to its Appeals Chamber, "the establishment of the International Tribunal falls squarely within the powers of the Security Council under Article 41"[217]. It concluded that the tribunal was "lawfully established as a measure under Chapter VII of the Charter"[218]. In addition, the same criticism was expressed in 1994 when the Security Council created a second *ad hoc* tribunal, the Rwanda Tribunal[219]. However, the creation of this second Tribunal could now rely on solid Security Council practice, that is, the establishment of the Yugoslav Tribunal in 1993 (notwithstanding the repeated claims by Brazil and China that this could not be considered as a precedent[220]).

2.2.2. Was the UN Human Rights Council Libya Inquiry Commission acting ultra vires *by including NATO operation Unified Protector in its report (2012)?*

In Libya, in early 2011, the opposition against the regime of Muammar Gaddafi – who had been in power since 1969 – became stronger than ever before, backed by the Arab Spring movement, and a

---

217. ICTY, *Prosecutor v. Dusko Tadic a/k/a/ "Dule"*, Decision on the Defence Motion for the Interlocutory Appeal on Jurisdiction, 2 October 1995, para. 36.
218. *Id.*, at para. 40.
219. SC Res. 955, 8 November 1994. During the meeting in which this resolution was adopted, Brazil stated: "Exceptional ad hoc initiatives by the Council may not be the best way to promote the consistent, balanced and effective application of international humanitarian law or to create an environment conducive to the enhancement of the rule of law in international public order. The Security Council's responsibilities lie not in the judicial or institution-building field, but in the maintenance of international peace and security. Therefore, the invocation of Chapter VII of the Charter for the purpose of establishing an international tribunal goes, in our view, beyond the competence of the Council as clearly defined in the Charter" (UN Doc. S/PV.3453, at p. 9). China expressed criticism similar to its comments when the Yugoslavia Tribunal was created (*id.*, at p. 11; also earlier, UN Doc. S/PV.3400, at p. 7).
220. UN Docs. S/PV.3217, at pp. 34-37; S/PV.3543, at p. 10.

civil war began. Demonstrators protested in a number of cities including Benghazi. A number of opposition leaders were arrested. Following allegations of serious and widespread human rights violations, the UN Human Rights Council on 25 February 2011 established the International Commission of Inquiry on Libya with the mandate "to investigate all alleged violations of international human rights law in Libya, to establish the facts and circumstances of such violations and of the crimes perpetrated and, where possible, to identify those responsible, to make recommendations, in particular, on accountability measures, all with a view to ensuring that those individuals responsible are held accountable" [221].

On 17 March 2011 the UN Security Council adopted Resolution 1973, in which it "authorized member states. . ., acting nationally or through regional organizations or arrangements . . . to take all necessary measures . . . to protect civilians and civilian populated areas under threat of attack in the Libyan Arab Jamahiriya, including Benghazi, while excluding a foreign occupation force of any form on any part of Libyan territory". NATO implemented this authorization in its Operation Unified Protector and carried out many airstrikes.

When carrying out its mandate, the Commission of Inquiry decided to cover not only the acts and activities of the Gaddafi government and of the opposition but also those of NATO. The Commission requested NATO to give information about its military operations in Libya. However, NATO questioned whether, in doing so, the Commission acted within its mandate. On behalf of NATO, its legal adviser, Peter Olson, answered in a letter of 20 December 2011 that "many of the queries in the 11 November letter, and all or virtually all of those in the Annexure to your letter of 15 December, appear to involve issues of international humanitarian law", whereas the mandate of the Commission is "to investigate alleged violations of international human rights law" [222]. In subsequent letters, NATO provided some information about its military operation in Libya and answered some of the questions of the Commission of Inquiry. NATO referred again to the mandate of the Commission, to look into the alleged violations of international human rights law, and stated: "Although NATO has in its letter responded in detail to the Commission's request for information, it is for a variety of reasons not evident that many of the queries posed in the Commission's

---

221. HRC Res. S-15/1, 25 February 2011.
222. The letter is reproduced in Annex II of the Report of the International Commission of Inquiry on Libya, UN Doc. A/HRC/19/68.

letters. . ., including those relating to the law of armed conflict, fall within that mandate." [223]

In its final report of 8 March 2012 the International Commission of Inquiry on Libya found that both the Gaddafi forces and the opposition forces committed international crimes. Regarding NATO, while the Commission concluded that it had conducted "a highly precise campaign with a demonstrable determination to avoid civilian casualties", it also found that "[o]n limited occasions, the Commission confirmed civilian casualties and found targets that showed no evidence of military utility" [224]. In its report, the Commission did not address the criticism by NATO that it could be questioned as to whether the Commission had acted within its powers. Earlier, in its first report, the Commission only indicated how it interpreted the scope of its mandate [225]:

> "With an armed conflict having developed in late February in Libya and continuing during the Commission's operations, the Commission looked into both violations of international human rights law and relevant provisions of international humanitarian law, the *lex specialis* which applies during armed conflict."

This interpretation implied that the Commission disagreed with the observation by NATO that the law of armed conflict was outside the scope of the Commission's mandate.

2.2.3. Julian Assange in the Embassy of Ecuador in London: Voluntary stay or arbitrary deprivation of liberty? Was the UN Working Group on Arbitrary Detention competent to consider the case of Julian Assange?

A further example involves the scope of powers of the UN Working Group on Arbitrary Detention. This working group was established in 1991 by the UN Human Rights Commission (the predecessor of the UN Human Rights Council) [226] and was tasked to investigate "cases of detention imposed arbitrarily or otherwise inconsistently with the

---

223. *Id.*, quotation at p. 35.
224. *Id.*, at pp. 1-2; pp. 16-17, p. 21.
225. UN Doc. A/HRC/17/44, 1 June 2011, https://www.ohchr.org/sites/default/files/english/bodies/hrcouncil/docs/17session/A.HRC.17.44_AUV.pdf, quotation at p. 14; in a footnote, the Commission refers to the 2004 Advisory Opinion of the ICJ (*Legal consequences of the construction of a wall in the Occupied Palestinian Territory, ICJ Reports 2004*, p. 178 *et seq.*, at para. 106). See also pp. 31-32 of this first report.
226. UN Commission on Human Rights, Res. 1991/42.

relevant international standards set forth in the Universal Declaration of Human Rights or in the relevant international legal instruments accepted by the States concerned" [227].

Julian Assange is the founder of WikiLeaks. In 2010 WikiLeaks published leaked information relating to, *inter alia*, US military operations in Iraq and Afghanistan. The US initiated criminal investigations against WikiLeaks. Later in 2010 a Swedish prosecutor issued a European arrest warrant for Assange relating to allegations of sexual misconduct. Assange was apprehended in the United Kingdom. He feared extradition to the US and political persecution, and sought refuge in the Embassy of Ecuador in London. A communication was brought before the UN Working Group on Arbitrary Detention, submitting *inter alia* that Assange was deprived of his liberty against his will. Sweden and the United Kingdom argued, *inter alia*, that Assange voluntarily decided to enter and stay in the Ecuadorian Embassy and was free to leave the Embassy at any time. Accordingly, he was not deprived of his liberty in violation of the criteria adopted by the Working Group [228].

The UN Working Group concluded the following in its Opinion: "The deprivation of liberty of Mr Assange is arbitrary and in contravention of articles 9 and 10 of the Universal Declaration of Human Rights and Articles 7, 9 (1), 9 (3), 9 (4), 10 and 14 of the International Covenant on Civil and Political Rights. It falls within category III of the categories applicable to the consideration of the cases submitted to the Working Group." [229] In order to perform its tasks, the Working Group has distinguished five different categories of arbitrary deprivation of liberty. A case falls within Category III "when the total or partial non-observance of the international norms relating to a fair trial, spelled out in the Universal Declaration of Human Rights and in the relevant international instruments accepted by the States concerned, is of such gravity as to give the deprivation of liberty an arbitrary character" [230].

One of the members of the Working Group, Vladimir Tochilovsky, disagreed. In a dissenting opinion, he expressed the view that the adopted Opinion "raises serious questions as to the scope of the mandate of the Working Group" and that "the Working Group is not competent to consider situations that do not involve deprivation of liberty . . .

---

227. *Id.*, at para. 2. The mandate of the commission has been extended for periods of three years, see e.g. UN Doc. A/HRC/RES/42/22, 8 October 2019.
228. UN Doc. A/HRC/WGAD/2015, Opinion No. 54/2015, in particular at paras. 37 and 46-47.
229. *Id.*, at para. 99.
230. See https://www.ohchr.org/en/about-arbitrary-detention.

issues related to the fugitives' self-confinement, such as asylum and extradition, do not fall into the mandate of the Working Group" [231].

As in the previous example, relating to the International Commission of Inquiry on Libya, there was disagreement about the scope of the mandate of a UN organ. In the Assange Opinion case as well, a broader interpretation of powers was given than the interpretation preferred by, in the case of the Working Group, one of its members. The Assange Opinion of the UN Working Group led to a heated debate in the media and in academic blogs [232].

2.2.4. Was the OPCW acting ultra vires *by deciding in June 2018 that the OPCW Secretariat may play a role in identifying "those who were the perpetrators, organisers, sponsors or otherwise involved" in the use of chemical weapons?* [233]

The Organization for the Prohibition of Chemical Weapons was established by the 1993 Convention on the Prohibition of Development, Production, Stockpiling and Use of Chemical Weapons and on their Destruction. This Convention entered into force in 1997. At present the OPCW has 193 member states.

In June 2018 the OPCW's plenary policymaking organ, the Conference, adopted a decision in which it stated that the OPCW Secretariat could investigate an alleged use of chemical weapons in order to facilitate the identification of those who were the perpetrators, organizers, sponsors or otherwise involved. The 1993 Convention (OPCW's constituent instrument) does not explicitly attribute such a power to the Secretariat and it was disputed by a number of member states as to whether the Conference could create it in this way. The matter was highly controversial. Normally, decisions of the Conference on matters of substance are adopted by consensus [234]. However, it was impossible to achieve consensus in this specific case. At the end of

---

231. *Id.*, at p. 18.
232. See M. Happold, "Julian Assange and the UN Working Group on Arbitrary Detention", *EJIL:Talk!*, 5 February 2016, https://www.ejiltalk.org/julian-assange-and-the-un-working-group-on-arbitrary-detention/, followed by a number of comments; L. Lazarus, "The United Nations Working Group on Arbitrary Detention Decision on Assange: 'Ridiculous' or 'Justifiable'?", *EJIL:Talk!*, 9 February 2016, https://www.ejiltalk.org/the-united-nations-working-group-on-arbitrary-detention-decision-on-assange-ridiculous-or-justifiable/, also followed by a number of comments.
233. OPCW Decision C-SS-4/Dec.3, at para. 19.
234. Convention on the Prohibition of the Development, Production, Stockpiling and Use of Chemical Weapons and on their Destruction, Art. VIII.B.18.

Legal Facets of the Practice of International Organizations 147

the day, a decision was taken by voting: eighty-two members voted in favour, twenty-four against [235]. Subsequently, the OPCW Secretariat established the Investigation and Identification Team, "responsible for identifying the perpetrators of the use of chemical weapons in the Syrian Arab Republic" [236].

The background to this profound disagreement was highly political. Some preceding events played a key role and were the main drivers for a number of countries to take the initiative for the OPCW decision of June 2018. First, in October 2017 the mandate of the OPCW-UN Joint Investigative Mechanism (JIM), established to identify perpetrators of chemical weapons attacks in Syria, was not renewed when the Russian Federation vetoed the relevant draft Security Council resolution [237]. A second example is the poisoning, on 4 March 2018 in Salisbury (UK), of Sergei Skripal (a former Russian spy and double agent who collaborated with M16 (the UK's secret intelligence service)) and his daughter Yulia. Investigations in the UK concluded that the poison used was a Novichok nerve agent. This was later confirmed by the OPCW [238]. The UK and other Western countries accused Russia of these murder attempts (both Sergei and Yulia Skripal survived), but the Russian government denied any involvement. Statements by a number of delegations during the meeting of the OPCW Conference in which the above-mentioned Decision was adopted referred to these two preceding events (some specifically, others in general terms) [239].

Those who voted in favour of the June 2018 Decision stated, for example, that "[t]he Convention can – and should – adapt and remain relevant to the changing security environment" (United States) [240]. In addition, the US stated [241]:

> "Removing the ability to use chemical weapons with impunity is a first step towards restoring deterrence against chemical weapons

---

235. See OPCW Doc. C-SS-4/3, at p. 6.
236. OPCW Doc. EC-90/DG.14, 7 March 2019.
237. See UN Doc. S/PV.8073, 24 October 2017. In this meeting, Russia stated that the draft resolution was premature, as the JIM would present an important report on 7 November and because its mandate would only end on 17 November. Following the presentation of the report on 7 November, Russia severely criticized its findings and the work of the JIM in general; see UN Doc. S/PV.8090, esp. at pp. 14-17.
238. See https://www.opcw.org/media-centre/news/2018/04/opcw-issues-report-technical-assistance-requested-united-kingdom.
239. See e.g. the statements by Brazil, Bulgaria (on behalf of the EU), Canada, Germany, Malaysia, the Republic of Korea, Sweden and the United States, https://www.opcw.org/csp-ss-4.
240. OPCW Doc. C-SS-4/NAT.6, 26 June 2018, https://www.opcw.org/csp-ss-4.
241. Id.

use. We must first empower the OPCW so that it can ably identify those who are responsible for the confirmed instances of chemical weapons use in Syria."

Germany explained this new power in the Decision (to identify the perpetrators) in the following way [242]:

"First and foremost, we need to enable the Technical Secretariat to identify the perpetrators of those chemical weapons attacks confirmed by the [Fact-Finding Mission]. There is nothing in the Convention that prevents the Secretariat from fulfilling this task. The policy-making bodies of this organisation would then have to draw appropriate conclusions from the findings. Let me be very clear. We are not proposing that the OPCW hold those identified accountable. Ensuring accountability would be a role for other institutions. What we are calling for is a solution that would enable the Secretariat to perform the technical work of independently and impartially investigating and identifying those responsible and reporting on its investigations to the Executive Council, the Conference of the States Parties and the United Nations Security Council for their consideration."

Canada stated [243]:

"It has been argued by some States that the OPCW does not have the mandate for attribution. These States should recall Article XII, which stipulates that the Conference of States Parties 'shall take the necessary measures . . . to ensure compliance with this Convention', including collective measures. This special session has the authority to put in place measures at the OPCW to address compliance issues. Period."

The main opponent of the decision, the Russian Federation, stated the following in the meeting of the Conference in which the decision was adopted [244]:

"The Russian Federation expresses its categorical disagreement with the decision taken. . . .

Neither the Conference, nor the Executive Council, nor the Technical Secretariat has a mandate that would allow it to assign

---

242. OPCW Doc. C-SS-4/NAT.9, 26 June 2018, https://www.opcw.org/csp-ss-4.
243. OPCW Doc. C-SS-4/NAT.31, 26 June 2018, https://www.opcw.org/csp-ss-4.
244. OPCW Doc. C-SS-4/NAT.42, 27 June 2018, https://www.opcw.org/csp-ss-4.

attribution for violating the Convention. . . . Granting the function of attribution to the Organisation by taking some kind of decisions at a special session of the Conference is not possible, and can only be done by introducing amendments to the Convention as stipulated in Article XV."

According to Russia, giving this attribution function "means transforming the OPCW, the objective of which is to provide technical assistance to States Parties in order to fulfil their obligations under the Convention, into a quasi-prosecutory, police, and medical forensics agency" [245].

In addition, Russia stated the following on the website of its Permanent Representation at the OPCW [246]:

"International organisations unlike States do not possess universal legal personality and therefor they are subjects of international law with a special status. It means that IOs have the right to act only within the mandate clearly stipulated in their founding documents.

Creation of attributive mechanism within the OPCW can be legitimate only through the adoption of a relevant amendment to the CWC. . . .

Should the OPCW be entrusted with such attributive functions in violation of provisions of the CWC it will inevitably create a detrimental precedent which can damage the credibility of this Organisation as well as of the system of international organisations and of international law and order on the whole."

It is clear therefore that there were two opposing views regarding this decision. According to the majority view, the OPCW Conference was fully utilizing its powers, in a changed security environment. According to the minority view, the Conference was acting *ultra vires* [247]; the "attribution power" could only be given to the OPCW by an amendment of its constituent instrument.

---

245. OPCW Doc. C-SS-4/NAT.40, 26 June 2018, https://www.opcw.org/csp-ss-4.
246. Text copied from the website of the Russian Permanent Representation, now no longer available.
247. This view is supported by A. Orakhelashvili, "The Attribution Decision Adopted by the OPCW's Conference of States Parties and Its Legality", *International Organizations Law Review*, Vol. 17 (2020), pp. 664-681. Orakhelashvili analyses this decision "from the viewpoint of consensual positivist approach to international law" (at p. 665).

As in the 1993 report by the UN Secretary-General about the creation of the ICTY, the June 2018 "attribution decision" could not refer to a specific precedent for the power concerned, in other words, a practice on which the organization could rely. In the alternative, what it could do was mention "stepping stones" or building blocks for such a power. In addition, the decision referred repeatedly (five times) to the object and purpose of the Convention and once to its objectives. Taking recourse to the teleology of the Convention, a majority of the member states took the view that the prevailing political and security circumstances required a reading of the Convention that included the "attribution power", whereas a minority rejected this and concluded that this was a power that could only be attributed to the organization by amending the Convention.

2.2.5. Does NATO have the power to carry out "out of area operations"?

The North Atlantic Treaty Organization was established by the 1949 Washington Treaty as a collective self-defence organization. Due to the beginning of the Cold War not too long after the beginning of the UN and the failed implementation of the plans for a UN force, member states could not fully rely on the collective security system of the UN Charter. NATO and other collective self-defence organizations were created. Article 5 of the Washington Treaty refers to the right of individual or collective self-defence recognized by Article 51 of the Charter and provides that an attack against one or more member states "shall be considered an attack against them all". Presumably to avoid the impression that they were turning away from the UN, the members made abundantly clear in the Washington Treaty that they "reaffirm their faith in the purposes and principles of the Charter" (Preamble, first sentence).

The end of the Cold War changed the security situation in Europe and initially took away much of the rationale of NATO. While its counterpart in Eastern Europe, the Warsaw Pact, was dissolved in 1991, NATO followed a different course. In the 1990s it adapted its functions to also include joint military operations "out of area", also referred to as "non-Article 5 operations", that is, not in reaction to an armed attack against one or more of its member states [248]. This fundamental adaptation

---

248. See for a brief overview of this development M. Zwanenburg, "NATO, Its Member States, and the Security Council", in N. Blokker and N. Schrijver (eds.),

was not implemented by amending the Washington Treaty; NATO's founding instrument has never been amended. In this context, Ress has referred to the Washington Treaty as a "Vertrag auf Rädern" (treaty on wheels) [249]. This raises questions about the principle of attributed powers. If functions and powers have been given to an organization for a particular purpose (collective self-defence), can this organization further develop or even shapeshift to also perform other functions and use its powers for different purposes ("non-Art. 5 operations") without constitutional amendment? While no such amendment took place, a number of declarations were adopted by high-level meetings of the North Atlantic Council, accompanying this transformation and providing some normative guidance [250]. However, is this good enough? Can new functions and powers be given to an international organization not only by treaty (or treaty amendment) but also by (high-level) political decisions?

These questions did not become very prominent in practice but were raised in the literature [251]. In addition, a group in the German Parliament brought a case before the Federal Constitutional Court (Bundesverfassungsgericht) against the German Government, claiming *inter alia* that the German Government infringed provisions of the German Basic Law by approving the decisions on NATO's 1999

The Security Council and the Use of Force, Leiden, Nijhoff, 2005, pp. 189-211, in particular pp. 197-203.

249. G. Ress, "Verfassungsrechtliche Auswirkungen der Fortentwicklung völkerrechtlicher Verträge", in Fürst (ed.), *Festschrift für Wolfgang Zeidler* (1987), p. 1175 *et seq.*, quotation at p. 1179, quoted in M. Ruffert and C. Walter, *Institutionalised International Law*, Baden-Baden, C. H. Beck/Hart/Nomos, 2015, at p. 94.

250. In particular the Rome Declaration, agreed in November 1991 by the Heads of State and Government participating in the Meeting of the North Atlantic Council to define the new security architecture in Europe. For the text, see https://www.nato.int/cps/en/natohq/official_texts_23847.htm.

251. For example, E. Klein and S. Schmahl, "Die neue NATO-Strategie und ihre völkerrechtlichen und verfassungsrechtlichen Implikationen", *Recht und Politik*, Vol. 35 (1999), pp. 198-209; H. Sauer, "Die NATO und das Verfassungsrecht: neues Konzept – alte Fragen", *Zeitschrift für ausländisches öffentliches Recht und Völkerrecht*, Vol. 62 (2002), pp. 317-346, esp. at pp. 339-341; I. F. Dekker and E. P. J. Myjer, "Air Strikes on Bosnian Positions: Is NATO Also Legally the Proper Instrument of the UN?", *Leiden Journal of International Law*, Vol. 9 (1996), pp. 411-416; N. Blokker and S. Muller, "NATO as the UN Security Council's Instrument: Question Marks From the Perspective of International Law?", *Leiden Journal of International Law*, Vol. 9 (1996), pp. 417-421; Peters, note 14, at pp. 368-375 (with extensive references to German literature); N. D. White, *The Law of International Organisations*, 3rd ed., Manchester, Manchester University Press, 2017, at p. 83 ("There appear to be strong legal arguments for saying that NATO members ought to make a new contract instead of trying to layer incompatible constitutional interpretations upon what is a narrow contractual treaty").

Strategic Concept [252]. If these decisions should be considered as treaties, amending the NATO Treaty, the German Parliament would need to give its approval. Or, if the relevant NATO decisions would amount to a *de facto* amendment of the NATO Treaty, this would circumvent the need for parliamentary approval. The Bundesverfassungsgericht rejected the claims. It stated that these decisions on the 1999 Strategic Concept are not treaties but rather "a consensus paper that describes NATO's new tasks and instruments only in general terms" [253]. The expansion of NATO tasks to "non-Article 5 operations" ("which has not been implied in the Treaty") "constitutes only a further development *["Fortentwicklung"]* of the NATO Treaty, which cannot be interpreted . . . as an inconsistency with, or as an expansion of the content of the existing Treaty" [254]. These operations "do not constitute . . . a fundamentally new type of operation" [255]. However, it is clear that this conclusion is far from obvious. It triggers the question of what the difference is between "a further development" and a new development, non-Article 5 operations being fundamentally different from the collective self-defence operations for which NATO was established. The judges of the Bundesverfassungsgericht fundamentally disagreed on this issue. Four judges voted in favour of the judgment. Four were against, taking the view that the new tasks were not covered by the NATO Treaty and constituted an implicit amendment of that Treaty [256]. In the case of such a tied vote, the Court cannot declare that constitutional law has been violated.

This example of "messy practice" demonstrates that the functions and powers of an international organization may fundamentally change in practice without constitutional amendment. NATO was established to carry out collective self-defence operations, but in the 1990s it was also mandated to perform "non-Article 5 operations". To a significant extent this was facilitated by the brief and general nature of the constituent instrument concerned. The Washington Treaty does not define in detail the functions and powers of the organization, thereby leaving more

---

252. Bundesverfassungsgericht, Judgment of the Second Senate of 22 November 2001 – 2 BvE 6/99 –, paras. 1-164; ECLI:DE:BVerfG:2001:es20011122.2bve000699; http://www.bverfg.de/e/es20011122_2bve000699en.html.
253. *Id.*, Section C.I.1 *(b)*.
254. *Id.*, Section C.I.2, at paras. 141, 139. As the Court indicates, such a further development "which does not constitute an amendment of the Treaty, does not require the consent of the *Bundestag*" (*id.*, Section II).
255. *Id.*, Section C.II.2.
256. See Ruffert and Walter, note 249, at p. 218.

room for informal change (or "further development", as concluded by the Bundesverfassungsgericht). Moreover, the alternative way in which new functions and powers have been given to NATO in practice has always been accepted by all member states; therefore, constitutional amendment was not considered necessary.

2.2.6. The power of the CTBTO PrepCom to use its verification installations not only for nuclear explosions but also for tsunami warning [257]

The 1996 Comprehensive Nuclear-Test-Ban Treaty (CTBT), which has not yet entered into force [258], provides for the establishment of a new international organization (the Comprehensive Nuclear-Test-Ban Treaty Organization (CTBTO)). The aim of the CTBT is to prevent the proliferation of nuclear weapons by prohibiting the testing of such weapons or any other nuclear explosions. The organization has to verify that no such tests are carried out. Pending the entry into force of the CTBT, a Preparatory Commission (PrepCom) has been established to make the necessary preparations, so that a verification regime is operational when the Treaty enters into force [259]. This PrepCom – itself an international organization – is responsible for building or establishing 337 facilities (321 monitoring stations and 16 laboratories) around the world to verify compliance with the Treaty [260]. These installations make use of sophisticated technology: seismic, hydroacoustic, infrasound and radionuclide stations are used to monitor vibrations in the earth, the oceans and the atmosphere, as well as to detect the presence of radionuclides in the air. The information gathered by these installations is sent directly to an international data centre at the headquarters in Vienna where it is transmitted to the state signatories, processed, analysed and reported [261]. It is clear that the collection and analysis

---

257. The section below is largely reproduced from Schermers and Blokker, note 2, at pp. 168-170.
258. The CTBT was concluded in 1996. As of July 2022, 186 states had signed this Treaty, and 173 had ratified it. For entry into force it is required that the forty-four states holding nuclear power or research reactors in 1996 have ratified the Treaty (Art. XIV and Annex 2 to the Treaty). Eight of these ratifications (China, Egypt, India, Iran, Israel, North Korea, Pakistan, US) are still lacking.
259. Established by Resolution CTBT/MSS/RES/1, adopted 19 November 1996.
260. See https://www.ctbto.org/, in particular at https://www.ctbto.org/verification-regime/background/overview-of-the-verification-regime/.
261. Information taken from https://www.ctbto.org/ and obtained from the CTBTO PrepCom Secretariat, February 2011.

of these data serves the purpose of verifying compliance with the prohibition to carry out nuclear weapons test explosions or any other nuclear explosion. But could they serve other purposes as well? The doctrine of attributed competences would suggest a negative answer to this question. Powers given for a purpose A cannot be used for a purpose B.

While it is likely that states, when signing the CTBT in 1996, would agree to such a negative answer, another answer was given in practice following the devastating tsunami of 26 December 2004, caused by an earthquake of the coast of Indonesia, killing over 230,000 people in fourteen countries. It appeared that the existing CTBT facilities generate data about earthquakes that could be made available to tsunami warning centres more rapidly than other sources of information. As a result, populations could be warned two to two-and-a-half minutes earlier in the event of a tsunami [262]. On 4 March 2005, the CTBTO PrepCom decided to make its facilities available for these purposes, which are clearly unrelated to the prohibition of the testing of nuclear weapons [263]. Since then, the PrepCom has concluded tsunami warning agreements and arrangements with a number of member states. In 2010 it signed an agreement with the United Nations Educational, Scientific and Cultural Organization (UNESCO) to enhance cooperation in this field (the Intergovernmental Oceanographic Commission of UNESCO has been responsible for intergovernmental coordination of tsunami warning since 1965) [264]. As of July 2022, tsunami warning centres in seventeen member states receive data from some 100 CTBTO stations [265]. The data are provided on a strictly confidential basis and can only be used for tsunami warning purposes [266].

---

262. See www.ctbto.org/press-centre/press-releases/2008/new-tsunami-arrangements/; P. A. Bernal, "The Importance of PTS Data for Tsunami Warning Centres", *CTBTO Spectrum*, Vol. 9 (January 2007), pp. 20-21.
263. In a Special Session held on 4 March 2005; see CTBTO PrepCom Doc.CTBT/PC-24/1, https://www.ctbto.org/press-centre/press-releases/2005/the-preparatory-commission-for-the-ctbto-holds-a-special-session-on-a-possible-contribution-to-a-tsunami-warning-system/. See also Doc. CTBT/PC-24/3/Annex II. The March 2005 PrepCom decision tasked the Provisional Technical Secretariat (PTS) to "*(a)* Explore and initially assess with national authorities and international tsunami warning organizations recognized by UNESCO, upon their request, which data and products might be useful and can be provided by the PTS for tsunami warning", and to "*(b)* Examine the legal framework . . .".
264. See W. Watson-Wright, "Buttressing the Global Tsunami Warning Network", *CTBTO Spectrum*, Vol. 18 (March 2012), pp. 33-35.
265. See https://www.ctbto.org/verification-regime/spin-offs-for-disaster-warning-and-science/.
266. *UNJY 2006*, at p. 256.

This demonstrates that, in extreme cases such as this one, strong societal needs can prevail over a stricter interpretation of the powers of an international organization that would normally be followed. While in theory this could be considered an example of "mission creep" of international organizations, in practice such mission creep should be welcomed. The formal adaptation of the constitution of the organization is of course the regular way to expand the organization's activities, but this is usually a process that takes years. In the meantime, it would be overly formalistic if the organization was prevented from acting. In such cases, there should be broad consensus among the members about the choices to be made, and the use of the powers of the organization should not violate the rules of the organization. In the case of the CTBTO PrepCom, the "tsunami warning use" of the powers of the organization should not hamper the use of these powers for their original purposes. Moreover, since the PrepCom is carrying out preparatory work pending the entry into force of the CTBT, the arrangements made should ultimately be approved by the CTBTO once it has started functioning.

Nevertheless, even though this tsunami warning evolution of the CTBTO PrepCom is to be welcomed, it raises questions in the light of the principle of attributed powers. What is the legal basis for the activities of this organization in the field of tsunami warning?

*

These examples – which could be complemented by many others – concern widely diverging situations and demonstrate the richness of practice, as well as the great variety of the activities of international organizations. At the same time, they have in common that these activities are beyond, sometimes far beyond, what the founders of these organizations could imagine. It is therefore hardly surprising that the organizations concerned lacked the necessary explicit powers for such activities. Essentially, the primary route of explicit constitutional power attribution falls short for two reasons: incompleteness and obsolescence. First, the explicit attribution of powers is always incomplete. Constituent instruments can never lay down a detailed list of all specific powers an organization needs for the performance of its functions. For example, in its first resolution, the UN Security Council requested "the permanent members of the Security Council to direct their Chiefs of Staff to meet, or to appoint representatives who shall meet, at London on 1 February 1946", and it directed the Military Staff Committee "as its first task, to draw up proposals for its organization . . . and procedure" [267]. The UN Charter does not explicitly empower the Security Council to take these two specific decisions, but the power to do so was not questioned at all during the relevant meeting of the Council [268] and the resolution was adopted without a vote. The second constraint of explicit power attribution is that it may soon fall short of what an organization needs to perform its functions, because, as Bob Dylan sang in the 1960s, "the times, they are a-changin'" [269]. The world in which an organization must perform its functions continues to evolve. If a proposal to create a new international organization was made five years later, its founders might agree to give it different functions and more or fewer powers, or perhaps they would not have created the organization at all.

Hence, each international organization is confronted every now and then with a tension between what action may be seen as necessary and what it is constitutionally explicitly empowered to do. In terms of the observation in Julian Barnes's novel quoted in the opening of this chapter, there are gaps between "theories" and "life". Obviously, there are always gaps between law and practice. But when such gaps are, or become, fundamental, the time has come to build bridges, by adapting the law and/or by correcting what is done in practice.

Here, gaps between rules and practice would be less problematic if international organizations had, like states, general powers and if they were ungoverned by the rule of law, that is, if the principle of attributed powers did not apply. However, international organizations are not states. Because it is long established that international organizations may only act if they have the power to do so, and because member states are often apprehensive of "mission creep" of "their" organization, the legality and the legitimacy of the activities mentioned in the above-mentioned examples have been questioned. Against this background, the next sections will discuss three key ways of bridging the gap between "clean theory" and "messy life" in this field: the attribution of new powers by amending the organization's constituent instrument, implying powers, and accepting customary powers emerging from an organization's practice.

---

267. SC Res. 1(1946), adopted 25 January 1946.
268. SC Official Records, First Year: First Series, No. 1, at pp. 12-14.
269. See his website, https://www.bobdylan.com/. This song was first played in 1963.

2.3. Bridging the gap (i): Amending the constituent instrument

Obviously, the formal way to give new powers to an international organization is to amend its constituent instrument [270]. Indeed, if the principle of attributed powers is strictly followed, members would amend this instrument to give new powers to their organization whenever they agree that this is necessary, because they want the organization to perform new functions or for other reasons. In this way, there would be no gap, or no big gap, between the formal powers of an organization and the powers that they exercise in practice. As the Institut de Droit International recognized in 2021, "the appropriate use of amendment procedures of constituent instruments of international organizations is conducive to maintaining the integrity and coherence of those instruments" [271].

However, this first and most formal way to bridge the gap in this field between "clean theory" and "messy practice" is rarely used. The constitutions of many international organizations have never been amended for the purpose of attributing new powers to the organization. One exception is the European Union. For example, in the (then) European Community, the European Commission had proposed since 1979 that the Community should become a party to the European Convention on Human Rights [272]. This involved a number of legal questions, including the question of whether the field of human rights was within the scope of the Community's powers and whether there was a constitutional basis for acceding to the European Convention. A number of member states questioned whether there was such a basis. The Council therefore decided to request an opinion of the Court of Justice about the proposal [273].

In its Opinion the Court referred to the principle of conferred powers (in the French text: *principe des compétences d'attribution*) and observed that "[n]o Treaty provision confers on the Community institutions any general power to enact rules on human rights or to conclude international

---

270. On the amendment of constitutions of international organizations, see Schermers and Blokker, note 2, at pp. 765-784, with references to further literature.
271. IDI, Resolution adopted 4 September 2021, Preamble (available at www.idi-iil.org). This Resolution is further discussed in the next chapter in Sec. 3.4.3.
272. See Memorandum on the Accession of the European Communities to the Convention for the Protection of Human Rights and Fundamental Freedoms, 4 April 1979, reproduced in the *Bulletin of the European Communities*, Supplement 2/79.
273. According to (then) Art. 228 (6) of the Treaty on European Union, the Council, the Commission or a Member State may obtain the opinion of the Court of Justice as to whether an agreement envisaged is compatible with the provisions of the Treaty.

conventions in this field" [274]. In addition, it considered that the intended accession of the Community to the Convention could not be based on the above-mentioned "catch-all clause", included in (now) Article 352, paragraph 1 (Sec. 2.1). The Court stated with respect to that clause [275]:

> "That provision, being an integral part of an institutional system based on the principle of conferred powers, cannot serve as a basis for widening the scope of Community powers beyond the general framework created by the provisions of the Treaty as a whole and, in particular, by those that define the tasks and the activities of the Community. On any view, Article 235 cannot be used as a basis for the adoption of provisions whose effect would, in substance, be to amend the Treaty without following the procedure which it provides for that purpose."

The Court concluded: "As Community law now stands, the Community has no competence to accede to the European Convention for the Protection of Human Rights and Fundamental Freedoms." [276] Community law therefore had to be changed. This is what the 2007 Lisbon Treaty did: it amended the Treaty on European Union so that it now includes the following provision: "The Union shall accede to the European Convention for the Protection of Human Rights and Fundamental Freedoms." [277] An explicit power having now been conferred, the European Commission could then take the initiative for accession [278].

There is a limited number of other examples of amendments of constituent instruments to attribute new powers to international organizations. These include two amendments of the Articles of Agreement of the International Finance Corporation, which empowered it to make investments of its funds in capital stock [279] and to lend to or borrow from the World Bank [280]. In addition, seven amendments have been made to the Articles of Agreement of the International Monetary Fund. Some of these have attributed new powers to the Fund: for example, the first (1969) amendment creating the Special Drawing

---

274. Opinion 2/94 (1996), at para. 27.
275. *Id.*, at para. 30. See also paras. 34-35.
276. Opinion 2/94 (1996).
277. Treaty on European Union, Art. 6.2.
278. The accession negotiations turned out to be complex, and the EU has not yet joined.
279. See 439 UNTS (1962), at p. 318 *et seq.*
280. See 563 UNTS (1967), p. 362 *et seq.*

Right as an international reserve asset and giving powers to the Fund in that context (e.g. the power to allocate SDRs to members)[281]; the 1990 amendment introduced new penalties[282]; the 2008 amendment expanded the investment authority of the International Monetary Fund (IMF)[283].

There may be different reasons why it is relatively rare that new powers are attributed to international organizations by constitutional amendment. First, the powers attributed in the original constituent instrument may simply suffice for the organization to carry out its functions, because they are sufficiently broad, because the use of implied or customary powers (see below) has made it unnecessary to take recourse to an amendment of the constitution, or for other reasons. Second, there is usually considerable reluctance to amend a constituent instrument of an international organization as the process may often take years (if it is successful at all)[284] and since this is often compared to opening Pandora's box (a proposal for a particular amendment may trigger proposals for other amendments that are not necessarily desired).

In a few international organizations the difficulty of amending the constitution has been recognized and a lighter procedure for amendment has been accepted. In these cases, amendments do not need the ratification of the members but are adopted by a decision of the plenary organ of the organization[285]. For example, the constitution of the European Coal and Steel Community (which ceased to exist in 2002) provided for a procedure for "small revision". If "unforeseen

---

281. See J. Gold, "Legal Technique in the Creation of a New International Reserve Asset: Special Drawing Rights and the Amendment of the Articles of Agreement of the International Monetary Fund", *Case Western Reserve Journal of International Law*, Vol. 1 (1969), pp. 105-123, reproduced in J. Gold, *Legal and Institutional Aspects of the International Monetary System: Selected Essays*, Washington, IMF, 1979, pp. 128-147.

282. See J. Gold, "The IMF Invents New Penalties", in N. Blokker and S. Muller (eds.), *Towards More Effective Supervision by International Organizations: Essays in Honour of Henry G. Schermers*, Vol. 1, Dordrecht, Nijhoff, 1994, pp. 127-147; F. Gianviti, "The Third Amendment to the IMF's Articles of Agreement", in R. C. Effros (ed.), *Current Legal Issues Affecting Central Banks*, Washington, IMF, 1995, pp. 14-17.

283. See IMF Press Release No. 11/52, https://www.imf.org/en/News/Articles/2015/09/14/01/49/pr1152; A. Viterbo, *International Monetary Fund (IMF)*, 3rd ed., Alphen aan den Rijn, Wolters Kluwer, 2019, at p. 43.

284. For example, in 1986 amendments to the ILO Constitution were adopted, changing *inter alia* the composition and the governance of the Governing Body and the procedure for appointment of the Director-General. However, in the absence of the required number of ratifications, these amendments have not yet entered into force.

285. See further Schermers and Blokker, note 2, at pp. 776-779. This has sometimes been referred to as "self-amendment" (see e.g. Gold, note 10, at p. 19).

difficulties emerging in the light of experience in the application of this Treaty, or fundamental economic or technical changes directly affecting the common market in coal and steel, make it necessary to adapt the rules for the High Authority's exercise of its powers, appropriate amendments may be made"[286]. Such amendments

> "shall be proposed jointly by the High Authority and the Council, acting by a five-sixths majority of its members, and shall be submitted to the Court for its opinion. In considering them, the Court shall have full power to assess all points of fact and of law. If as a result of such consideration it finds the proposals compatible with the provisions of the preceding paragraph, they shall be forwarded to the Assembly and shall enter into force if approved by a majority of three quarters of the votes cast and two thirds of the members of the Assembly".

These "small revision" amendments therefore did not require ratifications by the members[287]. However, the overwhelming majority of international organizations do not have such lighter procedures for amending the constitution. What may sometimes be seen as an advantage of such lighter procedures not requiring ratification by the members is also usually the main objection: they bypass approval by national parliaments and therefore lack the normal democratic legitimacy[288].

Apart from amendments of the constitution, there are two other key ways of bridging the gap between "clean theory" and "messy life" in the field of powers of international organizations: taking recourse to implied powers, or to customary powers.

2.4. Bridging the gap (ii): Implied powers

Implied powers are the main remedy for the two above-mentioned constraints of explicit power attribution, incompleteness and obsolescence. Both the PCIJ and the ICJ have pointed out that international organizations not only have explicit but also implicit (or implied)

---

286. Treaty establishing the European Coal and Steel Community (1951), Art. 95, para. 3.
287. Unlike an amendment of the Treaty on European Union in accordance with simplified revision procedures (see TEU, Art. 48.6).
288. This disadvantage was the main reason why it was decided not to accept proposals for self-amendment during the wartime negotiations of the IMF Articles of Agreement and during the drafting of the second amendment of these Articles. See Gold, note 10, at p. 19.

Legal Facets of the Practice of International Organizations 161

powers. They have done so mostly in regard to the specific organization that requested an advisory opinion, but the ICJ has also confirmed this in general terms. It observed in 1996 [289] that

"the necessities of international life may point to the need for organizations, in order to achieve their objectives, to possess subsidiary powers which are not expressly provided for in the basic instruments which govern their activities. It is generally accepted that international organizations can exercise such powers, known as 'implied' powers".

All international organizations have implied powers; without those they cannot function. This may not always be easy to accept for states, as they cannot fully control what powers may be implied in the life of an organization. The founding fathers of the OAS agreed in the Charter of the organization that it only has explicit powers [290], suggesting that it does not have implied powers. Nevertheless, in practice activities have been undertaken by the OAS, for example by its Secretary-General, which are difficult to base on *express* powers [291].

Implied powers are not *new* powers that are attributed to an international organization. They are powers that are connected to what the founding fathers agreed in the constituent instrument of an international organization: the purposes, functions or explicit powers of the organization (see Sec. 2.4.2 below) [292]. This is how they differ from customary powers (see Sec. 2.5 below).

However, while the notion of implied powers as such is indeed generally accepted, it raises as many questions as it solves. Two fundamental questions will be briefly discussed. First, the question of how implied powers are related to the principle of attributed powers

---

289. ICJ, *WHO Nuclear Weapons* Advisory Opinion, note 183, quotation at p. 79.
290. OAS Charter, Art. 1 ("The Organization of American States has no powers other than those expressly conferred upon it by this Charter").
291. See H. Caminos and R. Lavalle, "New Departures in the Exercise of Inherent Powers by the UN and OAS Secretaries-General: The Central American Situation", *American Journal of International Law*, Vol. 83 (1989), pp. 395-402. Another example of OAS practice is given by White: the 1991 Santiago Commitment to Democracy (that "certainly seems to go beyond the pro-democracy amendments to the OAS Charter that occurred in 1985 and, therefore, cannot be seen as the exercise of an express power"). See White, note 251, at p. 125.
292. As Weiß stated: "Bei impliziten Kompetenzen geht es aber . . . nicht um eine Erweiterung der Kompetenzen einer Organisation, sondern darum, ihr bereits zustehende – sozusagen verdeckt mitgeschriebene – Kompetenzen sichtbar zu machen"; N. Weiß, *Kompetenzlehre internationaler Organisationen*, Dordrecht, Springer, 2009, at p. 363.

(2.4.1). The second question concerns the scope of implied powers (2.4.2).

2.4.1. Implied powers and the principle of attribution

According to the principle of attribution, international organizations only have the powers that have been attributed to them. Unlike states, they do not have general powers. It is clear that powers that are expressly laid down in an organization's constituent instrument are attributed powers. However, is this also true for implied powers? This is sometimes rejected in literature, assuming that what is attributed should be stated explicitly [293]. In my opinion, however, a broader view of the attribution principle is warranted, accepting that implied powers are also attributed [294]. States, when creating an international organization, deliberately do not conclude a treaty with only mutual rights and obligations; they also establish a living instrument and give it powers to enable it (and themselves) to respond to future developments that are by definition unknown. If the future is unknown, how could an organization perform its functions with only powers that are known? To some extent, this could be remedied by attributing new powers to an organization by constitutional amendment, whenever this is considered necessary by the members (see Sec. 2.3 above). However, this remedy

---

293. E.g. J. Klabbers, *An Introduction to International Organizations Law*, 4th ed., Cambridge, Cambridge University Press, 2022, at pp. 53-63; Ruffert and Walter, note 249, at p. 94: "The most visible modification, if not breach, of the doctrine of speciality is the *doctrine of implied powers*" (italics in the original). Engström also presents attributed and implied powers as opposite doctrines, but observes at the same time that "while the attributed and implied powers doctrines *can* be used to present different constructions of powers of organizations, in a closer look the distinguishing features of the two begin to disappear" (italics in the original); see V. Engström, "Reasoning on Powers of Organizations", in J. Klabbers and Å. Wallendahl (eds.), *Research Handbook on the Law of International Organizations*, Cheltenham, Elgar, 2011, pp. 56-83, quotation at p. 76.

294. For a similar view: P. Klein, "Les compétences et pouvoirs de l'organisation internationale", in E. Lagrange and J.-M. Sorel (eds.), *Droit des organisations internationales*, Issy-les-Moulineaux Cedex, Librairie générale de droit et de jurisprudence, 2013, pp. 714-734. Klein correctly concludes: "la théorie des pouvoirs implicites ne remet pas en cause le principe fondamental des compétences d'attribution" (at p. 728). The ICJ also follows this broader view. In para. 25 of its 1996 WHO *Nuclear Weapons* Advisory Opinion (note 183), at pp. 78-79, the Court first refers to the principle of speciality, then mentions that "[t]he powers conferred on international organizations are normally the subject of an express statement in their constituent instruments", subsequently observes that it is generally accepted that organizations also have implied powers, and finally concludes: "to ascribe to the WHO the competence to address the legality of the use of nuclear weapons ... would be tantamount to disregarding the principle of speciality; for such competence could not be deemed a necessary implication of the Constitution of the Organization".

is often inadequate, and it is therefore generally accepted, as the ICJ observed in 1996, that international organizations have implied powers [295]. Such general acceptance is made explicit when the above-mentioned "catch-all clauses" are included in constituent instruments of international organizations (Sec. 2.1), but it may also be considered to be implied. Implied powers are not a violation of the principle of attribution but rather one of its most dynamic manifestations [296].

2.4.2. The scope of implied powers

Accepting powers that are not explicitly attributed may provide an international organization with the necessary flexibility. At the same time, implied powers are not without limits. For example, they must respect any restrictions laid down in the constituent instrument and may not be used against explicit powers of the organization [297]. The scope of what may be implied is also, to a significant extent, in the eye of the beholder. Are powers to be implied in the organization's purposes or functions? Or, more restrictively, in its explicit powers? This was a well-known source of disagreement within the ICJ. In its 1949 *Reparation for Injuries* Advisory Opinion, the Court made two important observations relating to implied powers. The first observation was made in the context of the first, general part of the Advisory Opinion in which the Court examined the preliminary question of whether the UN is an international legal person. In this context, the Court raised the question of whether "the sum of the international rights of the Organization comprises the right to bring a claim . . . against a State to obtain reparation in respect of damage caused by the injury of an agent of the Organization in the course of the performance of his duties" [298]. The Court stated [299]:

---

295. As Klabbers writes: "[t]here is virtual agreement among diplomats, statesmen, and scholars alike that implied powers exist and are, generally, a good thing", note 293, at p. 56. As Ruffert and Walter write: "the implied powers doctrine continues to be linked to an organisation's founding treaty and thus to the intentions of the founding members", note 249, at p. 95.
296. As Chaumont concluded long ago: "[l]'utilisation de la notion de 'pouvoir implicites' ne consiste donc pas à violer les textes et à détourner l'organisation de l'affectation qui lui a été donnée, mais au contraire est le résultat de l'affectation continue et renouvelée, et du fait que l'organisation est un instrument réel et pratique, non une structure hypothétique et artificielle", note 181, at p. 59.
297. See PCIJ, *Danube* Advisory Opinion, note 181, at p. 64. See further Schermers and Blokker, note 2, at pp. 197-199.
298. ICJ, *Reparation for injuries suffered in the service of the United Nations*, Advisory Opinion, *ICJ Reports 1949*, p. 174 *et seq.*, quotation at pp. 179-180.
299. *Id.*, at p. 180.

"Whereas a State possesses the totality of international rights and duties recognized by international law, the rights and duties of an entity such as the Organization must depend upon its purposes and functions as specified or implied in its constituent documents and developed in practice."

This first observation is, strictly seen, not about implied *powers* but about implied *purposes* and *functions*. Nevertheless, in a wider sense, it is also relevant for implied powers. The quoted observation is a stepping stone to what the Court stated in the next sentence: the functions of the UN cannot be effectively performed if "fifty-eight or more Foreign Offices" would have to bring the claim concerned, instead of the UN [300]. The UN therefore has the implied power [301] to bring an international claim whenever this is necessary in the exercise of its functions. In this first observation, the ICJ contrasted the rights and duties of the UN (and similar "entities") with those of states. States enjoy "the totality" of international rights and duties; those of international organizations are limited; they depend on their purposes and functions. Needless to say, the broader those purposes and functions are, the wider the limits. However, there will always be limits. International organizations are not states (enjoying "the totality" of international rights and duties).

The second observation was made in the context of the specific question of whether the UN has the capacity to bring an international claim "in respect of the damage caused ... *(b)* to the victim or to persons entitled through him" [302]? Here, the Court compared the capacity for the UN to bring such a claim against "[t]he traditional rule that diplomatic protection is exercised by the national State" [303]. It noted that it "is here faced with a new situation", and that the Charter "does not expressly confer upon the Organization the capacity to include, in its claim for reparation, damage caused to the victim or to persons entitled through him" [304]. The question therefore was whether such a capacity should be *implied*. Before answering this specific question in the affirmative, the Court first made the following famous general observation [305]:

---

300. *Id.*
301. The Court used the word "capacity", which is the word used in the General Assembly's request for an advisory opinion.
302. *Id.*, at p. 181.
303. *Id.*
304. *Id.*, at p. 182.
305. *Id.*, at pp. 182-183.

> "Under international law, the Organization must be deemed to have those powers which, though not expressly provided in the Charter, are conferred upon it by necessary implication as being essential to the performance of its duties. This principle of law was applied by the Permanent Court of International Justice to the International Labour Organization in its Advisory Opinion No. 13 of 23 July 1926 (Series B, No. 13, p. 18), and must be applied to the United Nations."

In this second observation the Court points out that there is a principle of law, according to which the UN has implied powers. The *raison d'être* of such powers are the duties that the UN has to perform. Not just almost any power can be implied; it must be "essential" for the performance of the relevant duties. As this is essential, the implication of powers is "necessary".

Judge Hackworth did not agree with the Court's observations concerning implied powers. In his dissenting opinion, he favoured a narrower view of implied powers. Applied to the specific question requested by the General Assembly, he denied that the UN had the capacity to bring a claim for the damage caused to its agent (and only accepted the UN's capacity to bring a claim for the damage caused to itself) [306]:

> "Powers not expressed cannot freely be implied. Implied powers flow from a grant of expressed powers, and are limited to those that are 'necessary' to the exercise of powers expressly granted.
>
> . . . .
>
> No necessity for the exercise of the power here in question has been shown to exist. There is no impelling reason, if any at all, why the Organization should become the sponsor of claims on behalf of its employees, even though limited to those arising while the employee is in line of duty. These employees are still nationals of their respective countries, and the customary methods of handling such claims are still available in full vigour."

Ever since then, the question of whether implied powers should be defined broadly or more narrowly has been the subject of much debate, in practice and in doctrine. Following *Reparation for Injuries*, the ICJ has generally adhered to the broader interpretation. In its *Effect of*

---

306. *Id.*, at p. 198.

Awards Advisory Opinion, it quoted and applied the *Reparation* phrase (second observation mentioned above), and found that the power to establish the UN Administrative Tribunal "was *essential* to ensure the efficient working of the Secretariat, and to give effect to the paramount consideration of securing the highest standards of efficiency, competence and integrity. Capacity to do this arises *by necessary intendment* out of the Charter"[307].

In *Certain Expenses*, the Court went further, by stating that "when the Organization takes action which warrants the assertion that it was appropriate for the fulfilment of one of the stated purposes of the United Nations, the presumption is that such action is not *ultra vires* the Organization"[308]. This "presumption of legality" merely requires that the action undertaken by an organ of the UN is appropriate for the fulfilment of one of the purposes of the UN. Since these purposes are very broad (e.g. "to maintain international peace and security"), a lot of leeway is given for the exercise of powers.

Finally, in 1996, the Court stated in its *WHO – Legality of the Use of Nuclear Weapons* Advisory Opinion that "the necessities of international life may point to the need for organizations, in order to achieve their objectives, to possess subsidiary powers which are not expressly provided for in the basic instruments which govern their activities. It is generally accepted that international organizations can exercise such powers, known as 'implied' powers"[309]. Thus, here the Court linked implied powers to the organization's objectives (more or less as in *Certain Expenses*), although it only referred to the formula used in *Reparation*, reproduced in *Effect of Awards*. However, the Court applied the implied powers doctrine in a restrictive way in this Advisory Opinion, finding that the competence to address the legality of the use of nuclear weapons "could not be deemed a necessary implication of the Constitution of the Organization in the light of the purposes assigned to it by its member States"[310]. A broader application of the implied powers doctrine would also have been possible in this case, as is illustrated in some of the dissenting opinions[311].

---

307. ICJ, *Effect of awards of compensation made by the United Nations Administrative Tribunal*, Advisory Opinion, *ICJ Reports 1954*, p. 57 *et seq.*
308. ICJ, *Certain expenses of the United Nations (Art. 17, para. 2, of the Charter)*, Advisory Opinion, 20 July 1962, *ICJ Reports 1962*, p. 151 *et seq.*, quotation at p. 168.
309. ICJ, *WHO Nuclear Weapons* Advisory Opinion, note 183, quotation at p. 79.
310. *Id.*
311. See the Dissenting Opinions by Judge Koroma (note 183, p. 172, in particular at p. 198) and by Judge Weeramantry (*id.*, p. 101 *et seq.*).

2.4.3. Inherent powers

In the 1960s, Seyersted went one step further than implying powers. He advanced the view that international organizations even have *inherent* powers. Seyersted later wrote that the ICJ originally used the doctrine of implied powers "until it in 1962 turned to the contrary principle of inherent powers submitted to the judges by the present writer"[312]. The ICJ in *Certain Expenses* did not explicitly refer to "inherent powers". This notion was based on the idea that once states have established an international organization, this organization enjoys its own objective legal personality. Inherent in such personality is a wide variety of powers. According to Seyersted, inherent powers "include jurisdiction and international (and legal) capacity which all States, IGOs and other self-governing communities exercise as a matter of general customary law – *i.e.* without specific legal basis – unless there is a *contrary provision*"[313].

Seyersted's views did not find broad support in literature, and certainly not in practice. Most likely the main reason for this lack of support is Seyersted's assumption that states, once they establish an international organization, automatically (inherently) attribute a number of powers to it. This brings the powers of international organizations even closer than implied powers to the "general powers" reserved for states. As a result of this assumption, international organizations are "removed" or detached from their members to a degree that does not correspond

---

312. F. Seyersted, *Common Law of International Organizations*, Leiden, Nijhoff, 2008, at p. 31. Seyersted indicates that he has presented his principle of inherent powers "to the judges". It is not clear how he has done so. The text of the ICJ *Certain Expenses* Advisory Opinion, note 308, does not explicitly refer to such a principle; the same is true for the text of the separate opinions to this advisory opinion. But traces of it can be found in the written proceedings and oral statements (in particular the oral statement by the US, p. 415 of the oral statements, published on the ICJ website). See also F. Seyersted, "Can the United Nations Establish Military Forces and Perform Other Acts Without Specific Basis in the Charter?", *Österreichische Zeitschrift für Öffentliches Recht*, Vol. 12 (1962), pp. 190-229, in particular at pp. 201-214 (at pp. 210-211: "while intergovernmental organizations, unlike states, are restricted by specific provisions in their constitutions as to the aims for which they shall work, such organizations are, like states, in principle free to perform any sovereign acts, or any act under international law, which they are in a factual position to perform, to attain these aims, provided that their constitutions do not preclude such acts. . . . Thus, it is not necessary to look for specific provisions in the constitution or to resort to strained interpretations of texts and intentions or to other constructions to justify legally the performance by an intergovernmental organization of a sovereign or an international act not specifically authorized in its constitution. As an intergovernmental organization it has an *inherent power* to do so, which need not be justified by construing a special delegation in each case", italics in the original).
313. *Id.*, at p. 35 (italics in the original).

to the reality of a world that is territorially and politically divided into some 200 sovereign states that (still?) primarily call the shots.

2.5. Bridging the gap (iii): Organizational practice and the conundrum of customary powers

"Yes", said Viktor, "of course today's theory is tomorrow's practice. But I don't need to tell *you* how reluctant our authorities are to accept that"[314].

A defining characteristic of implied powers is that they are implied through something that has been agreed in the organization's constituent instrument (purposes, functions or powers). As the ICJ stated in 1949, international organizations are not states[315]. Their rights and duties must depend upon their "purposes and functions as specified or implied in [their] constituent documents and developed in practice", whereas a State "possesses the totality of international rights and duties recognized by international law"[316]. But it may happen in the life of an international organization[317] that it is agreed that the organization should exercise powers *that cannot be implied through anything that was agreed at the time of its creation*. In such situations, it may be impossible, too forced or too artificial, to found a proposed decision or action on implied powers since this proposed decision or action is simply too far removed from what was agreed at the organization's creation. "The times they are a-changin'"[318]: there are limits to what can be anticipated when establishing a new international organization. Certainly when an organization grows older, parts of its constitution may become obsolete, or – this is not necessarily the same – may no longer be seen by members as in their best interest. What was agreed at the organization's creation may become too far removed from reality as it presents itself later.

---

314. V. Grossman, *Life and Fate*, trans. Robert Chandler, London, Harvill Press, 1985, at p. 672 (first published in Russian as Жизнь и судьба in 1980, completed in 1960).

315. ICJ, *Reparation for Injuries*, note 298, at p. 179: "Accordingly, the Court has come to the conclusion that the Organization is an international person. That is not the same thing as saying that it is a State, which it certainly is not, or that its legal personality and rights and duties are the same as those of a state."

316. *Id.*, at p. 180.

317. ICJ, *Reparation for Injuries*, note 298, at p. 178 ("the requirements of international life"); ICJ, *WHO Nuclear Weapons* Advisory Opinion, note 183, at para. 25 ("the necessities of international life").

318. Dylan, note 269.

Obviously, it could be argued that in such situations the constituent instrument of an organization should be amended to attribute the necessary additional powers to the organization, whenever this is considered necessary. However, as discussed above, it may take a number of years before such amendments enter into force (assuming that agreement can be reached about them), or the amendment procedure may not be suitable for other reasons. In such situations it has happened that constitutions have been amended "informally", or *de facto* [319]. In such cases, a pragmatic spirit prevails. As has been said in Dutch politics, "if things cannot be done in the way they *should* be done, they should be done in the way they *can* be done" [320]. This is certainly not happening on a daily basis in all international organizations, but it is happening often enough to require closer analysis and also to distinguish between cases where this technique is used as a pretext for acting *ultra vires* and cases of a sincere, good-faith evolution of an organization's powers.

Here, almost automatically, the key question arises of how such giving of new powers to international organizations "simply" *by practice* is to be reconciled with the attribution principle, the core principle governing powers of international organizations. Is this generation of powers by practice a phenomenon that occurs in reality but that we have so far failed to fully understand in legal terms? Einstein's aphorism comes to mind: "[d]ie Welt vor uns, ein geöffnetes Buch. Wenn wir es nur lesen können" [321]. It is suggested that the concept of customary powers may be helpful in this context, as will be discussed now in some more detail.

It may happen in the life of an international organization that it is proposed or agreed to adopt a decision or take action even if the organization does not have the necessary express or implied powers. Such proposed or agreed decisions or actions may then be based on customary powers, which postdate the organization's constitution. To a limited extent, this has been recognized in the existing literature. Some important early observations are the following. Pollux (the pseudonym for E. Hambro, who was involved in the UN Charter negotiations

---

319. See e.g. S. Engel, "Procedures for the De Facto Revision of the Charter", in *Proceedings of the American Society of International Law at Its Annual Meeting (1921-1969)*, Vol. 59 (1965), pp. 108-116; S. Engel, "'Living' International Constitutions and the World Court (The Subsequent Practice of International Organs under their Constituent Instruments)", in *International and Comparative Law Quarterly*, Vol. 16 (1967), pp. 865-910.
320. This expression is attributed to the Dutch politician Jan de Koning (1926-1994). In Dutch: "als het niet kan zoals het moet, dan moet het maar zoals het kan".
321. Neffe, note 12.

and in the early practice of the UN) wrote in 1946: "A constitutional customary law will grow up and the Charter itself will merely form the framework of the Organization which will be filled in by the practice of the different organs." [322] In 1965 Higgins stated that "it seems to me, that the repeated practice here of the organ, in interpreting the treaty, establishes a *practice* and ultimately *custom*" [323]. In addition, she concluded: "Decisions which UN organs take concerning their own jurisdiction and competence, when acquiesced in by sufficient members over a period of time, form 'Charter Law' if they fall into some recognizable pattern. A customary practice of internal Charter practice thus becomes established." [324]

More recently, White quite rightly observed that this "legal development by practice, regarded by the organs of an IGO as normative, is a product of the separate will of the organization, as opposed to the doctrines of express and implied powers, which are tied to the will or intention of the (founding) member states" [325]. In addition, Alvarez has correctly noted that "it has become common for charter interpreters to rely on institutional (or 'customary') practice as evidence of the meaning of a constitutional provision, at least so long as that practice is within the purposes of the organization" [326]. Wood and Sthoeger have observed that "[t]he terms of the Charter *and the established practice of the Council* are sufficiently flexible that it is difficult to conceive of circumstances actually arising that could raise serious doubts about the legality of the Council's actions or whether it abused its discretion" [327]. In doctrinal terms, Seidl-Hohenveldern and Loibl have briefly indicated how they see the role of customary law in the internal law of international organizations: "Because the rules of internal law of an organization are particular *international law*, they can be modified by contrary, *particular international law*, not only by treaties of any kind but also by particular *customary international law*." [328] They refer to decision-

---

322. Pollux, note 167, at p. 54.
323. R. Higgins, "The Development of International Law by the Political Organs of the United Nations", *Proceedings of the Annual Meeting (American Society of International Law)*, Vol. 59 (1965), pp. 116-124, quotation at p. 119 (italics in the original).
324. *Id.*, at p. 121.
325. White, note 251, at p. 122.
326. J. E. Alvarez, *International Organizations as Law-Makers*, Oxford, Oxford University Press, 2005, in particular at pp. 87-95, quotation at p. 88.
327. M. Wood and E. Sthoeger, *The UN Security Council and International Law*, Cambridge, Cambridge University Press, 2022, at p. 61 (italics added).
328. Seidl-Hohenveldern and Loibl, note 199, at p. 224, para. 1513. The quote is a translation from the original text in German: "Da die Regeln des internen Rechtes

making in the UN Security Council, where abstention by one or more of the permanent members does not prevent the adoption of resolutions, even though the text of Article 27.3 requires their "concurring votes". This view suggests that existing powers of an international organization may be modified or supplemented by customary powers.

While these quotations show that there are traces of the recognition of customary powers in the literature [329], such powers have not (yet?) been generally accepted as such, neither in doctrine nor in practice. This lack of general acceptance is what the concept of customary powers has in common with the concept of inherent powers. However, the difference between inherent and customary powers is that the former are based on the organization's formal status as an international organization (even if created long ago), while the latter are based on a (current) agreement in practice that an international organization should adopt a particular decision or undertake a certain action.

To some extent, the ICJ's *Reparation* Advisory Opinion provides support for the existence of customary powers of international organizations. To quote the Court again [330]:

> "Whereas a State possesses the totality of international rights and duties recognized by international law, the rights and duties of an entity such as the Organization must depend upon its purposes and functions as specified or implied in its constituent documents *and developed in practice*."

The Court did not exclusively base the rights and duties of the UN on the Charter ("its purposes and functions as specified or implied in its constituent documents") but also took into account how these purposes and functions were developed in practice. At the same time, by keeping the link to the purposes and functions of the organization, the Court made clear that the rights and duties of the organization could not go

---

einer Organisation partikuläres *Völkerrecht* sind, können sie durch entgegenstehendes, *partikuläres Völkerrecht*, also durch völkerrechtliche Verträge jeder Art . . ., aber auch durch partikuläres *Völkergewohnheitsrecht abgeändert* werden" (italics in the original). See also p. 114, para. 0907, where the authors mention that international organizations enjoy some privileges and immunities on the basis of customary international law.

329. Another, somewhat different example is L. Arditi, "The Role of Practice in International Organizations: The Case of Government Recognition by the International Monetary Fund", *International Organizations Law Review*, Vol. 17 (2017), pp. 531-585, who refers to "a power recognized by the customary law of international organizations" (in the context of the power of the IMF to recognize governments, at p. 546).

330. ICJ, *Reparation for Injuries*, note 298, quotation at p. 180 (italics added).

beyond these. The same is true for its powers. However, if the powers of an international organization cannot go beyond what was agreed in its constituent instrument, what is the legal basis of customary powers, if they cannot be implied by anything that was agreed at the time of the creation of the organization?

There is something paradoxical about the concept of customary powers. Powers originate from somewhere. For states, powers originate from statehood. A state, from its origin, automatically has the rights, duties and powers that international law bestows on states. International organizations are not states. For international organizations, powers do not originate from "international organizationhood"[331] but from attribution by their founding fathers. However, unlike implied powers, customary powers lack a "hook" in the attributed purposes, functions or explicit powers of the organization. Do they not need a legal basis? Are they self-standing, providing in a somewhat circular way "their own legal basis"?

These questions are particularly pertinent, not when an organizational practice is already well-established and has become routine, but at its beginning. This is *new* conduct by the organization. It may live or it may die. It may develop into a new practice and into the exercise of customary powers. But such new conduct may also lack the necessary subsequent support by membership, remain isolated and extinguish. Or it may be adjusted. New conduct may be a response to a particular crisis, urgency or emergency, receiving the necessary majority vote but lacking robust support[332]. However, after a briefer or longer period of time, members may generally accept the exercise of new powers by international organizations until the point is reached that these may be

---

331. Unlike what Seyersted's notion of inherent powers claims. The expression "international organizationhood" is from Klabbers. See Klabbers, note 293, at p. 65.

332. See N. Bonucci, G. Marceau, A.-P. Ouellet and R. Walker, "IGO's Initiatives as a Response to Crises and Unforeseen Needs", *International Organizations Law Review*, Vol. 19 (2022), pp. 423-482. See also C. Kreuder-Sonnen, *Emergency Powers of International Organizations*, Oxford, Oxford University Press, 2019. The concept of "emergency powers" in this book is not related to the legal powers of international organizations but rather to the political power, the authority to act in exceptional, emergency circumstances. Kreuder-Sonnen defined these powers as "the constitutionally deviant widening of executive discretion at the expense of the political autonomy of the rule-addressees that is justified by exceptional necessity" (at p. 23). He compares this to emergency powers of states to act internally, in exceptional circumstances, based on necessity. However, as the ICJ stated: unlike states, international organizations do not have general powers but attributed powers. They also take action in emergency circumstances, but ultimately such action must be based on legal powers given to the organization (explicit or implied powers, customary powers).

considered customary powers [333]. Until that point is reached, the legality of the relevant conduct of the organization is uncertain; it is taking place in a twilight zone. This is somewhat similar to the coming into being of a rule of customary international law, although that is taking place in a more anarchic way. The emergence of new, customary powers of international organizations occurs within the legal framework of the relevant organization.

An example is the establishment of the UN Emergency Force by the General Assembly in 1956. Some UN member states questioned whether it was within the powers of the General Assembly to create such a peacekeeping force. Even though the ICJ concluded in 1962 that this was not enforcement action, and was therefore *intra vires*, almost all subsequent peacekeeping operations were established by the Security Council. At present, it is difficult to argue that the creation of peacekeeping forces is within the Assembly's customary powers. The power to create peacekeeping forces is not explicitly mentioned in the Charter. But via emergency action in the General Assembly during the Suez crisis, practice by states and the UN Secretariat, and further development under the aegis of the Security Council, it became one of the key instruments of the UN to maintain international peace and security.

The twilight period between the start of new conduct with the first exercise of new powers by an organization and the general acceptance of such new powers is an uncertain period. There is disagreement about whether the new conduct is a violation of the law or the beginning of new law, *ultra* or *intra vires* [334]. Such a twilight period gradually comes to an end, the end being either the light of the day or the darkness of the night. This end is less fixed than when new powers would be given by constitutional amendment, entering into force on a specific

---

333. See Higgins, note 323, at p. 120 ("the gradual acceptance by states of a deviating norm will, in time, establish a new custom"). See also Salmon, in the *Annuaire de l'Institut de Droit International 2021* (hereinafter *IDI Annuaire 2021*), at p. 250, quoted in note 418 in the next chapter (Sec. 3.7).

334. Cf. R. Higgins, *Problems and Process: International Law and How We Use It*, Oxford, Oxford University Press, 1994, at p. 19: "One of the special characteristics of international law is that violations of law can lead to the formation of new law." Earlier, Higgins, note 323, refers to Tammes, who wrote the following about the coming into being of customary international law: "a new rule is often initially established by a succession of unlawful individual acts. . . . It might be paradoxically said that the first illegal acts must already have contained an element of law"; A. J. P. Tammes, "Decisions of International Organs as a Source of International Law", *Recueil des cours*, Vol. 94 (1958), pp. 265-363, quotation at p. 349.

day [335]. The end has arrived when it is generally recognized either that the new conduct is *ultra vires* and therefore should stop or that it is *intra vires* and can continue. The *vires* concerned could either be implied or customary powers.

Ultimately, it is the acceptance by the membership that practice may require the organization to exercise new, additional powers. This acceptance is normally linked to the organization's constituent instrument and to relevant "building blocks" in its practice. For example, as mentioned above (2.2.1), when the UN Secretary-General proposed the creation by the Security Council of an *ad hoc* criminal tribunal for the former Yugoslavia, he referred to a number of elements as part of the legal basis for the establishment of this tribunal. Thus the creation of the ICTY did not come out of the blue but was grounded in a combination of general acceptance by the members and UN constitutional law and practice. In this way, with the necessary support (when there is general acceptance), a new power may quickly turn into a customary power. This may go very fast (instant customary power, the younger sister of instant customary law) [336]. Exceptionally, the general acceptance that an organization may need to exercise new powers is not linked to the organization's constituent instrument. This is illustrated by the above-mentioned example of the power of the CTBTO Prepcom to use its verification installations not only for nuclear explosions but also for tsunami warning. But in such exceptional cases it is particularly important that there is very robust support from membership, in particular from those members that are most relevant and/or most affected.

Assuming now that customary powers can be based on organizational practice, there is another fundamental question. Since customary powers postdate the attribution of powers in an organization's constituent instrument, how should they be reconciled with the doctrine of attributed powers?

---

335. As is the case for the coming into being of rules of customary international law. See W. G. Werner, "Custom as Rewritten Law: The Text and Paratext of Restatement Reports", *ESIL Reflections*, Vol. 11, No. 3 (29 September 2022), https://esil-sedi.eu/esil-reflection-custom-as-rewritten-law-the-text-and-paratext-of-restatement-reports/, at p. 2: "Customary law . . . is unable to articulate its own beginning."

336. Cf. Engel (1965), note 319, at p. 116: "The closer and more frequent contacts between Members caused by their participation in a permanent organization may facilitate and accelerate the creation of customary law (a sort of pressure-cooked customary law which UN organs help create – as midwives – but which they do not create themselves)."

Two answers may be possible to this question. One answer is to consider customary powers as an exception to the doctrine of attributed powers. A disadvantage of this approach would be that it may wrongly give the impression that these powers are not attributed (and therefore not supported by membership), but originate spontaneously or in some other way, escaping state consent. Another answer is to employ a broad definition of the attribution principle so that it encompasses not only express and implied powers but also customary powers. This answer comes in two variants. Under variant *(a)*, states accept *from the outset, when a new international organization is established*, that it may be agreed later, during the life of the organization, that practice may require the organization to exercise new, additional powers, even without constitutional amendment. This brings customary powers close to Seyersted's inherent powers, but there is a subtle difference. Whereas inherent powers come with "international organizationhood" and therefore exist from the birth of an international organization, customary powers come later, when a specific need arises in practice and broad agreement exists that and how new powers of the organization should meet that need. Under variant *(b)*, member states only accept *later, during the life of an international organization*, the need to attribute new, customary powers to the organization. This variant is perhaps closer to reality than variant *(a)*. It would avoid what may largely be a fiction: the need to accept that states, already upon the creation of an international organization, agree that they may in the future need to agree to customary powers for the organization. It would recognize that member states may only later agree on this, under the pressure of the circumstances.

Some support for the above-mentioned variant *(a)* may be found in what was written long ago by Elihu Lauterpacht [337]:

> "It is probably necessary to recognize that recourse to the practice of international organizations now stands on an independent legal basis; that is to say, that there exists a specific rule of the law of international organization to the effect that recourse to such practice is admissible and that States, *on joining international organizations*, impliedly accept the permissibility of constitutional development in this manner."

---

337. E. Lauterpacht, "The Development of the Law of International Organization by the Decisions of International Tribunals", *Recueil des cours*, Vol. 152 (1976), pp. 379-478, at p. 460 (italics added).

Many years later, the German Bundesverfassungsgericht accepted a somewhat similar "constitutional flexibility" for the European Union in its *Lisbon Urteil*. The Court stated [338]:

> "Every integration into peacekeeping systems ['friedenserhaltene Systeme'], in international or supranational organizations opens up the possibility for the institutions thus created of developing independently, and showing, in doing so, a tendency of political self-enhancement, even, and particularly if, their bodies act according to their mandate. An Act that grants powers to embark on integration, like the Act approving the Treaty of Lisbon, can therefore, in spite of the principle of conferral, only outline a programme in whose boundaries a political development will take place which cannot be determined in advance in every respect."

There are two elements that these two quoted observations have in common. First: organizational practice may evolve in a way not foreseen at the creation of the organization. Second, this is something that states accept or need to accept. It does not at all mean that the member states cannot influence the scope of such constitutional flexibility. Represented in the organization, and in accordance with the powers attributed to the relevant organs, they are fully involved. Constitutional amendment by practice is unlikely to take place in the absence of general support from the membership. However, it is not required that each and every member gives its support, and the necessary support may also emerge over time. After all, at the end of the day, member states are not powerless when confronted with a constitutional amendment by practice to which they are fundamentally opposed. Ultimately, they may decide to leave the organization. Here, a parallel can be drawn with what is laid down in the Declaration of interpretation on withdrawal from the UN, adopted in 1945 at the creation of the UN. The UN Charter does not contain a provision on withdrawal from the organization. However, according to this Declaration of interpretation, it would not be

> "the purpose of the Organization to compel a Member to remain in the Organization if its rights and obligations as such were changed by Charter amendment in which it has not concurred and which it finds itself unable to accept, or if an amendment duly accepted by

---

338. Judgment of 30 June 2009, quotation at para. 237, available at https://www.bundesverfassungsgericht.de/SharedDocs/Entscheidungen/EN/2009/06/es20090630_2bve000208en.html.

the necessary majority in the Assembly or in a general conference fails to secure the ratification necessary to bring such amendment into effect" [339].

Essentially, this reflects the understanding that membership of an international organization does not have to be permanent; members cannot be forced to stay against their sovereign will and may decide to withdraw under certain circumstances.

At the same time, as true as this may be, it is also question-begging. Is Lauterpacht's observation true for *any* practice of an international organization? If not, where is the borderline between a practice that is "admissible" and a practice that is inadmissible? Is this borderline the same as for state practice? It is suggested that this is not the case. State practice is *unilateral*; it is for an individual state only to decide whether it is in accordance with international law to act in a particular way. When Russia invaded Ukraine in 2022, it took the view that this was lawful. In contrast, the practice of international organizations is *multilateral*. International organizations can only act if this has the necessary support of the members and in some cases also of organs of the organization. If these members and/or organs were to consider the proposed act *ultra vires*, it is unlikely that it would be adopted. It is therefore more difficult (although not impossible) for an international organization to act *ultra vires* than it is for a state to act unlawfully. This will be further discussed in Chapter 3, in the context of the role of practice as an interpretative device.

2.6. How to read the "open book" of "messy practice" in the light of express, implied and customary powers?

Returning now to the examples of "messy practice" (discussed above in Sec. 2.2), this section will briefly examine to what extent express, implied and customary powers can bridge the gap with the "clean theory" of attributed powers. Is this a solid bridge or rather some pontoon waiting for more definite structures to be developed?

2.6.1. *The establishment of* ad hoc *criminal tribunals by the UN Security Council*

It could be argued that it is within the *express* powers of the Security Council to establish *ad hoc* criminal tribunals. After all, the text of

---
339. For the text of this Declaration, see 7 UNCIO, at 267.

Article 41 of the Charter provides that the Security Council "may decide what measures not involving the use of armed force are to be employed to give effect to its decisions". This is indeed what the Appeals Chamber of the ICTY concluded in 1995: "the establishment of the International Tribunal falls squarely within the powers of the Security Council under Article 41" [340]. However, if this argument was not accepted, for example because the Security Council lacks powers in the field of international criminal justice and therefore could not delegate such powers to the ICTY, it could be argued that the creation of *ad hoc* criminal tribunals is within the Council's *customary* powers. There was broad support by UN membership for the creation of such tribunals by the Council. As mentioned above (Sec. 2.2.1), when this happened for the first time, when the ICTY was established, the UN Secretary-General referred to a number of elements as part of the legal basis for the establishment of this tribunal. Thus the creation of the ICTY did not come out of the blue but was grounded in a combination of general acceptance by the members and UN constitutional law and practice.

2.6.2. Was the UN Human Rights Council Libya Inquiry Commission acting ultra vires *in discussing NATO operation Unified Protector in its report?*

It was understandable that NATO raised objections against the inclusion of its operation in Libya in the report of the Libya Inquiry Commission given that the legal framework applied by NATO was international humanitarian law whereas the Commission, as a subsidiary body of the Human Rights Council, was competent in the field of human rights. However, it is also understandable that the Commission, investigating "all alleged violations of international human rights law in Libya, to establish the facts and circumstances of such violations and of the crimes perpetrated", did not want to exclude any actor or individuals operating in Libya at the time of the investigation. It could be argued that the Commission's power to also include NATO in its investigation was based on *implied* or *customary* powers. The Commission itself did not pay much attention to this question in its report. It only indicated that it interpreted the scope of its mandate so as to include international humanitarian law, "the *lex specialis* which applies during armed conflict" [341].

---

340. ICTY, *Tadic* Decision October 1995, note 217, at para. 36.
341. See note 225.

2.6.3. Was the UN Working Group on Arbitrary Detention competent to consider the case of Julian Assange?

In this example there was disagreement within the UN Working Group about the scope of its mandate. One of the members of the Working Group argued that the case of Julian Assange did not involve a situation of deprivation of liberty. The majority of the members however gave a broader interpretation of the powers of the Working Group. It is clear that the situation of self-chosen diplomatic asylum is not included in the *explicit* mandate of the Working Group. However, it could well be argued, under the special circumstances of this case, that it is within the *implied* or *customary powers* of the Working Group to give a broader interpretation of its powers, as explained in the report.

2.6.4. Was the OPCW acting ultra vires *by deciding in June 2018 that the OPCW Secretariat may play a role in identifying "those who were the perpetrators, organisers, sponsors or otherwise involved" in the use of chemical weapons?*

It was not within the express powers of the OPCW to adopt its June 2018 Decision. Russia and a minority of other members argued that the OPCW was acting *ultra vires* by adopting this decision and that the organization could only exercise the "attribution powers" mentioned in the decision by amending the Chemical Weapons Convention. A broad majority of the members however took another view. Taking recourse to the teleology of the Convention, they argued that the prevailing political and security circumstances required a reading of the Convention that included the "attribution power". It could be interpreted that such a reading is within the *customary powers* of the organization. Depending on how broadly implied powers are defined, and on how the objectives of the organization are perceived, it could also be argued that such a reading is within the organization's *implied powers*.

2.6.5. Does NATO have the power to carry out "out of area operations"?

This example seems to cross the borderline of cases in which an organization's actions or decisions could be covered by its *implied powers*, as was also concluded by the German Bundesverfassungsgericht [342].

---

[342]. The expansion of NATO tasks to "non-Article 5 operations" "has not been implied in the Treaty"; it "constitutes only a further development *["Fortentwicklung"]* of the NATO Treaty", note 252, Section C.I.2, paras. 141, 139.

There is nothing in the Washington Treaty, NATO's constituent instrument, that suggests that the organization was originally empowered to carry out anything other than self-defence operations. However strategic high-level decisions taken by the organization since the 1990s to initiate "out of area operations" had the unanimous support of the members, who did not consider it necessary to amend the Washington Treaty for this purpose. It can be argued that it is within NATO's *customary powers* to decide to conduct "out of area operations" and *de facto* amend its constitution in this way.

2.6.6. The power of the CTBTO Prepcom to use its verification installations not only for nuclear explosions but also for tsunami warning

As in the previous example, it does not seem possible to argue that it was within the *express* or *implied powers* of the CTBTO PrepCom to use its verification installations for a purpose that is entirely outside the scope of its constituent instrument. The only way to justify the relevant decisions is to consider them as an exercise of *customary powers* of the organization, even though this requires novel ways of reasoning and therefore also needs to rely on very strong support by the membership.

2.7. In conclusion: Practice, the attribution principle, and beyond

This chapter has demonstrated that and how one important facet of the practice of international organizations is its power-generating capacity. It has shown that this facet is dominated by the attribution principle. Although it is not always clear what precisely this principle entails and how it plays out in practice, it is of fundamental importance. It is the key, overarching principle governing the legal basis and scope of powers of international organizations, as is generally recognized in practice, in the case law of the PCIJ and the ICJ, and in doctrine.

At the same time, without detracting from its fundamental importance, a rigid interpretation and application of the attribution principle is not desirable. When it comes to its employment in practice, this principle should not be interpreted and applied in isolation, as an end in itself, but rather against the background of the idea that whatever international organizations do is not the only result of "the rule of (voting) power" but also a corollary of the rule of law. It should be seen against the backdrop of the implementation of the predetermined objectives, functions and powers of international organizations, and of the wider interests that this principle serves, that is, the general need for states to cooperate in a globalizing world. Seen from this wider perspective, it is easier to understand why, for example, the CTBTO PrepCom's activities in the field of tsunami warning should not be considered *ultra vires*. More generally, this wider perspective also explains the general acceptance of implied powers of international organizations. In addition, this chapter has also identified other categories of powers: inherent and customary powers. There is not much support for the doctrine of inherent powers. Not much consideration has yet been given to customary powers, which can be distinguished as an additional category of powers, based on the practice of international organizations.

In the analysis of the power-generating capacity of the practice of international organizations, issues of interpretation have often played a role. The next chapter will fully focus on the role of practice in the interpretation of the law of international organizations as a third facet of their practice.

CHAPTER 3

PRACTICE IN INTERPRETATION:
PRACTICE OF INTERNATIONAL ORGANIZATIONS
AS AN INTERPRETATIVE DEVICE

3.1. Introduction

A third legal facet of the practice of international organizations is its role in the context of the interpretation of their law. Issues of interpretation have already figured prominently in the previous chapter. Questions relating to the powers of international organizations have always been closely intertwined with questions of interpretation. For example, in its second Advisory Opinion, the PCIJ observed [343]:

> "It was much urged in argument that the establishment of the ILO involved an abandonment of rights derived from national sovereignty, and that the competence of the Organization therefore should not be extended by interpretation. There may be some force in this argument, but the question in every case must resolve itself into what the terms of the Treaty actually mean, and it is from this point of view that the Court proposes to examine the question."

And when the UN Security Council established the ICTY, Brazil stated the following [344]:

> "Just as the authority of the Council does not spring from the Council itself but derives from the fact that certain responsibilities have been conferred upon it by all the Members of the United Nations, the powers of the Council cannot be created, recreated or reinterpreted creatively by decisions of the Council itself, but must be based invariably on specific Charter provisions."

This chapter will now fully focus on the role of practice of international organizations in the interpretation of their law. Analysing this third facet will require a different *modus operandi* than the one used in the previous chapter. Unlike the field of powers of international

---
343. PCIJ, Advisory Opinion No. 2, note 192, at p. 23.
344. UN Doc. S/PV.3175, at p. 6.

organizations, "interpretation of international organizations law" as such is not a well-developed sub-area in legal doctrine. Obviously, general textbooks on the law of international organizations pay more or less attention to the interpretation of this law, with some writings focusing on the interpretation of the law of specific organizations [345]. However, while there are books about interpretation in international law in general [346] and about the interpretation of treaties [347], a comprehensive book on the interpretation of international organizations law is yet to be written. Moreover, unlike the field of powers of international organizations, there is not one dominant theory or overarching principle governing the interpretation of the law of international organizations. In addition, partly related to this or not, there has always been debate on the nature of interpretation [348]. Is it not more art than science [349]?

However, these three factors do not imply that those who research issues of interpretation of the law of international organizations have to proceed with empty hands. Their analysis does not need to start from scratch. The most obvious starting point are the rules on treaty

---

345. For example, E. Canal-Forgues, "Sur l'interprétation dans le droit de l'OMC", *Revue générale de droit international public*, Vol. 1 (2001), pp. 5-24; G. Letsas, *A Theory of Interpretation of the European Convention on Human Rights*, Oxford, Oxford University Press, 2007; M. C. Wood, "The Interpretation of Security Council Resolutions", *Max Planck Yearbook of United Nations Law*, Vol. 2 (1998), pp. 73-95. In a follow-up analysis eighteen years later, Wood writes that developments in these eighteen years confirm his earlier conclusions. Moreover, "questions of interpretation have become more important and more frequent. There is perhaps a greater awareness of the need to bear in mind, when interpreting Security Council resolutions, the differences between treaties and resolutions, and indeed the differences between various kinds of resolutions". See M. Wood, "The Interpretation of Security Council Resolutions, Revisited", *Max Planck Yearbook of United Nations Law*, Vol. 20 (2016), pp. 3-35, quotation at p. 35.
346. For example, S. Sur, *L'interprétation en droit international public*, Paris, Librairie générale de droit et de jurisprudence, 1974.
347. For example, R. K. Gardiner, *Treaty Interpretation*, 2nd ed., Oxford, Oxford University Press, 2015.
348. The ILC Commentary on the Draft Articles on the Law of Treaties even starts its commentary on the rules on treaty interpretation by observing the following: "The utility and even the existence of rules of international law governing the interpretation of treaties are sometimes questioned." See *Yb. ILC 1966*, Vol. 2, at p. 38, para. 1.
349. *Id.*, at p. 38, para. 4: principles and maxims of interpretation "are, for the most part, principles of logic and good sense valuable only as guides to assist in appreciating the meaning which the parties may have intended to attach to the expressions that they employed in a document. Their suitability for use in any given case hinges on a variety of considerations which first have to be appreciated by the interpreter of the document; ... recourse to many of these principles is discretionary rather than obligatory and the interpretation of documents is to some extent an art, not an exact science". See also P. Merkouris, "Introduction: Interpretation is a Science, is an Art, is a Science", in M. Fitzmaurice *et al.* (eds.), *Treaty Interpretation and the Vienna Convention on the Law of Treaties: 30 Years On*, Leiden, Brill Nijhoff, 2010, pp. 1-13.

interpretation included in the 1969 and 1986 Vienna Conventions on the Law of Treaties. Therefore, Section 3.2 will first give a brief general overview of these rules, and the place of subsequent practice therein. The Vienna rules on treaty interpretation are relevant both for treaties to which international organizations are parties (instruments of their external relations) and for their own rules. Section 3.3 will briefly pay attention to the former. The remaining sections will be devoted to the role of practice of international organizations in the interpretation of their own rules. First, Section 3.4 will focus on the constituent instruments of international organizations. Is a special approach required for the interpretation of these instruments? Are there any limits to the dynamic or "evolutive" interpretation of their provisions? The role of organizational practice in the interpretation of the further rules of international organizations (resolutions, decisions, etc.) will be discussed in Section 3.5. Next, Section 3.6 will examine what types of organs are relevant for the development of an organization's subsequent practice. Section 3.7 will focus on the need of support by membership of an interpretation in the organization's practice. Should all members support a certain practice before it can be accepted as a way to "read" this instrument, or is a certain majority of the membership sufficient? Are there any limits to this interpretative device? Section 3.8 will offer some concluding observations.

3.2. The rules on treaty interpretation in the 1969 and 1986 Vienna Conventions and practice of international organizations

When a treaty provision is applied, it is also interpreted. Its meaning is "translated" to a factual situation. Parties do not operate in a normative vacuum; their conduct in this factual situation is not unguided. The relevant treaty provision prescribes how to act. Needless to say, this act of "translation" is hardly ever a plain and simple exercise, in which the law automatically dictates how parties should act. It requires interpretation of the relevant treaty provision(s). Interpretation is not a purely mechanical operation and has been characterized in different ways: a technique, an art, or otherwise.

As long as treaties have existed, there has been treaty interpretation. A wide variety of means of treaty interpretation have been used in practice. An opportunity to codify rules on treaty interpretation came when the ILC started to work on the law of treaties, as one of the first three topics that it selected in 1949 for its codification activity [350]. This work resulted in the 1969 and 1986 Vienna Conventions on the Law of Treaties, which will be discussed in Subsection 3.2.1. Subsection 3.2.2 will focus specifically on the role of the practice of international organizations in treaty interpretation.

3.2.1. The Vienna rules on treaty interpretation

As mentioned, the most obvious starting point in an analysis of the role of the practice of international organizations in the interpretation of their law are the rules on treaty interpretation included in the 1969 and 1986 Vienna Conventions on the Law of Treaties. Obviously, even though these rules are a good starting point, they are also the tangible result of centuries of evolution of relevant practice and writings, and of years of codification preparations in the ILC, in the General Assembly, and finally in Diplomatic Conferences in Vienna. Practice and writings reflect widely diverging views on treaty interpretation. Should the intentions of the parties prevail, the text, the object and purpose, or even other factors? The draft rules on treaty interpretation prepared by the ILC in the 1960s are a synthesis of these different views and means of interpretation. They were adopted almost without any change in Vienna in 1969. The same text was adopted in 1986, as part of the Vienna II Convention.

Articles 31 and 32 of the 1969 and 1986 Vienna Conventions provide the following [351]:

> "*Article 31*
>
> *General rule of interpretation*
>
> 1. A treaty shall be interpreted in good faith in accordance with the ordinary meaning to be given to the terms of the treaty in their context and in the light of its object and purpose.
>
> 2. The context for the purpose of the interpretation of a treaty shall comprise, in addition to the text, including its preamble and annexes:

---

350. *Yb. ILC 1949*, Vol. 1, at p. 281.
351. A third article dealing with interpretation, Art. 33 ("Interpretation of treaties authenticated in two or more languages") will not be discussed here as it is less relevant in the context of the role of practice of international organizations in the interpretation of treaties.

(a) any agreement relating to the treaty which was made between all the parties in connection with the conclusion of the treaty;

(b) any instrument which was made by one or more parties in connection with the conclusion of the treaty and accepted by the other parties as an instrument related to the treaty.

3. There shall be taken into account, together with the context:

(a) any subsequent agreement between the parties regarding the interpretation of the treaty or the application of its provisions;

(b) any subsequent practice in the application of the treaty which establishes the agreement of the parties regarding its interpretation;

(c) any relevant rules of international law applicable in the relations between the parties.

4. A special meaning shall be given to a term if it is established that the parties so intended.

Article 32

Supplementary means of interpretation

Recourse may be had to supplementary means of interpretation, including the preparatory work of the treaty and the circumstances of its conclusion, in order to confirm the meaning resulting from the application of article 31, or to determine the meaning when the interpretation according to article 31:

(a) leaves the meaning ambiguous or obscure; or

(b) leads to a result which is manifestly absurd or unreasonable."

Article 31, paragraph 1, lays down the key rule for treaty interpretation. Essentially, it has three elements: the text, the context and the object and purpose. The text is described as "the ordinary meaning to be given to the terms of the treaty". The context is defined in paragraph 2. Paragraph 3 refers to three additional means of interpretation that must be taken into account together with the context, the second of which is "any subsequent practice in the application of the treaty which establishes the agreement of the parties regarding its interpretation". There is no hierarchy between paragraphs 2 and 3, as is clear from the opening words of paragraph 3 ("together with the context"). The main difference between paragraphs 2 and 3 is that paragraph 2 is about agreements *(a)* and instruments *(b)* that were made "in connection with the conclusion of the treaty", therefore *at the same time* as when the treaty was concluded. Subparagraphs *(a)* and *(b)* of paragraph 3 are about relevant *later* developments, *after* the treaty has been concluded: "any subsequent agreement" *(a)* and "any subsequent practice" *(b)*. Subparagraph *(c)* of paragraph 3 is not limited to such later developments [352]. Although Article 31 is presented as a "General rule of interpretation" (not: general *rules* [353]), paragraph 4 leaves flexibility to treaty parties, to give "special meaning" to a term, that is, a meaning that might be different from the "ordinary" (para. 1) meaning that would otherwise be given by application of the means of interpretation laid down in paragraphs 1-3.

While there is no hierarchy among the different means of interpretation mentioned in Article 31, there *is* a hierarchy between Articles 31 and 32. Article 32 covers *supplementary* means of interpretation, two of which are explicitly mentioned (the *travaux préparatoires* and the circumstances under which the treaty is concluded). These supplementary means are not the first to be employed when it comes to treaty interpretation. They only come into play later, either to confirm the meaning that results from the application of Article 31, or to determine the meaning of the relevant treaty provision if the application of Article 31 "leaves the meaning ambiguous or obscure", or if this "leads to a result which is manifestly absurd or unreasonable".

While it is a remarkable achievement that agreement was reached on the text of Articles 31 and 32, and while these rules on treaty interpretation are considered to be a reflection of customary international law and are widely supported and extensively applied [354], it is also clear that they themselves also leave a lot of room for interpretation. For example, what may be a provision's ordinary meaning for some may

---

352. See ILC Commentary, note 348, at p. 42, para. 16.
353. See ILC Commentary, note 348, at p. 39, para. 8 ("The Commission, by heading the article 'General rule of interpretation' in the singular and by underlining the connection between paragraphs 1 and 2 and again between paragraph 3 and the two previous paragraphs, intended to indicate that the application of the means of interpretation in the article would be a single combined operation. All the various elements, as they were present in any given case, would be thrown into the crucible, and their interaction would give the legally relevant interpretation"); Corten and Klein, note 28, at p. 814, para. 21; Gardiner, note 347, at pp. 35-38.
354. See e.g. I. Sinclair, *The Vienna Convention on the Law of Treaties*, 2nd ed., Manchester, Manchester University Press, 1984, at p. 154 ("The Convention rules do mark a major advance in resolving some of the doctrinal disputes which have divided jurists in the past in their approach to treaty interpretation").

be *extra*ordinary for others. Some parties to treaties may have another recollection of their original intention than others, and the object and purpose of a treaty are far from automatically leading to one specific interpretation. Much is in the eye of the beholder [355]. Those who, unlike the present author, hold a cynical (or, as they might prefer, realistic) view will not only say that treaties are "disagreements reduced to writing" [356] but may also see the interpretation of what has been written down as a technique to continue these disagreements.

At the same time, this flexibility is what may also to some extent explain the success of these provisions, allowing treaties to stay relevant and evolve with the needs of a changing international society. In addition, fundamentally, these provisions offer a predetermined legal framework to the "beholders" so that treaty interpretation does not take place fully in limbo but in a more organized way, in accordance with the rule of law. Those who see treaty interpretation as an art now have "rules for practicing that art" at their disposal [357]. These rules are a "common lexicon" for these "beholders" and may assist courts "to give more substantiated and clearly argued judgments" [358].

3.2.2. *Treaty interpretation and the practice of international organizations*

In the almost two decades of *travaux préparatoires* of the 1969 Vienna Convention, no attention was given to the role of practice of international organizations in treaty interpretation [359]. This may come as no surprise, as this Vienna Convention only covers treaties concluded between states. However, throughout these negotiations in the 1950s and 1960s, the rapidly developing treaty practice of international

---

355. See therefore Klabbers's warm plea for the virtues of the interpreter: "individuals should approach the interpretation of texts with humility, acquiescence, integrity and candour, as Powell proposes, rather than with the mechanic sense of applying a rule as if it were mathematics"; J. Klabbers, "Virtuous Interpretation", in M. Fitzmaurice *et al.* (eds.), *Treaty Interpretation and the Vienna Convention on the Law of Treaties: 30 Years On*, Leiden, Brill Nijhoff, 2010, pp. 17-37, quotation at p. 37.
356. P. Allott refers to this expression in "The Concept of International Law", *European Journal of International Law*, Vol. 10 (1999), pp. 31-50, at p. 43.
357. Cf. Ago's criticism of the view ("too glibly") that treaty interpretation is an art: "The question was whether there were any rules for practicing that art" (*Yb. ILC 1964*, Vol. 1, at p. 23, para. 34).
358. P. Merkouris, "Debating Interpretation: On the Road to Ithaca", *Leiden Journal of International Law*, Vol. 35 (2022), pp. 461-468, at p. 466.
359. On these negotiations, see Sinclair, note 354; Gardiner, note 347, esp. chap. 2; Corten and Klein, note 28. More specifically on the attention paid to international organizations treaties, see Brölmann, note 27.

Legal Facets of the Practice of International Organizations 189

organizations was often taken into consideration more generally. From the beginning, the question of whether the outcome of the *travaux* should also cover treaties concluded by international organizations was discussed. Even at the concluding Vienna Conference, after the ILC had decided to limit its draft to state treaties, the US delegation proposed an amendment to enlarge the scope of the Convention to "treaties concluded between two or more states or other subjects of international law" [360]. This amendment was rejected, but at the same time a recommendation to the General Assembly was adopted, to refer to the ILC "the study, in consultation with the principal international organizations, of the question of treaties concluded between States and international organizations or between two or more international organizations" [361].

Even though the treaty practice of international organizations was taken into account in the *travaux* of the 1969 Convention, this was mostly limited to the fundamental question of whether some or all international organizations have the capacity to conclude treaties, and to the question of to what extent treaties concluded by international organizations have special characteristics, distinguishing them from state treaties. No serious attention was given to more specific issues such as the role of practice of international organizations in treaty interpretation. The preparations for the 1986 Convention could have been an occasion to study this practice, but that did not happen. These preparations focused on other issues [362]. At the end of the day, the

---
360. UN Doc. A/Conf/39/C.1/L.15, quoted by Brölmann, note 27.
361. Resolution annexed to the Final Act of the Conference, UN Doc. A/Conf.39/26 and Corr. 2.
362. See G. Limburg, "The United Nations Conference on the Law of Treaties Between States and International Organizations or between International Organizations", *Netherlands International Law Review*, Vol. 33 (1986), pp. 195-203; G. E. do Nascimento e Silva, "The 1986 Vienna Convention and the Treaty-Making Power of International Organizations", *German Yearbook of International Law*, Vol. 29 (1986), pp. 68-85; J. P. Dobbert, "Evolution of the Treaty-Making Capacity of International Organizations", in *The Law and the Sea: Essays in Memory of Jean Carroz*, Rome, FAO, 1987, pp. 22-42; Gaja, note 169; P. Reuter, "La conférence de Vienne sur les traités des organisations internationales et la sécurité des engagements conventionnels", in F. Capotorti *et al.* (eds.), *Du droit international au droit de l'intégration : Liber Amicorum Pierre Pescatore*, Baden-Baden, Nomos, 1987, pp. 545-564; W. Riphagen, "The Second Round of Treaty Law", in F. Capotorti *et al.* (eds.), *Du droit international au droit de l'intégration : Liber Amicorum Pierre Pescatore*, Baden-Baden, Nomos, 1987, pp. 565-581; Ph. Manin, "The European Communities and the Vienna Convention on the Law of Treaties between States and International Organizations or between International Organizations", *Common Market Law Review*, Vol. 24 (1987), pp. 457-481; K. Zemanek, "The United Nations Conference on the Law of Treaties between States and International Organizations or between Inter-

substance of the 1986 Convention was almost completely identical to that of its older sister. As mentioned, the rules on treaty interpretation are exactly the same.

A distinction must be made between two types of practice of an international organization [363]. A first type of practice is when a particular treaty provision is applied – and therefore interpreted – by the organization for the first time ("new practice"). An example is the first case in which a permanent member of the UN Security Council abstained from voting on a non-procedural matter. In this case, all means of interpretation of the relevant treaty provision (in the example: Art. 27.3 of the Charter) can potentially be employed in search of support for the new practice, except one, subsequent practice, because there is no subsequent practice yet or because the new practice deviates from the existing practice. A second type of practice of an international organization occurs when a particular treaty provision has already been applied before, and may even have become – more or less – a routine. In this scenario, the earlier application(s) – and therefore: interpretation(s) – of the rules are relevant as "subsequent practice" and may be relied upon as a means of treaty interpretation.

In the case law, discussions and literature about the role of subsequent practice in treaty interpretation, the focus has almost entirely been on the subsequent practice of *states*. For example, in the Commentary by the ILC to the 1986 Vienna Convention on Treaties between States and International Organizations or between International Organizations, there is hardly any reference to the practice of international organizations in the context of "subsequent practice" as a means of treaty interpretation [364]. In addition, as is further discussed in the next chapter, in its 1996 Advisory Opinion at the request of the World Health

---

national Organizations: The Unrecorded History of its 'General Agreement'", in K.-H. Böckstiegel *et al.* (eds.), *Law of Nations, Law of International Organizations, World's Economic Law: Liber Amicorum Honouring Ignaz Seidl-Hohenveldern*, Dordrecht, Kluwer Law International, 1988, pp. 665-679; F. Morgenstern, "The Convention on the Law of Treaties between States and International Organizations or between International Organizations", in Y. Dinstein (ed.), *International Law at a Time of Perplexity: Essays in Honour of Shabtai Rosenne*, Dordrecht, Nijhoff, 1989, pp. 435-447; G. E. do Nascimento e Silva, "The 1969 and the 1986 Conventions on the Law of Treaties: A Comparison", in Y. Dinstein (ed.), *International Law at a Time of Perplexity: Essays in Honour of Shabtai Rosenne*, Dordrecht, Nijhoff, 1989, pp. 461-487; Brölmann, note 27; Corten and Klein, note 28.
363. See also the Introduction to this special course.
364. See *Yb. ILC 1982*, Vol. 2, Part 2. The 1969 Vienna Convention is limited to treaties concluded by states. Nevertheless, in the preparations for this Convention, the Netherlands government considered with respect to the draft provision that finally became Art. 31.3 *(b)*: "that to require the 'understanding of all the parties' may

Legal Facets of the Practice of International Organizations 191

Organization (WHO), the ICJ referred extensively to the practice of the WHO but it did so in terms of subsequent (state) practice under Article 31 of the 1969 Vienna Convention. This focus on subsequent practice of states is in line with the more general primary orientation to states in the two Vienna Conventions, as is also reflected in the decision to first conclude a convention on the law of treaties between states, using this as a basis for a later convention on the law of treaties to which international organizations are parties [365]. In spite of the similarity between the Vienna I and II Conventions, the wish to make clear in treaty law that international organizations are fundamentally different from states is also apparent from the terminology for the expression of consent to be bound, which is different for international organizations ("act of formal confirmation") [366] than for states. Furthermore, it was decided that exclusively state ratifications are relevant for the entry into force of the Vienna II Convention. International organizations'

---

restrict unduly the influence of what is 'conventional' (customary usage?) within an international organization" (*Yb. ILC 1966*, Vol. 2, at p. 98, para. 17).

365. While there is indeed such a general primary orientation to states, it is also clear from the *travaux préparatoires* of the Vienna II Convention that states held differing views as to what extent international organizations should be seen as similar to states for the purpose of the law of treaties. Cf. the observations by Reuter in this regard: "Certains gouvernements sensibles à l'extraordinaire expansion de l'activité conventionnelle des organisations internationales souhaitaient consacrer, au regard du droit des traités, dans les termes les plus simples, l'assimilation des organisations aux Etats. D'autres au contraire, étaient frappés du caractère 'artificiel' des organisations, de leur dépendance totale des Etats qui les créent presque toujours par un traité, impriment à chacune une physionomie originale; mais surtout, ces gouvernements redoutaient leur dynamisme spontané, les conduisant à dépasser le cadre des traités qui les instituent et à bouleverser au profit de leurs secrétariats ou de certains organes la répartition interne des pouvoirs et des fonctions. Ce dernier état d'esprit a marqué d'une manière permanente certaines délégations, mais rares sont celles qui lui ont complètement échappé", note 362, at p. 546.

366. Defined in Art. 2.1*bbis* as "an international act corresponding to that of ratification by a State, whereby an international organization establishes on the international plane its consent to be bound by a treaty". In the ILC there was "considerable discussion" about the use of the term ratification by international organizations, see *Yb. ILC 1982*, Vol. 2, Part 2, at p. 19, para. 96. The Commission considered "that the term 'ratification' should be reserved for States, since in accordance with a long historical tradition it always denotes an act emanating from the highest organs of the State, generally the Head of State, and there are no corresponding organs in international organizations" (*id.*, at para. 8). The Commission therefore created the term "act of formal confirmation". Riphagen (leading the delegation of the Netherlands to the UN Diplomatic Conference where the Vienna Convention was adopted) expressed annoyance at this special terminology for a consent to be bound by an international organization: "if one can express one's consent to be bound 'by any means if so agreed' [Art. 11.1], what is the difference between an 'act of formal confirmation' and a 'ratification' (or, for that matter, the sending of a bunch of flowers)? Even a perfunctory knowledge of information theory could have saved our international legislators from such nonsense", note 362, at p. 570.

expressions of their consent to be bound do not count towards the thirty-five ratifications that are required [367]. Therefore, while there are currently forty-five parties to the Vienna II Convention, it has not yet entered into force because thirty-three of these parties are states and twelve are international organizations [368].

The focus on *state* practice is not unwarranted. States are the principal centres of political authority, the supreme form of political organization in the world. However, international organizations have become increasingly relevant in our primarily state-organized world to cope with the consequences of globalization and increasing interdependence and to deal with global challenges that require global solutions (such as peace and security, climate change and infectious diseases). The subsequent practice of international organizations has become important, including for treaty interpretation, although this has not always been fully appreciated and well understood.

There are numerous questions that arise when more closely analysing the role of practice of international organizations in treaty interpretation. Some of these are similar to those arising in the context of subsequent state practice, for example whether there are any limits to this interpretative device and how robust a certain practice should be before it can be accepted as a way to "read" the relevant treaty. Other questions are unique to international organizations. For example, questions relating to the role of practice of international organizations in the interpretation of their constituent instruments, the question of whether all members or only a certain majority need to support a certain interpretation of the constituent instrument by organs of the organization when they apply it in practice, and the question of what organs of an organization are relevant for the development of its subsequent practice. The remainder of this chapter will focus on the latter type of questions.

In the context of treaty interpretation, the practice of international organizations is relevant in a number of situations. First, where an international organization is a party to a treaty, its practice together with that of the other party or parties is a means of interpretation of the treaty if this establishes the agreement of the parties (Sec. 3.3). Second, the practice of international organizations is relevant for the interpretation

---

367. Vienna II Convention, Art. 85.
368. See the Status of Treaties Deposited with the Secretary-General at https://treaties.un.org/Pages/ViewDetails.aspx?src=TREATY&mtdsg_no=XXIII-3&chapter=23&clang=_en.

of their constituent instruments. Even though the organization itself is formally not a party to its own constituent instrument, its practice is highly relevant for the interpretation of this instrument (Sec. 3.4). Third, it is relevant for the interpretation of other rules and decisions of international organizations (Sec. 3.5).

3.3. The role of practice of international organizations in the interpretation of treaties to which they are parties

The practice of international organizations is not only relevant for the interpretation of their own law but also for the interpretation of treaties to which they are parties [369]. International organizations are parties to a great variety of treaties. Examples are headquarters agreements (concluded between an international organization and its host state) and Status of Forces Agreements (SOFAs) concluded by the UN with host states for its peacekeeping operations (but also by military organizations such as NATO). Treaties may also be concluded between international organizations only. Examples are the relationship agreements concluded by the UN with its specialized agencies and with other organizations (such as the International Atomic Energy Agency, the World Trade Organization (WTO) and the OPCW). Another example is the Agreement between the International Criminal Court and the European Union on Cooperation and Assistance [370]. Crawford has observed succinctly that "the parties to a treaty ... own the treaty. It is their treaty. It is not anyone else's treaty" [371]. Therefore, not only the practice of the states that are parties to all the above-mentioned treaties shall be taken into account in the interpretation of these treaties, but also the practice of the international organizations that are parties to these treaties. It is their treaty as well.

The question could still be raised whether it matters that one (or more) of the parties to a treaty is not a state but an international organization. After all, what counts is that the "subsequent practice in the application of the treaty" must establish "the agreement of the parties regarding

---

369. Such treaties are instruments for the conduct of the external relations of international organizations. See further Schermers and Blokker, note 2, at chap. 12.
370. Concluded on 10 April 2006, https://www.icc-cpi.int/sites/default/files/NR/rdonlyres/6EB80CC1-D717-4284-9B5C-03CA028E155B/140157/ICCPRES010106_English.pdf.
371. J. Crawford, "A Consensualist Interpretation of Article 31(3) of the Vienna Convention on the Law of Treaties", in G. Nolte (ed.), *Treaties and Subsequent Practice*, Oxford, Oxford University Press, 2013, pp. 29-33, at p. 31.

its interpretation"[372]. Since this means of interpretation is all about the agreement of the parties, does it make a difference that one of them is an international organization? This question is still waiting to be answered. There are many treaties to which international organizations are parties, and therefore there is extensive subsequent practice in the application of these treaties. However, not only is there no complete collection in which all these treaties are published, but there is also no general repository for the relevant treaty *practice* of international organizations. In the absence of this information, there are two reasons why it should not simply be assumed that it does not matter that one (or more) of the parties to a treaty is an international organization: the layered nature of international organizations and their great variety.

First, although international organizations are independent international legal persons, their members are mostly sovereign states. No matter how supranational international organizations are, as long as they are international organizations they have sovereign member states. Even in the European Union, the member states are still sometimes called the "masters of the treaties" *(Herren der Verträge)*. Behind their legal personality veils, more or less thin, the member states remain visible. To varying degrees, they control the life and work of the organization. Being such a "layered" treaty partner may well have implications for the organization's application of a treaty.

Second, there is an immense variety of international organizations, in terms of membership, functions, powers, structure and more. This may have implications for the way in which they apply treaties to which they are parties. A very small technical organization that does not have its own legal counsel may rely to a significant extent on the host state when it comes to the application and interpretation of its treaties. This is likely to be very different for organizations such as the UN and the EU.

The above-mentioned two reasons justify paying special attention to the subsequent practice of international organizations. On the one hand, the same rules of treaty interpretation apply to states and international organizations. However, the way in which these rules themselves are interpreted, including the rule on subsequent practice, also depends on the subsequent practice in the application of the Vienna II Convention. Obviously, this Convention has not yet entered into force, but, leaving this aside, little is known about the treaty practice of international organizations.

---

372. Art. 31.3 *(b)* of the two Vienna Conventions.

3.4. The role of practice of international organizations in the interpretation of their constituent instruments

3.4.1. A special approach for the interpretation of constituent instruments?

Apart from treaties to which international organizations are parties, there is an important category of treaties to which almost exclusively states are parties but for the interpretation of which the practice of the relevant organization is key: constituent instruments of international organizations [373]. To what extent is it true that the parties to such constituent instruments "own the treaty"? Is it really "their treaty", and not "anyone else's" [374]? It is true to the extent that the founders of an international organization may also agree to dissolve it. This has sometimes happened. For example, the International Institute of Agriculture was dissolved in 1946, the Organization for European Economic Cooperation in 1960 and the League of Nations in 1946. However, even though these examples show that the founders of an organization indeed "own the treaty" in this way, they also demonstrate that these dissolutions did not mean the end of institutionalized international cooperation in these areas but rather the transition to more intense institutionalized cooperation through the creation of new international organizations: respectively the Food and Agriculture Organization (FAO) of the UN, the Organisation for Economic Co-operation and Development and the United Nations. It rarely happens that an international organization is dissolved because its members no longer want to cooperate in the area concerned [375].

Leaving aside the special situation of dissolutions, during the life of international organizations its constituent instrument is continuously interpreted, not only by its members but also by the organization itself. In this sense, this instrument is owned as much by the members as by the organization itself, even though the latter is not a party to its founding instrument. It may be presumed that this is in fact what the

---

373. Another category of treaties for which this is also true are multilateral agreements on privileges and immunities (such as e.g. the 1946 Convention on Privileges and Immunities of the UN and the 2002 Agreement on the Privileges and Immunities of the International Criminal Court).
374. Crawford, note 371.
375. See for a further analysis, R. A. Wessel, "Dissolution and Succession: The Transmigration of the Soul of International Organizations", in J. Klabbers and Å. Wallendahl (eds.), *Research Handbook on the Law of International Organizations*, Cheltenham, Elgar, 2011, pp. 342-362.

founding states wanted when establishing the organization, giving it legal personality and powers of its own. "You can't have your cake and eat it." Once created, an international organization has a legal life of its own, and its subsequent practice must be taken into account when interpreting its constituent instrument. This does not mean that the position of the members is no longer relevant. On the contrary, their views about interpretation of the constituent instrument are of key importance. But it would be a denial of the organization's independent position, its autonomy, if its own practice was not taken into account. The role of this practice in the interpretation of constituent instruments will now be analysed in more detail.

Constituent instruments of international organizations are a special type of treaty. It has long been recognized that their special characteristics should affect the interpretation of their provisions [376]. For example, Judge Hersch Lauterpacht observed in 1955 that "[a] proper interpretation of a constitutional instrument must take into account not only the formal letter of the original instrument, but also *its operation in actual practice* and in the light of the revealed tendencies in the life of the organization" [377]. However, these special characteristics were not sufficiently special for the drafters of the 1969 and 1986 Vienna Conventions to prepare special rules for the interpretation of constitutions of international organizations. The above-discussed Vienna rules on treaty interpretation apply to treaties generally. At the same time, these Vienna Conventions open two doors for taking into account the special nature of constitutions of international organizations. First, both Vienna Conventions apply to any treaty "which is the constituent instrument of an international organization and to any treaty adopted within an international organization *without prejudice to any relevant rules of the organization*" [378]. Constituent instruments or other rules of international organizations may therefore contain provisions that deviate from the Vienna rules on treaty interpretation. Second, these Vienna rules encompass a rich variety of means of interpretation. The question may

---

376. See e.g. R. Monaco, "Le caractère constitutionnel des actes institutifs d'Organisations internationals", in *Mélanges offerts à Charles Rousseau – La communauté internationale*, Paris, Pedone, 1974, pp. 153-172; Rosenne, note 26, at pp. 181-258; Amerasinghe, note 96, in particular pp. 25-61; Brölmann, note 27, in particular pp. 113-123.

377. *South West Africa – Voting procedure*, Advisory Opinion, 7 June 1955, Separate Opinion of Judge Lauterpacht, *ICJ Reports 1955*, p. 67 *et seq.*, quotation at p. 106 (italics added).

378. Art. 5 of both Vienna Conventions (italics added).

Legal Facets of the Practice of International Organizations   197

be raised as to whether these different means of interpretation have the same weight and should be used in the same way when interpreting constituent instruments of international organizations as when interpreting other treaties.

Generally, practice and doctrine support the view that the interpretation of constitutions of international organizations requires a different approach [379]. According to this view, particular attention must be given to the object and purpose of the relevant constitution and the aims of the international organization concerned [380]. One comprehensive study of the case law of a number of international courts has demonstrated that these courts base their interpretation of the relevant constituent instruments on one fundamental principle: to give a meaning to constitutional provisions that is most favourable for giving effect to the objectives of the organization ("la poursuite de l'effectivité des finalités institutionnelles") [381]. At the same time, these Courts have also used this principle to establish limits to the scope of interpretation (*auto-limitation judiciaire*, or self-restraint; judicial caution) [382].

---

379. See the literature mentioned above, note 376, and below, note 380. A few authors criticize this view. See e.g. G. Arangio-Ruiz, "The Normative Role of the General Assembly of the United Nations and the Declaration on Principles of Friendly Relations: With an Appendix on the Concept of International Law and the Theory of International Organization", *Recueil des cours*, Vol. 137 (1972-III), pp. 409-742, in particular at pp. 708-720; also Klabbers, note 293, at pp. 89-90.

380. P. Pescatore, *Les objectifs de la Communauté européenne comme principes d'interprétation dans la jurisprudence de la Cour de Justice* (W. J. Miscellanea Ganshof van der Meersch, Vol. 2), Brussels, Bruylant, 1972, at pp. 325-363; Monaco, note 376, esp. at p. 170; K. Skubiszewski, "Remarks on the Interpretation of the United Nations Charter", in R. Bernhardt *et al.* (eds.), *Völkerrecht als Rechtsordnung, Internationale Gerichtsbarkeit, Menschenrechte, Festschrift für Hermann Mosler*, Heidelberg, Springer, 1983, pp. 891-902, esp. at pp. 891-894; G. Fitzmaurice, *The Law and Procedure of the International Court of Justice*, Vol. 1, Cambridge, Grotius, 1986, at p. 341; Seidl-Hohenveldern and Loibl, note 199, at p. 247; Alvarez, note 326, chap. 2 ("Constitutional" Interpretation), at pp. 65-108 (2005) (an earlier version of this chapter was published in J.-M. Coicaud and V. Heiskanen (eds.), *The Legitimacy of International Organizations*, Tokyo/New York, UN University Press, 2001, at pp. 104-154); Ruffert and Walter, note 249, at pp. 63-64; T. Clark, "The Teleological Turn in the Law of International Organisations", *International and Comparative Law Quarterly*, Vol. 70 (2021), pp. 533-567. According to Judge Weeramantry, in the interpretation of constitutions of international organizations, "particularly one which sets before itself certain sociological or humanitarian goals, the task of interpretation should be guided by the object and purpose. . . . A literal interpretation, using strict methods of anchoring interpretation to the letter rather than the spirit . . . would be inappropriate", ICJ, *WHO Nuclear Weapons*, note 183, Dissenting Opinion, quotation at p. 148.

381. D. Simon, *L'interprétation judiciaire des traités d'organisations internationales*, Paris, Pedone, 1981, at p. 317. The same conclusion is drawn by P. Sands and P. Klein, *Bowett's Law of International Institutions*, 6th ed., London, Sweet & Maxwell, 2009, at pp. 455-456.

382. Simon, note 381, at pp. 309-315.

The most fundamental special characteristic of constitutions of international organizations is the fact that (almost always) a new international legal person is created. By doing so, the founding fathers of international organizations implicitly accept that it is not only for them to give interpretations of the relevant constitution but also for organs of the organization they have created. It is also their treaty. Indeed, it is often these organs that interpret constitutional provisions in their practice. Virally, representing France at the UN Conference that adopted the 1969 Vienna Convention, correctly stated at this conference [383]:

> "At the conclusion stage it [the constituent instrument of an organization] was comparable to any other treaty, but the position changed when it entered into force. Ordinary treaties were applied by the States parties to them through their executive, legislative and judicial organs. A treaty which was the constituent instrument of an organization was applied both by the parties as members of the organization and by organs of the organization. That produced a whole series of consequences which the draft convention [Vienna I] could not cover."

In its 1962 *Certain Expenses* Advisory Opinion the ICJ famously stated [384]:

> "In the legal systems of States, there is often some procedure for determining the validity of even a legislative or governmental act, but no analogous procedure is to be found in the structure of the United Nations. Proposals made during the drafting of the Charter to place the ultimate authority to interpret the Charter in the International Court of Justice were not accepted; the opinion which the Court is in course of rendering is an advisory opinion. *As anticipated in 1945, therefore, each organ must, in the first place at least, determine its own jurisdiction.*"

These words apply not only to the UN General Assembly but also to organs of other international organizations that – like the UN – lack judicial review procedures. In general, it is these organs themselves that first of all give an interpretation of the rules of the constitution that they apply, unless constitutions give specific powers in this respect to other organs.

---

383. UN Doc. A/CONF.39/11, at pp. 45-46.
384. ICJ, *Certain Expenses* Advisory Opinion, note 308, at p. 168 (emphasis added).

3.4.2. Interpretation of constituent instruments: The 1996 ICJ Advisory Opinion requested by the WHO

A key question relevant for this chapter focusing on questions of interpretation is how the organs of the newly created legal person interpret the constituent instrument of the organization. In their interpretative work, do they operate like states interpreting their treaties? Do they follow, explicitly or implicitly, the rules on interpretation of the two Vienna Conventions? Are some of these rules particularly relevant for these organs? The 1996 Advisory Opinion of the ICJ requested by the WHO is of particular importance in this context. The next chapter will discuss this Advisory Opinion more generally. Its relevance for the interpretation of constituent instruments will be analysed here.

This Advisory Opinion offers much more than merely an answer to the question about the legality of the use of nuclear weapons posed by the WHO. It includes a number of general observations highly relevant for the law of international organizations, one of which relates to the interpretation of their constituent instruments. Before the conclusion of the 1969 Vienna Convention, in particular in 1948, 1950 and 1962, the ICJ had already made some general observations on the interpretation of the UN Charter [385]. Now, in 1996, the Court not only states that "[f]rom a formal standpoint" constituent instruments of international organizations are multilateral treaties, "to which the well-established rules of treaty interpretation apply" [386], but also fully details and appreciates their special nature. While previously, in *Certain Expenses*, the Court had only observed in an "elliptical statement" [387] that such constitutions have "certain special characteristics" [388], it now specifies what these characteristics are. Having said that constituent instruments

---

385. In its 1948 and 1950 Advisory Opinions, the Court strongly relied on the text of the relevant Charter provision (see ICJ, *Admission of a State* Advisory Opinion, note 188, at pp. 62-63; ICJ, *Competence of Assembly regarding admission to the United Nations*, Advisory Opinion, *ICJ Reports 1950*, p. 4 *et seq.*, in particular at pp. 8-9). In its 1962 *Certain Expenses* Advisory Opinion, the Court referred to the 1950 *Competence of Assembly* Advisory Opinion, not mentioning the text of the applicable provision, but, instead, "the structure of the Charter", "the relations established by it between the General Assembly and the Security Council", and the fact that "[t]he Court sustained its interpretation of Article 4 by considering the manner in which the organs concerned 'have consistently interpreted the text' *in their practice*", note 308, at p. 157 (italics added).
386. ICJ, *WHO Nuclear Weapons* Advisory Opinion, note 183, at p. 74, para. 19.
387. The term was coined by Rosenne, note 26, at p. 239. Later, it was also used by Arsanjani in her report for the IDI discussed below in Section 3.4.3, note 401, at p. 216.
388. ICJ, *Certain Expenses* Advisory Opinion, note 308, at p. 157.

of international organizations are formally multilateral treaties, the Court continues as follows [389]:

> "But the constituent instruments of international organizations are also treaties of a particular type; their object is to create new subjects of law endowed with a certain autonomy, to which the parties entrust the task of realizing common goals."

The Court is exactly right in identifying the creation of a new legal person as the most fundamental special characteristic of constitutions of international organizations. It also distinguishes two interrelated features of this newly created legal person – again, in general terms, so not only with respect to the WHO that had requested the Advisory Opinion: the new legal person is "endowed with a certain autonomy", and its creators "entrust" to it "the task of realizing common goals". The Court did not go so far as fully recognizing that international organizations are independent international legal persons. Previously, in particular in its *Reparation for Injuries* Advisory Opinion, the Court used the word "independent", both for the UN and for its agents, now it uses the more restrictive words "a certain autonomy". The second feature is that those who establish an international organization "entrust" it with "the task of realizing common goals". These words are well chosen. The background of the creation of a new international organization is always that it is in the common interest of its founders to cooperate in pursuing certain aims that they can no longer realize in isolation. This cooperation is executed not by the states concerned themselves but by their newly created organization, in which they place the necessary trust to perform this task.

Next, the Court also specifies in this 1996 Advisory Opinion what implications these special characteristics of constituent instruments may have for their interpretation, in the following way [390]:

> "Such treaties can raise specific problems of interpretation owing, *inter alia,* to their character which is conventional and at the same time institutional; the very nature of the organization created, the objectives which have been assigned to it by its founders, the imperatives associated with the effective performance of its functions, as well as its own practice, are all elements which may

---

389. ICJ, *WHO Nuclear Weapons* Advisory Opinion, note 183, at p. 75, para. 19.
390. *Id.*

deserve special attention when the time comes to interpret these constituent treaties."

In this sentence, the Court mentions not only why constituent instruments of international organizations "can raise specific problems of interpretation" (in a non-exhaustive way). It also lists four more specific reasons, mentioned after the semicolon. The semicolon – which also appears in the French text of the Advisory Opinion – seems to separate the preceding words from the remainder of the sentence. If the preceding few words were of the same "rank" as the words following the semicolon, the Court would have used a comma. The best interpretation of this important paragraph is that the Court first points out the dual nature of constituent instruments of international organizations ("conventional and at the same time institutional"); next, it fleshes out this dual nature, by giving four specific reasons why constitutions are special treaties [391]. These are the following:

"the very nature of the organization created"

This – somewhat elliptical – reason may have a variety of meanings. It could refer, for example, to the political or technical nature of the organization, to its universal or regional membership, or perhaps also to its more intergovernmental or more supranational character.

"the objectives which have been assigned to it by its founders"

This could be perceived as a reference to teleological interpretation, a means of interpretation that is particularly well suited to serve the aims that an organization is expected to achieve.

"the imperatives associated with the effective performance of its functions"

This reason is a reminder of the functional nature of international organizations. They are not created to serve themselves, as *l'art pour l'art*, but have been brought into life to perform a particular task in an outside social environment, and to do so effectively.

"as well as its own practice"

---

391. For that reason, it may have been better if the Court used a colon rather than a semicolon because colons are used more commonly to introduce an explanation or illustration. Semicolons are commonly used to separate parts of a sentence in a more robust way than commas would do.

This element is of particular importance. Here the Court fully recognizes an implication of one of the unique characteristic of constituent instruments of international organizations. These are not only treaties with rights and obligations that the parties to it must comply with and implement. They also create a new legal person that leads its own life in practice. The Court correctly refers to the organization's *own* practice [392].

Following the above-quoted paragraph, having mentioned that constituent instruments of international organizations can raise specific problems of interpretation, the Court orients itself on the general rules for interpretation of treaties, in the following way [393]:

> "According to the customary rule of interpretation as expressed in Article 31 of the 1969 Vienna Convention on the Law of Treaties, the terms of a treaty must be interpreted 'in their context and in the light of its object and purpose' and there shall be 'taken into account, together with the context:
>
> . . .
>
> *(b)* any subsequent practice in the application of the treaty which establishes the agreement of the parties regarding its interpretation'."

Some comments can be given concerning this quoted passage from the Advisory Opinion. First, the Court chooses to use as its reference framework *the customary rule of interpretation* as expressed in Article 31 of the 1969 Vienna Convention, not the Vienna Convention as such. The Court does not mention the 1986 Vienna Convention, which, even though it was not yet in force, could have some relevance because the interpretation of a constituent instrument of an international organization is at issue. Although the organization as such is not a party to this instrument, international organizations are bound by their constitutions. It is therefore relevant for their application and interpretation of these instruments that exactly the same rules apply to the interpretation of treaties to which international organizations are parties as to the interpretation of state treaties. It reinforces the reference legal framework used by the Court.

---

392. Although it does not *apply* this correctly in the subsequent paragraphs of the advisory opinion, as will be discussed later (see Chap. 4).
393. *Id.*

Second, the Court does not use all treaty interpretation articles of the 1969 Vienna Convention as its reference framework (Arts. 31 to 33), but only Article 31. Thereby it excludes from the outset supplementary means of interpretation (Art. 32) and the rules on the interpretation of treaties authenticated in two or more languages (Art. 33) [394].

Third, the Court does not use the full text of Article 31 as its reference framework but selected parts of it. To be more precise, the Court leaves out the references to the following:

- "good faith";
- the first means of interpretation mentioned in Article 31, textual interpretation ("the ordinary meaning to be given to the terms of the treaty"). This is notable since textual interpretation has often been used by the Court as a key way to interpret treaties, including constitutions of international organizations [395];
- paragraph 2, specifying what "the context" shall comprise for the purpose of a treaty (although the Court does refer in general to "the context");
- subparagraphs 3 *(a)* and 3 *(c)*;
- paragraph 4.

It is not certain whether or not the omission of these elements would have had any implication for the subsequent application of this framework in this Advisory Opinion. But it is clear that the Court has selected two of the three main means of interpretation (context, but only in part; object and purpose). In particular, it has singled out "subsequent practice".

Following the above-mentioned quotation, the Court observes that it "has had occasion to apply this rule of interpretation several times", referring to four judgments [396]. However, in only one of these judgments the Court mentions "subsequent practice", and this is not in the context

---

394. The WHO Constitution has five authentic languages.
395. For example, in its Advisory Opinion in *Competence of Assembly*, note 385, the Court stated that "the first duty of a tribunal which is called upon to interpret and apply the provisions of a treaty, is to endeavor to give effect to them in their natural and ordinary meaning in the context in which they occur. If the relevant words in their natural and ordinary make sense in their context, that is an end of the matter" (quotation at p. 8). See also the Court's first Advisory Opinion in *Admission of a State*, note 188, at p. 62. In addition (not with respect to a constitution of an international organization): *Territorial Dispute (Libyan Arab Jamahiriya/Chad)*, *ICJ Reports 1994*, p. 22 *et seq.*, at para. 41 ("Interpretation must be based above all upon the text of the treaty").
396. *Id.*

of the interpretation of a constituent instrument of an international organization [397].

It is not fully clear whether the Court has made this selection only for the purpose of this specific Advisory Opinion or whether it would also apply in general to the interpretation of constituent instruments of international organizations. Irrespective of this, the singling out of "subsequent practice" is on the one hand commendable, as it is doing justice to the nature and work of international organizations in ever-changing times. On the other hand, strictly understood, it does not match with the earlier reference by the Court to "its own practice" as one of the four specific reasons why constitutions are different from other treaties and can raise problems of interpretation. As will be further discussed below [398], this earlier reference is to the practice of the organization, whereas "subsequent practice" in Article 31 of the Vienna Convention is about practice of the member states.

In this approach of constituent instruments of international organizations, the Court has found a balanced approach. While they are treaties, they are also treaties of a special kind. While the general rules of treaty interpretation apply, the Court has selected some of those as being the ones that are most relevant as the reference framework.

3.4.3. Limits to the interpretation of constitutions? The work of the Institut de Droit International

There is general support for the view that the interpretation of constitutions of international organizations requires an approach that is different from that used for the interpretation of other treaties, with particular attention given to the object and purpose of the relevant constitution and the aims of the organization. This may give the impression that such constitutions can be interpreted *à gogo*, to the full discretion of their interpreters. Some or most of the examples discussed in Chapter 2 may also support this view. If this were fully true, this would mean in practice that any interpretation is possible as long as the required majority (whatever it may be) supports it in the relevant decision of the organization. It would give maximum leeway to whatever interpretation by political or policymaking organs of an

---

397. *Land, Island and Maritime Frontier Dispute (El Salvador/Honduras: Nicaragua intervening)*, *ICJ Reports 1992*, p. 586 *et seq.*, at para. 380.
398. See Sec. 4.3.4.

international organization and amount to "legal nihilism"[399]. It raises the question of whether there are any *legal* limits to such interpretation. In other words: while the two Vienna Conventions are of an "enabling" nature, laying down generally recognized means of treaty interpretation, they only contain rather general limits for such interpretation (such as the obligation to interpret treaties in good faith).

This question of limits to treaty interpretation is particularly pertinent with regard to the interpretation of constituent instruments of international organizations. What is true for the UN is true for most other international organizations: at the establishment of the organization, its founding fathers did not give one particular organ the ultimate authority to interpret these instruments. Hence, it is for each of the organs themselves to apply and interpret the relevant provisions, including in particular the provisions defining their powers. This enables the organization to perform its functions as effectively as possible, in a rapidly changing world that was unpredictable at the organization's creation. Whenever the creators of a new organization feared that such powers could be abused or used excessively, and wanted to include the necessary checks and balances, they created judicial organs and provided for judicial review procedures. However, this is the exception rather than the rule. In a large majority of international organizations such checks and balances are absent. That does not mean that creating these organizations is a leap in the dark (or, more positively, a leap of trust), in the sense that states when creating an organization need to accept that it may eventually develop into a Frankenstein's monster (or, more positively, a sorcerer's apprentice). Constituent instruments may be amended if members wish to change the organization's work or direction. Finally, as *ultimum remedium*, members are not obliged to remain members; they may decide to withdraw if they decide, at a certain point in time, that membership is no longer in their interest. Therefore: there are always certain checks and balances. Nevertheless, it is also true that constitutional amendments and withdrawals are steps that are only exceptionally taken. It is therefore understandable that the question of limits to constitutional interpretation by organs of the organization has been raised, as a lighter check on the wide interpretative powers of these organs.

Against this background, the Institut de Droit International (hereinafter: Institut or IDI) decided in 2003 to examine the question:

---

399. This expression is from Rosenne, note 26, at p. 225; see also p. 227.

"Are there Limits to Dynamic Interpretation of the Constitution and Statutes of International Organizations by the Internal Organs of such Organizations, having Special Reference to the United Nations System"[400]. Institut member Mahnoush Arsanjani prepared a thorough report on these questions[401], which led to extensive discussions within the IDI[402]. The Resolution proposed by Rapporteur Arsanjani was amended significantly.

The Arsanjani report focuses mainly on the UN. It discusses the San Francisco *travaux* of the Charter, where it was deliberately decided not to give to one organ (in particular: the General Assembly or the ICJ) the exclusive competence to give an authoritative interpretation of the Charter. The report also analyses how the two Vienna Conventions on the Law of Treaties deal with the constituent instruments of international organizations and their interpretation. An important part of the report presents an overview of interpretations of the UN Charter by the General Assembly, the Security Council and the Secretary-General. Some attention is also given to the interpretative practice of selected specialized agencies, in particular the IMF and the World Bank. A final section of the report discusses relevant judgments and advisory opinions of the ICJ.

The conclusion of the report is that there are hardly any limits for organs of international organizations when they interpret their constituent instruments: "although certain interpretations of constituent instruments by international organizations amount to *de facto* amendment of their constituent instruments, the level of oversight or limitation upon such interpretations is practically nonexistent or ineffective"[403]. As

---

400. *IDI Annuaire*, Vol. 71, Book 2 (session de Bruges, 2004, deuxième partie), at p. 352. The original proposal used the words "pragmatic interpretation", but following discussions within the IDI this was changed into "dynamic interpretation", at the proposal of IDI member Tomuschat (see *id.*, at pp. 59, 71).
401. Published in *IDI Annuaire*, Vol. 79 (session de la Haye, 2019), p. 87 *et seq*. Also available at https://www.idi-iil.org/app/uploads/2019/06/Commission-7-Interpretation-constitution-of-international-organizations-Arsanjani-Travaux-La-Haye-2019.pdf.
402. See *IDI Annuaire*, Vol. 80 (session de La Haye, 2019), p. 235 *et seq*. At the end of its somewhat chaotic discussion of the report during the Institut's meeting in 2019, it was decided by twenty-eight votes in favour and twenty-seven against (with seven abstentions) to postpone the deliberations on the report; see *IDI Annuaire 2019*, at p. 285. The discussions concluded two years later, when a resolution was adopted.
403. Arsanjani Report, note 401, at p. 237. During the subsequent discussions in the Institut, Rapporteur Arsanjani "expressed her dissatisfaction not to have been able to find too many limits to the interpretation of constituent instruments by international organizations but reminded that her task was to provide for an effective representation of the reality as it stood", *IDI Annuaire 2019*, at pp. 246-247.

Rapporteur Arsanjani explains, the overall absence or ineffectiveness of oversight or limitation was a deliberate choice when the UN was created, and this is also true for many other international organizations. States have generally preferred to allow the organs of the organization to interpret their own constituent instrument "in their daily work, in the light of an endless stream of novel legal and factual issues" [404]. This "has permitted a broad and permissive jurisprudence of 'constitutional' interpretation to flourish within each organization, subject only to infrequent – and merely advisory – oversight" [405]. For constitutional interpretations by organs to be authoritative, they must be generally accepted by the members of the organization. This is the main limit to the wide interpretative discretion of these organs. According to Arsanjani, this interpretative practice fits within the Vienna rules on treaty interpretation, which are sufficiently flexible to take into account the special nature of constituent instruments of international organizations. This flexibility "contains no tangible outer limits. . . . In practice the limits are to be found in the world political process" [406]. The conclusion of the report is reflected in the draft Resolution prepared by Rapporteur Arsanjani [407].

During the subsequent discussion about this report, it was decided to change the words "dynamic interpretation" into "evolutive interpretation" [408]. The resolution on this topic adopted in 2021 by the Institut defines evolutive interpretation as "interpretation of constituent instruments in order to achieve perceived needs of an international organization that are consistent with its object, purpose and functions" [409]. There are two elements in this definition. First, it refers to the goal of evolutive interpretation "to achieve perceived needs of an international organization". Second, these perceived needs must be consistent with the organization's object, purpose and functions. This is somewhat similar to the more detailed description of characteristics of constitutions given by the ICJ in 1996 (see 3.4.2 above). The Institut notes that "highly significant activities of some international organizations owe their existence to the evolutive interpretation by these

---

404. *Id.*, at p. 234.
405. *Id.*
406. *Id.*, at p. 235.
407. *Id.*, at pp. 241-242.
408. See the suggestion made by Institut member Nolte, in *IDI Annuaire 2019*, at p. 244.
409. IDI Resolution adopted 4 September 2021, Preamble, available at https://www.idi-iil.org/en/.

organizations of their constituent instruments"[410]. As stated in the first paragraph of the Resolution, "[i]nternational organizations may resort to evolutive interpretation of their constituent instruments to address current challenges and to fill unforeseen gaps". Such instruments may be "ambiguous or silent on a specific issue"[411].

The Institut identifies five limits to evolutive interpretation by international organizations of their constituent instruments[412]:

– it "shall be consistent with those instruments and in particular with their object and purpose";
– it "shall take account of the fundamental principles of international law, often reaffirmed, initiated and promoted by these organizations themselves";
– it "may not violate jus cogens including internationally protected fundamental human rights";
– "[i]n exercising their competence to interpret their constituent instruments, international organizations shall pay due regard to the functions of other international organizations";
– "[u]nless otherwise provided in the constituent instrument of the international organization, when there is a general agreement among the membership of the international organization as to an interpretation, the interpretation should be presumed to be valid and intra vires".

While the core of these five limits was also mentioned in the draft resolution prepared by Rapporteur Arsanjani, there are significant differences. First, the draft does not mention the Vienna Conventions and their rules on treaty interpretation. In contrast, the final version of the resolution states that "[a]rticles 31 to 33 of the Vienna Convention of the Law of Treaties which reflect customary international law shall be applied in the interpretation of the constituent instruments of international organizations, taking into account any relevant rules of the organizations as provided in Article 5 of the aforesaid Convention". This reference to the Vienna Convention rules on treaty interpretation is relevant as it makes clear that the Institut does not propose special rules for the interpretation of constituent instruments of international organizations, outside the framework of the Vienna rules[413].

---

410. *Id.*, Preamble, last para.
411. *Id.*, Preamble.
412. *Id.*, paras. 3-7.
413. This is not what Rapporteur Arsanjani proposed, see in particular pp. 234-235 of her report, but the absence of any reference to the Vienna rules on treaty interpretation in her draft resolution could create this impression.

Second, the resolution adopted in 2021 starts by explicitly stating – unlike the draft resolution – that international organizations "may resort to evolutive interpretation of their constituent instruments to address current challenges and to fill unforeseen gaps". This is a full recognition of the need to allow evolutive interpretation, in order to enable international organizations to perform their functions in circumstances that were not foreseen at their creation.

Third, at the same time the resolution, in its preamble, acknowledges the value of amendment procedures of constituent instruments. Whereas the draft resolution stated that these procedures "may be cumbersome and inefficient", the resolution recognizes that the appropriate use of them "is conducive to maintaining the integrity and coherence of those instruments". There are limits to what dynamic or evolutive interpretation may achieve in order to enable an organization to adapt to changing circumstances. If these limits are reached, and if a constituent instrument (and with it: its organization) risks becoming too far removed from the reality in which it is expected to perform its functions, it may lose its normative grip on this reality. When the European Court of Justice concluded in 1996 that European Community law could not be interpreted so that the Community's competences would include the competence to accede to the European Convention on Human Rights, an amendment of the Community's constitution was necessary. This was done in the 2007 Lisbon Treaty [414]. When there was broad agreement that the European Community should accede to the FAO of the UN, the latter's constitution first had to be amended. Originally only states ("nations") could become members of the FAO. There is not much support for the view that a dynamic or evolutive interpretation of "state", "nation" or "country" could also cover international organizations [415]. Therefore, the FAO constitution was amended to introduce the possibility for regional economic integration organizations to become a member, and the EC was able to join in 1991 [416].

---

414. See Sec. 2.3 above.
415. Schermers and Blokker, note 2, at p. 81.
416. R. Frid, "The European Economic Community: A Member of a Specialized Agency of the United Nations", *European Journal of International Law*, Vol. 4 (1993), pp. 239-255, at pp. 253-254; J. Schwob, "L'amendement de l'acte constitutif de la FAO visant à permettre l'admission en qualité de membre d'organisations d'intégration économique régionale et la Communauté économique européenne", *Revue trimestrielle de droit européen*, Vol. 29 (1993), pp. 1-16, at pp. 10-11.

The five limits mentioned in the resolution are rather general, and can be interpreted in different ways. The first three limits seem to reflect generally accepted views, as expressed in practice and in literature. The fourth limit is perhaps the most innovative. Literature only has scant references to an obligation of international organizations to take into account each other's functions [417]. The fifth and final limit will be discussed below (Sec. 3.7).

The rules on interpretation of the two Vienna Conventions do not mention "dynamic" and "evolutive" interpretation. The definition of evolutive interpretation given by the Institut is somewhat question-begging. Should *any* interpretation of an organization's constituent instrument not be done "in order to achieve perceived needs of an international organization that are consistent with its object, purpose and functions"? Is a purely textual interpretation by definition unsuitable to achieve this? It seems that what is "evolutive" (or, previously, "dynamic", and, at the beginning of this project, "pragmatic") is not so much a means of interpretation, added to those mentioned in the two Vienna Conventions regarding the constitutions of international organizations, but rather a renewed, updated position assumed by an international organization in a changed *milieu* in which it is expected to perform its functions, at risk of becoming obsolete, irrelevant [418]. *Tempora mutantur, nos et mutamur in illis*. Times change, and we with them. Times change, and international organizations with them. As UN Secretary-General Annan wrote in 2005 [419]:

> "[T]he principles and purposes of the United Nations, as set out in the Charter, remain as valid and relevant today as they were in 1945 ... the present moment is a precious opportunity to put them into practice. But while purposes should be firm and principles constant, practice and organization need to move with the times."

3.5. The role of organizational practice in the interpretation of other rules of international organizations

The previous two sections have discussed the relevance of organizational practice for the interpretation of two types of treaties: those to

---

417. See e.g. Schermers and Blokker, note 2, at pp. 1145-1147.
418. As Institut member Salmon observed: "l'interprétation évolutive n'est que le reflet de l'instauration de nouvelles circonstances de fait, de nouveaux rapports de force, qui nécessitent une adaptation souple", *IDI Annuaire 2019*, at p. 250.
419. In Larger Freedom: Towards Development, Security and Human Rights for All, Report of the Secretary-General, UN Doc. A/59/2005, at para. 153.

which international organizations are parties and treaties establishing a new international organization. This section will examine the role of organizational practice in the interpretation of their rules (other than constitutions). A main difference here, in contrast with the treaties discussed in the two previous sections, is that a general legal framework is lacking; while there are the two Vienna Conventions on the Law of Treaties, there is no "Vienna Convention on the Law of Decisions, Resolutions and other Acts of International Organizations" (and it is far from certain whether it would be necessary or useful to have such an additional Vienna Convention).

Rules of international organizations include a wide variety of legal instruments. Most recently, they have been defined in the context of the ILC ARIO [420]:

> "For the purposes of the present draft articles,
>
> *(a)* ...
>
> *(b)* "rules of the organization" means, in particular, the constituent instruments, decisions, resolutions and other acts of the international organization adopted in accordance with those instruments, and established practice of the organization."

Even though this definition applies only to these ILC articles, it can be used as well for broader purposes, and, moreover, because somewhat similar definitions have been used in other legal instruments [421]. The list of legal instruments mentioned is broad but not exhaustive [422]. It also covers established practice, analysed in Chapter 1. As the ILC notes in its Commentary to these articles, "[o]ne important feature of the definition of 'rules of the organization' in subparagraph *(b)* is that it gives considerable weight to practice" [423].

There is no reason to assume that what has been observed in the previous section on the constitutions of international organizations applies equally to their other rules. Constitutions are drafted and adopted

---

420. ILC ARIO, Art. 2 *(b)*, published in *Yb. ILC 2011*, Vol. 2, Part 2, at p. 39 *et seq.* See Ahlborn, note 27.
421. For example, the Vienna II Convention, Art. 2 *(j)*.
422. See the ILC Commentary to Art. 2 of ARIO, *Yb. ILC 2011*, Vol. 2, Part 2, at p. 51, para. 16: "the rules of the organization may also include such instruments as agreements concluded by the organization with third parties and judicial or arbitral decisions binding the organization".
423. *Id.*, at para. 17. As an example, the ILC refers to NATO, where the key rule for decision-making (decision-making by consensus) is not laid down in the NATO rules but is the result of the practice of that organization.

almost exclusively by states, yet the other rules are drafted and adopted by organs of international organizations, in accordance with their decision-making rules. The process of treaty-making is fundamentally different from that of decision-making. This may have implications for interpretation, including for the role played by organizational practice.

As is the case for the interpretation of constituent instruments of international organizations, the ICJ has also provided some guidance for the interpretation of their other rules. However, while the Court's observations on the interpretation of constitutions – discussed in 3.4.2 above – have been made in general terms, its guidance on the interpretation of other rules is limited to a specific type of decision: resolutions of the UN Security Council.

In its 2010 Advisory Opinion on Kosovo's unilateral declaration of independence, the Court observed the following [424]:

> "Before continuing further, the Court must recall several factors relevant in the interpretation of resolutions of the Security Council. While the rules on treaty interpretation embodied in Articles 31 and 32 of the Vienna Convention on the Law of Treaties may provide guidance, differences between Security Council resolutions and treaties mean that the interpretation of Security Council resolutions also require that other factors be taken into account. Security Council resolutions are issued by a single, collective body and are drafted through a very different process than that used for the conclusion of a treaty. Security Council resolutions are the product of a voting process as provided for in Article 27 of the Charter, and the final text of such resolutions represents the view of the Security Council as a body. Moreover, Security Council resolutions can be binding on all Member States (*Legal Consequences for States of the Continued Presence of South Africa in Namibia (South West Africa) notwithstanding Security Council Resolution 276* (1970), Advisory Opinion, *ICJ Reports 1971*, p. 54, para. 116), irrespective of whether they played any part in their formulation. The interpretation of Security Council resolutions may require the Court to analyse statements by representatives of members of the Security Council made at the time of their adoption, other resolutions of the Security

---

424. ICJ, *Accordance with international law of the unilateral declaration of independence in respect of Kosovo*, Advisory Opinion, *ICJ Reports 2010*, p. 403 *et seq.*, quotation at p. 442, para. 94.

Legal Facets of the Practice of International Organizations 213

Council on the same issue, as well as the subsequent practice of relevant United Nations organs and of States affected by those given resolutions."

While these observations concern the interpretation of UN Security Council resolutions, they may also to a greater or lesser degree be relevant for the interpretation of decisions of other international organizations. A few comments may be made on this point.

First, it is understandable that the Court refers to the Vienna rules on treaty interpretation as "guidance". After all, there is no reason why the rich variety of means of interpretation in these Vienna rules should not be relevant for the interpretation of decisions, in this case Security Council resolutions. But it is equally understandable that the Court observes that "other factors" must also be taken into account in the interpretation of the latter, to do justice to their special nature. After all, decisions of international organizations (such as Security Council resolutions) are not treaties concluded between two or more parties, but unilateral acts [425]. The difference between these two legal instruments is therefore more pronounced than the distinction between constituent instruments of international organizations and other treaties made by the Court in 1996 (there the Court stated that a number of elements "may deserve special attention when the time comes to interpret these constituent treaties" [426]).

Second, the Court mentions five differences between treaties and Security Council resolutions:

– the latter "are issued by a single, collective body"

In this respect, the Security Council is fundamentally different from an *ad hoc* gathering of states, not meeting within a given legal framework. Security Council resolutions are unilateral acts, in contrast to treaties, which are concluded between two or more parties.

– they are drafted "through a very different process than that used for the conclusion of a treaty"

---

425. The EU Court drew the same conclusion, in cases in which Italy claimed that certain decisions adopted by the Council of Ministers were in fact international agreements. See Case 38/69, Judgment of the Court of 18 February 1970, *ECR 1970*, at p. 47, para. 11: "a measure which is in the nature of a Community decision on the basis of its objective and of the institutional framework within which it has been drawn up cannot be described as an 'international agreement'". See also Case 91/79, Judgment of the Court of 18 March 1980, *ECR 1980*, at p. 1099, para. 7.

426. ICJ, *WHO Nuclear Weapons* Advisory Opinion, note 183, at p. 75, para. 19.

The Court does not specify what these differences are. They may be more pronounced for certain treaties than for others. The process of treaty-making is far from uniform. Some treaties are rather simple bilateral exchanges of letters; at the other end of the spectrum there are multilateral treaties prepared over many years (e.g. by the ILC and the UN General Assembly), like the Vienna Conventions on the Law of Treaties. Nevertheless, in general terms, key differences include the speed and flexibility with which Security Council resolutions in many cases are adopted and the possibility in the case of treaties to require ratification and to allow reservations [427]. In two publications, Wood has also warned that "caution is required" when applying the rules on interpretation of the Vienna Convention in the case of interpretation of resolutions of the UN Security Council [428].

– they are "the product of a voting process" laid down in Article 27 of the Charter

For the conclusion of treaties, no standard voting procedure exists.

– they represent "the view of the Security Council as a body"

This is related to the first element mentioned above. Treaties do not represent the view of a single, collective body, but the views of the parties. It is their treaty [429].

– they "can be binding on all Member States . . ., irrespective of whether they played any part in their formulation"

As is stipulated in Article 34 of the two Vienna Conventions on the Law of Treaties, "[a] treaty does not create either obligations or rights for a third State without its consent". This is different for Security

---

427. For the process of treaty-making, see A. Aust, *Modern Treaty Law and Practice*, 3rd ed., Cambridge, Cambridge University Press, 2013, esp. chaps 2 and 6; G. Korontzis, "Making the Treaty", in D. B. Hollis (ed.), *The Oxford Guide to Treaties*, Oxford, Oxford University Press, 2012, pp. 177-207, at p. 178: "for all its formality and customary character, treaty-making remains a remarkably flexible process". For the process of decision-making by the UN Security Council, see L. Sievers and S. Daws, *The Procedure of the UN Security Council*, 4th ed., Oxford, Oxford University Press, 2014, esp. chaps 5 and 6; Wood and Sthoeger, note 327, at pp. 28-58.

428. Wood (1998), note 345, at p. 95: "given their essentially political nature and the way they are drafted, the circumstances of the adoption of the resolution and such preparatory work as exists may often be of greater significance than in the case of treaties. The Vienna Convention distinction between the general rule and supplementary means has even less significance than in the case of treaties. In general, less importance should attach to the minutiae of language. And there is considerable scope for authentic interpretation by the Council itself". On Wood's follow-up analysis, see note 345.

429. Crawford, note 371.

Council resolutions (although parties to the UN Charter have accepted in Article 25 of the Charter that they "agree to accept and carry out the decisions of the Security Council in accordance with the present Charter").

Third, the Court mentions three "implications for interpretation" that flow from the above-mentioned differences between Security Council resolutions and treaties. It may be required for the Court:

– "to analyse statements by representatives of members of the Security Council made at the time of their adoption"

Such statements may shed light on the meaning of sentences or words in the relevant resolution, or it may show that Security Council members have different views on how a resolution is to be interpreted. In addition, if members have difficulties with elements of a draft resolution but do not want to prevent its adoption, a statement may be somewhat similar to a reservation to a treaty (although it cannot "exclude or . . . modify the legal effect" of the contested parts of the resolution "in their application to that State" [430]). In terms of the Vienna rules on interpretation, statements made by members at the time of the adoption of a Security Council resolution may be seen as forming part of the relevant resolution's *travaux préparatoires*, one of the supplementary means of interpretation mentioned in Article 32 of the two Vienna Conventions.

– "other resolutions of the Security Council on the same issue"

Such resolutions may contain, for example, particular words that are interpreted in a certain way. If there are no statements to the contrary, a similar interpretation should be followed for resolutions that are subsequently adopted on the same issue. In terms of the Vienna rules on interpretation, this comes perhaps closest to "context" in the interpretation of treaties.

– "the subsequent practice of relevant United Nations organs and of States affected by those given resolutions"

Just as it emphasized the importance of subsequent practice in the interpretation of constitutions of international organizations, the Court also mentions subsequent practice here, with regard to the interpretation of Security Council resolutions.

---

430. The quoted words are taken from the definition of reservations in the 1969 and 1986 Vienna Conventions, Arts. 2 *(d)*.

The ICJ's approach is different from the one of its 1996 Advisory Opinion, in which the Court quoted the 1969 Vienna Convention and selected some particularly relevant means of interpretation. In this Advisory Opinion, the Court mentions three "implications for interpretation" without explicitly putting these three into the context of the Vienna Convention. Perhaps this was not done because, after all, resolutions of the Security Council are not treaties.

The three mentioned "implications for interpretation" are also relevant for the interpretation of decisions of other UN organs and of organs of other international organizations. It is true that such decisions differ from each other, they may be binding or not, and may cover very different matters. To mention some examples: the resolution of the UN General Assembly in which it *"[d]eplores in the strongest terms* the aggression by the Russian Federation against Ukraine in violation of Article 2 (4) of the Charter"[431]; the Resolution *Covid-19 response* adopted by the World Health Assembly[432]; the Decision on Decolonization of Mauritius adopted by the Assembly of the African Union[433]; the Resolution adopted by the General Assembly of the Organization of Vine and Wine about the valuation and importance of microbial biodiversity in a sustainable vitiviniculture context[434]. Thousands of very different kinds of resolutions, decisions and other acts are adopted by organs of international organizations every year. However, no matter how different they are, they have in common that they are adopted not by states (as treaties) but by an organ of an international organization, on the basis of powers attributed to that organ, as interpreted by it, and in accordance with the decision-making rules and the practice of the organ concerned. In all these cases, statements of members of these organs made at the adoption of these decisions may be relevant for their interpretation, as are decisions taken by these organs on the same issue, as well as the subsequent practice of the organs of the organization concerned and of its members. Other factors may also play a role, such as the political or technical nature of the organization concerned and the involvement of the secretariat of the organization in the drafting of the relevant decisions[435].

---

431. A/RES/ES-11/1, adopted 2 March 2022, at para. 2.
432. Resolution WHA73/1, adopted 19 May 2020.
433. AU Doc. Assembly/AU/Dec. 836(XXXV), adopted 5-6 February 2022.
434. Resolution OIV-VITI 655-2021, adopted 12 July 2021.
435. For example, UN Secretariat lawyers are not generally involved in the drafting of Security Council resolutions, and the Council is often inconsistent in its practice. See Wood and Sthoeger, note 327, at p. 36.

Organs of international organizations are a kind of biotope, a habitat where individuals in different capacities regularly meet (discussed in the next section), the *raison d'être* of which lies in the aims and functions of the international organization concerned. They adopt resolutions, decisions and other acts within a predetermined legal framework, and follow practices that are key when it comes to the interpretation of their output.

3.6. The interpreter I: (Organs of) the organization

As discussed above (3.2.1), the Vienna rules on treaty interpretation provide a legal framework for those who need to apply and interpret a treaty so that treaty interpretation does not take place fully in limbo but in a more organized way, in accordance with the rule of law. The previous two sections have illustrated how the ICJ has benefited from these rules. At the same time, it remains true that it is to some extent in the eye of the beholder how a certain treaty provision is interpreted. Who is the beholder when it comes to the interpretation of the law of international organizations? First, this is the organization itself, or rather its organs (discussed in this section). In their daily practice they interpret the relevant rules of the organization. Second, the members of the organization are closely involved, in different ways, in the interpretation of the organization's rules (discussed in Sec. 3.7).

An international organization's practice must be distinguished from the practice of its organs. On the one hand, an international organization acts through its organs. They have their own composition, their own powers and also their own practice. For example, the practice of the UN General Assembly in adopting resolutions is different from that of the Security Council. On the other hand, international organizations also have practices that apply throughout the entire organization. For example, within the UN, it is not for each individual principal organ (let alone each organ) to decide about questions concerning the representation of member states in the organization. For that reason, recognizing the "risk that conflicting decisions may be reached by its various organs", the General Assembly recommended in 1950 that

> "whenever more than one authority claims to be the government entitled to represent a Member State in the United Nations and this question becomes the subject of controversy in the United Nations, the question should be considered in the light of the

Purposes and Principles of the Charter and the circumstances of each case;

. . . .

when any such question arises, it should be considered by the General Assembly. . .; . . .

the attitude adopted by the General Assembly . . . concerning any such question should be taken into account in other organs of the United Nations and in the specialized agencies" [436].

In making this recommendation, the Assembly considered that "in virtue of its composition", the General Assembly "is the organ of the United Nations in which consideration can best be given to the views of all Member States in matters affecting the Organization as a whole" [437].

In practice, this recommendation has usually been followed. When in 1971 the General Assembly for the first time accepted the credentials signed by the government in Beijing and no longer those signed by the government in Taiwan, this choice for the representation of China in the UN was followed not only in the General Assembly but across the UN. There are a number of other examples [438]. Difficulties arose in some cases, for instance with regard to the representation in the UN of Myanmar following the military coup that occurred in February 2021, overthrowing the civilian government. The civilian government continued to represent Myanmar in the General Assembly in 2021, while the military junta represented Myanmar in the same year in the UN Human Rights Council and in the UN's Economic and Social Commission for Asia and the Pacific. In December 2021 the General Assembly was unable to make a choice between the two when adopting the report of its Credentials Committee [439]. As a result, it allowed for the time being the sitting (civilian) representative to continue to represent Myanmar in the General Assembly. The situation only became more complex because the issue of the representation of Myanmar also arose in the proceedings before the ICJ, instituted in 2019, by The Gambia against Myanmar under the Genocide Convention. Originally the civilian

---

436. GA Res. 396 (V).
437. *Id.*, 3rd preambular paragraph.
438. See further Schermers and Blokker, note 2, at pp. 213-223.
439. GA Res. 76/15 (report of the Credentials Committee: UN Doc. A/76/550 (at the proposal of its Chair, the Committee decided to defer its decision on the credentials of representatives of Myanmar)). See further R. Barber, "The Role of the General Assembly in Determining the Legitimacy of Governments", *International and Comparative Law Quarterly*, Vol. 71 (2022), pp. 627-656.

government represented Myanmar (in December 2019 Foreign Minister and Nobel Prize laureate Aung San Suu Kyi herself appeared before the Court). However, in the hearings on the preliminary objections raised by Myanmar (February 2022), Myanmar was represented by the military government. Both the civilian government and a group of Rohingya in Bangladesh wrote to the Court that it should not recognize the military junta as the representative of Myanmar [440]. In its judgment of 22 July 2022 the Court merely noted the change in representation of Myanmar before the Court [441]. Obviously the Court was in a difficult position and any decision it would take would be criticized. The Court is an independent institution, but it is also a principal organ of the UN. In this case, the General Assembly – in its own words, best placed to decide these matters of representation – has not yet taken a final decision. This example illustrates both the importance and the difficulties of a unitary practice within the UN concerning the representation of member states.

When a new international organization is created, its founding fathers may discuss whether the competence to interpret the constitution and other rules of the organization should be given to a particular organ. A well-known example is the UN Charter negotiations. As noted by the ICJ, "[p]roposals made during the drafting of the Charter to place the ultimate authority to interpret the Charter in the International Court of Justice were not accepted" [442]. In contrast, in some other organizations it was decided to give a prominent role in this regard to judicial organs [443].

---

440. See C. Amirfar, R. Zamour and D. Pickard, "Representation of Member States at the United Nations: Recent Challenges", *ASIL Insights*, Vol. 26, No. 6 (August), https://www.asil.org/insights/volume/26/issue/6, at p. 2. See also the Declaration by judge *ad hoc* Kress to the 22 July 2022 Judgment of the Court, and M. Weller, "Is the ICJ at Risk of Providing Cover for the Alleged Genocide in Myanmar?", *EJIL:Talk!*, 11 February 2022, with reactions, see https://www.ejiltalk.org/is-the-icj-at-risk-of-providing-cover-for-the-alleged-genocide-in-myanmar/. For the letter by 807 Rohingyas (2 February 2022), see https://www.legalactionworldwide.org/gender-equality-gbv/807-rohingya-call-on-icj-to-reject-military-junta.

441. ICJ, *Application of the Convention on the Prevention and Punishment of the Crime of Genocide (The Gambia v. Myanmar)*, Judgment of 22 July 2022 (Preliminary Objections), para. 8. Judge *ad hoc* Kress criticizes what he calls the "laconic formulation", in para. 8, in paras. 2-5 of his Declaration. While there was a change in the representation of Myanmar before the ICJ, judge *ad hoc* Kress (chosen by the civilian government of Myanmar when it was still in power) continued as judge *ad hoc* following the regime change in February 2021.

442. ICJ, *Certain Expenses* Advisory Opinion, note 308, at p. 168. These proposals made during the UN Charter negotiations will be further discussed in Sec. 3.7.

443. For example, the ILO (International Court of Justice), the European Union (Court of Justice of the EU), and also other regional organizations, e.g. the Andean Community (the Andean Court of Justice), the African Union and the International Conference on the Great Lakes Region (African Court of Justice) and the East African Community (East African Court of Justice).

In yet other organizations, the competence to interpret constitutional provisions was given to policymaking organs or to the secretariat [444]. Within financial and commodity organizations, the competence to give interpretations is usually given to their executive organs [445]. Good examples are the IMF and the World Bank.

When states established these two financial organizations at Bretton Woods in 1944, they deliberately decided that questions of interpretation of the constituent instruments of these organizations should be submitted to their (non-plenary) Executive Boards. If these Boards adopt a certain interpretation, any member state of these organizations may require that these decisions be referred to the (plenary) Board of Governors, "whose decision shall be final" [446]. This choice by the founding fathers of these organizations is not, or not only, marked by the era of the construction of a post-war liberal international order, and now out of date. When in 2015 the Asian Infrastructure Investment Bank was created, exactly the same interpretative competences were given to the non-plenary and plenary policymaking organs of that organization [447].

Early legal advisers of the IMF and the World Bank referred to these broad interpretative powers of the Executive Boards and the Boards of Governors as quasi-legislative and quasi-judicial powers [448]. In her report for the IDI, Rapporteur Arsanjani examined whether there are any limits to these powers. She notes that the constitutions of the IMF and the World Bank "do not provide for judicial control" [449]. In addition, Arsanjani quotes a study by Hexner, former legal adviser of the IMF. According to Hexner, interpretation should not in fact amend

---

444. For example, in the WTO the exclusive authority to interpret the constitution is given to the Ministerial Conference and the General Council (Art. IX.2 of the Agreement establishing the WTO). In ASEAN, member states may request the Secretariat to interpret the ASEAN Charter (ASEAN Charter, Art. 51.1).

445. E.g. IMF, Art. XXIX; World Bank, Art. IX; Asian Development Bank, Art. 60; Caribbean Development Bank, Art. 59 (1); International Coffee Organization (International Coffee Agreement 2022, Art. 43); International Cocoa Organization (2010 International Cocoa Agreement, Art. 50); the European Stability Mechanism, Art. 37 (if the ESM member concerned contests the interpretation by the Board of Governors, the dispute shall be submitted to the Court of Justice of the EU).

446. Articles of Agreement IMF, Art. XXIX; Articles of Agreement World Bank, Art. IX.

447. Articles of Agreement of the Asian Infrastructure Investment Bank, Art. 54.

448. See the analysis by Arsanjani in her report for the IDI, note 401, pp. 194-202. See also F. Gianviti, "Members' Rights and Obligations Under the IMF's Articles of Agreement: The Role of Practice in the Interpretation of an Organization's Charter", in R. C. Effros (ed.), *Current Legal Issues Affecting Central Banks*, Washington, IMF, 1995, pp. 1-13.

449. *Id.*, at p. 198.

the organization's constituent instrument, although it is difficult to draw the line between the two [450]:

> "The question may be asked whether the interpretative power includes the right to determine the limits of the interpretative power, and whether it extends to interpretation of provision relative to amendments of the Agreement. . . . The answer to this question is in the affirmative, subject, of course, to the fact that matters touching on *competence de la competence* frequently border on political aspects and involves problematical elements of *ultra vires* actions."

These examples demonstrate that whenever a new international organization is established (or later in its life), its founding fathers have choices to make about the interpretation of the law of their creation. If nothing is decided, interpretation is entirely left to practice. During the life of the organization, its organs will interpret the law of the organization that is relevant for the performance of their functions, and the members of the organization will also play a role (see Sec. 3.7). If it is decided to give the competence of the ultimate, authoritative interpretation of the law of the organization to a specific organ, the main choice concerns the nature of this organ: an organ composed of representatives of the members or an organ composed of independent individuals. In case of the former, the members stay more in control of actions and decisions of the organization. In case of an organ composed of independent individuals, the members consider such a body, which is at greater distance from the members, better placed to flesh out what is in the common interest and entrust to it the task of determining the organization's actions and decisions. At the same time, this does not necessarily mean that an organ composed of representatives of the members gives a more restrictive interpretation of the powers of the organization than the interpretation by an independent organ. An example is the question of whether it is within the powers of the WHO to deal with the legality of the use of nuclear weapons. The World Health Assembly – the WHO's plenary policymaking organ composed of representatives of the members – gave an affirmative answer to this question, but the ICJ concluded that this is not within the WHO's powers [451].

---

450. *Id.*
451. ICJ, *WHO Nuclear Weapons* Advisory Opinion, note 183.

In organs composed of representatives of the members, the distinction between the organization (and its practice) and its members (and their practice) is blurred because these organs *are* composed of representatives of these very same members. Nevertheless, even though it is blurred, the distinction is important as the members act in different capacities. First, in their *external* capacity, they are sovereign states, which created the organization (or joined the organization later), they are addressees of the organization's decisions, and so forth. For example, Article 25 of the UN Charter refers to member states in this capacity ("The Members of the United Nations agree to accept and carry out the decisions of the Security Council in accordance with the present Charter"). Second, in their *internal* capacity, they are constituent elements of one or more organs of the organization [452]. For example, the UN General Assembly consists of "all the Members of the United Nations" (Art. 9.1 of the UN Charter), and each of them has one vote (Art. 18.1 UN Charter). In addition, in non-plenary organs such as the Security Council, its members have a broader responsibility. They are not only acting in an external and internal capacity but also have to take into account that the Security Council acts on behalf of the entire UN membership (Art. 24.1 UN Charter). Acting in their *internal* capacity, as members of the General Assembly and the Security Council, they must comply with the obligations of these organs under the UN Charter. Therefore, as the ICJ observed in its first Advisory Opinion [453], they do not have a "free vote" to decide whatever they want when these organs take a decision on the admission of new members to the UN [454], but they are bound by applying (and thus: interpreting) the conditions for membership mentioned in Article 4.1 of the Charter.

The situation is different for organs of international organizations that are composed of independent staff or experts. In the UN, as far as its six principal organs are concerned, this is the case for the ICJ and

---

452. See further on these two capacities Schermers and Blokker, note 2, at pp. 65-69. Also L. M. Goodrich and E. Hambro, *Charter of the United Nations: Commentary and Documents*, 2nd rev. ed., Boston, World Peace Foundation, 1949, at p. 549 ("Every organ naturally would have to decide questions of its own competence and procedure, and Members, in their individual capacities and as members of organs, would find it necessary to express judgments on questions of interpretation").

453. ICJ, *Admission of a State* Advisory Opinion, note 188, at p. 62: "All these conditions [of Art. 4.1] are subject to the judgment of the Organization. The judgment of the Organization means the judgment of the two organs mentioned in paragraph 2 of Article 4, and, in the last analysis, that of its Members."

454. In the words of the Court: "an indefinite and practically unlimited power of discretion in the imposition of new conditions", *id.*, at p. 63.

the Secretariat. The performance of their functions inherently requires interpretations of the Charter. The angle from which such interpretations are given is different from that of interpretations by organs composed of representatives of the members. A *vue d'ensemble* is required to prevail, having in mind the interests of the organization as a whole. This is not to say that such an angle is absent in organs composed of representatives of the members, but it is fair to assume that the self-interest of members is dominant in such organs.

In practice, interpretations of the UN Charter by the Secretariat may be given during meetings of UN organs and are often laid down in legal memoranda [455]. The same is done by secretariats of other international organizations, for example the ILO and ASEAN [456]. Interpretations by the secretariat may be different from those of policymaking organs of an organization. An example is the advice given by the Legal Counsel of the WHO during the discussions preceding the request of an advisory opinion from the ICJ on the legality of the use of nuclear weapons [457]. In the interpretation of the World Health Assembly, in contrast with the advice of the Legal Counsel, it was *intra* the *vires* of the organization to deal with this question (and to ask an Advisory Opinion). In the interpretation of the ICJ, however, this was not within the WHO's powers. Another example is a legal opinion of the Legal Adviser of OPCW, emphasizing that the appointment of the Director-General is for a period of four years and that there are no constitutional provisions allowing for the dismissal of the Director-General [458]. The principal organ of the OPCW, the Conference, disagreed and decided in a special session in 2002 to terminate the appointment of Director-General Bustani (who was reappointed in 2001 for a second term of four years). Subsequently, the ILO Administrative Tribunal agreed with the Legal Adviser's views and set the decision of the Conference to terminate Bustani's appointment aside [459].

---

455. Many important legal memoranda have been published in the *UNJY*. For an example of legal advice given during a meeting of the UN General Assembly, see UN Doc. A/71/PV.66, at pp. 20-21.
456. See Schermers and Blokker, note 2, at pp. 894-895.
457. The WHO Legal Counsel's view was that this question was not within the normal competence or mandate of the WHO. He expressed his views on several occasions, mentioned in the Separate Opinion of Judge Oda to the Court's Advisory Opinion (ICJ, *WHO Nuclear Weapons*, at pp. 88-96). The WHO's Assembly did not follow the legal advice and decided to request the Advisory Opinion.
458. See OPCW Doc. C-SS-1/DG.6, 21 April 2002.
459. See, with further references, C. Wickremasinghe, "Casenote: The Bustani Case before the ILOAT", *International Organizations Law Review*, Vol. 1 (2004), pp. 197-207.

No matter how the organs are composed, in their daily practice the rules of the organization are applied and interpreted. Their interpretations must be distinguished from those by the member states, to be discussed in the next section.

3.7. The interpreter II: The members – membership support for an interpretation by the organization

There are good arguments in favour of giving an important role to the members of an international organization in the interpretation of its rules. A well-known principle is *eius est interpretare legem cuius condere* (whoever is authorized to establish the law is authorized to interpret it)[460]. Both the original members (who adopted the organization's constituent instrument) and those who joined later must have a say in the interpretation of this instrument. However, it is not *only* for them to do this. As discussed in Section 3.6, the organs of the organization also play an important part here. Ultimately, this is what the founding fathers want, as will now be illustrated by reviewing the relevant part of the *travaux préparatoires* of the UN Charter.

During the 1945 United Nations Conference on International Organization, Committee IV/2 (Legal Problems) discussed on 28 May "how and by what organ or organs of the Organization the Charter should be interpreted"[461]. Since "some articles of the Charter might give rise to a conflict of jurisdiction", states felt the need that this Committee "should determine the proper interpretative organ for the several parts of the Charter"[462]. A wide variety of views was expressed. Some delegations favoured the General Assembly as the main organ for interpretation, others the ICJ. Still others suggested to not include a provision about interpretation in the Charter and to leave the matter to practice (as was the case for the League of Nations)[463]. Against this background, the matter was referred to a subcommittee[464].

---

460. This principle was mentioned by the PCIJ, *Question of Jaworzina (Polish-Czechoslovakian Frontier)*, Advisory Opinion, *PCIJ Reports, Series B, No. 8 (1923)*, p. 37. The Court referred to it as "an established principle that the right of giving an authoritative interpretation of a legal rule belongs solely to the person or body who has power to modify or suppress it".

461. *Documents of The United Nations Conference on International Organization (San Francisco, 1945)*, Vol. XIII, at p. 633.

462. *Id.*

463. *Id.*, at pp. 633-634.

464. As suggested by the Chair. However, some members questioned whether it was necessary to refer the matter to a subcommittee. Others suggested that a decision could be taken by vote. Finally, the Chair's suggestion was put to a vote. With sixteen votes in favour and thirteen against, a subcommittee was established; *id.*, at p. 634.

The subcommittee was composed of delegations from six states: United Kingdom, United States, Norway, Yugoslavia, Belgium and France [465]. It delivered its report within a few days, on 2 June. Essentially, the report has three components. First, it states that, in the daily operation of organs of the UN, "it is inevitable that each organ will interpret such parts of the Charter as are applicable to its particular functions" [466]. For this purpose, "it is not necessary to include in the Charter a provision either authorizing or approving the normal operation of this principle" [467]. A second component is about what should happen if difficulties arise. If there is a difference of opinion among UN organs about the correct interpretation of a Charter provision, the report distinguishes two scenarios. First, if two member states disagree about the correct interpretation of the Charter, they can submit their dispute to the ICJ. Second, the General Assembly or the Security Council could request an advisory opinion from the Court; in the alternative, they could create an *ad hoc* committee of jurists or could take recourse to a joint conference (as mentioned in Art. 12 of the ICJ Statute). However, according to the subcommittee "[i]t would appear neither necessary nor desirable to list or to describe in the Charter the various possible expedients" [468]. Finally, as a third component of its report, the subcommittee observed the following: "It is to be understood, of course, that if an interpretation made by any organ of the Organization or by a committee of jurists is not generally acceptable it will be without binding force. In such circumstances, or in cases where it is desired to establish an authoritative interpretation as a precedent for the future, it may be necessary to embody the interpretation in an amendment to the Charter." [469]

Committee IV/2 adopted the report of its subcommittee on 7 June [470]. It adopted the final report of its work on 12 June [471]. This final report

---

465. *Id.*, at p. 635.
466. *Id.*, at p. 831.
467. *Id.*
468. *Id.*, at p. 832.
469. *Id.*
470. *Id.*, at p. 653. In this meeting, Belgium "disapproved of according equal weight to opinions of the Court and an ad hoc interpreting committee", and suggested that UN organs should refer their interpretation disputes to the ICJ, "in the interest of objectivity and uniformity of jurisprudence". Other delegations however took the view that the Court and an *ad hoc* committee "perform a function of equal weight: The Court deciding disagreements of a serious nature where time is not a factor; the committee deciding everyday routine disagreements where time is a factor". The Committee rejected the suggestion by Belgium.
471. *Id.*, at p. 701.

fully reproduced the substance of the subcommittee's report. Each of the three components of the subcommittee's report, now included in the final report of Committee IV/2, will now be further analysed.

The first component ("daily operation of UN organs") fully recognizes that the daily functioning in the practice of UN organs by definition involves a permanent interpretation of Charter provisions. The application of the rules of the Charter in practice implies an interpretation of these rules. It is the task of UN organs to translate the words of the Charter into deeds, in a world unknown to the drafters but for which they collectively wanted to prepare. The drafters were fully aware that UN organs would need flexibility for this "translation work", and therefore decided "not to include in the Charter a provision either authorizing or approving the normal operation of this principle" [472]. This is also demonstrated in publications by members of delegations to the 1945 San Francisco Conference. The author Pollux (E. Hambro) wrote in 1946: "A constitutional customary law will grow up and the Charter itself will merely form the framework of the Organization which will be filled in by the practice of the different organs." [473] Together with L. Goodrich, Hambro (but now not using the pseudonym Pollux) wrote in an authoritative early commentary on the UN Charter that [474]

> "the interpretation of the Charter is as much a political as a juridical function, and . . . therefore it must be left to the various organs of the United Nations and to Members to determine the meaning of the document in the light of circumstances. Every organ naturally would have to decide questions of its own competence and procedure, and Members, in their individual capacities and as members of organs, would find it necessary to express judgments on questions of interpretation".

This quotation from this Charter commentary also correctly distinguishes between the internal and external capacities of UN members (as mentioned in 3.6) in their daily Charter interpretation work.

The second component of the report ("difference of opinion about the correct interpretation") rightly distinguishes between two scenarios: a dispute between member states submitted to the ICJ and three ways in which the organ in which the dispute arose could deal with it (request an advisory opinion from the ICJ, create an *ad hoc* committee of

---

472. *Id.*, at p. 831.
473. Pollux, note 167, at p. 54.
474. Goodrich and Hambro, note 452, at p. 549.

Legal Facets of the Practice of International Organizations 227

jurists or take recourse to a joint conference). In practice, since 1945, member states have not normally brought their disputes over the correct interpretation of the Charter before the ICJ. Only exceptionally such disputes have been an element in bilateral disputes before the Court that essentially concerned other issues [475]. Typically, whenever disputes over the interpretation of the Charter were submitted to the ICJ, this was done through a request for an advisory opinion. In most cases, such requests were made by the General Assembly [476]; in one case by the Security Council [477]. The other routes mentioned in the report (*ad hoc* committee of jurists, joint conference) have not been used. It seems that practice has confirmed the subcommittee's conclusion ("It would appear neither necessary nor desirable to list or to describe in the Charter the various possible expedients"). Although this can never be proven, it seems unlikely that explicit provisions in the Charter detailing the various available options to deal with interpretation disputes would have made any difference.

The third component of the report ("interpretations by an organ must be generally acceptable") is probably the most enigmatic. What is *generally acceptable*, and how can this be ascertained? Is this a percentage of UN membership supporting the interpretation that is very high, much higher than 50 per cent? Presumably not all members need to give their support, but how close to 100 per cent does it need to be? It is mentioned as something obvious ("It is to be understood, of course. . ."). However, is it *really* obvious? And if it was at all obvious in 1945, is it still obvious today? For example, if the Security Council adopts a resolution that is binding upon the member states (Art. 25 of the Charter), why should the interpretation of the Charter in this resolution *not* be binding upon the member states? Why would, in addition, such an interpretation have to be "generally acceptable"?

---

475. See e.g. the Lockerbie cases, in which the UK and the US argued that Libya could not exercise its rights under the Montreal Convention because they had been superseded by two Security Council resolutions. The ICJ rejected this argument. See *Questions of Interpretation and Application of the 1971 Montreal Convention arising from the Aerial Incident at Lockerbie (Libyan Arab Jamahiriya v. United Kingdom)*, Preliminary Objections, Judgment, *ICJ Reports 1998*, p. 9 *et seq.*, at pp. 23-24; *Questions of Interpretation and Application of the 1971 Montreal Convention arising from the Aerial Incident at Lockerbie (Libyan Arab Jamahiriya v. United States of America)*, Preliminary Objections, Judgment, *ICJ Reports 1998*, p. 115 *et seq.*, at pp. 128-129.
476. E.g. ICJ, *Certain Expenses* Advisory Opinion, note 308.
477. *Legal Consequences for States of the Continued Presence of South Africa in Namibia (South West Africa) notwithstanding Security Council Resolution 276* (1970), Advisory Opinion, *ICJ Reports 1971*, p. 16 *et seq.*

Furthermore, if an interpretation made by a UN organ is *not* generally acceptable, is it realistic to assume that there is enough support for adopting its substance as an amendment to the Charter? If there is not enough support, would this not prevent the UN from performing its functions in a rapidly changing world? To use a specific example, if the interpretation that the General Assembly can establish a peacekeeping operation is not generally acceptable, why should states that oppose such an interpretation of the Assembly's powers be in favour of an amendment of the Charter through which such a power would be given to the Assembly?

The question of what the requirement for interpretations of the Charter by UN organs to be "generally acceptable" really means was not only pertinent in 1945, but also today. This was put to the test when the IDI discussed the topic of limits to the dynamic or evolutive interpretation of constituent instruments of international organizations. In her report for the Institut, Rapporteur Arsanjani extensively discussed the above-mentioned negotiations in San Francisco in June 1945, including the report of the subcommittee on the interpretation of the Charter. Reflecting the importance of "general acceptance" of an interpretation by an organ of an international organization, the draft resolution that she proposed stated that "when there is a general agreement among the membership of the international organization as to an interpretation, the interpretation should be presumed to be *intra vires* and lawful"[478].

In the discussions within the Institut about this report and the proposed draft resolution, a number of comments and questions related to this requirement of "general acceptance"[479]. Some confusion arose due to the French version of the proposed resolution, which referred to the requirement of "un consensus général"[480]. In revised versions of the draft resolution, the French words "consensus général" were first changed into "généralement acceptable"[481], and subsequently into "généralement acceptée"[482].

---

478. *IDI Annuaire 2019*, at p. 237.
479. For example, Nolte proposed to delete "general" (*id.*, at p. 244); Hafner, at pp. 244-245; Corten, at pp. 264-265; Meron, at p. 266: "what kind of majority was necessary for such acceptance (e.g., consensus, simple majority)"; Kohen, proposed to replace "general agreement" by "consensus", at p. 267.
480. *Id.*, at p. 238. According to Pellet, "consensus général" is a pleonasm; he proposed to delete "general", at p. 245. See also Kolodkin (asking whether "general agreement" "is equivalent to 'consensus' and/or to the French 'consensus'", at p. 249.
481. *Id.*, at p. 253.
482. *Id.*, at p. 262.

In the final version of the Resolution, adopted by the Institut in 2021, the above-quoted text was slightly amended, as follows: "Unless otherwise provided in the constituent instrument of the international organization, when there is a general agreement among the membership of the international organization as to an interpretation, the interpretation should be presumed to be valid and *intra vires*." [483] The "general acceptance" requirement was therefore not merely something put forward long ago, under the unique circumstances of the UN Charter negotiations, as part of a report that was prepared within a few days by a subcommittee composed of six delegations in San Francisco, while there was only minimal support for creating this subcommittee. Instead, this requirement is indeed something much more fundamental, as a counterbalance for wide interpretation powers of UN organs. In 1945 it obtained the necessary support from the representatives of fifty states negotiating the UN Charter. Seventy-six years later, it also received the support from the IDI, as one of the limits to evolutive interpretation of constituent instruments of international organizations by their organs.

Given that the "general agreement" requirement is fundamental when it comes to the interpretation of constituent instruments of international organizations by their organs, it is important to explore what this entails. Three observations may be made in this context. First, "general agreement" is not defined in the Arsanjani report [484]. This suggests that no fixed percentage of membership (supporting a particular interpretation) is required. For example, if the opposition to a particular interpretation of the Charter adopted by the UN General Assembly were to include a few member states such as Liberia and Panama, this would not necessarily stand in the way of a "general agreement". In the International Maritime Organization, however, in which these states have a prominent position, this might be different. Arsanjani mentions in her report the *Uniting for Peace* Resolution adopted by the UN General Assembly in 1950, by fifty-two votes in favour, five against (including the Soviet Union) and two abstentions; she concludes that the interpretation of the Charter in this resolution was "generally acceptable" [485]. Should the same conclusion be drawn regarding the interpretation of the constituent instrument of the OPCW

---

483. Available at https://www.idi-iil.org/en/. The final French version of the Resolution refers in para. 7 to the requirement of "un accord général".
484. In the subsequent discussion about the report within the Institut, Rapporteur Arsanjani mentioned that she "did not think that it would be appropriate to provide for a definition of it in her work", Arsanjani Report, note 401, at p. 246.
485. *Id.*, at p. 123 *et seq.*

in the above-discussed 2018 Resolution adopted by the Conference, adopted by eighty-two votes in favour and twenty-four against (including China, India, Russia and South Africa)[486]? How "general" the "agreement" is required to be varies according to the organization. Ultimately, this is decided by each individual organization where this issue arises. The bottom line for a dissenting member is its right to withdraw from the organization.

Second, "general agreement" is to be distinguished from consensus. If organs of international organizations adopt decisions by consensus, this usually means that there is no formal opposition against the adoption of the relevant decision. There is no voting; rather, the chair concludes at the end of a meeting that "the sense of the meeting" is that a particular text is adopted. In rules of procedure of UN organs, there is no formal definition of consensus. Most other international organizations also lack such a definition. An exception is the WTO. Its constituent instrument defines consensus as follows: "if no member, present at the meeting where the decision is taken, formally objects to the proposed decision"[487]. The bottom line of decision-making by consensus is that members of the relevant organ can always prevent the adoption of a decision. In the case of "general agreement", this is different: some members may be opposed, even strongly. Rapporteur Arsanjani emphasized this difference in her report for the Institut[488], and in particular in her statements during the subsequent discussions[489].

Third, the question is relevant at what point in time the requirement of "general acceptance" must be fulfilled. Is this at the moment of adoption of the relevant decision, interpreting the organization's constituent instrument? Or could such "general acceptance" of this interpretation also emerge later? The latter view is preferable. It allows an adopted

---

486. See above Chap. 2.2.4.
487. Agreement establishing the WTO, Art. IX.1, note 1. A definition that is not only negative but has some positive elements as well is given in Art. 2 of the constitution of the Common Market for Eastern and Southern Africa: "'consensus' means general agreement, characterized by the absence of objection to issues secured by a process that involves seeking to take into account the views of all parties concerned and to reconcile any conflicting arguments".
488. See e.g. p. 107: "the absence of a requirement of unanimity. The words 'generally acceptable' anticipate that there may be States that will not agree to a particular interpretation, but their disagreement will not undermine the authoritative character of the interpretation". See also p. 123.
489. See e.g. p. 263 ("revising the draft Resolution so as to require unanimous support for a particular interpretation would vest any individual State with the power to paralyze the work of the organization"); p. 269 ("a requirement of consensus in this provision would risk endorsing the paralysis of international organizations through a differing interpretation by any individual State").

decision to be implemented in practice, it gives it a chance, and the passage of time may make it clearer to all those involved whether the interpretation given was the right way to proceed. IDI member Salmon articulated this very well. His remarks about the Arsanjani report deserve to be quoted in full [490]:

> "[L]e rapport met le point sur un des problèmes permanents du droit international, le problème temporel. Il est particulièrement difficile de déterminer le moment où l'appréciation de l'acceptabilité d'une interprétation doit être faite. Au début, certaines interprétations peuvent apparaître contraires à l'acte constitutif et être contestées par une minorité, mais alors c'est la règle de la majorité qui s'impose. Et même si des objections persistent pendant une certaine période, la pratique peut se consolider."

A closely related question is whether the existence of "general acceptance" is permanent, or whether it could also cease to exist, for example due to changes in membership of the organization. It seems that the latter view is preferable. If there is broad support for a revised interpretation, why could that not be followed, just like the previous interpretation received the necessary support in earlier times?

3.8. In conclusion: Practice, interpretation, and beyond

This chapter has analysed a third legal facet of the practice of international organizations: the role of this practice in the interpretation of their law. International organizations are not states. It was therefore decided to limit the 1969 Vienna Convention to the law of treaties concluded between states. However, the subsequent work on and the conclusion of the 1986 Vienna II Convention has demonstrated that there are hardly any differences between states and international organizations as far as the law of treaties concluded by them is concerned. The rules on treaty interpretation are even fully identical. At the same time, there is diversity within unity. In two different ways, these identical rules can take into account that international organizations are not states, that constituent instruments of international organizations are different from other treaties and that treaties concluded by international organizations are not the same as treaties concluded between states. First, the rules on treaty interpretation are sufficiently broad and flexible to take into

---

490. *IDI Annuaire 2021*, at p. 250.

account these differences. For example, as illustrated by the 1996 ICJ Advisory Opinion requested by the WHO, greater weight may be given to subsequent practice when interpreting the organization's constituent instrument. It is also generally recognized that particular attention must be given to the object and purpose of constituent instruments and the aims of the organization concerned when these instruments are interpreted. Second, the two Vienna Conventions explicitly state that they apply to constitutions of international organizations and to treaties adopted within an international organization "without prejudice to any relevant rules of the organization"[491]. Each international organization may therefore have its own rules and arrangements for the interpretation of its rules. Apart from constitutions, the Vienna rules on interpretation are also relevant for the interpretation of other rules of international organizations, although such rules are often not treaties but unilateral acts. For example, the Vienna rules "may provide guidance" for the interpretation of Security Council resolutions, as the ICJ stated in its 2010 Advisory Opinion on Kosovo's unilateral declaration of independence[492]. But the Court also emphasized that other factors, including the relevant practice of the organ concerned, play an important role in the interpretation of unilateral decisions such as Security Council resolutions.

Since the art of interpretation is not an automatic process, and since the Vienna rules on interpretation offer considerable flexibility, the outcome of interpretative work is determined to a considerable extent by the interpreter. When it comes to the interpretation of the law of international organizations, there are two main interpreters: the organization and its members. As to the former, it is to be decided by the founding fathers of an organization whether rules on interpretation are included in the constituent instrument and, in particular, whether the competence to interpret rules of the organization is attributed to a specific organ. In some organizations, this competence is given to a judicial organ or to a policymaking organ. But in most organizations, specific rules on interpretation are absent and no organ is specifically charged with the task of interpreting the organization's rules. Regardless of whatever is decided by the founding fathers, in their daily practice the organs of international organizations interpret the rules of the organization that apply to them. This is unavoidable, otherwise they

---

491. Art. 5 of both Vienna Conventions.
492. ICJ, *Kosovo* Advisory Opinion, note 424, at p. 442, para. 94.

Legal Facets of the Practice of International Organizations 233

cannot perform their functions in a rapidly changing world. At the same time, it has raised questions about the role of the members in the interpretation of the organization's rules. This role is certainly not limited to the moment of establishment of the organization, when key decisions can be taken for the future interpretation of the organization's law. If no specific provisions apply, giving the task of ultimate interpretation to specific organs of the organization, the members must generally agree with interpretations given by organs. If this is the case, these interpretations are valid and *intra vires*. In 2021 the IDI adopted a resolution in which it made clear that what was decided in this respect in the 1945 UN Charter negotiations is applicable also today, and more generally. This is probably the most important limit to the evolutive interpretation of constituent instruments of international organizations. The relationship between an international organization and its members is fundamental for understanding the law and functioning of international organizations. This is also true for the role of an organization's practice in the interpretation of its rules. First and foremost, in their daily practice, it is for organs of the organization to interpret the latter's rules. But second, the requirement that members generally agree with such interpretations is an important check.

The previous chapter demonstrated the power-generating capacity of the practice of international organizations, while this chapter has discussed the important role of this practice in the interpretation of their law. The next two chapters will follow a different approach. Having analysed the role of practice of international organizations in two key areas in Chapters 2 and 3, the next two chapters will examine how two UN organs that are most relevant for the topic of this course, the ICJ and the ILC, have viewed the practice of international organizations in their work. First, an overview will be given of how the ICJ and its predecessor have dealt with the practice of international organizations in their work. Some examples from their advisory opinions have already been given in this chapter, but a more complete and in-depth analysis will be provided in Chapter 4. While, obviously, the PCIJ and the ICJ have developed their approach towards the practice of international organizations in the context of legal questions put to them, the ILC has dealt with that practice in the context of its own lawmaking work, as will be discussed in Chapter 5.

CHAPTER 4

THE INTERNATIONAL COURT OF JUSTICE AND PRACTICE OF INTERNATIONAL ORGANIZATIONS

4.1. Introduction

As discussed in Chapter 3, Articles 31-33 of the 1969 and 1986 Vienna Conventions are far from a fixed prescription that automatically leads to a particular treaty interpretation. Much is in the eye of the beholder, including the role given to the practice of international organizations. Therefore, perhaps the biggest change in this area – next to the Vienna codification of rules on treaty interpretation – is the impressive increase in the number of "beholders". Over the years, treaty interpretation has become less the exclusive prerogative of states. On the one hand, since the days of preparation of the Vienna Conventions, the number of international organizations has grown rapidly. In all these cases, the interpretation of their constituent instruments is not only in the hands of the founding fathers (almost exclusively states), but also in their own hands. On the other hand, in particular since the 1990s, the number of international courts and tribunals has increased from some six in 1990 to more than thirty at present, even more than fifty if international administrative tribunals are also included [493]. Therefore, the arena of the beholders of treaty interpretation has become steadily busier over the years.

Both international organizations and international courts and tribunals interpret and apply relevant treaties, and they do so from their own perspective. What *is* their perspective on the practice of international organizations in their interpretative work? The eyes of these beholders are different from those of states. Who is to provide guidance in this field? This chapter will offer a judicial perspective, focusing in particular on the role that the ICJ and its predecessor have given to the practice of international organizations in treaty interpretation. The next chapter will give a "legislative" perspective, analysing in particular the

---

493. See C. P. R. Romano, K. J. Alter and Y. Shany (eds.), *The Oxford Handbook of International Adjudication*, Oxford, Oxford University Press, 2014; K. J. Alter, *The New Terrain of International Law: Courts, Politics, Rights*, Princeton, NJ, Princeton University Press, 2014.

work of the UN's ILC on two topics on its agenda. Treating these two perspectives separately should not suggest that the work of the ICJ and the ILC is neatly separated. Both fully use and take into account each other's work [494], and this is without even mentioning that ICJ judges and ILC members are all part of the "invisible college of international lawyers" [495]. However, their tasks and proceedings are fundamentally different.

It is far beyond the scope of this special course to give a full overview of the relevant practice of all existing international organizations: how their practice might generate powers, how they use their practice in the interpretation of their constituent instruments, and so on. As mentioned in Chapter 1, this is a vast object of research. There are hundreds of international organizations. They all have their own practice, sometimes spanning more than a century. Instead of trying to do the impossible, giving an overview of the relevant practice of international organizations, the aim of this special course is to obtain a better understanding of legal facets of this practice.

In view of this aim, it is useful to analyze the decisions of the many international courts and tribunals that currently exist. Some of these courts and tribunals are confronted in some of their work with legal questions concerning the practice of international organizations, for example the question of whether a certain practice is in accordance with the rules of the organization and the question as to what extent they can or shall use the practice of an organization in interpreting these rules. As judicial bodies, their role is important in finding answers to such questions, and more generally in understanding the legal relevance of practice

---

494. For example, Chairman Nolte of the ILC Working Group on subsequent agreements and subsequent practice in relation to the interpretation of treaties started his work by analysing the case law of international courts and tribunals, in particular the ICJ; see *Yb. ILC 2008*, Vol. 2, Part 2 (UN Doc. A/CN.4/SER.A/2012/Add. 1 (Part 2)), at p. 159, para. 40; also UN Doc. A/65/10, at pp. 334-335. Likewise, Special Rapporteur Wood in his First Report on formation and evidence of customary international law analysed the relevant jurisprudence of international courts and tribunals, in particular the ICJ (see UN Doc. A/CN.4/653, p. 4, para. 18 and UN Doc. A/CN.4/663, at pp. 127-135). The ICJ referred to the work of the ILC in, for example, *Military and Paramilitary Activities in and against Nicaragua (Nicaragua v. United States of America)*, Merits, Judgment, *ICJ Reports 1986*, p. 14 *et seq.*, at p. 100, para. 190 and in *Difference Relating to Immunity from Legal Process of a Special Rapporteur of the Commission on Human Rights*, Advisory Opinion, *ICJ Reports 1999*, p. 62, at p. 87, para. 62.

495. O. Schachter, "The Invisible College of International Lawyers", *Northwestern University School of Law Review*, Vol. 72 (1977), pp. 217-226, at p. 217. Many ICJ judges have been members of the ILC before being elected to the Court (the other way around rarely if ever happens).

of international organizations. Some of the examples mentioned in Chapter 2 have illustrated this. In cases in which a judicial or quasi-judicial organ is tasked with giving an authoritative interpretation, the relevant answers are given on the basis of legal arguments. The UN Working Group on Arbitrary Detention concluded (its member Tochylovski dissenting) that it was within its competence to consider the case of Julian Assange. In the EU (at the time still the European Community), the Court of Justice established in 1996 that the Community lacked the competence to accede to the European Convention for the Protection of Human Rights and Fundamental Freedoms. In contrast, in organizations without such a judicial organ having the task of giving authoritative interpretations of the organization's rules (such as the UN), their practice is shaped largely or completely through political decision-making, and when its legality is questioned, this resulting uncertainty is likely to linger longer.

This chapter will first examine whether or to what extent the PCIJ has referred to the practice of international organizations in its decisions (Sec. 4.2). Next, in the most important part of this chapter, Section 4.3 will focus on the relevant advisory opinions of the ICJ. Within this section particular attention will be given to the 1962 *Certain Expenses* Advisory Opinion. This Opinion, and the rich diversity of views expressed by the Court's judges in the individual and separate opinions to this Opinion, is without doubt of key importance for understanding legal facets of the practice of international organizations more generally. Section 4.4 will offer some concluding observations.

4.2. The Permanent Court of International Justice

The PCIJ referred to the practice of international organizations in a few of its advisory opinions. The Court did not identify this as a distinct notion or concept, but that can hardly be surprising since only a very limited number of international organizations existed at the time, the two most important of which (the League of Nations and the ILO) were still very young. One of the ways in which the PCIJ referred to the practice of international organizations later became a common technique for the ICJ. According to this technique, a reference to such practice is used as an argument supporting a conclusion drawn by the Court on the basis of a legal analysis of the question to be addressed. It is a secondary, subsidiary argument that can be convincing and question-begging at the same time, as will be further discussed below (Sec. 4.4).

4.2.1. Competence of the ILO in regard to international regulation of the conditions of the labour of persons employed in agriculture (1922)

In its second Advisory Opinion (1922), the PCIJ was requested to answer the following question: "Does the competence of the International Labour Organization extend to international regulation of the conditions of labour of persons employed in agriculture?" [496] On the basis of "the construction of the text itself" the Court reached the conclusion that agricultural labour was within the competence of the ILO [497]. In the relevant text (Part XIII of the 1919 Versailles Peace Treaty), "read as a whole", the Court was "unable to find . . . any real ambiguity", and it concluded that it had "no doubt that agricultural labour is included in it" [498]. However, for the Court this was not the end of the matter. In addition, it stated the following: "If there were any ambiguity, the Court might, for the purpose of arriving at the true meaning, consider the action which has been taken under the Treaty." [499] Even though there was no "real ambiguity", the Court did consider briefly the relevant practice ("the action which has been taken under the Treaty"). This action consisted of

– the fact that the question of whether agricultural labour was within the ILO competences was not raised by any of the parties to the treaty in the first two years and four months since the signature of the Treaty, while in this period the subject of agriculture was repeatedly discussed (from this the Court concluded: "All this might suffice to turn the scale in favour of the inclusion of labour, if there were any ambiguity" [500]);
– the fact that the Conference of ILO devoted its second session almost entirely to seaman, and also adopted a recommendation regarding the fishing industry; however, "[i]t was never even suggested that either of these great industries was not within the competence of the ILO" [501].

---

496. PCIJ, *Competence of the ILO in regard to international regulation of the conditions of the labour of persons employed in agriculture*, Advisory Opinion, *PCIJ Reports*, Series B., No. 2 (1922).
497. *Id.*, at p. 41.
498. *Id.*, at p. 39.
499. *Id.*
500. *Id.*, at p. 41.
501. *Id.*

These arguments, which were derived from practice, were used by the PCIJ as additional, secondary arguments. It was not necessary for the Court to mention this, and the Court did not specify why it nevertheless wanted to do so. The practice to which the Court referred was practice within the ILO. It was partly practice by the parties to the Treaty, partly by the Conference of the ILO.

4.2.2. Competence of the ILO to regulate incidentally the personal work of the employer (1926)

Four years later, the PCIJ was requested to answer another question concerning the competences of the ILO: "Is it within the competence of the International Labour Organization to draw up and to propose labour legislation which, in order to protect certain classes of workers, also regulates incidentally the same work when performed by the employer himself?" [502] The Court gave an affirmative answer to the question. It did so by first examining the context of the discussions leading to the request for an advisory opinion, and subsequently by interpreting and applying the text of Part XIII of the 1919 Versailles Peace Treaty. Next, it mentioned several examples from ILO and member state practice, relating to the regulation of hours of work, the use of white phosphorus in the manufacture of matches and the use of white lead in paining. It concluded that in these examples, "it may be assumed that the incidental regulation of the personal work of the employers is potentially involved" [503]. Finally, it made a general analogy with the use of arguments derived from practice by domestic courts, when performing constitutional review functions, as follows [504]:

> "It is not an unusual thing, in countries in which legislative power is limited by a fundamental charter, for the Courts, in deciding whether certain legislation is constitutional, or intra vires, to resort to practice, national or international, for the determination of the extent of a particular governmental power. On this principle illustrations from existing labour legislation might be multiplied; but the examples already given are precise and pertinent and will suffice."

---

502. PCIJ, *Competence of the ILO to regulate incidentally the personal work of the employer*, Advisory Opinion, *PCIJ Reports, Series B.*, No. 13 (1926), p. 7 et seq.
503. *Id.*, at p. 18.
504. *Id.*, at p. 20.

It appears from this quotation that the PCIJ perceived a certain need to justify the part of its reasoning that related to practice. Since "[i]t is not an unusual thing" for national courts to do this, when reviewing whether the legislator has acted *ultra vires*, the PCIJ could also do so when asked to answer the question of whether it was within the ILO's powers to draw up and propose the labour legislation mentioned.

4.2.3. Jurisdiction of the European Commission of the Danube *(1927)*

One year later, another advisory opinion was requested from the Court concerning the powers of an international organization, this time the European Commission for the Danube (established by the Treaty of Paris in 1856) [505]. In its Advisory Opinion, the PCIJ fully took into account the practice of this organization. One of the questions in this Advisory Opinion was "where the powers of the European Commission [of the lower or maritime Danube], whatever they may be, terminate and are replaced by those of the International Commission [of the upper or fluvial Danube]" [506]. The Court decided that "[i]f the upstream limit is formed by a line across the river, this line must be placed immediately above the port of Braila" [507]. The port of Braila was therefore within the jurisdiction of the European Commission (and outside that of the International Commission). The Court mentioned a number of arguments for this conclusion, including the fact that the European Commission had taken fifteen decisions in the period from 1888 to 1909 that "refer clearly to the port of Braila itself" [508]. These fifteen decisions concern practice of the organization concerned. Another question in the Advisory Opinion concerned the delimitation of powers between the European Commission and Romania in relation to the ports of Galatz and Braila [509]. The Court rejected the Romanian view that such a delimitation should be of a territorial nature (instead of defining specific jurisdictional functions). One of the arguments used by the Court was derived from the practice of the European Commission: "It is also to be noted that, amongst the sentences of the European Commission. . ., there are no less than 36 cases which . . . relate to occurrences 'in the

---

505. PCIJ, *Danube* Advisory Opinion, note 181.
506. *Id.*, at p. 56.
507. *Id.*
508. *Id.*, at p. 58.
509. *Id.*, at p. 60.

port' *(dans le port)* or 'in the roads' *(en rade)* of Galatz or Braila."[510] It is not relevant that the Court did not use the term "practice of the organization". Neither did it in the two aforementioned earlier advisory opinions relating to the competences of the ILO. This term only became a term of art much later. What matters here is that the Court used an argument of this nature to support its conclusion.

The next section will analyse to what extent (and if so, how) the Court's successor has also referred to the practice of international organizations in its judicial reasoning.

4.3. The International Court of Justice

4.3.1. Early references to the practice of (organs of) the organization

From its beginning, the ICJ has consistently taken into account the practice of international organizations, in particular in its advisory opinions. Without analysing in detail the relevant opinions of the Court, this section will briefly mention the instances where the Court refers to such practice.

(i) Conditions of Admission *(1948)*

In its first advisory opinion, the Court answered the General Assembly's question of whether UN members, when voting in the Assembly and in the Security Council on the admission of a new member state, were "juridically entitled" to make their consent to admission "dependent on conditions not expressly provided for" by Article. 4.1, in particular "on the condition that other States be admitted to membership in the United Nations together with that State"[511]. The Court gave a negative answer, because "the text [of Art. 4.1] is sufficiently clear"[512]. Nevertheless, in addition, it referred to one specific element of the relevant practice of the Security Council, and that was the first paragraph of Rule 60 of the Council's Provisional Rules of Procedure: "The Security Council shall decide whether in its judgment the applicant is a peace-loving State and is able and willing to carry out the obligations contained in the Charter, and accordingly whether

---

510. *Id.*, at p. 62. See also p. 63, where the Court concludes that neither the instruments in force *nor the practice* support the Romanian argument.
511. ICJ, *Admission of a State* Advisory Opinion, note 188.
512. *Id.*, at p. 63.

to recommend the applicant State for membership."[513] The Court did not extensively comment on this paragraph, but simply concluded that it was "based on this interpretation"[514], that is, the textual interpretation of Article 4.1. In other words, the text of the first paragraph of Rule 60 confirmed the Court's interpretation.

(ii) Reparation for Injuries *(1949)*

One year later, the Court used the "practice of the organization argument" again. Following the assassination of UN mediator Count Bernadotte on the territory of Israel – not a UN member at the time – the General Assembly had asked, *inter alia*, whether the UN had the capacity to bring an international claim against Israel[515]. The Court noted that, before answering this question, it first needed to answer the preliminary question whether the UN possessed international personality. The Court stated that, in somewhat of an understatement, "[t]his [international personality] is no doubt a doctrinal expression, which has sometimes given rise to controversy"[516]. Primarily on the basis of its analysis of the UN Charter and the characteristics of the UN, the Court concluded that the UN is an international person. For the UN to achieve its ends, "the attribution of international personality is indispensable"[517]; "it could not carry out the intentions of its founders if it was devoid of international personality"[518]. However, the Court did not only base its conclusion on its Charter analysis. In addition, it took into account UN practice. Having concluded that the Charter has defined the position of the members in relation to the organization, the Court stated: "*[p]ractice has confirmed* this character of the Organization, which occupies a position in certain respects in detachment from its Members"[519]. In this context the ICJ mentions the 1946 Convention on the privileges and immunities of the UN, observing that "[i]t is

---

513. *Id.*
514. *Id.*
515. ICJ, *Reparation for Injuries*, note 298.
516. *Id.*, at p. 178. Indeed, during the UN Charter negotiations there had been considerable debate about the question of whether or not to include in the Charter a provision explicitly attributing international legal personality to the UN. It was finally decided not to do so, and the fear of creating a "super-State" was mentioned in that context (to which the Court refers on p. 179 of its Advisory Opinion). See in more detail Schermers and Blokker, note 2, at pp. 1028-1029.
517. *Id.*, at p. 178.
518. *Id.*, at p. 179.
519. *Id.* (italics added).

difficult to see how such a convention could operate except upon the international plane and as between parties possessing international personality" [520]. Hence, the Court used the "practice of the organization argument" as a supplementary argument, "confirming" the correctness of its conclusion, which was based on an analysis of the rules of the Charter and the character of the organization. The Court did not mention the *travaux* of the Charter. Its conclusion is not based on a reading of the Charter in light of these *travaux* but rather in light of the intentions of the founders of the UN. They "have clothed it with the competence required to enable those ... functions to be effectively discharged" [521].

In addition, as a general stepping stone to its conclusion that the status of international legal person afforded the UN the right to bring an international claim, the Court made the following general observation: "whereas a State possesses the totality of international rights and duties recognized by international law, the rights and duties of an entity such as the Organization must depend upon its purposes and functions as specified or implied in its constituent documents *and developed in practice*" [522]. In this way, the Court fully recognized, in the early years of the UN, the need for the organization to be able to pursue its aims and functions effectively in a world that already in 1949 was considerably different from the one existing at the time of the signing of the Charter.

(iii) Second Admission Case *(1950)*

Again one year later, the General Assembly requested a second advisory opinion relating to the procedure for the admission of new members to the UN. In the period preceding this request, the Security Council had been unable to recommend the admission to the UN of a number of applicant states, as required by Article 4.2 of the Charter. It was suggested that the Assembly could perhaps also admit candidate members without a recommendation of the Security Council, since it is not bound by such recommendations anyway (as they are not legally binding). The ensuing discussions and disagreements in the Assembly resulted in the question to the Court of whether states could be admitted to the UN "by a decision of the General Assembly when the Security Council has made no recommendation for admission by reason of the

---

520. *Id.*
521. *Id.*
522. *Id.*, at p. 180 (italics added).

candidate failing to obtain the requisite majority or of the negative vote of a permanent Member upon a resolution so to recommend" [523]?

The Court did not need much time nor many words to give a negative answer to this question; without a recommendation by the Security Council, states cannot be admitted to the UN by the General Assembly. The Court considered that, when it "can give effect to a provision of a treaty by giving to the words used in it their natural and ordinary meaning, it may not interpret the words by seeking to give them some other meaning. In the present case the Court finds no difficulty in ascertaining the natural and ordinary meaning of the words in question and no difficulty in giving effect to them" [524]. Even though the Court had stated a few sentences earlier "[i]f the relevant words in their natural and ordinary meaning make sense in their context, that is an end of the matter", it nevertheless took other arguments into consideration. It added that its conclusions based on the text of Article 4.2 "are fully confirmed by the structure of the Charter, and particularly by the relations established by it between the General Assembly and the Security Council" [525]. These two organs "have consistently interpreted the text in the sense that the General Assembly can decide to admit only on the basis of a recommendation of the Security Council" [526]. In this way, as before, the ICJ used the interpretation practice of these two UN organs as a supplementary argument for its conclusion.

(iv) International Status of South West Africa *(1950)*

Four months later, the ICJ rendered another advisory opinion at the request of the General Assembly [527]. The Assembly's request related to the international status of South West Africa. South Africa did not want to place what is now Namibia under the UN trusteeship system. It took the view that the Mandate agreement concluded during the existence of the League of Nations had lapsed, "because the League ha[d] ceased to exist" [528]. One of the questions examined by the Court was whether the UN General Assembly could continue to perform the functions previously performed by the League of Nations. The Court

---

523. ICJ, *Competence of Assembly* Advisory Opinion, note 385, at p. 5.
524. *Id.*, at p. 8.
525. *Id.*
526. *Id.*, at p. 9.
527. ICJ, *International status of South West Africa*, Advisory Opinion, *ICJ Reports 1950*, p. 128 *et seq.*
528. *Id.*, at p. 132.

stated that "[t]he competence of the General Assembly of the United Nations to exercise such supervision and to receive and examine reports is derived from the provisions of Article 10 of the Charter" [529]. It found support for this in the fact that "[t]his competence was in fact exercised by the General Assembly" in three resolutions [530]. Therefore, this practice of the Assembly confirmed the finding by the Court that the Assembly could continue the supervisory functions over mandates previously carried out by the League of Nations.

 (v) Judgments of the ILO Administrative Tribunal in cases against UNESCO *(1956)*

In 1956 the ICJ delivered an Advisory Opinion requested by the Executive Board of UNESCO [531]. The request concerned judgments of the ILO Administrative Tribunal (ILOAT) in cases brought by four UNESCO officials against UNESCO, because the renewal of their fixed-term contracts had been refused. The four officials challenged the argument that the holders of a fixed-term contract had no right to the renewal of their contract. "They alleged that, on the contrary, they had an acquired right to the renewal of their contracts. In doing so they relied, apart from general considerations relating to the international civil service and *the practice of international organizations*, on the position taken with regard to the renewal of fixed-term contracts by the Director-General." [532]

The ILOAT declared itself competent to entertain these complaints, and issued judgments in 1955. However, subsequently UNESCO's Executive Board raised a number of questions relating to ILOAT's competence in these four cases. Under the Statute of ILOAT, the Board was entitled to challenge ILOAT judgments, in a request for an advisory opinion to the ICJ. Under such a procedure, the opinion of the Court is binding.

The Court was "of the opinion that, in order to decide on the competence of the Administrative Tribunal, it is necessary to consider these contracts not only by reference to their letter but also in relation

---

529. *Id.*, at p. 137.
530. *Id.*
531. ICJ, *Judgments of the Administrative Tribunal of the ILO upon complaints made against the UNESCO*, Advisory Opinion, *ICJ Reports 1956*, p. 77 *et seq.*
532. *Id.*, at p. 88 (italics added).

to the actual conditions in which they were entered into and the place which they occupy in the Organization" [533]. It observed [534]:

> "In the practice of UNESCO – as well as in the practice of the United Nations and of the Specialized Agencies – fixed-term contracts are not like an ordinary fixed-term contract between a private employer and a private employee. At the crucial period a large number of the employees of UNESCO held fixed-term contracts. A similar situation seems to have obtained in the United Nations and in the Specialized Agencies. There is no need here to go into the reasons which have prompted that form of contracts. The fact is that *there has developed in this matter a body of practice* to the effect that holders of fixed-term contracts, although not assimilated to holders of permanent or indeterminate contracts, have often been treated as entitled to be considered for continued employment, consistently with the requirements and the general good of the organization, in a manner transcending the strict wording of the contract . . . *The practice as here surveyed is a relevant factor in the interpretation of the contracts in question.*"

The Court concluded that the ILOAT was competent to hear the complaints in these cases. This Advisory Opinion demonstrated the extent to which the ICJ took into consideration the practice of UNESCO, in addition to the text of the relevant contracts of the officials concerned.

(vi) Constitution of the Maritime Safety Committee of IMCO *(1960)*

In 1959, the Assembly of the Inter-Governmental Maritime Consultative Organization (IMCO) requested an advisory opinion from the ICJ, on the question of whether the Maritime Safety Committee of this organization "which was elected on 15 January 1959, [was] constituted in accordance with the Convention for the Establishment of the Organization" [535]. According to Article 28 *(a)* of this Convention, this Committee "shall consist of fourteen members. . ., of which not less than eight shall be the largest ship-owning nations" [536]. Liberia and Panama claimed that they belonged to these eight largest ship-owning nations,

---
533. *Id.*, at p. 91.
534. *Id.* (italics added).
535. ICJ, *Constitution of the Maritime Safety Committee of the Inter-Governmental Maritime Consultative Organization*, Advisory Opinion, *ICJ Reports 1960*, p. 150 *et seq.*
536. *Id.*, at p. 154.

but they were not elected on 15 January 1959. They claimed that the sole test to decide which are the eight largest ship-owning nations is the so-called registered tonnage, the total weight of the ships registered in a country. Other countries argued that the IMCO Assembly had much more flexibility in deciding which are the largest ship-owning nations. The Netherlands even argued that "the term 'ship-owning nations' is . . . not suitable for legal analysis" [537].

The Court concluded "that where in Article 28 *(a)* 'ship-owning nations' are referred to, the reference is solely to registered tonnage" [538]; "the test of registered tonnage is that which is most consonant with international practice and with maritime usage" [539]. It arrived at this conclusion by interpreting relevant articles of the constituent instrument of IMCO "*and the actual practice* which was followed in giving effect to them" [540]. It found that "*[t]he practice followed by the Assembly* . . . reveals the reliance placed upon registered tonnage" [541].

4.3.2. Certain Expenses *(1962)*

(i) *Background*

The background to a request for an advisory opinion from the ICJ by an organ or organization always pertains to the existence of a political dispute with one or more legal dimensions. The background to the request for the advisory opinion in *Certain Expenses* was a political dispute of particular intensity, concerning fundamentally opposing positions among the permanent members and among the three Western permanent members, first with regard to the 1956 Suez crisis and subsequently about the major, innovative way in which the UN dealt with this crisis: the establishment by the General Assembly of the first true UN peacekeeping operation [542]. The legal dimensions of this major political dispute were of a constitutional nature, concerning the scope of the powers of the General Assembly and how these powers relate to those of the Security Council.

---

537. *Id.*, at p. 165.
538. *Id.*, at p. 170.
539. *Id.*, at p. 169.
540. *Id.*, at p. 167 (italics added).
541. *Id.*, at p. 168 (italics added).
542. Some broader definitions of peacekeeping also include observer missions, which had already been created before 1956 (e.g. the UN Truce Supervision Organization, established in 1948).

The history of international organizations is not only the history of what is in the individual and collective interest of their members, the prevailing power relations, as well as immediate costs and benefits, and so on. It is also the history of individuals who have made a difference and have turned the scale. The *dramatis personae* in the functioning of the UN during the Suez crisis are numerous. However, if one person should be singled out it is UN Secretary-General Dag Hammarskjöld. It was Hammarskjöld who made an exceptional and courageous statement of principle in the Security Council on 31 October 1956, when he was shocked by the events of the time and outraged by the conduct of the permanent members France and the United Kingdom. He reiterated and highlighted his perceptions of the duties of a UN Secretary-General, and implicitly offered to step down if member states did not agree with those perceptions [543]. This statement deserves to be quoted in full [544]:

> "The principles of the Charter are, by far, greater than the Organization in which they are embodied, and the aims which they are to safeguard are holier than the policies of any single nation or people. As a servant of the Organization, the Secretary-General has the duty to maintain his usefulness by avoiding public stands on conflicts between Member nations unless and until such an action might help to resolve the conflict. However, the discretion and impartiality thus imposed on the Secretary-General by the character of his immediate task may not degenerate into a policy of expediency. He must also be a servant of the principles of the Charter, and its aims must ultimately determine what for him is right and wrong. For that he must stand. A Secretary-General cannot serve on any other assumption than that – within the necessary limits of human frailty and honest differences of opinion – all Member nations honour their pledge to observe all Articles of the Charter. He should also be able to assume that those organs which are charged with the task of upholding the Charter will be in a position to fulfil their task. The bearing of what I have just said must be obvious to all without any elaboration from my side. Were the members to consider that another view of the duties of the Secretary-General than the one here stated would better

---

543. See J. P. Lash, *Dag Hammarskjöld*, London, Cassell, 1961, at p. 81; Urquhart, note 17, at pp. 174-175.
544. Security Council Official Records, 751st meeting, UN Doc. S/PV.751, at pp. 1-2.

serve the interests of the Organization, it is their obvious right to act accordingly."

Following this statement, members of the Security Council expressed their support for Secretary-General Hammarskjöld. In the next few days, it was also Hammarskjöld who translated his perception of his position into practice by contributing majorly to the establishment by the General Assembly of the first true UN peacekeeping operation, the UN Emergency Force (UNEF) [545].

Several member states were against the creation of a peacekeeping force by the UN General Assembly, for a variety of reasons. Obviously, France and the United Kingdom had their reservations. The Soviet Union was fundamentally opposed as it considered the creation of UNEF a violation of the Charter. In its view, only the Security Council would have the power to take such action. For this reason, the Soviet Union refused to meet the expenses of the force [546]. France did not question the constitutionality of the force [547], but it also refused to contribute to the expenses of UNEF, and also of ONUC, the peacekeeping force that was subsequently established [548]. As a result of the refusal by these and some other countries to pay for UNEF and ONUC [549], the UN entered into what was termed a financial crisis but what was at its core a major political and constitutional crisis. Against the background of these circumstances, the General Assembly decided in 1961 to request an advisory opinion from the ICJ, "*[r]ecognizing* its need for authoritative legal guidance as to obligations of Member States under the Charter of the United Nations in the matter of financing the United Nations operations in the Congo and in the Middle East" [550]. In its question, the General Assembly asked whether the expenditures concerning these operations, authorized in a number of specified resolutions, "constitute

---

545. See in particular Urquhart, note 17, at pp. 178-194.
546. See R. Higgins, *United Nations Peacekeeping 1946-1967: Documents and Commentary*, London, Oxford University Press, Vol. 1: *The Middle East* (1969); Vol. 2: *Asia* (1970); Vol. 3: *Europe and Africa* (1980). See Vol. 1, at p. 264.
547. *Id.*, at p. 261.
548. In 1964, the arrears in payment of France and the Soviet Union reached such a level that it amounted to two full years of the contributions of these countries, as a result of which the sanction of the suspension of their votes would become applicable, as foreseen in Art. 19 of the Charter. The Soviet Union threatened that it would withdraw from the UN if this were to happen; see Higgins, note 546, Vol. 1, at p. 450. The General Assembly finally found a compromise solution avoiding the application of Art. 19. See Higgins, note 546, Vol. 1, at pp. 453-456. See also Higgins, note 546, Vol. 3, at p. 303.
549. For details, see Higgins, note 546, Vol. 1, at pp. 415-456; Higgins, note 546, Vol. 3, at pp. 274-303.
550. GA Res. 1731 (XVI), Preamble.

'expenses of the Organization' within the meaning of Article 17, paragraph 2, of the Charter of the United Nations" [551].

(ii) *The Advisory Opinion*

In its Advisory Opinion, the Court relied extensively on arguments derived from the practice of the UN and the practice of the General Assembly. Before doing so, it referred to its 1950 Advisory Opinion (*Second Admission Case*, discussed above in 4.3.1.(iii)), in which it had already referred to the practice of the Security Council and the practice of the General Assembly in its interpretation of the Charter. Following this precedent, the Court referred to the practice of the UN and the General Assembly as follows:

— Following a legal analysis of the word "budget" in Article 17.1 of the Charter, the Court concludes that this refers to one budget (for both administrative and operational expenses). While discussions have taken place concerning the idea of an operational budget, these did not result in the adoption of two separate budgets. Following this conclusion, the Court states: "[a]ctually, *the practice of the Organization* is entirely consistent with the plain meaning of the text" [552], and it refers to numerous examples of expenses included in the budget that were not administrative expenses.
— In addition, the Court observes that "[i]t is *a consistent practice of the General Assembly* to include in the annual budget resolutions, provision for expenses relating to the maintenance of international peace and security" [553].
— With respect to Article 17.2 of the Charter, the Court finds that the term "expenses of the Organization" means all expenses and not just some. It refers to Chapters IX and X of the Charter dealing with international economic and social cooperation and to Article 98 (which obliges the Secretary-General to perform such functions as are entrusted to him by UN organs). Subsequently, the Court concludes that it "does not perceive any basis for challenging the legality of *the settled practice* of including such expenses as these in the budgetary account which the General Assembly apportions among the Members" [554].

---

551. GA Res. 1731, at para. 1.
552. ICJ, *Certain Expenses*, note 308, at p. 160 (italics added).
553. *Id*. (italics added).
554. *Id*., at p. 162 (italics added).

- Following its analysis of Article 17, the ICJ analyses "its place in the general structure and scheme of the Charter", in order to see whether this could provide "any basis for implying a limitation upon the budgetary authority of the General Assembly which in turn might limit the meaning of 'expenses' in [Art. 17.2]" [555]. In this context, the Court considers the claim that Article 11.2 is such a limit. This Article stipulates, *inter alia*, that questions "on which action is necessary shall be referred to the Security Council". The Court observes that "action" means coercive or enforcement action [556]. It does not mean that the General Assembly can only make recommendations "of a general character affecting peace and security in the abstract, and not in relation to specific cases" [557]. Following this interpretation of Article 11.2, the Court states: "*The practice of the Organization throughout its history* bears out the foregoing elucidation of the term 'action' in the last sentence of Article 11, paragraph 2." [558]
- In the second part of this Advisory Opinion, the Court examines the specific expenditures relating to UNEF and ONUC mentioned in the request for an advisory opinion by the General Assembly. These expenditures "must be tested by their relationship to the purposes of the United Nations in the sense that if an expenditure were made for a purpose which is not one of the purposes of the United Nations, it could not be considered an 'expense of the Organization'" [559]. The Court chooses to apply this test in a rather liberal way, by a "presumption of legality": "when the Organization takes action which warrants the assertion that it was appropriate for the fulfilment of one of the stated purposes of the United Nations, the presumption is that such action is not *ultra vires* the Organization" [560]. In addition, the Court notes that proposals made in 1945 to give the final authority of interpreting the Charter to the ICJ were not accepted, and concludes that "[a]s anticipated in 1945, therefore, each organ must, in the first place at least, determine its own jurisdiction" [561]. Against this background, the Court examines the specific General Assembly resolutions dealing

---

555. *Id.*
556. *Id.*
557. *Id.*, at p. 165.
558. *Id.* (italics added).
559. *Id.*, at p. 167.
560. *Id.*, at p. 168.
561. *Id.* In this respect, Judge Fitzmaurice was right when he stated in his separate opinion that "[t]he argument drawn from practice, if taken too far, can be question-begging" and "it is indeed the validity of some part of that practice [of the United Nations] which is put in issue by the present Request"; *id.*, at p. 201.

with the expenses of UNEF and ONUC. It concludes that these resolutions were adopted both without a dissenting vote or by the required majority, and that the Assembly has always treated the expenses concerned as expenses of the Organization. Again, this is an argument based on the practice of (organs of) the organization, although the Court does not explicitly say this. As will be further discussed below (Sec. 4.5), there is a certain "danger of circularity" involved in this argument. Essentially, it boils down to answering the Assembly's question of whether particular expenses are expenses of the Organization by stating that the Assembly has consistently treated such expenses as expenses of the Organization. It may be questioned whether this fully meets the General Assembly's "need for authoritative legal guidance" [562].

It is therefore clear that the ICJ in this Advisory Opinion strongly relies on the practice of the UN and the General Assembly. In doing so it uses different terms: "consistent practice", "settled practice", and "the practice of the Organization throughout its history".

(iii) *Separate and Dissenting Opinions: Judge Spender*

The Advisory Opinion was given by nine votes to five. It was accompanied by a declaration from Judge Spiropoulos, Separate Opinions by Judges Spender, Fitzmaurice and Morelli, and dissenting opinions by President Winiarski and Judges Basdevant, Moreno Quintana, Koretsky and Bustamante y Rivero. For the purpose of the present analysis, in particular the Separate Opinion by Judge Spender is relevant. The last ten pages of his opinion are devoted to the topic coined by him as "*Practice within the United Nations* – Its effect on or value as a criterion of interpretation" [563]. His conclusion is:

> "In the present case, it is sufficient to say that I am unable to regard any usage or practice followed by any organ of the United Nations which has been determined by a majority therein against the will of a minority as having any legal relevance or probative value."

The great merit of Spender's analysis is that it distinguishes between practice of the member states and practice of the organization (something

---

562. GA Res. 1731 (XVI), Preamble.
563. ICJ, *Certain Expenses*, note 308, Separate Opinion of Judge Sir Percy Spender, p. 182 *et seq.*, at p. 187.

that the ICJ has not always done). The great demerit of his analysis is that it does not accept the legal relevance of the practice of organs of the UN. This part of Judge Spender's opinion will now be analysed in detail, also because views not unlike those of Judge Spender are still sometimes expressed [564].

Judge Spender took issue with the proposition advanced by some states during the proceedings in this case that "the uniform practice pursued by the organs of the United Nations should be equated with the "subsequent conduct" of contracting *parties* as in the case of a bilateral treaty" [565]. His reasoning follows a number of steps, reproduced below, using mostly his own words:

> *(i)* The conduct of one party to a bilateral instrument may throw light upon its intentions when entering into it while that of both parties may have considerable probative value in aid of interpretation, even though there is an element of artificiality in this principle (p. 189). The essence, the roots of the principle of subsequent conduct are deeply embedded in the experience of mankind. The meaning of a compact between two parties may well be affected, even determined, by the manner in which both parties in practice have carried it out. Their conduct "expresses their common understanding of what the terms of their compact, at the time they entered into it, were intended to mean, and thus provides direct evidence of what they did mean" (p. 190).
>
> *(ii)* In the case of multilateral treaties, the admissibility and value as evidence of subsequent conduct of one or more parties thereto encounter particular difficulties. This occurs first of all when not all of the parties by their subsequent conduct interpret the text in the same way. Second, these difficulties are even more serious if the parties to a multilateral treaty include not only the original parties but also parties who have joined later. For example, if the intention of the original members of the UN is that which provides a criterion of interpretation, then it is the subsequent conduct of *those* members which may be equated with the subsequent conduct of the parties to a bilateral or multilateral treaty where the parties are fixed and constant (p. 191).
>
> *(iii)* It is not permissible to move the principle of subsequent conduct of parties to a bilateral or multilateral treaty into another field and

---

564. For examples, see Chap. 5 below.
565. Separate Opinion of Judge Sir Percy Spender, at p. 188 (italics in the original).

seek to apply it, not to the *parties* to the treaty, but to an *organ* established under the treaty (p. 192). The above-mentioned element of artificiality (see *(i)*) is greatly magnified when the principle is sought to be extended from the field of bilateral instruments to that of multilateral instruments of an organic character and where the practice (or subsequent conduct) relied upon is that, not of the parties to the instrument, but of an organ created thereunder (p. 189). With regard to organs of the UN: "Not only is such an organ not a party to the Charter but the inescapable reality is that both the General Assembly and the Security Council are but the mechanisms through which the Members of the United Nations express their views and act" (p. 192).

(iv) Finally, Judge Spender disagrees with those who find authority for the contention that the practice of the General Assembly and the Security Council has a particular probative value of its own in the jurisprudence of the ICJ and that of its predecessor. He analyses various cases and concludes that "they throw little light upon the matter" (p. 192). In some of these cases, the Court had already drawn a conclusion, and added that this was in fact confirmed in practice. Moreover, some of these cases did not concern the practice of organs, but rather the practice of states.

As mentioned above, while the great merit of Judge Spender's analysis is that it distinguishes between practice of the member states and practice of the organization, its great demerit is that it fails to see the legal relevance of the practice of organs of the UN. First, Judge Spender attaches great value to the intention of the parties to a treaty ("the subsequent conduct of the parties to a bilateral – or a multilateral – instrument may throw light on the intention of the parties at the time the instrument was entered into and thus may provide a legitimate criterion of interpretation" (p. 189)). However, it is generally recognized that the intention of the parties is not the only means of interpretation, and in the case of constituent instruments of international organizations not the most important one.

Second, even if the intention of the parties was used as an important means of interpreting the Charter, it must be underscored that the fifty states negotiating the Charter intended to not only conclude a multilateral treaty but also the constituent instrument of an international organization, with *its own* international legal personality and with organs having *their own* powers, including the power to take binding and non-binding decisions, that are not agreements between states but unilateral acts emanating from an organ whose will is to be distinguished from that of the member states. As the ICJ stated in 1949 [566], "we must consider what characteristics it [the Charter] *was intended* thereby to give to the Organization" . . . "The Charter has not been content to make the Organization created by it merely a centre 'for harmonizing the actions of nations in the attainment of these common ends' (Art. 1, para. 4). It has equipped that centre with organs, and has given it special tasks." The Organization "could not carry out *the intentions of its founders* if it was devoid of international personality". Spender fails to recognize that states, when establishing an international organization, deliberately do more than concluding a multilateral treaty or starting an informal framework of cooperation such as the G7 or the G20. Definitions of international organizations generally contain at least two elements: not only the requirement that the organization is (normally) created by treaty but also the requirement that it is a separate legal person, and/or that it has a will of its own (or better, in French, a *volonté distincte*) [567]. Failing to recognize this second element makes it difficult if not impossible to distinguish the organization from its members and to identify the organization's practice as different from that of the members.

Third, Judge Spender is neglecting the institutional or organizational characteristics of the UN Charter and overemphasizes the fact that it is a multilateral treaty that "cannot be altered at the will of the majority of the member States, no matter how often that will is expressed or asserted against a protesting minority and no matter how large be the majority of Member States which assert its will in this manner or how small the minority" [568]. Already in the same case, one of the other judges, Judge Fitzmaurice, explained that this view is erroneous, in his Separate Opinion: "even if a majority vote cannot in the formal sense bind the minority, it can, if consistently exercised in a particular way, suffice to establish a settled practice which a tribunal can usefully and properly take account of" [569].

---

566. ICJ, *Reparation for Injuries*, note 298. The following quotations are at pp. 178-179 of the Court's Opinion (italics added).
567. See e.g. Schermers and Blokker, note 2, at pp. 48-50 (with references to further literature). See also the definition of "international organization" in the ILC ARIO: "an organization established by a treaty or other instrument governed by international law and possessing its own international legal personality", UN Doc. A/66/10.
568. Separate Opinion of Judge Sir Percy Spender, note 563, at p. 196.
569. Separate Opinion of Judge Sir Gerald Fitzmaurice, note 561, at pp. 201-202.

Fourth, Judge Spender's overview of the jurisprudence of the PCIJ and the ICJ is incomplete and partly incorrect. He does not refer to several of the above-mentioned advisory opinions (such as *Reparation for Injuries*, *Judgments of the ILO Administrative Tribunal in cases against UNESCO* and *IMCO*) and he neglects to take account of the distinct nature of the argument based on the practice of the organization. Instead, Judge Spender states that the Court in some of these cases "had already arrived at its conclusion on the interpretation which should be given to the text; its observation was accordingly *obiter dicta*" [570]. "Again, whatever is the significance to be attached to this purely factual observation on a coincidence [the consistent interpretation of the text of Article 4 of the Charter by the General Assembly and the Security Council], it was unnecessary and irrelevant to the Court's opinion" [571]. As will be further discussed below, the reference to the practice of the organization or of the organ is not an *obiter dictum*; neither is it a coincidence. It is a deliberate attempt by the Court to demonstrate that its interpretation is in touch with reality. In doing so, the Court only confirms what Spender wrote: the roots of the principle of subsequent conduct "are deeply embedded in the experience of mankind" [572].

Spender's views have also been criticized by others. Already in 1965, Higgins commented: "Sir Percy Spender's objections are irrelevant. For although *organ* practice may not be good evidence of the intention of the original parties, it *is* of probative value as customary law." [573] In addition, in 1976, Elihu Lauterpacht observed that "the conclusions of Sir Percy Spender are ones which are largely – and increasingly – contradicted by the practice of international tribunals themselves" [574]. In 1984, Reuter wrote: "L'opinion de sir Percy Spender est discutable dans ses bases théoriques et dans la forme extrême qu'il a donnée à son expression, mais pose un problème de principe et répond à des réalités politiques." [575] More recently, Alvarez stated: "Justice Spender was wrong: institutional practice, even when controverted by some members, has an inherent value and is not simply a sometimes misleading alternative to 'original intent'." [576] Finally, the notion of "established practice of the organization" is now included in multilateral treaties and

---

570. *Id.*, at p. 193.
571. *Id.*, at p. 195.
572. Separate Opinion Judge Spender, note 563, at p. 190.
573. Higgins, note 323, quotation at p. 119.
574. Lauterpacht, note 337, at p. 447.
575. Reuter, note 4, at pp. 202-203.
576. Alvarez, note 326, at p. 89.

in the ILC ARIO [577]. Not only academic writings but also practice (of states *and* of international organizations) has demonstrated that Judge Spender's views are erroneous and outdated.

4.3.3. Namibia *(1971)*

Nine years after *Certain Expenses*, the Court was faced with another challenge relating to the legal appreciation of the practice of the UN. In its 1971 *Namibia* Advisory Opinion, the only opinion ever requested by the Security Council, the practice concerned was the practice of the decision-making of the Security Council regarding substantive (non-procedural) issues, according to which abstentions by one or more permanent members were not considered to prevent the lawful adoption of a resolution, in spite of the language of Article 27.3 of the Charter.

The immediate background to this unique request by the Security Council was the declaration of the Security Council in 1970 that the continued presence of South Africa in its former mandate South West Africa/Namibia was illegal [578]. South Africa did not withdraw from Namibia following the adoption of this resolution. Subsequently, the Security Council agreed to request the following question from the ICJ: "What are the legal consequences for States of the continued presence of South Africa in Namibia, notwithstanding Security Council resolution 276 (1970)?" [579] The more general background to this request was the strong and ever-growing opposition in the UN to South Africa in general, not only because of its presence in Namibia but also in view of its apartheid policy (practised not only in South Africa but also in Namibia). In addition, the request for an advisory opinion was seen as a way to reactivate the ICJ [580], and also to "to provide an opportunity for the International Court to redeem its impaired image" caused by the "unfortunate Judgment of the Court in 1966" [581].

---

577. Vienna Convention on the Representation of States in their Relations with International Organizations of a Universal Character, Art. 1.1 (34); Vienna Convention on the Law of Treaties between States and International Organizations or Between International Organizations (1986), Art. 2.1 *(j)*; ILC ARIO, Art. 2 *(b)*.
578. SC Res. 276 (1970), adopted 30 January 1970.
579. SC Res. 284 (1970), adopted 29 July 1970.
580. See in particular the statement by Finland in the meeting of the Security Council where the resolution requesting the advisory opinion was adopted, UN Doc. S/PV.1550, at p. 5: "An organ which is left unused is in danger of atrophy. The decline in the authority of the Court is damaging to the interests of the United Nations system as a whole and to the structure of international law. The request for an advisory opinion on a question of great interest to the international community would reactivate the Court at a particularly difficult time in its existence."
581. Statement by Nepal in the Security Council, UN Doc. S/PV.1550, at p. 9. A number of other members of the Council also referred to this "impaired image" of

Before the Court, South Africa made a number of preliminary objections. One of these was that in the voting on Resolution 284 (requesting the opinion of the Court) two permanent members of the Council abstained. South Africa contended that "the resolution was consequently not adopted by an affirmative vote of nine members, including the concurring votes of the permanent members, as required by Article 27, paragraph 3, of the Charter of the United Nations" [582]. A plain reading of the text of this provision seems to provide much support for South Africa's position and would appear to seriously question the lawfulness of the practice of the adoption of substantive resolutions with one or more permanent members abstaining from voting [583]. A textual analysis of this provision not only in English but also in the other authentic languages of the Charter would lead to the same conclusion [584]. However, the ICJ rejected the South African objection in three sentences, which contain a number of legal arguments essential for the topic of this course and are therefore quoted in full [585]:

> "However, the proceedings of the Security Council extending over a long period supply abundant evidence that presidential rulings and the positions taken by members of the Council, in particular its permanent members, have consistently and uniformly interpreted the practice of voluntary abstention by a

---

the Court because of its 1966 judgment, e.g. Sierra Leone (*id.*, at p. 5), Zambia (*id.*, at p. 12), Poland (*id.*, at p. 15) and Burundi (*id.*, at p. 15).

582. *South West Africa* Advisory Opinion, note 477, at p. 22, at para. 21. Already in 1962, in his Dissenting Opinion in *Certain Expenses*, ICJ Judge Bustamante pointed to the possibility that the conformity of the Security Council practice with Art. 27.3 could be challenged: "It is already well known that an unwritten amendment to the Charter has taken place in the practice of the Security Council, namely, to the effect that the abstention of a permanent Member present at a meeting is not assimilated to the exercise of the right of veto. No doubt this type of amendment may be legally repudiated in a given case by invoking the text of the Charter (Art. 27, para. 3), since no permanent Member has undertaken to apply it without reservations" (note 308, at p. 291; footnote omitted).

583. In his Separate Opinion, Judge Dillard argued that the text of Art. 27.3 does not unequivocally lead to the conclusion that it is required that permanent members vote in favour, in order for a resolution to be lawfully adopted. He wrote that "[h]ad the critical clause read: '*all five* permanent members, *who must be present and voting*. . .'", the contention might have been justified. In the absence of such a precise prescription the subsequent conduct of the parties is clearly a legitimate method of giving meaning to the Article in accordance with the expectations of the parties, including, in particular, the permanent members" (italics in the original).

584. See e.g. the French text: "un vote affirmatif de neuf de ses membres dans lequel sont comprises les voix de *tous* les membres permanents" (italics added). The following observations have been reproduced from Schermers and Blokker, note 2, at pp. 880-881.

585. *South West Africa* Advisory Opinion, note 477, at p. 22, para. 22.

permanent member as not constituting a bar to the adoption of resolutions. By abstaining, a member does not signify its objection to the approval of what is being proposed; in order to prevent the adoption of a resolution requiring unanimity of the permanent members, a permanent member has only to cast a negative vote. This procedure followed by the Security Council, which has continued unchanged after the amendment in 1965 of Article 27 of the Charter, has been generally accepted by Members of the United Nations and evidences a general practice of that Organization."

These three sentences are carefully composed and illustrate the importance attached by the Court to the organization's practice and the far-reaching implications that the "recourse to practice" technique may have – it may result in an interpretation that some would consider *contra legem* [586]. This also raises the question of how much practice is needed before it would qualify as a supporting argument for a certain interpretation. In *Namibia*, the Court used a temporal requirement ("extending over a long period"), a frequency requirement ("abundant evidence"), an interest requirement ("members of the Council, in particular its permanent members"), a stability requirement ("consistently and uniformly") and the fact that the practice continued following the 1965 amendment (that did not codify this interpretation). In addition, the Court did not consider it sufficient to take into account exclusively the position of the members of the Security Council; it also

---

586. See further C. A. Stavropoulos, "The Practice of Voluntary Abstentions by Permanent Members of the Security Council under Article 27, Paragraph 3, of the Charter of the United Nations", *American Journal of International Law*, Vol. 61 (1967), pp. 737-752; B. Simma (ed.), *The Charter of the United Nations: A Commentary*, 2nd ed., New York, Oxford University Press, 2002, at pp. 493-499 (analysing the relevant literature, in which "two fundamentally different opinions can be found": according to one view, this practice is based on an interpretation of Art. 27.3, according to the other view, this is a "progressive modification of the Charter" – e.g. "[a]ccording to a widespread view, Art. 27 (3) has been modified by customary law between the contracting States" (*id.*, at pp. 493, 495)). The third edition of the last-mentioned UN Charter commentary prefers the first, "interpretation view": "this accepted interpretation of Art. 27 (3) has become binding upon all member States of the Organization. . . . There is therefore no need to further consider the possibility of a customary law norm having superseded Art. 27 (3)"; see B. Simma *et al.* (eds.), *The Charter of the United Nations: A Commentary*, 3rd ed., New York, Oxford University Press, 2012, at 915; see also B. Conforti and C. Focarelli, *The Law and Practice of the United Nations*, 5th rev. ed., Leiden, Brill Nijhoff, 2016, at pp. 80-84. This case of the interpretation of Art. 27.3 of the Charter could also be seen as an example of "established practice" of the organization, which (in accordance with the definition of "rules of the organization" given in the 1986 Vienna Convention and in the 2011 ARIO) is not required to be in accordance with the constitution of the organization (i.e. the UN Charter).

observed that the practice concerned "has been generally accepted by Members of the United Nations". It is therefore clear that the attitude of both the organization and its members is relevant. This is in line with the *travaux préparatoires* of the Charter. Committee IV/2 of the San Francisco conference not only stated in its report that "each organ will interpret such parts of the Charter as are applicable to its particular functions", it continued [587]:

> "It is to be understood, of course, that if an interpretation made by any organ of the Organization or by a committee of jurists is not *generally acceptable* it will be without binding force. In such circumstances, or in cases where it is desired to establish an authoritative interpretation as a precedent for the future, it may be necessary to embody the interpretation in an amendment to the Charter."

4.3.4. WHO Nuclear Weapons *(1996)*

In 1993 the World Health Assembly decided to request an advisory opinion from the ICJ on the following question: "In view of the health and environmental effects, would the use of nuclear weapons by a State in war or other armed conflict be a breach of its obligations under international law including the WHO Constitution?" [588] The relevant resolution of the Assembly was adopted following heated discussions, by a vote of seventy-three in favour, forty against (forty-one members absent, ten abstentions) [589]. During these discussions and in preceding meetings, the WHO Legal Counsel had repeatedly indicated that in his view it was not within the competence of the WHO to deal with the legality of the use of nuclear weapons [590]. A majority of the member states however took another view and the resolution was adopted, requesting the ICJ to give an advisory opinion on the above-mentioned question. The Court found that it was not able to give the requested advisory opinion because one of the conditions to exercise its jurisdiction was not met: the question was not one arising within the scope of the WHO's

---

587. Doc. 933, IV/2/42(2), 13 UNCIO, at 709 (emphasis added).
588. ICJ, *WHO Nuclear Weapons* Advisory Opinion, note 183.
589. See WHO Doc. A46/VR/13, at p. 282; see also the official records of the meeting of the Assembly in WHO, Forty-Sixth World Health Assembly, Verbatim records of plenary meetings, Doc. WHA46/1993/REC/2, at p. 273 *et seq.*
590. See the Separate Opinion of Judge Oda to the Court's Advisory Opinion, referring to the relevant statements of the WHO Legal Counsel (note 183, at pp. 88-96).

activities [591]. In the Court's arguments for this conclusion, the "practice of the organization argument" plays an important role.

The ICJ has always considered it important to take into account the practice of the organization in giving an interpretation of constituent instruments of international organizations, but only in its 1996 *WHO Nuclear Weapons* Advisory Opinion was some legal underpinning of this approach given [592]. As discussed in Chapter 3, having observed that "constituent instruments of international organizations are also treaties of a particular type", the ICJ stated that "[s]uch treaties can raise specific problems of interpretation owing, *inter alia,* to their character which is conventional and at the same time institutional". The Court specified this as follows: "the very nature of the organization created, the objectives which have been assigned to it by its founders, the imperatives associated with the effective performance of its functions, as well as its own practice, are all elements which may deserve special attention when the time comes to interpret these constituent treaties". In the interpretation of constitutions of international organizations, their institutional nature should be taken into account.

At the same time, the Court did not explicitly indicate what this means. To what extent should the Vienna rules on treaty interpretation be applied differently when interpreting constitutions of international organizations? For example, when compared to the interpretation of other treaties, should "the ordinary meaning" of the terms of the treaty be less important and their "object and purpose" more important? Should the *travaux préparatoires* be less important and subsequent practice more important? In the 1996 *WHO Nuclear Weapons* Advisory Opinion, the ICJ does not refer to Articles 31-33 of the 1969 and 1986 Vienna Conventions in their entirety. Instead, the Court singles out some of the means of interpretation laid down in these articles, as follows:

> "According to the customary rule of interpretation as expressed in Article 31 of the 1969 Vienna Convention on the Law of Treaties, the terms of a treaty must be interpreted "in their context

---

591. As required by Art. 96.2 UN Charter. The Court notes in its Advisory Opinion that Art. X.2 of the 1948 relationship agreement concluded between the UN and the WHO, as well as Art. 76 of the WHO Constitution, use different language, requiring questions for an advisory opinion to arise within the scope of the WHO's "competence". However, it considered that "for the purposes of this case, no point of significance turns on the different formulations" (note 183, at p. 74, para. 18).

592. The following comments on this 1996 Advisory Opinion of the Court are largely reproduced from Schermers and Blokker, note 2, at pp. 882-884.

and in the light of its object and purpose" and there shall be "taken into account, together with the context:

...

(b) any subsequent practice in the application of the treaty which establishes the agreement of the parties regarding its interpretation."

Next, the Court recalls that it has applied this rule of interpretation earlier (referring to four cases) and states that "it will also apply it in this case for the purpose of determining whether, according to the WHO Constitution, the question to which it has been asked to reply arises 'within the scope of [the] activities' of that Organization" [593].

It is noteworthy that the Court in its reference to Article 31 does not explicitly refer to textual interpretation [594], which is laid down in the first part of Article 31.1 of the 1969 and the 1986 Vienna Conventions ("A treaty shall be interpreted in good faith in accordance with the ordinary meaning to be given to the terms of the treaty"), but, instead, starts its reference to Article 31 by quoting the final part of paragraph 1 ("in their context and in the light of its object and purpose").

In addition, the Court selects another means of interpretation mentioned in Article 31: "any subsequent practice in the application of the treaty which establishes the agreement of the parties regarding its interpretation". This is remarkable as the Court has usually been reluctant to conclude that a specific method of interpretation should be followed *because* of the "constitutional" character of the treaty in question [595]. In the subsequent sections of this Advisory Opinion, the Court pays ample attention to the practice of the WHO, sometimes referring to the "practice of the Organization" [596], sometimes to "a practice establishing an agreement between the members of the Organization to interpret its Constitution as empowering it to address the question of the legality of the use of nuclear weapons" [597].

Two further comments are called for. First, the ICJ has now attempted to formulate a legal basis for referring to the practice of the organization. However, second, it may be questioned whether this legal basis is accurate because "subsequent practice" as a canon of interpretation laid

---

593. *Id.*
594. As it has done earlier, for example in ICJ, *Competence of Assembly* Advisory Opinion, note 385, at p. 8.
595. Lauterpacht, note 337, at pp. 414-416.
596. ICJ, *WHO Nuclear Weapons* Advisory Opinion, note 183, at paras. 21 and 27.
597. *Id.*, at p. 66, para. 27.

down in the 1969 Vienna Convention refers to the practice of the *states* that are party to a particular treaty ("the application of the treaty which establishes the agreement of the parties regarding its interpretation") and not to the practice of the *organization* itself. In this sense, Article 31 (3) *(b)* of the Vienna Convention seems to be incorrect as a foundation on which the "practice of the organization" may rest [598]. This also has a very practical implication: whereas it is required that *all parties* to the constitution must agree to a certain interpretation if it were to be considered as "subsequent practice", such unanimous support is not required for the "practice of the organization".

Following the above-quoted references to Article 31 of the Vienna Convention, the Court analyses the WHO Constitution, in particular the list of functions given to the WHO in Article 2. It concludes that these functions authorize the WHO to deal with the effects of the use of nuclear weapons on health. The question of the legality of the use of those weapons is not relevant in this regard and is therefore *ultra vires* ("Whatever those effects might be, the competence of the WHO to deal with them is not dependent on the legality of the acts that caused them") [599]. Applying the principle of speciality, the Court concludes that this question is outside the explicit and implied powers of the WHO. In addition, the Court refers to the "logic of the overall system contemplated by the Charter": the WHO is a *specialized* agency; its task is to focus on health issues, whereas "questions concerning the use of force, the regulation of armaments and disarmament are within the competence of the United Nations and lie outside that of the specialized agencies" [600].

However, this does not conclude the ICJ's Advisory Opinion. The Court does not limit its answer to a legal analysis of the WHO

---

598. A few authors have, briefly or in more detail, paid attention to the distinction between subsequent practice (Art. 31.3 *(b)* of the Vienna Convention) and the "practice of the organization". See Rosenne, note 26, at p. 195 ("It is doubtful if the equation may legitimately be made") and at p. 241; Brölmann, note 27, at pp. 120-121; Boisson de Chazournes, note 4; I. Buga, "Subsequent Practice and Treaty Modification", in M. J. Bowman and D. Kritsiotis (eds.), *Conceptual and Contextual Perspectives on the Modern Law of Treaties*, Cambridge, Cambridge University Press, 2018, pp. 363-391, in particular at pp. 368-369. Nolte, in the context of his work for the ILC on the topic "Treaties over Time", has briefly observed that "the distinction between the practice of the organization itself and that of its member states must be taken into account". See his Introductory Report for the ILC Study Group on Treaties over Time. This report has not been published as a UN document but is reproduced in G. Nolte (ed.), *Treaties and Subsequent Practice*, Oxford, Oxford University Press, 2013, at p. 204. The only more extensive studies are by Peters, notes 14 and 34.
599. ICJ, *WHO Nuclear Weapons* Advisory Opinion, note 183, at p. 76.
600. *Id.*, at p. 80.

Constitution (which resulted in the conclusion that the question asked is *ultra vires* the WHO). Instead, it supplements its legal analysis by adding another section devoted to the practice of the WHO (not the practice of the WHO *member states*). The first sentence of this section is: "[a] consideration of the practice of the WHO bears out these conclusions"[601]. The WHO reports and resolutions reviewed by the Court are not "in the nature of a practice of the WHO in regard to the legality of the threat or use of nuclear weapons"[602]. However, this practice *of the organization* is not covered by the 1969 Vienna Convention to which the Court has referred earlier in this Advisory Opinion (as quoted above), since this Convention's reference to subsequent practice as a means of treaty interpretation refers to practice *of states*. The Court refers to the WHO member states only in a final sentence of this section of the Advisory Opinion, where it concludes with regard to the WHO resolution requesting the advisory opinion that this resolution "could not be taken to express or to amount on its own to a practice establishing an agreement between the members of the Organization to interpret its Constitution as empowering it to address the question of the legality of the use of nuclear weapons"[603].

In conclusion, the Court uses the "practice argument" as an additional argument to support its preceding legal analysis, as it has done in earlier advisory opinions. What is new, however, is that the Court has now explicitly referred to the 1969 Vienna Convention's rules on treaty interpretation and has specifically mentioned "subsequent practice" as a legal basis for its subsequent taking into account of WHO practice. This reference to the Vienna Convention is unfortunate since its rules only apply to states and their subsequent practice. They do not cover the practice of international organizations (such as the WHO in this case).

4.3.5. Further references to organizational practice, post WHO Nuclear Weapons

Following the 1996 Advisory Opinion requested by the WHO, the ICJ used the "practice argument" in several advisory opinions that will now be briefly examined.

---

601. *Id.*, at p. 81.
602. *Id.*
603. *Id.*

(i) Cumaraswamy *(1999)*

There are brief references to the practice of the UN in this Advisory Opinion [604], requested by the Economic and Social Council in the context of the dispute between the UN and Malaysia on the immunity of Dato' Param Cumaraswamy, Special Rapporteur on the Independence of Judges and Lawyers of the UN Commission on Human Rights. In 1995 Cumaraswamy (a Malaysian national) gave an interview published in a journal in which he made comments on litigations in Malaysian courts. Two companies filed a suit against Cumaraswamy, *inter alia* for damages for slander. The UN Secretary-General determined that Cumaraswamy had given the interview in his capacity as UN Special Rapporteur and therefore enjoyed immunity from legal process. Malaysian courts did not recognize this immunity. The dispute was brought before the ICJ under Article VIII, Section 30, of the 1946 UN Convention on Privileges and Immunities; advisory opinions given on this basis are legally binding [605].

The Court, when scrutinizing the Secretary-General's determination that Cumaraswamy had acted in his official capacity and therefore enjoyed immunity, noted "that it has become *standard practice* of Special Rapporteurs of the Commission to have contact with the media" [606]. This was one of the elements of the Court's reasoning, leading it to the conclusion that the Secretary-General correctly found that Cumaraswamy had acted in the course of the performance of his mission as Special Rapporteur.

(ii) Legal consequences of the construction of a wall in the Occupied Palestinian Territory *(2004)*

In the context of its 10th Emergency Special Session, the General Assembly requested an advisory opinion relating to the legal consequences arising from the construction of a wall by Israel in the Occupied Palestinian Territory [607]. However, according to Article 12.1

---

604. ICJ, *Immunity from Legal Process* Advisory Opinion, note 494.
605. Section 30 of this Convention does not refer to disputes but uses the term "difference". It provides that the opinion given by the court "shall be accepted as decisive by the parties".
606. ICJ, *Immunity from Legal Process* Advisory Opinion, note 494, at p. 85 (italics added).
607. ICJ, *Wall* Advisory Opinion, note 225, at p. 136.

of the Charter: "While the Security Council is exercising in respect of any dispute or situation the functions assigned to it in the present Charter, the General Assembly shall not make any recommendation with regard to that dispute or situation unless the Security Council so requests." Israel argued that the ICJ lacked jurisdiction in this case, "given the active engagement of the Security Council with the situation in the Middle East, including the Palestinian question". In its view, "the General Assembly acted *ultra vires* under the Charter" when it requested this advisory opinion [608].

In order to deal with this objection to the exercise of jurisdiction, the Court examined relevant rules of the Charter and "the practice of the United Nations" [609]. It concluded that in this practice, the Assembly and the Council "initially interpreted and applied Article 12 to the effect that the Assembly could not make a recommendation on a question concerning the maintenance of international peace and security while the matter remained on the Council's agenda" [610]. However, next, the Court concluded that "this interpretation of Article 12 has evolved subsequently" [611]. It noted that there has been "an increasing tendency over time for the General Assembly and the Security Council to deal in parallel with the same matter" [612]. It concluded "that *the accepted practice of the General Assembly*, as it has evolved, is consistent with Article 12, paragraph 1, of the Charter", and that the Assembly therefore "did not exceed its competence" by submitting the request for an advisory opinion [613].

In addition, the *Wall* Advisory Opinion has two further references to relevant practice: it referred to "*the constant practice* of the Human Rights Committee" and to its 1995 judgment in the *East Timor* case, in which it had stated that "the right of peoples to self-determination, as it evolved from the Charter *and from United Nations practice*, has an *erga omnes* character" [614].

---

608. *Id.*, at p. 148.
609. *Id.*
610. *Id.*, at p. 149 (the Court gave a number of examples from this early practice of the Assembly and the Council).
611. *Id.*
612. *Id.* As the Court further specified, it often happened that the Council focused on peace and security matters, while the Assembly took a broader view, also considering humanitarian, social and economic aspects (*id.*, at p. 150).
613. *Id.*, at p. 150 (italics added).
614. *Id.*, at p. 199 (first italics added, second italics *("erga omnes")* in the original).

(iii) Accordance with international law of the unilateral declaration of independence in respect of Kosovo *(2010)*

In 2008 the General Assembly requested the Court to render an advisory opinion on the following question: "Is the unilateral declaration of independence by the Provisional Institutions of Self-Government of Kosovo in accordance with international law?"[615] In 2010 the ICJ delivered its opinion.

In the proceedings before the Court, some participants invoked resolutions of the Security Council condemning particular declarations of independence. The ICJ noted however that in all those cases the illegality of those declarations did not stem from their unilateral character but from "the unlawful use of force or other egregious violations of norms of general international law, in particular those of a peremptory character *(jus cogens)*. In the context of Kosovo, the Security Council has never taken this position"[616]. The Court concluded "that no general prohibition against unilateral declarations of independence may be inferred from *the practice of the Security Council*"[617].

In addition, the Court took into consideration the role played by the Special Representative of the Secretary-General. This Special Representative had significant supervisory powers with regard to the Provisional Institutional of Self-Government established under the authority of the UN Mission in Kosovo. On a number of occasions, he declared acts by the Assembly of Kosovo *ultra vires*. However, he remained silent after the declaration of independence of 17 February 2008. The Court concluded: "*As the practice shows*, he would have been under a duty to take action with regard to acts of the Assembly of Kosovo which he considered to be ultra vires."[618] Hence, the actual practice of the Special Representative (specifically here: his silence) was a factor in the Court's reasoning.

Finally, and most importantly, the Court made a number of general observations in this advisory opinion in relation to the interpretation of resolutions of the Security Council. In this context, it referred to Articles 31 and 32 of the 1969 Vienna Convention, stating that these "may provide guidance". However, it also emphasized that[619]

---

615. ICJ, *Kosovo* Advisory Opinion, note 424, at p. 403.
616. *Id.*, at p. 437, para. 81.
617. *Id.*, at p. 438, para. 81 (italics added).
618. *Id.*, at p. 447, para. 108 (italics added).
619. *Id.*, at p. 442, para. 94 (italics added).

"differences between Security Council resolutions and treaties mean that the interpretation of Security Council resolutions also require that other factors be taken into account. Security Council resolutions are issued by a single, collective body and are drafted through a very different process than that used for the conclusion of a treaty. Security Council resolutions are the product of a voting process as provided for in Article 27 of the Charter, and the final text of such resolutions represents the view of the Security Council as a body. Moreover, Security Council resolutions can be binding on all Member States. . ., irrespective of whether they played any part in their formulation. The interpretation of Security Council resolutions may require the Court to analyze statements by representatives of members of the Security Council made at the time of their adoption, other resolutions of the Security Council on the same issue, as well as *the subsequent practice of relevant United Nations organs and of States affected by those given resolutions*".

In this way, the Court specified elements that are of particular relevance for the interpretations of Security Council resolutions. One of these elements is "subsequent practice", and the Court correctly distinguishes here between states (those that are affected by these resolutions) and "relevant United Nations organs" (therefore: not only the Security Council itself).

(iv) Chagos *(2019)*

In 2017 the General Assembly requested the ICJ to render an advisory opinion on several questions regarding the separation of the Chagos Archipelago from Mauritius. The Court concluded, *inter alia*, that Mauritius's decolonization was not lawfully completed in 1968 and that the United Kingdom is obliged to end its administration of the Chagos Archipelago as rapidly as possible [620]. In the context of its overview of the applicable law, the Court observed that it needed "to determine the nature, content and scope of the right to self-determination applicable to the process of decolonization of Mauritius, a non-self-governing territory recognized as such, from 1946 onwards, both in *United Nations*

---

620. ICJ, *Legal Consequences of the Separation of the Chagos Archipelago from Mauritius in 1965*, Advisory Opinion, *ICJ Reports 2019*, p. 95 *et seq.*

practice and by the administering Power itself" [621]. When mentioning the functions of the General Assembly with regard to decolonization, the Court noted that the Assembly "has overseen the implementation of the obligations of Member States in this regard, such as they are laid down in Chapter XI of the Charter and as they arise from *the practice which has developed within the Organization*" [622]. More specifically, it concluded that "[i]t has been *the Assembly's consistent practice* to adopt resolutions to pronounce on the specific situation of any non-self-governing territory" [623], and that the Assembly "has consistently called upon administering Powers to respect the territorial integrity of non-self-governing territories, especially after the adoption of resolution 1514 (XV) of 14 December 1960" [624]. This demonstrates that the ICJ, in applying international law to this particular situation, in particular the relevant UN law on self-determination, fully took into account relevant practice of the UN, in particular that of the General Assembly.

4.4. Concluding observations

This chapter has analysed how the PCIJ and in particular the ICJ have dealt with the practice of international organizations in their decisions. Only a small number of international organizations existed during the life of the PCIJ. Nevertheless, even in their early years the Court has mentioned their practice, albeit in passing. In 1926, whether or not to pre-empt potential future criticism of its use of an argument derived from practice, the PCIJ observed that "it is not an unusual thing, in countries in which legislative power is limited by a fundamental charter, for the Courts, in deciding whether certain legislation is constitutional, or intra vires, to resort to practice, national or international, for the determination of the extent of a particular governmental power" [625]. Subsequently, arguments derived from practice became a common phenomenon in the advisory opinions of the ICJ.

Ten years ago, James Crawford wrote in his General Course that "the life of international law has not been logic but experience" [626].

---

621. *Id.*, at p. 131, para. 144 (italics added).
622. *Id.*, at p. 135, para. 163 (italics added).
623. *Id.*, at p. 136, para. 167 (italics added).
624. *Id.*, para. 168 (italics added).
625. PCIJ, *Competence of the ILO to Regulate* Advisory Opinion, note 502, quotation at p. 20.
626. J. Crawford, "Chance, Order, Change: The Course of International Law", *Recueil des cours*, Vol. 365 (2013), at p. 111. The expression "[t]he life of law has

This is illustrated by the fact that the ICJ has consistently taken into consideration the practice experienced by international organizations in its reasoning, as well as in the interpretation and application of the relevant law. The way it has sometimes done so may be subject to criticism, but this first observation is an important finding that should not be seen as stating the obvious. The fundamental differences of opinion among the judges in the 1962 *Certain Expenses* case, in particular the Separate Opinion by Judge Spender, show that it has not always been self-evident for the Court to use the practice of an (organ of an) international organization in its reasoning.

A second concluding observation concerns issues of definition and terminology. The PCIJ and the ICJ have referred to the practice of international organizations in different ways. In several advisory opinions (for example, in *Reparation* and in *Kosovo*), the Court only referred to practice as such, without any further qualification. However, in other advisory opinions the Court added a qualifier: the practice was consistent (*Second Admission, Certain Expenses* (twice), *Namibia, Chagos*); the practice was uniform *(Namibia)*; "settled practice" *(Certain Expenses)*; "a body of practice" *(Judgments of the ILOAT in cases against UNESCO)*; "standard practice" *(Cumaraswamy)*; "constant practice" *(Wall)*; the practice of the Organization "throughout its history" *(Certain Expenses)* or "extending over a long period" *(Namibia)*; the practice "has been generally accepted by Members of the United Nations" *(Namibia)*; "a general practice of that Organization" *(Namibia)*; "accepted practice" *(Wall)*. In the *IMCO* Advisory Opinion, the ICJ referred to "actual practice", but that seems to be closer to a pleonasm rather than to a qualifier. The Court has not yet referred to the notion of established practice.

Third, how should the Court's recourse to the practice of international organizations be seen in relation to the Vienna rules on treaty interpretation? The Court explicitly refers to those rules in particular in its *WHO Nuclear Weapons* and *Kosovo* Advisory Opinions. It is clear from those references that the way in which particular rules or decisions are interpreted "in practice" or in "subsequent practice" are key or even

---

not been logic: it has been experience" is from Oliver Wendell Holmes Jr. (associate justice of the US Supreme Court from 1902 to 1932). See his book *The Common Law*, originally published in 1881. In the 2009 edition of this book, the quoted sentence is on p. 3 (the text continues as follows: "The felt necessities of the time, the prevalent moral and political theories, intuitions of public policy, avowed or unconscious, even the prejudices which judges share with their fellow-men, have had a good deal more to do than the syllogism in determining the rules by which men should be governed").

leading for the Court in its interpretation of both constituent instruments of international organizations and resolutions of the Security Council. The almost standard references to organizational practice in the Court's advisory opinions are generally confirming preceding conclusions drawn by the Court on the basis of legal arguments. In this "confirming" role, such references perform the same functions as the "supplementary means of interpretation" means of interpretation mentioned in Article 32 of the 1969 and the 1986 Vienna Conventions. However, paradoxically, the recourse to practice is far from being "supplementary". It is core business when it comes to the interpretation of constituent instruments and decisions of international organizations.

This brings us to a fourth and final concluding observation, or rather set of observations. The ICJ's recourse to the practice of international organizations has fulfilled two main functions: a supportive and an independent function. The former function can be recognized in a number of the advisory opinions analysed in this chapter. In these cases, the Court has referred to such practice in support of a preceding conclusion based on legal arguments (*Reparation*, *Second Admission*, *IMCO*, *Certain Expenses*, *WHO* (1996), *Chagos*). In some of these cases, the Court even considered the relevant practice after it had concluded that the text of the applicable rule was sufficiently clear and did not require any further exegesis (already in 1922 (PCIJ); for the ICJ, see for example its two *Admissions* advisory opinions (1948 and 1950)))[627].

The use of the "practice argument" in this supplementary, supportive way has an important advantage but also a significant disadvantage. The advantage is that the Court's "preliminary" conclusion based on legal arguments has already proved itself to be acceptable and/or effective in practice. The Court's approach to the matter is therefore not detached from reality. It is a "reality check" or, as the Dutch expression goes, it is no *luchtfietserij* ("cycling in the air"), but it fully recognizes the relevance of the organization's experience in practice (see also the first observation, above). However, there is also a significant disadvantage. As Judge Fitzmaurice observed in his Separate Opinion in *Certain Expenses*: "The argument drawn from practice, if taken too far, can be question-begging . . . (it is indeed the validity of some part of that

---

627. See in particular the *Second Admission* Advisory Opinion, in which the Court stated that "[i]f the relevant words in their natural and ordinary meaning make sense in their context, that is an end of the matter"; ICJ, *Competence of Assembly* Advisory Opinion, note 385, at p. 8.

practice [of the United Nations] which is put in issue by the present Request)."[628] A danger of circularity is constantly looming when this argument is used. The request for an advisory opinion normally concerns certain issue(s) in practice having a legal dimension. Basically, the question is whether a certain practice is consistent with international law. If the Court would then, essentially, reply by pointing to that same practice, this could hardly if at all be considered as a satisfactory answer to the question.

However, the ICJ's recourse to the practice of international organizations has also fulfilled another, independent function. It is not necessary to mention that threats of circularity are looming even more here. The *locus classicus* is the Court's *Namibia* Advisory Opinion. Essentially, the question was whether a certain Security Council practice was lawful. Essentially, the Court's answer was permeated with that very same practice. The text of the relevant Charter provision (Art. 27.3) in all authentic languages seems to suggest that, for a non-procedural Security Council resolution to be lawfully adopted, all permanent members need to vote in favour of that resolution. Nevertheless, since almost the earliest meetings of the Security Council, a robust practice has evolved, according to which the adoption of a resolution while one or more permanent members abstained was accepted and was not considered a violation of the Charter. As analysed in this chapter, in *Namibia*, the Court went to great lengths to arrive at the conclusion that the practice of voluntary abstention by a permanent member was accepted as not constituting a bar to the adoption of resolutions. It had to leave no means of interpretation untouched and used a list of qualifiers to the practice of the Security Council and of the UN, generally accepted by the member states. This example demonstrates the importance of subsequent practice in the interpretation of Security Council resolutions, to which the Court referred in general terms in its 2010 *Kosovo* Advisory Opinion. Apart from *Namibia*, the *Wall* Advisory Opinion is the other main example of a case in which the "practice argument" fulfilled this independent function. The practice of the General Assembly and the Security Council dealing in parallel with the same matter evolved considerably as compared to the rule in Article 12 of the Charter and early practice, and although this practice was not as long-standing as the voluntary abstentions of permanent members,

---

628. ICJ *Certain Expenses* Advisory Opinion, note 308, at p. 201.

it was still sufficiently robust for the Court to accept this as a "further development of the law" rather than a violation.

Following the analysis in this chapter of the way in which the ICJ and its predecessor have dealt with the practice of international organizations in their judicial work, the next chapter will focus on the relevant "legislative" work of the ILC.

CHAPTER 5

THE INTERNATIONAL LAW COMMISSION AND PRACTICE OF INTERNATIONAL ORGANIZATIONS

5.1. Introduction

As mentioned in the introduction to the previous chapter, when it comes to treaty interpretation, including the role given to the practice of international organizations, much is in the eye of the beholder. Over the years, the number of "beholders" has increased significantly. Many new international organizations and international courts and tribunals have been established. The eyes of these beholders are different from those of states. They apply and interpret relevant treaties from their own perspectives. Treaty interpretation has become less and less the exclusive prerogative of states. The previous chapter analysed the extent to which the ICJ and its predecessor have offered some judicial guidance in this field, analysing the role they have given to the practice of international organizations in treaty interpretation. This chapter will focus on the ILC. It will examine whether there has also been "legislative" guidance in our search for a better understanding of legal facets of practice of international organizations.

While the ICJ and the ILC are the central international law bodies of the UN, their functions are completely different. To a certain degree, taking into account the fundamental differences between the international legal order and national legal orders, their functions may be compared to those of courts and legislators at the national level. More precisely, the function of the ICJ is essentially twofold: "to decide in accordance with international law such disputes as are submitted to it" and to give advisory opinions "on any legal question" requested by the General Assembly, the Security Council or other organs of the UN and specialized agencies authorized to do so by the General Assembly [629]. The ICJ, therefore, similar to any other court, acts on demand [630].

---

629. ICJ Statute, Art. 38.1; UN Charter, Art. 96.
630. As Tomka (the then President of the ICJ) observed when addressing the ILC in 2012: "The Court was not in such a comfortable position as was the Commission: it could not select topics, but had to consider the cases submitted to it. Moreover, it could not engage in theoretical debates; it had to decide specific cases and consider only those issues relevant to its decision", *Yb. ILC 2012*, Vol. 1, at p. 147, para. 100.

The ILC has a different position and function within the UN. While the ICJ is one of the six principal organs of the UN, as well as its principal judicial organ [631], the ILC is not mentioned in the Charter. There was no support for the idea to give legislative powers to the UN; a proposal to that effect was rejected in San Francisco [632]. At the same time, the drafters of the Charter were convinced of the need to codify and develop international law. This is mentioned in the Charter as part of the powers of the General Assembly [633]. It was thus left to the Assembly, under the control of the entire UN membership, to further substantiate these powers. Following proposals by a subcommittee [634], the Assembly decided in 1947 to establish the ILC and adopt its Statute [635]. In line with Article 13.1 *(a)* of the UN Charter, the ILC's task is "the promotion of the progressive development of international law and its codification" [636]. This twofold task is defined in Article 15 of the ILC Statute, as follows:

> "In the following articles the expression 'progressive development of international law' is used for convenience as meaning the preparation of draft conventions on subjects which have not yet been regulated by international law or in regard to which the law has not yet been sufficiently developed in the practice of States. Similarly, the expression 'codification of international law' is used for convenience as meaning the more precise formulation and systematization of rules of international law in fields where there already has been extensive state practice, precedent and doctrine."

The work of the ILC over the years reflects the increasing activities of international organizations since 1945. Some of this work included specific topics of international organizations law, such as the preparation

---

631. UN Charter, Arts. 7.1, 92.
632. See *UNCIO Docs*, Vol. 9, at p. 316 (proposal by the Philippine Commonwealth) and at p. 70 (rejection of the proposal by twenty-six votes to one). It was only agreed that Security Council decisions should be binding on all member states (Art. 25 Charter). However, such decisions are not legislative acts but rather specific decisions related to issues on the agenda of the Security Council.
633. Notably, the Charter mentions the progressive development of international law before its codification (see Charter, Art. 13.1). In their early commentary on the Charter, Goodrich and Hambro quite rightly observe, regarding Art. 13: "International law may also be developed through the practice of states in response to General Assembly recommendations, *and by the practice of the United Nations itself*", Goodrich and Hambro, note 452, at p. 177 (italics added).
634. UN Doc. A/331.
635. GA Res. 174(II).
636. ILC Statute, Art. 1.1.

of the Vienna II Convention on the law of treaties concluded by international organizations and the 2011 ARIO. But the ILC has also taken into account the role and activities of international organizations in its work on other topics. This chapter will analyse two topics that have been on the agenda of the ILC in recent years, where the Commission had to consider the practice of international organizations. First, Section 5.2 will analyse the "identification of customary international law". Partly in parallel, the ILC discussed another relevant topic: "subsequent agreements and subsequent practice in relation to interpretation of treaties"; this will be covered in Section 5.3. Section 5.4 will offer some concluding observations. The overall question in this chapter is whether the ILC has taken the practice of international organizations seriously in its work.

5.2. The ILC, customary international law and practice of international organizations

The creation and functioning of international organizations, the recognition of their international legal personality, the attribution of significant powers to them and, indeed, their functioning in practice all raise the question of their relationship with customary international law. There are two sides to this relationship. First: are international organizations bound by customary international law? Second: can international organizations contribute to the formation of customary international law? There has been some discussion of these questions in the literature [637], as well as in professional organizations such as the ILC [638]. As to the first side of the coin, there is much support for an

---

637. See for an in-depth study Cahin, note 171.
638. See Statement of Principles Applicable to the Formation of General Customary International Law, the final report of the committee on the formation of customary (general) international law, adopted at the ILA's London Conference (2000), https://www.law.umich.edu/facultyhome/drwcasebook/Documents/Documents/ILA%20Report%20on%20Formation%20of%20Customary%20International%20Law.pdf. This statement of principles to some extent recognizes the relevance of international organizations for the creation of customary international law. A rule of customary international law is defined as "one which is created and sustained by the constant and uniform practice of States *and other subjects of international law* in or impinging upon their international legal relations, in circumstances which give rise to a legitimate expectation of similar conduct in the future" (*id.*, at p. 8, italics added). However, immediately following this definition, the report makes clear that the position of international organizations is still fundamentally different from that of states: "If a sufficiently extensive and representative number of States participate in such a practice in a consistent manner, the resulting rule is one of 'general customary international law'". The participation of international organizations in such practice is thus not considered relevant for emergence of rules of general customary international law.

affirmative answer to the question, even though it is not always fully clear how and to what extent international organizations are bound by customary international law [639]. As to the other side, there is much more uncertainty, with some authors and states taking the view that customary international law must (almost) exclusively be based on state practice, while others are of the opinion that international organizations themselves may contribute to the formation of customary international law [640]. A myriad of further, more specific questions arise. If the latter opinion is held, how ought the practice of international organizations be distinguished from that of their members? How can it be established whether an international organization has the necessary *opinio iuris*?

This section will solely focus on the way the ILC has dealt with international organizations in the context of its work on the "identification of customary international law". Following some introductory remarks in Subsection 5.2.1, Subsection 5.2.2 will discuss the work of the ILC on this topic.

5.2.1. Introduction

The ILC has a specific obligation relating to customary international law. Article 24 of its Statute provides the following:

> "The Commission shall consider ways and means for making the evidence of customary international law more readily available, such as the collection and publication of documents concerning State practice and of the decisions of national and international courts on questions of international law, and shall make a report to the General Assembly on this matter."

This statutory obligation only refers to the collection and publication of documents concerning *state* practice, as a way or means for making

---

In addition, this ILA report pays specific attention to resolutions of the UN General Assembly (*id.*, at p. 55 *et seq.*).

639. See e.g. K. Daugirdas, "How and Why International Law Binds International Organizations", *Harvard International Law Journal*, Vol. 57 (2016), pp. 325-381 (arguing, *inter alia*, that customary international law binds international organizations "as a default matter", "like states, IOs may contract around such default rules" (at 327)). See also A. Reinisch, "Sources of International Organizations' Law: Why Custom and General Principles are Crucial", in S. Besson and J. d'Aspremont (eds.), *The Oxford Handbook on the Sources of International Law*, Oxford, Oxford University Press, 2017, pp. 1007-1024.

640. Cahin, note 171, at p. 252 ("les opinions doctrinales sont encore réticentes à admettre, sinon la possibilité de principe [of international organizations having their own practice], du moins celle de distinguer la pratique des organes de celle des Etats membres").

the evidence of customary international law more readily available. While this provision does not exclude other ways and means for fulfilling this purpose, it does not refer to the practice of international organizations. This is hardly surprising since the life and work of international organizations was just beginning and the process of their establishment in the international legal order, with its implications, was still in its early stages when the General Assembly adopted the ILC Statute in 1947 [641], two years before the ICJ rendered its *Reparation for Injuries* Advisory Opinion.

It *is* therefore remarkable that the ILC, in its work on this topic in its first two sessions (1949 and 1950) referred to the relevance of the practice of international organizations. The UN Secretary-General prepared an extensive report for the first session of the ILC, in the context of the obligation in Article 24 of the ILC Statute [642]. In this report, he observed that "opinions and decisions of international organs . . . have frequently been regarded as evidence of international law" [643]. The Secretary-General refers in this context to the work of the League of Nations and that of the UN. In particular, he cites the following from his third Annual Report on the Work of the Organization [644]:

> "Particular importance attaches to the development of those rules of international law which have found expression in the Charter, and to the legal precedents which are constantly being built up in the practice of the various organs of the United Nations. Hardly any problem comes before the United Nations which does not raise questions of a legal character and does not require a study of the previous application and interpretation of the Articles of the Charter and of the practice and precedents in the various organs. . . . In addition, apart from the Charter, rules of international law are constantly being applied and interpreted in the organs of the United Nations and by the Secretariat. The widespread activities of the Organization are a fertile source of questions which require legal analysis and opinions, and the legal precedents thus established in the day-to-day work of the

---

641. GA Res. 174 (II).
642. Ways and Means of Making the Evidence of Customary International Law More Readily Available: Preparatory Work Within the Purview of Article 24 of the Statute of the International Law Commission (1949), UN Doc. A/CN.4/6/Corr. 1.
643. *Id.*, at p. 76.
644. UN Doc. A/565, at pp. 108-109.

Organization are an important part of the process of developing international law under the auspices of the United Nations."

For the reasons indicated, the UN Secretariat had therefore already started to compile a systematic annotation of the Charter provisions as interpreted or applied by UN organs, as well as a systematic collection and arrangement of legal opinions [645].

On the basis of this report, the ILC approved the topic "ways and means for making the evidence of customary international law more readily available (Art. 24 of the Statute of the Commission)" as one of the six items on its agenda for its first session in 1949 [646]. It discussed the Secretariat report in this first session, and decided that one of its members should prepare a working paper, to be discussed at the next session [647]. Manley Hudson, former ICJ judge and president of the first session of the ILC, prepared this working paper. In this paper, he mentioned the "practice of international organizations" among the sources that could provide evidence of customary international law, as follows [648]:

> "G. Practice of international organizations
>
> 78. Records of the cumulating practice of international organizations may be regarded as evidence of customary international law with reference to States' relations to the organizations. The *Repertoire of Questions of General International Law before the League of Nations, 1920-1940,* published by the Geneva Research Centre in 1942, contained chiefly statements in the *Official Journal* of the League of Nations concerning questions of international law. It is understood that a *répertoire* of its practice is planned by the Secretariat of the United Nations."

---

645. *Id.*, at p. 109. In 2018 the UN Secretariat prepared a similar survey, at the request of the ILC ("to prepare a memorandum on ways and means for making the evidence of customary international law more readily available, which would survey the present state of the evidence of customary international law and make suggestions for its improvement"); see UN Doc. A/CN.4/710. As the Secretariat notes, compared to its earlier report prepared in 1949, "both the scope of customary international law and the availability of evidence thereupon have changed strikingly" (*id.*, at p. 4). A few years after 1949, the General Assembly authorized the Secretariat to prepare the Repertoire of the Practice of the Security Council (GA Res. 686 (VII)) and the Repertory of Practice of United Nations Organs (GA Res. 796 (VIII)). In 1959, the Assembly decided that the *UNJY* should be published (GA Res. 1451 (XIV)); see also above Sec. 1.2.3*(i)*.
646. *Yb. ILC 1949*, at p. 279.
647. *Id.*, at pp. 228-235.
648. UN Doc. A/CN.4/16.

This working paper was discussed by the ILC during its second session (1950)[649]. It was revised in light of these discussions in the second session and was included as part of the ILC report to the General Assembly[650]. This completed the work of the ILC on this topic during its early years[651].

5.2.2. The work of the ILC on the "identification of customary international law"

In 2012 the ILC decided to include the topic "Formation and evidence of customary international law" in its programme of work and appointed its member Michael Wood as Special Rapporteur for the topic[652]. In 2013 the Commission decided to change the name of this topic into "Identification of customary international law"[653]. The Special Rapporteur has prepared five reports and has actively promoted discussions on the topic[654]. In 2018 the ILC adopted a set of sixteen "draft conclusions on identification of customary international law"[655]. The work of the ILC on this topic will now be analysed from one particular perspective: to what extent did the ILC take into account the practice of international organizations in its work on this topic[656]? Particular attention will therefore be paid to those sections in the reports of the Special Rapporteur and of the ILC in which this practice is discussed, and to the relevant conclusions that were adopted in 2018. Given what are generally considered to be the two constituent elements of customary international law, practice and *opinio iuris*, it was clear from the outset of the ILC's work on this topic that a major issue was to what extent the first element ("practice") only covered the practice

---

649. *Yb. ILC 1950*, Vol. 1, at pp. 4-8.
650. *Id.*, at pp. 275-277; *Yb. ILC 1950*, Vol. 2, at pp. 367-374 (for the reference to practice of international organizations, see p. 372, para. 78).
651. *Yb. ILC 1950*, Vol. 2, at p. 366.
652. *Yb. ILC 2012*, Vol. 2, Part 2, UN Doc. A/CN.4/SER.A/2012/Add. 1, Part 2, at p. 69.
653. *Yb. ILC 2013*, Vol. 2, Part 2, UN Doc. A/CN.4/SER.A/2013/Add. 1, Part 2, at p. 64.
654. By contributing to conferences and by organizing informal meetings. See also his 2014 Jonathan J. Charney Distinguished Lecture in Public International Law: M. Wood, "International Organizations and Customary International Law", *Vanderbilt Journal of Transnational Law*, Vol. 48 (2015), at pp. 609-620.
655. Report ILC 2018, UN Doc. A/73/10, at pp. 117-156.
656. The following partly builds on N. Blokker, "International Organizations and Customary International law: Is the International Law Commission taking International Organizations Seriously?", *International Organizations Law Review*, Vol. 14 (2017), pp. 1-12.

of states or also the practice of international organizations (and if so, to what extent). However, as the overview below will demonstrate, some other issues are relevant as well, and these will also be very briefly addressed.

(i) *Direct relevance of the practice of international organizations, "in certain cases". . .*

When proposing this topic to the ILC in 2011, Wood indicated that, following the Commission's work on the law of treaties, the time was now ripe to put customary international law on the ILC's agenda. As the ultimate aim of the ILC's work on this topic, he proposed "to provide a practical aid to those called upon to investigate rules of customary international law"[657]. In addition, when introducing the topic to the ILC in 2012, he cautiously expressed the hope that "[p]erhaps the Commission's study of the topic would contribute to the acceptance of the rule of law in international affairs"[658]. One possible outcome of the ILC's work on this topic would be "a series of propositions, with commentaries"[659]. Wood made clear that the ILC "would not be drafting a 'Vienna convention on customary international law', because a convention in that field would be inappropriate and inconsistent with the need to retain the necessary degree of flexibility"; instead, he proposed that the Commission would prepare "conclusions", or "guidelines", with commentaries[660].

From the outset, the Special Rapporteur did not restrict this topic to the role of states in the development of international law. In his proposal, he stated that "[t]he formation of customary international law now has to be seen in the context of a world of nearly 200 States and numerous and varied international organizations, both regional and universal"[661]. At the same time, although relevant, the practice of international organizations was not among the key elements of the details of the proposal. Wood referred to it in two contexts. First, when mentioning state practice as a central issue, he questioned what acts other than State acts would be relevant practice for customary international law.

---

657. *Yb. ILC 2011*, Vol. 2, Part 2, UN Doc. A/CN.4/SER.A/2011/Add. 1, Part 2, at p. 184, para. 7(e).
658. *Yb. ILC 2012*, Vol. 1, at p. 135, para. 2.
659. *Yb. ILC 2011*, Vol. 2, Part 2, UN Doc. A/CN.4/SER.A/2011/Add. 1, Part 2, at p. 183, para. 4.
660. *Yb. ILC 2012*, Vol. 1, at p. 136, para. 14.
661. *Id.*, at p. 183, para. 2. Also UN Doc. A/CN.4/653 (Note prepared in 2012 for the ILC), at p. 5, para. 19.

The acts of "[c]ertain international organizations, like the European Union" [662]? Second, as a particular topic, he mentioned "[r]esolutions of organs of international organizations, including the General Assembly of the United Nations, and international conferences, and the formation of customary international law; their significance as possible evidence of customary international law" [663].

In order to assist its work on this topic, the ILC requested the UN Secretariat "to prepare a memorandum identifying elements in the previous work of the Commission that could be particularly relevant to this topic" [664]. In 2013, the Secretariat submitted its memorandum [665]. One of the elements it mentions in this report is the relevance of the practice of international organizations [666]. In this regard, the Secretariat makes the following two observations [667]:

(ii) *Observation 13*

Under certain circumstances, the practice of international organizations has been relied upon by the Commission to identify the existence of a rule of customary international law. Such reliance has related to a variety of aspects of the practice of international organizations, such as their external relations, the exercise of their functions, as well as positions adopted by their organs with respect to specific situations or general matters of international relations.

(iii) *Observation 14*

On some occasions, the Commission has referred to the possibility of the practice of an international organization developing into a custom specific to that organization. Such customs may relate to various aspects of the organization's functions or activities, for example the treaty-making power of an international organization or the rules applicable to treaties adopted within the organization.

Special Rapporteur Wood paid particular attention to the role of international organizations in relation to the identification of customary

---

662. *Id.*, at p. 184, para. 8 *(a)*.
663. *Id.*, at p. 185, para. 9 *(c)*.
664. *Yb. ILC* 2012, Vol. 2, Part 2, at p. 69, para. 159.
665. UN Doc. A/CN.4/659.
666. *Id.*, at pp. 23-24.
667. *Id.* (footnotes omitted).

international law in his second and third report. In his second report (2014), he started by stating that "the acts of international organizations on which States have conferred authority may also contribute or attest to the formation of a general practice in the fields in which those organizations operate"[668]. The report correctly distinguishes between internal practice ("practice relating to the internal affairs of the organization") and external practice (practice in the organization's external relations (with states, other international organizations, etc.)), and also between "products of the secretariats of international organizations" and products of their intergovernmental organs[669]. Furthermore, for good reason, the report equates the practice of international organizations to which members have attributed exclusive competences with the practice of states. If this would not be accepted, not only could the organization's practice not contribute to the identification of customary international law, but also their member states would have lost that capacity[670]. On this basis, the Special Rapporteur proposed the following draft conclusion (7.4): "The acts (including inaction) of international organizations may also serve as practice."[671]

The Special Rapporteur's third report (2015) includes a chapter devoted to "[t]he relevance of international organizations", in which a number of the observations, distinctions, as well as the conclusion from the second report are repeated and slightly more explained[672]. In addition, it demonstrates numerous dimensions of the interrelationship of the practice of international organizations and that of their member states. For example, acts of organizations may reflect the practice of their members but may also serve to catalyse it[673]. When introducing his third report in the ILC in 2015, Special Rapporteur Wood referred to this chapter as "probably the most sensitive section of the third report"[674].

There was much support within the ILC for what the Special Rapporteur wrote about the role of international organizations in these two reports. However, there was also criticism, in particular by ILC

---

668. UN Doc. A/CN.4/672, at pp. 29-30 (with extensive references in footnote 128, including to observation 13 in the Memorandum prepared by the UN Secretariat (quoted above)).
669. *Id.*, at p. 30.
670. *Id.*, at p. 31.
671. *Id.*, at p. 35.
672. UN Doc. A/CN.4/682, at p. 46 *et seq.*
673. *Id.*, at p. 51.
674. *Yb. ILC 2015*, Vol. 1, at p. 42, para. 37.

members Murphy, Hmoud, Wisnumurti, Singh and Gevorgian[675]. For example, ILC member Murphy stated in 2014[676]:

> "Perhaps it would be wiser to consider that they were different types of actors who operated in different realms of customary law. It appeared, however, that it was widely believed that the practice of an international organization was not an independent source of practice relevant to identifying the customary international law that was binding upon States. If the Commission said otherwise, it should base its view on a very thorough and careful analysis of practice, case law and scholarship that was accompanied by appropriate examples."

In 2015 Murphy repeated his criticism. He agreed "with the Special Rapporteur's emphasis on the centrality of States in the formation of customary international law" but also observed the following with regard to Wood's proposition that the practice of international organizations could be relevant to the identification of customary international law[677]:

> "[This proposition] had not been substantiated by any references to international case law, and it had been rejected by several States in the Sixth Committee. Only a handful of States and some academics were in favour, and even they seemed to recognize that it owed more to theory than to reality. Even the European Union, which was widely regarded as supranational, had itself emphasized that its practice was pertinent to the formation of customary international law only in its areas of exclusive competence."

While some other members also continued to criticize the views of the Special Rapporteur regarding the relevance of practice of international organizations, although somewhat less pronounced than in 2014[678], overall there was sufficient support to keep the suggested

---

675. *Yb. ILC 2014*, Vol. 1, at p. 120 (Murphy), at pp. 130-131 (Hmoud; para. 16: "it was solely the practice of States that created the rules of custom"), at p. 133 (Wisnumurti; in particular para. 48), at p. 135 (Singh; in particular para. 80), at p. 136 (Gevorgian; para. 86: "the practice of international organizations was simply an additional means of shedding light on State practice").

676. *Id.*, at p. 120, para. 28.

677. *Yb. ILC 2015*, Vol. 1, at p. 43, para. 5. See also Murphy's overview of the work of the ILC during its 67th session, in S. D. Murphy, "Identification of Customary International Law and Other Topics: The Sixty-Seventh Session of the International Law Commission", *American Journal of International Law*, Vol. 109 (2015), pp. 822-844, in particular pp. 827-832.

678. In particular ILC members Hmoud, *id.*, at p. 48, para. 52 (practice of international organizations is "a subsidiary form of practice") and Singh, *id.*, at p. 69, para. 31.

draft conclusion, which remained unchanged until it was finally adopted in 2018:

> "*Conclusion 4 – Requirement of practice*
>
> 1. The requirement of a general practice, as a constituent element of customary international law, refers primarily to the practice of States that contributes to the formation, or expression, of rules of customary international law.
>
> 2. In certain cases, the practice of international organizations also contributes to the formation, or expression, of rules of customary international law.
>
> 3. Conduct of other actors is not practice that contributes to the formation, or expression, of rules of customary international law, but may be relevant when assessing the practice referred to in paragraphs 1 and 2."

This conclusion only partly meets the stated objective of these conclusions on the identification of customary international law, which is to offer clear, practical guidance on "how the existence of rules of customary international law, and their content, are to be determined" [679]. First, it is fundamental that the ILC fully recognizes that one of the two constituent elements of customary international law, the requirement of general practice, does not only refer to the practice of states but also to the practice of international organizations. The practice of international organizations may, as such, directly contribute to the formation, or expression, of rules of customary international law and, in this respect, is of equal rank as state practice. It is not included in paragraph 3 of Conclusion 4, covering conduct of other actors, which "is not practice that contributes to the formation, or expression, of rules of customary international law, but may be relevant when assessing the practice referred to in paragraphs 1 and 2". This approach reflects the independent legal personality of international organizations. If they use their powers, this is their own practice, not that of their members, and this practice "also contributes to the formation, or expression, of rules of customary international law"; obviously this is only if those rules concern a subject matter for which the relevant organization is competent. As logical and straightforward as this may seem to be, in a world primarily governed by sovereign states, Conclusion 4.2 was not a fully predictable outcome of the ILC work on this topic, as is also

---

679. General commentary to the conclusions, paras. (2) and (4).

demonstrated by the criticism expressed by ILC members (during the *travaux préparatoires* of the Conclusions) and by UN member states (in the UN General Assembly). Here, the ILC has offered clear, practical guidance. Courts and others can no longer convincingly argue that the practice of international organizations is irrelevant for the identification of customary international law.

Second, this being accepted, the ILC has not been able to offer similar clarity and practical guidance to those who need to know under what specific conditions the practice of international organizations contributes to the formation, or expression, of customary international law. According to the ILC in Conclusion 4.2, not unlike the reference to "[u]nder certain circumstances" in the 2013 Memorandum of the UN Secretariat, this is only "[i]n certain cases". In the commentary, the ILC has made an attempt to give some guidance as to what "certain cases" are:

"1. the practice of international organizations 'will not be relevant to the identification of all rules of customary international law' (commentary (5));
2. 'it may be the practice of only some, not all, international organizations that is relevant' *(id.)*;
3. the practice of international organizations is only relevant if the subject matter of the relevant rules of customary international law falls within their mandate, and/or if these rules are addressed specifically to them *(id.)*;
4. 'certain cases' exist 'most clearly where member States have transferred exclusive competences to the international organization' (commentary (6));
5. they may also exist 'where member States have not transferred exclusive competences, but have conferred competences upon the international organization that are functionally equivalent to powers exercised by States'. Examples given are: the conclusion of treaties, serving as treaty depositaries, deploying military forces, administering territories, and taking positions on the scope of the privileges and immunities of the organization and its officials *(id.)*."

During the meetings of the ILC, the phrase "in certain cases" in Conclusion 4, paragraph 2, was criticized since this lacked the necessary clarification that these Conclusions aimed to provide[680]. As

---

680. See in particular the comments by ILC member Escobar Hernández, *Yb. ILC 2015*, Vol. 1, at p. 54, para. 32.

summarized above, the ILC has to some extent explained the meaning of this phrase in the Commentary, but these explanations are partly rather general (Nos. 1 and 2), partly ambiguous (what are competences of international organizations that are "functionally equivalent to powers exercised by States"? (No. 5)), and only partly more specific (the examples in No. 5). The commentary is most specific where it mentions examples (in No. 5 above). It is noteworthy that these examples concern areas in which the UN Secretariat has concluded that there are many "established practices of the organization" (forming part of the rules of the organization). At the same time, the ILC did not want to include this dimension in its work on the topic [681]. However, even though this "in certain cases formula" may be criticized, it has to be seen against the background of the lack of agreement within the ILC (which has prevented the Commentary from being more specific), the lack of more extensive information about the practice of the hundreds of existing international organizations, and the need to keep a certain level of necessary flexibility, for the future development of both customary international law and international organizations. Against this background, while the "in certain cases formula" lacks clarity, it is also an example of what is sometimes referred to as constructive ambiguity [682].

(iv) *Resolutions of international organizations*

Conclusion 12 and its commentaries deal with resolutions of international organizations and intergovernmental conferences. A disadvantage of not separating resolutions of international organizations and resolutions of intergovernmental conferences is that the authors of these two categories of resolutions are fundamentally different [683]. In the case of the former, the authors are international organizations; in the case of the latter, the authors are normally states [684]. Resolutions of international

---

681. See footnote 32 at commentary (5) to Conclusion 4: "'Established practice' of the organization . . . is not within the scope of the present conclusions".
682. See Barkholdt, note 13, at pp. 35-38. Barkholdt distinguishes four situations that "are conceivable as constituting 'certain cases'".
683. Within the ILC, only ILC member Petrič recognized the importance of distinguishing between (resolutions of) international organizations and (resolutions of) intergovernmental conferences: "The resolutions of international organizations expressed the will of the organizations. . . . On the other hand, international conferences usually adopted resolutions by consensus, and consequently they represented the sum of the will of participating States", *Yb. ILC 2015*, Vol. 1, at p. 62, para. 34.
684. "Normally", because exceptionally international organizations may, together with states, adopt resolutions of intergovernmental conferences.

organizations are unilateral acts; resolutions of intergovernmental conferences are multilateral acts. This distinction is relevant, and important in the context of the topic of the identification of customary international law. With regard to resolutions of intergovernmental conferences, the statements and views expressed by representatives of governments at the adoption of these resolutions are part of the practice and/or *opinio iuris* of states. This is also the case for statements and views expressed by representatives of governments at the adoption of resolutions of international organizations, but here another dimension must be taken into account. Here, the resolution itself is also relevant for the identification of customary international law, as an act of an international organization, as part of the practice of the organization, which may – as stated in Conclusion 4 – contribute to the formation, or expression, of rules of customary international law.

Perhaps the ILC did not consider it necessary to separate resolutions of international organizations from resolutions of intergovernmental conferences because the primary focus in this Conclusion is on states. As it appears from the Commentary to Conclusion 12, the ILC seems to regard resolutions predominantly as a means by which the practice and/or *opinio iuris* of states can be determined; it does not seem to fully recognize them as acts of the organization, emanating from a separate legal person [685]. Commentary (3) to this Conclusion is telling in this regard:

> "Although resolutions of organs of international organizations (unlike resolutions of intergovernmental conferences) emanate, strictly speaking, not from the States members but from the organization, in the context of the present draft conclusion what is relevant is that they may reflect the collective expression of the views of such States: when they purport (explicitly or implicitly) to touch upon legal matters, the resolutions may afford an insight into the attitudes of the member States towards such matters."

This comment demonstrates that the ILC is fully aware of the difference between resolutions of international organizations and resolutions of intergovernmental conferences. However, it does not want to focus on this formal difference ("strictly speaking") but on what it *does*

---

685. See also S. Mathias, "The Work of the International Law Commission on Identification of Customary International Law: A View from the Perspective of the Office of Legal Affairs", *Chinese Journal of International Law*, Vol. 15 (2016), pp. 17-31, in particular at pp. 25-30.

consider most important here ("what is relevant"), namely the views and the attitudes of states. Therefore, a better title of this Conclusion would have been: "The views of states at the adoption of resolutions of international organizations and intergovernmental conferences".

The primary relevance of the views of states for the identification of customary international law, in the context of this Conclusion, is also demonstrated by its paragraph 1: "A resolution adopted by an international organization or at an intergovernmental conference cannot, of itself, create a rule of customary international law." As is explained in the Commentary (under (4)), "the mere adoption of a resolution (or a series of resolutions) purporting to lay down a rule of customary international law does not create such law: it has to be established that the rule set forth in the resolution does in fact correspond to a general practice that is accepted as law. ... There is no 'instant custom' arising from such resolutions on their own account". In this respect, the Statement of principles applicable to the formation of general customary international law, adopted in 2000 by the International Law Association, is slightly less prohibitive and recognizes, with respect to resolutions of the UN General Assembly, that they "are capable, very exceptionally, of creating general customary law by the mere fact of their adoption", if they are accepted unanimously or almost unanimously, and evince a clear intention on the part of their supporters[686]. In addition, the practice of the UN Security Council also offers support for a slightly less absolute view than the one expressed in paragraph 1 of ILC's Conclusion 12[687]. In a number of resolutions the Security Council has explicitly stated that these resolutions "shall not be considered as establishing customary international law"[688]. If it would be generally accepted that Security Council resolutions cannot establish customary international law, such provisions would not need to be included in the

---

686. ILA Statement of Principles, note 638, Principle 32.

687. See for a similar view: ILC member Jacobsson, *Yb. ILC 2015*, Vol. 1, at pp. 65-66, para. 6 (at p. 65: "it was overly restrictive to say that, although such resolutions could be evidence of customary international law, they could not 'in and of themselves, constitute it'").

688. For example, in Resolution 1816 (Somalia, piracy), the Security Council affirms that the authorization provided in this resolution "shall not be considered as establishing customary international law". This authorization was given to states cooperating with the Transitional Federal Government of Somalia in the fight against piracy and armed robbery at sea off the coast of Somalia, to enter the territorial waters of Somalia and use there "all necessary means to repress acts of piracy and armed robbery". See Wood and Sthoeger, note 327, at p. 194, in footnote 78, where the authors mention fifteen other resolutions in which the Security Council made similar explicit statements.

resolutions of the Council. In conclusion, it seems therefore that the ILC has underestimated the independent contribution that resolutions of international organizations can make to the development of a rule of customary international law.

(v) *Other issues and comments*

Finally, the ILC has failed to deal consistently with international organizations and their practice in a number of other conclusions on the identification of customary international law. For example, Conclusion 5 deals with "Conduct of the State as State practice"; however, a similar conclusion for the "conduct of international organizations as practice of international organizations" is lacking, even though some organizations (such as the European Union and other regional integration international organizations) also exercise executive, legislative, judicial or other functions. Conclusion 6 ("Forms of practice") in paragraph 2 refers to "Forms of State practice"; there is no similar paragraph about forms of practice of international organizations. Conclusion 7 is about "Assessing a State's practice". There is no parallel conclusion for international organizations; is it not necessary to assess their practice? These omissions are remedied to some extent by one sentence in the Commentary: "In those cases where the practice of international organizations themselves is of relevance (as described below), references in the draft conclusions and commentaries to the practice of States should be read as including, *mutatis mutandis*, the practice of international organizations." [689] However, such a superficial, feather-light *mutatis mutandis* "solution", hidden in the Commentary, does not only leave uncertain where and how the conclusions should be changed in the context of (the practice of) international organizations, it also fails to fully recognize, as *is* done in Conclusion 4, the relevance of international organizations' practice for the identification of customary international law [690].

---

689. Commentary (4) to Conclusion 4, last sentence.
690. Cf. in this context the following comment by the EU in the General Assembly, concerning the Commentary to Conclusion 4 under (4) ("In those cases where the practice of international organizations themselves is of relevance . . . references in the draft conclusions and commentaries to the practice of States should be read as including, *mutatis mutandis*, the practice of international organizations"): the EU "understood that to be a way to consider more systematically the contribution of the practice of such organizations, where relevant, to the formation or expression of rules of customary international law", UN Doc. A/C.6/73/SR.20.

5.3. Subsequent agreements and subsequent practice in relation to interpretation of treaties: What role for the practice of international organizations?

5.3.1. Introduction

When proposing the topic "treaties over time" to the ILC in 2008, ILC member Georg Nolte suggested that the Commission should "revisit the law of treaties as far as the evolution of treaties over time is concerned" because "[p]roblems arise frequently in this context" and "are even more likely to arise in the future" as "certain important multilateral treaties reach a certain age"[691]. The goal of this proposal was to first prepare a sufficiently representative repertory of practice, and then develop general conclusions or guidelines for the interpretation of treaties in time[692]. Nolte distinguished four aspects of this topic; in doing so he did not mention issues relating to international organizations. However, when subsequently answering the question of whether the ILC should examine this topic, Nolte paid specific attention to constituent instruments of international organizations, distinguishing between the internal and external capacity of the members in their relations with their organizations: "By virtue of operating in and engaging with international organizations, member States display forms of subsequent agreement and subsequent practice that are relevant to the evolving interpretation of the constituent treaties of such organizations."[693] While he noted that the ILC had previously dealt separately with international organizations in its work on treaty law and international responsibility, he also observed that the areas of practice in the context of constituent instruments of international organizations and practice under "ordinary" inter-state treaties "are so closely interrelated", that "it would be artificial to distinguish between them"[694].

As to the possible scope of the proposed topic, Nolte mentioned eight specific issues that could be addressed by the ILC. One of these was entitled "Special types of treaties"; in this context Nolte referred to the WTO, the EU and to the European Convention on Human Rights. While the primary focus would be on the practice of states, Nolte also

---

691. *Yb. ILC 2008*, Vol. 2, Part 2, UN Doc. A/CN.4/SER.A/2012/Add. 1, Part 2, at p. 152, para. 6.
692. *Id.*, at p. 156, paras. 19-22 and p. 159, para. 37.
693. *Id.*, at p. 155, para. 18.
694. *Id.*

suggested that "[t]he analysis of the international pronouncements on the topic would be completed by looking at subsequent agreement and practice with respect to and by international organizations. It is expected that certain specific understandings and practices will emerge in this context which could then become the basis for corresponding guidelines" [695].

On the basis of this proposal by Nolte and the ensuing discussion within the ILC, the Commission included the topic "Treaties over time" in its programme of work, and decided to establish a study group for this topic at its next session [696].

5.3.2. The ILC Study Group on "Treaties over time" (2009-2012)

In 2009 the ILC established a Study Group to deal with this topic, chaired by Nolte [697]. Nolte prepared three reports for this study group. His first report still pays specific attention to the practice of international organizations. Since they "fulfil their purposes in typically dynamic circumstances", this "may have made it easier for international courts and tribunals to recognize certain modifications of their treaty basis by way of subsequent conduct" [698]. The report does not specify what such "dynamic circumstances" are, and why this would not also be true for "ordinary" inter-state treaties. Noting that "subsequent conduct may play a special role in the context of international organizations" [699], and the need to distinguish between the practice of international organizations and that of their members, this first report mentions twice that a later report will be devoted to subsequent conduct with respect to international organizations [700]. Nolte's second report analysed the jurisprudence of a number of international courts and tribunals and the Human Rights Committee, relating to subsequent agreements and subsequent practice [701]. This analysis did not contain examples relating to the practice of international organizations. Nolte's final report covers subsequent agreements and subsequent practice of states outside of

---
695. *Id.*, at p. 159, para. 42. See also *Yb. ILC 2012*, Vol. 2, Part 2, UN Doc. A/CN.4/SER.A/2012/Add. 1, Part 2, at p. 79, para. 238.
696. *Yb. ILC 2008*, Vol. 2, Part 2, UN Doc. A/CN.4/SER.A/2008/Add. 1, Part 2, at p. 148, para. 353.
697. *Yb. ILC 2009*, Vol. 2, Part 2, UN Doc. A/CN.4/SER.A/2009/Add. 1, Part 2, at p. 148, para. 218.
698. This report has not been published as a UN document, but is included in Nolte, note 598, at pp. 169-209, quotation at p. 203.
699. *Id.*, at p. 204.
700. *Id.*, at p. 199 and p. 204. Such a report never came.
701. *Id.*, at pp. 210-306.

judicial or quasi-judicial proceedings, and deliberately "does not address subsequent agreements or subsequent practice relating to constituent instruments of international organizations and by their organs", while also noting that "[i]nternational organizations merit separate treatment in that regard" [702].

Nolte's three reports were discussed within the ILC Study Group, but according to the brief overviews of these discussions in the reports of the ILC, no separate attention was paid to subsequent agreements and the subsequent practice of international organizations [703]. The preliminary research on the topic by the Study Group also included the question of whether a broad approach should be followed (which would also cover the termination and formal amendment of treaties) or a narrow approach (which would solely focus on subsequent agreements and subsequent practice only) [704]. There was a preference for the latter approach [705]. This would allow the ILC to define the topic more precisely. At the recommendation of the Study Group, the ILC decided to change the format of the work on the topic, with effect from its 2013 session, and it appointed Nolte as Special Rapporteur [706]. The topic was renamed into "Subsequent agreements and subsequent practice in relation to the interpretation of treaties" [707].

5.3.3. The ILC work on the topic "Subsequent agreements and subsequent practice in relation to the interpretation of treaties" (2013-2018)

In 2012 Nolte envisaged that he would prepare new reports following the change of format of the work on the topic. A first report would synthesize the earlier three reports, taking into account the discussions in the Study Group. Next, "one or two further reports should be submitted . . . on the practice of international organizations and the

---

702. *Id.*, at pp. 307-386, quotation at p. 311.
703. See *Yb. ILC 2010*, Vol. 2, Part 2, UN Doc. A/CN.4/SER.A/2010/Add. 1, Part 2, at pp. 194-195; *Yb. ILC 2011*, Vol. 2, Part 2, UN Doc. A/CN.4/SER.A/2011/Add. 1, Part 2, at pp. 168-171; *Yb. ILC 2012*, Vol. 2, Part 2, UN Doc. A/CN.4/SER.A/2012/Add. 1, Part 2, at pp. 77-80.
704. *Yb. ILC 2012*, Vol. 2, Part 2, UN Doc. A/CN.4/SER.A/2012/Add. 1, Part 2, at pp. 78-79, para. 237.
705. *Id.*
706. *Yb. ILC 2012*, Vol. 2, Part 2, UN Doc. A/CN.4/SER.A/2012/Add. 1, Part 2, at p. 77.
707. *Id.*

Legal Facets of the Practice of International Organizations 293

jurisprudence of national courts" [708]. Those additional reports should suggest "additional conclusions or guidelines that would complement or modify, as appropriate, the work based on the first report" [709]. In 2013, in his first report as Special Rapporteur, Nolte indicated that he planned to devote his third report to the practice of international organizations, to be submitted in 2015 [710]. However, the subsequent work on this topic was limited to one aspect of this practice, namely the practice relating to their constituent instruments.

Special Rapporteur Nolte prepared five reports, on a variety of topics. None of these were specifically devoted to subsequent agreements and subsequent practice of international organizations. Most relevant for the theme of this special course is his third report (2015), on "subsequent agreements and subsequent practice in the interpretation of constituent instruments of international organizations" [711]. That report indicates that it

> "does not concern the interpretation of treaties adopted within an international organization or those concluded by international organizations. The latter category is addressed by the Vienna Convention on the Law of Treaties between States and International Organizations or between International Organizations (hereinafter, '1986 Vienna Convention'). Whereas the interpretation of such treaties does, in principle, fall within the scope of the topic, the Special Rapporteur is inclined to agree with Gardiner, who has expressed the following view: 'It seems reasonable to predict that the rules on interpretation as replicated in the 1986 [Vienna] Convention will be subject to gravitational pull and will come to be regarded as stating customary international law in the same way as those of the 1969 [Vienna] Convention; but there is insufficient practice to assert this definitely'" [712].

The topics which were excluded (the interpretation of treaties adopted within an international organization or those concluded by

---

708. *Id.*, at p. 79, para. 238 (repeated later by the Special Rapporteur, at the conclusion of the ILC discussion of his third report; see *Yb. ILC 2015*, Vol. 1, at p. 135, para. 4.
709. *Id.*
710. UN Doc. A/CN.4/660, at p. 56 (see also p. 51). The envisaged third report would also cover the jurisprudence of national courts.
711. UN Doc. A/CN.4/683.
712. *Id.*, at p. 5 (in a footnote, Nolte refers to R. Gardiner, *Treaty Interpretation* (2008), p. 111).

international organizations) were not analysed in subsequent reports of the Special Rapporteur nor discussed within the ILC [713]. Nolte mentions that one of the two excluded topics, treaties concluded by international organizations, is addressed by the 1986 Vienna Convention. While this is true, it does not seem to be a convincing argument to exclude such treaties. Article 31 of the 1986 Vienna Convention is fully similar to Article 31 of the 1969 Vienna Convention. Therefore, if it is necessary for the ILC to work on the topic of subsequent agreements and subsequent practice in the interpretation of treaties, it is not clear why that would only be relevant for treaties concluded by states and not for those concluded by international organizations. Nolte quotes approvingly Gardiner, who suggests that the practice and authority ("gravitational pull") of the interpretation of treaties concluded by states is such that the same will apply to the interpretation of treaties concluded by international organizations. However, while this may be true, it may also not be true. We simply do not know. It is not in line with Nolte's original approach, which still recognized the specific nature of subsequent agreements and subsequent practice of international organizations, and therefore mentioned the need to deal with this in a specific report. Furthermore, Nolte does not explain why he excludes the other topic, the interpretation of treaties adopted within an international organization [714]. This is even explicitly mentioned in Article 5 of the 1969 Vienna Convention, together with constituent instruments of international organizations.

Although some members of the ILC criticized this limitation of the scope of the third report of the Special Rapporteur to constituent instruments of international organizations [715], excluding treaties concluded by and within international organizations, there was also much support for it [716].

---

713. ILC reports incidentally refer to the intention that subsequent agreements and subsequent practice relating to international organizations would be the subject of a later report (e.g. ILC, Annual Report on the work of the sixty-sixth session (2014), at p. 118, para. 25 and p. 128, footnote 728), but this did not materialize.
714. When criticized for this by ILM member Murphy, the Special Rapporteur replied by asking Murphy "for his understanding for leaving out, for reasons of convenience and for the time being, treaties adopted within an international organization, on the understanding that such a limitation was not definitive", *Yb. ILC 2015*, Vol. 1, at p. 135, para. 4.
715. E.g. ILC members Forteau, *Yb. ILC 2015*, at p. 113, para. 14 and Murphy, *Yb. ILC 2015*, at p. 129, para. 5. One year later, also ILC member Kolodkin, *Yb. ILC 2016*, at p. 125, para. 68.
716. *Yb. ILC 2015*, in particular pp. 134-135, paras. 4-5.

The Special Rapporteur's third report usefully distinguishes between three forms of conduct that "may constitute relevant subsequent practice for the purpose of the interpretation of a constituent instrument of an international organization"[717]:

> "*(a)* the subsequent practice of the parties to constituent instruments of international organizations under Articles 31 (3) *(b)* and 32 of the Vienna Convention;
> *(b)* the practice of organs of an international organization;
> *(c)* a combination of practice of organs of the international organization of subsequent practice of the parties."

A narrower approach would have involved fully leaving out the practice of international organizations[718], and only focusing on the subsequent practice of the parties to constituent instruments of international organizations (under *(a)* above). However, while this would indeed allow the ILC to fully focus on subsequent practice by states, parties to the 1969 Vienna Convention, it is obvious that this would also leave the analysis of subsequent practice as a means for the interpretation of constituent instruments of international organizations incomplete. While in theory the subsequent practice of the parties to such constituent instruments can be separated from the practice of organs of the relevant international organization, in practice these two may often be intertwined, as is recognized in the third above-mentioned form of conduct *(c)*. For this third form of conduct, a particular kind of subsequent practice of the parties is relevant, their acceptance of practice of organs of the organization[719].

One year later, in his fourth report (2016), the Special Rapporteur noted that several states had proposed in the General Assembly that the ILC should take more account of the practice of international organizations[720]. However, he proposed that the interpretation of treaties concluded by international organizations "should be dealt with separately, as the Commission did in its previous work on the

---

717. UN Doc. A/CN.4/683, at p. 12, paras. 30-31.
718. Because this practice is, strictly seen, not subsequent practice of the parties as covered by Article 31 of the 1969 Vienna Convention. See the criticism by ILC members Wood, Kamto, Murphy, Kolodkin and Peter, *Yb. ILC 2015*, at p. 125, para. 53, at p. 126, para. 63, at p. 129, paras. 7-8, at p. 131, para. 23 and p. 133, para. 41.
719. *Id.*, at p. 19, para. 52.
720. UN Doc. A/CN.4/694, at p. 4. For example, Malaysia (see UN Doc. A/C.6/70/SR.23, at p. 10, para. 50) and Estonia, UN Doc. A/C.6/73/SR.21, at p. 9, para. 54.

law of treaties" [721]. In addition, he did not consider it necessary "that subsequent agreements and subsequent practice regarding treaties that are 'adopted within an international organization' in the sense of Article 5 of the Vienna Convention on the Law of Treaties be addressed specifically" [722]. As he explained later that year, when introducing his fourth report to the ILC, "the project was limited to the scope of application of the 1969 Vienna Convention and did not therefore address the practice of international organizations and their organs, with the exception of practice relating to their constituent instruments, in keeping with Article 5 of the Convention" [723]. He admitted that other aspects related to the practice of international organizations could be added to the topic. However [724],

> "on previous occasions, the Commission had dealt with such treaties and practice separately. Given the character of the present topic as an elucidation of particular means of interpretation under the rules of interpretation set forth in the 1969 Vienna Convention, it seemed neither necessary nor reasonable to aim for completeness. As was the case for certain other topics, it should be sufficient to cover the most important aspects. It would, of course, be possible to add a saving clause, should the Commission consider that to be necessary".

Another year later, in 2017, while some states still favoured more attention for the practice of international organizations, the Special Rapporteur noted that

> "[m]ost States, however, agreed with the approach of the Commission to limit the draft conclusions to treaties to which the rules of interpretation of the Vienna Convention [of 1969] would apply . . . and not to extend the scope of the draft conclusions to treaties that would fall under the [Vienna II Convention]. Whereas it would certainly be desirable to also clarify the role of subsequent agreements and subsequent practice under the 1986 Vienna Convention, the Special Rapporteur recommends that the Commission maintain its approach of distinguishing between the law between States and the law of international organizations, as

---

721. *Id.*, at p. 44.
722. *Id.*
723. *Yb. ILC 2016*, at p. 110, para. 49.
724. *Id.*, at p. 112, para. 65.

it did when working on the two topics that resulted in the two Vienna Conventions of 1969 and 1986 and on its two projects on responsibility of States and international organizations, respectively"[725].

It is therefore clear, from the five reports prepared by the Special Rapporteur, from the discussions within the ILC and from the majority support in the General Assembly, that it was finally decided to exclude the practice of international organizations from the work of the ILC on this topic (except practice relating to their constituent instrument), in spite of the original intention to cover this. This evolution in the relevant *travaux* of the ILC is not unlike its *travaux* for the 1969 Vienna Convention, where attention was paid as well to treaties concluded by international organizations but where it was also ultimately agreed to leave these out. However, a key difference is that, when this was decided in the context of the 1969 Vienna Convention, it was also agreed, as a compromise, that the ILC would subsequently commence working on treaties concluded by international organizations. Following the adoption in 2018 by the ILC of its draft conclusions on subsequent agreements and subsequent practice, no decision was taken that the ILC should start working on subsequent agreements and subsequent practice of international organizations.

5.3.4. *Draft conclusions on subsequent agreements and subsequent practice in relation to the interpretation of treaties (2018)*

The final outcome of the ILC work on this topic is contained in the "Draft conclusions on subsequent agreements and subsequent practice in relation to the interpretation of treaties". Following the adoption of these draft conclusions by the ILC in 2018, the General Assembly took note of them, as "conclusions"[726]. Below, they will be referred to as Conclusions (or, abbreviated: CSASP, or SASP Conclusions).

The SASP Conclusions are exclusively based on the 1969 Vienna Convention, and not on the 1986 Vienna II Convention. This reduces their relevance for the purpose of this special course since subsequent practice of international organizations in the interpretation of treaties

---

725. UN Doc. A/CN.4/715, at p. 34, para. 113.
726. GA Res. 73/202.

to which they are parties is excluded ("not dealt with generally") [727]. On the one hand, this exclusion may be criticized. Does the ILC take international organizations (and their agreements, their practice) seriously? There is a wealth of treaties concluded by international organizations. They are continuously interpreted and applied. At present, there is an enormous amount of subsequent practice in relation to the interpretation of treaties concluded by international organizations. For example, by excluding subsequent agreements and subsequent practice in relation to treaties concluded between states and international organizations or between international organizations, the ILC excludes from the scope of these Conclusions the many treaties concluded by the EU with states and with other international organizations, including treaties that are the constituent instrument of an international organization (such as the constituent instruments of the FAO, the WTO, the various commodity organizations (such as the Olive Council), fisheries and river organizations, the International Renewable Energy Organization, the World Customs Organization, etc.), but also the many treaties concluded by or within other international organizations.

On the other hand, the exclusion of (subsequent agreements and) subsequent practice of international organizations is in line with the earlier practice of the ILC itself. In its work on the law of treaties it decided to first work on treaties concluded between states, and only after this was completed did it begin working on treaties concluded by international organizations. The same separation and sequence was followed with regard to responsibility for internationally wrongful acts. However, after the ILC completed its work that resulted in the SASP Conclusions, it did not take any initiatives to commence work on subsequent agreements and subsequent practice in relation to the interpretation of treaties concluded by international organizations. Obviously, many of the SASP Conclusions potentially also apply, *mutatis mutandis*, to subsequent agreements and subsequent practice in relation to the interpretation of treaties concluded by international organizations [728]. However, such an *ad hoc*, *mutatis mutandis* application (by states, by individual courts in individual cases, etc.) is far less

---

727. CSASP, Commentaries (2) and (3) to Conclusion 1. Conduct of international organizations "does not constitute subsequent practice under articles 31 and 32 [of the 1969 Vienna Convention]. Such conduct may, however, be relevant when assessing the subsequent practice of parties to a treaty" (Conclusion 5.2).

728. Such a potential is recognized by the ILC in Commentary (33) with respect to the relevance of practice of international organizations for the interpretation of their constituent instruments (*id.*, at p. 103).

thorough and reliable than a separately prepared text that is adopted on the basis of years of preparation and discussion within the ILC and the General Assembly (as was the case for the Vienna II Convention (1986) and the ARIO (2011)).

The only SASP Conclusion that is of direct relevance for this special course is Conclusion 12 ("Constituent instruments of international organizations"). This Conclusion is limited to constituent instruments; it does not apply to decisions of international organizations [729]. In particular, paragraphs 2 and 3 are relevant for the purpose of this special course:

> "2. Subsequent agreements and subsequent practice of the parties under article 31, paragraph 3, or subsequent practice under Article 32, may arise from, or be expressed in, the practice of an international organization in the application of its constituent instrument.
>
> 3. Practice of an international organization in the application of its constituent instrument may contribute to the interpretation of that instrument when applying Articles 31 and 32".

The ILC rightly distinguishes in these two paragraphs between practice of the parties and practice of the organization, even though it is sometimes difficult to neatly separate the two, as is illustrated in the Commentary [730]. The focus of paragraph 2 is on the former, that of paragraph 3 on the latter. Strictly seen, the substance of paragraph 3 is outside the scope of these SASP Conclusions, which are generally limited to (subsequent agreements and) subsequent practice of states. Paragraph 2 is within that scope, as its point of departure is subsequent agreements and subsequent practice of states. Such agreements and practice "may arise from, or be expressed in, the practice of an international organization in the application of its constituent instrument". The terms "may arise from" and "be expressed in" are explained in the Commentary. "'Arise from' is intended to encompass the generation and development of subsequent agreements and subsequent practice by State parties" [731]. Hence, the *origin* of the relevant agreement or practice of states is to be found in a practice of the organization. "'[E]xpressed in' is used in the sense of reflecting

---

729. CSASP, Commentary (5) to Conclusion 12.
730. See also Gasbarri, note 13.
731. *Id.*, at p. 97, para. 15.

and articulating such agreements and practice."[732] Here, the *origin* of the relevant agreement or practice is with the states (and it is reflected in the practice of the organization). Therefore, even though the focus of this paragraph 2 is on the practice of states, it also shows how such practice (in the context of the interpretation of constituent instruments of international organizations) is intimately related to the practice of organizations. The main reason for this is what Dupuy has referred to as the "transparency" of international organizations[733]: behind the legal personality veil of the organization its sovereign members remain visible.

This "transparency" may obscure the difference between the internal and the external capacity of member states of international organizations[734]. In the former capacity, states are the constituent parts of organs of the organization, and in pursuing their objectives these organs are dependent upon the will of the member states to cooperate. For example, the UN Security Council is at times unable to perform the task for which it was created, mainly because of fundamental disagreements among its permanent members.

It is easier to recognize the internal capacity of member states in the composition and functioning of non-plenary organs than in organs in

---

732. *Id.*
733. R.-J. Dupuy, *Le droit international*, 4th ed., Paris, Presses universitaires de France, 1972, at p. 121: "En dépit de son autonomie juridique, elle laisse voir les Etats toujours présents derrière ses structures". See also P. Reuter, *Institutions internationales*, 7th ed., Paris, Presses universitaires de France, 1972, at pp. 192-193, 200-201. Brölmann has demonstrated how the law of treaties and the law of international responsibility have difficulties in dealing with such "transparent" actors: C. Brölmann, "A Flat Earth? International Organizations in the System of International Law", *Nordic Journal of International Law*, Vol. 70 (2001), pp. 319-340; Brölmann, note 27.
734. The following is largely reproduced from Schermers and Blokker, note 2, at pp. 65-69. See further on this distinction between the internal and external capacities of members of international organizations: Tammes, note 334, at pp. 353-359; L.-J. Constantinesco, *Das Recht der Europäischen Gemeinschaften – Das institutionelle Recht*, Baden-Baden, Nomos, 1977, at pp. 286-287; Higgins, note 334, at pp. 93-94; R. Higgins, "The Legal Consequences for Member States of the Non-fulfilment by International Organizations of their Obligations Toward Third Parties", *Annuaire de l'Institut de Droit International*, Session de Lisbonne, Vol. 66-I (1995), https://www.idi-iil.org/app/uploads/2017/06/1995_lis_02_en.pdf, pp. 260-261, 388; R. A. Lawson, *Het EVRM en de Europese Gemeenschappen – Bouwstenen voor een aansprakelijkheidsregime voor het optreden van internationale organisaties*, Deventer, Kluwer, 1999, at p. 465 *et seq.*; A. Pellet, "Le droit international à la lumière de la pratique: l'introuvable théorie de la réalité", *Recueil des cours*, Vol. 414 (2021), at p. 64, paras. 63-64; Barkholdt, note 13, at esp. pp. 13-16. Within the ILC, several of its members have referred to this distinction; see e.g. ILC member Nolte, in *Yb. ILC 2015*, at p. 61, para. 25. Within the General Assembly, e.g. the Republic of Korea mentioned it, UN Doc. A/C.6/70/SR.23, at p. 12, para. 59.

which all members of the organization are represented [735]. Members of non-plenary organs are often expected to act on behalf of all members of the organization [736]. For this reason, the constitutions of most universal organizations contain provisions requiring that all geographic areas of the world are represented in these non-plenary organs [737]. In practice, non-permanent members of the Security Council sometimes explicitly refer to their duty to take into account not only their own interests but also the concerns or interests of their regions [738].

The responsibility to also represent other members is lacking in plenary organs. Moreover, particularly when these organs adopt decisions unanimously or by consensus, it may be difficult to see whether, or to what extent, a member of the organization is not only acting in its external but also in its internal capacity. Nevertheless, it is important to recognize this internal capacity of member states also in these organs. For example, in 2005 the Dutch Senate informed the Minister of Justice that it was of the opinion that he should not participate in consultations in the EU Council relating to a specific item on the agenda. The Minister of Justice however refused to implement this wish of the Senate. One of the reasons for his refusal was his view that "the Minister as member of the Council is not exclusively a Dutch Minister, but also a member of an EU organ. His functioning as such is also governed by what is necessary in the general interest of the Union" [739].

In their external role, states are the counterparts of the organization. Organizations are created to influence the policies of the member states; and in pursuing its objectives, the organization takes decisions directed at the outside world. In their external role, members are part of this outside world. They are confronted with these decisions that may

---

735. See also J. Wouters and P. De Man, "International Organizations as Law-Makers", in J. Klabbers and Å. Wallendahl (eds.), *Research Handbook on the Law of International Organizations*, Cheltenham, Elgar, 2011, pp. 190-224, at p. 208 ("The distinction between state practice and the practice of international organizations will typically be rather difficult to make in universal organizations, especially when the decisions in question have been taken by a plenary body").
736. E.g. Art. 24.1 of the UN Charter ("the Security Council acts on their [all UN members'] behalf"). Cf. also H. Kelsen, *The Law of the United Nations*, London, Stevens, 1951, at p. 280; J. Delbrück in Simma, note 586, 2nd ed., at pp. 448-449; A. Peters in Simma *et al.*, note 586, 3rd ed., at pp. 775-777.
737. E.g. ICAO, Art. 50 *(b)*; IMO, Art. 18 *(c)*; UNESCO, Art. V.A.2; WHO, Art. 24; IRENA, Art. X.A.
738. E.g. UN Docs. S/PV.2977 (Part II)(closed resumption 3), at p. 322 (Cuba); S/PV.3413, at p. 9 (Brazil).
739. Letter by the Minister of Justice of 20 June 2005, Senate document 2004-2005, 23490, AS.

have a direct or indirect impact on them, and they must respect such decisions to a degree which is commensurate with their legal effect.

The Commentary to SASP Conclusion 12 [740] demonstrates that it is difficult to identify these two different capacities, and that it is therefore difficult to assess whether a certain practice is a practice of (member) states, of their organization, or perhaps even of both. It is probably realistic to conclude that a not unimportant part of the relevant practice is an inextricable mix of the conduct of both states and the organization that acts in their common interest (with varying degrees of autonomy), as was recognized by the Special Rapporteur in his third report, when distinguishing between three forms of conduct, the third of which being "a combination of practice of organs of the international organization [and] of subsequent practice of the parties" [741].

5.4. Concluding observations: Does the ILC take the practice of international organizations seriously?

The way in which the ILC has dealt with the practice of international organizations is fundamentally different from the approach of the ICJ. This may be explained mainly by the different nature of the work of these two main international law organs of the UN. A request for an advisory opinion of the Court almost always requires the Court to consider the relevant practice of the UN or other international organizations. For the ILC, however, its lawmaking task is first of all oriented towards states. Only a few of the topics on its agenda have concerned the law of international organizations, and that part of its work has not always been the most successful [742].

---

740. In particular Commentaries (15) and (22). Commentary (22), first sentence: "Subsequent agreements and subsequent practice of the parties, which may 'arise from, or be expressed in' the practice of an international organization, may sometimes be very closely interrelated with the practice of the organization as such." See also the Third Report of Special Rapporteur Wood, UN Doc. A/CN.4/682, at pp. 48-49, para. 71.

741. UN Doc. A/CN.4/683, at p. 12, para. 31.

742. P. H. F. Bekker, "The Work of the International Law Commission on 'Relations between States and International Organizations' Discontinued: an Assessment", *Leiden Journal of International Law*, Vol. 6 (1993), pp. 3-16. P. Webb, "Should the *2004 UN State Immunity Convention* Serve as a Model/Starting point for a Future UN Convention on the Immunity of International Organizations?", *International Organizations Law Review*, Vol. 10 (2013), pp. 319-331, in particular at pp. 329-330. Two Vienna Conventions prepared by the ILC and of special relevance to international organizations have not yet entered into force: the 1975 Vienna Convention on the Representation of States in their Relations with International Organizations of a Universal Character and the 1986 Vienna Convention on the Law of Treaties between States and International Organizations or between International Organizations.

In its preparations for the Vienna Convention on the Law of Treaties (1969), it was difficult for the ILC to decide whether the future Convention should only cover treaties concluded by states, or also international organizations' treaties. In this respect, history repeated itself during the ILC's work on the SASP Conclusions. Originally these conclusions would also cover subsequent agreements and subsequent practice in relation to international organizations' treaties, but over time this work was narrowed down to (subsequent agreements and subsequent practice in relation to) treaties concluded by states. As mentioned above, the exclusion of subsequent agreements and subsequent practice of international organizations is in line with the earlier practice of the ILC itself (law of treaties, law of international responsibility). However, in this earlier practice, after the ILC had completed its work on the law of treaties concluded by states and on the articles on state responsibility, it began working on the law of treaties concluded by international organizations and the ARIO. However, after the ILC completed its work that resulted in the SASP Conclusions, it did not take any initiatives for commencing work on subsequent agreements and subsequent practice in relation to the interpretation of treaties concluded by international organizations.

In this respect, the ILC's work on the identification of customary international law is different. From the outset, the ILC and its Special Rapporteur took a broader, more integrative approach, not limiting this project to the role of states but also covering the role of international organizations and other non-state actors [743]. At the same time, it appears that it has not been easy for the ILC to implement this broader approach. The ILC Conclusions on the identification of customary international law reveal a certain ambivalence. On the one hand, the practice of international organizations is considered as equivalent to state practice, as far as its contribution to the formation, or expression, of rules of customary international law is concerned (even though this is only "in certain cases"). On the other hand, international organizations and their practice are not fully integrated in the ILC Conclusions; these Conclusions are primarily "state oriented".

---

743. Only exceptionally have members of the ILC suggested that customary international law applicable to states should be distinguished from customary international law for international organizations. See e.g. ILC member Murphy: "Perhaps it would be wiser to consider that they [international organizations] were different types of actors who operated in different realms of customary law", *Yb. ILC 2014*, Vol. 1, at p. 120, para. 28.

Both in the ILC and in the General Assembly (when it discussed the annual reports of the ILC), views on the role and relevance of international organizations and their practice regarding the two topics discussed in this chapter varied quite considerably [744]. Hence, the Special Rapporteurs had to act as tightrope walkers, taking the lead in the ILC's defining of the course on the two topics concerned [745]. Whereas some members of the ILC and some states in the General Assembly were in favour of a stronger recognition of the role and relevance of international organizations and their practice, others were opposed to this. In the ILC, in particular its member Murphy – not unlike ICJ Judge Spender in *Certain Expenses* – was reluctant to accept that the practice of international organizations may contribute to the formation, or expression, of rules of customary international law. In the General Assembly, in particular the three most powerful permanent members of the Security Council all took a stance against an independent role for international organizations in regard to both topics. For example, the Russian Federation "held that only the practice of States could contribute to the formation of customary law. The practice of international organizations in and of itself could not have the same effect; rather, it was the reaction of States to such practice that was important" [746]. The United States criticized Conclusion 4.2 on the identification of customary international law by stating that this provision "inaccurately suggested that international organizations

---

744. See for a detailed analysis: Barkholdt, note 13.
745. In doing so, it was to be expected that they would sometimes be criticized for being either too conservative or too progressive. For example, ILC member Saboia criticized Special Rapporteur Wood thus: "Contrary to what he had announced in his second report, the Special Rapporteur did not deal in detail with the question of the role of international organizations in the formation and identifications of customary international law. The Special Rapporteur devoted a great deal of attention to highlighting the differences, in terms of nature and scope, between the practice of international organizations and that of States and, although he quoted academic sources that ascribed increasing significance to those organizations in the formation of customary international law, it was the opposite view that he favoured in the report", *Yb. ILC 2015*, Vol. 1, at p. 55, para. 45. Special Rapporteur Nolte, summarizing the ILC debate on his third report, stated in his conclusion that "the statements of many of the members of the Commission who had taken the floor seemed to reflect an underlying concern that he wished to diminish the primary role of States in the interpretation of treaties and to elevate the role of international organizations to an inappropriate level. Those concerns were somewhat surprising because he had been careful in trying to adhere strictly to the case law of international courts, in particular that of the International Court of Justice. Furthermore, he had refrained from adopting a 'constitutionalist' approach to the interpretation of constituent instruments of international organizations or any other theoretical approach that was not well established" (*id.*, at p. 139, para. 28).
746. UN Doc. A/C.6/73/SR.22, at p. 8, para. 45.

could contribute to the formation of customary international law in the same way as States" [747]. It also stated that SASP Conclusion 12.3 "was incorrect"; "an international organization was not a party to its own constituent instrument. Consequently, the practice of an international organization 'as such' could not constitute subsequent practice of a party to the agreement of the kind contemplated in Article 31, Paragraph 1, of the Vienna Convention and could not contribute to establishing the agreement of the parties regarding the interpretation of the instrument" [748]. Other states in the General Assembly, as well as members in the ILC, were in favour of a full recognition of the role and relevance of international organizations and their practice. For example, Estonia stated in the General Assembly, with regard to the Conclusions on the identification of customary international law: "[e]xcluding such practice [of international organizations] would preclude States that directed an international organization to execute in their place actions falling within their own competences from contributing to the creation, or expression, of customary international law" [749]. With respect to Conclusion 12 on the identification of customary international law, Spain criticized the "very restrictive approach to the acts of international organizations, disregarding the fact that the practice of such organizations had the potential to influence the process of establishing customary international law in the same way that a treaty did" [750].

On balance, the impression prevails that the ILC's approach towards international organizations and their practice is somewhat ambivalent, at least in respect of the two topics discussed in this chapter. To some extent, this is understandable. Dealing with these topics has been full of challenges already as far as states and their practice is concerned. Moreover, fundamentally different views exist regarding international organizations and their practice in relation to these two topics, but apparently also more generally. There has been no systematic study of how the ILC has dealt with international organizations in its activities over the years, but similar "understandable ambivalences" can be seen in its work on other topics. For example [751], with respect to "Diplomatic protection", Special Rapporteur John Dugard wrote in his first report

---

747. UN Doc. A/C.6/73/SR.29, at p. 4, para. 18.
748. *Id.*, at p. 5, para. 23.
749. UN Doc. A/C.6/73/SR.21, at p. 9, para. 55.
750. *Id.*, at p. 14, para. 90.
751. I thank Dr Zsuzsanna Deen-Racsmány for drawing my attention to this example, and for the references to the relevant documents.

(2000): "The protection of an agent of an international organization by the organization – 'functional protection' – raises special issues distinct from diplomatic protection. At the current stage, the Special Rapporteur has not decided whether to include this topic in his study." [752] Two years later, the Special Rapporteur indicated that he was opposed to including functional protection by international organizations for the following reasons [753]:

> "That is a complex topic that would take the Commission beyond diplomatic protection as it is traditionally understood and ensure that the completion of the present draft articles within the present quinquennium would become impossible. This is not to say that functional protection is not an important subject. It certainly is. However, it is suggested that if the Commission believes it should consider this topic, it should do so as a separate study. The Special Rapporteur would welcome such a decision, as such a study would draw on and complement the present articles. During the previous quinquennium this issue was frequently raised, with a clear majority of members opposed to the inclusion of functional protection in the present study. The time has come for an immediate and final resolution of the matter."

However, just like the more recent experience regarding the topic "subsequent agreements and subsequent practice in relation to interpretation of treaties", here the ILC also failed to subsequently start working on the "stepsister" topic of functional protection, relating to international organizations. A disadvantage of the "efficiency choice" to focus on states is that the ILC does not give the "stepsister topic" relating to international organizations the attention that it may deserve – irrespective of the outcome. The ILC could take international organizations and their practice more seriously.

---

752. UN Doc. A/CN.4/506, at p. 61, para. 187.
753. UN Doc. A/CN.4/523, at p. 5, para. 17.

CONCLUDING OBSERVATIONS

The preceding journey along five legal facets of the practice of international organizations has offered some impressions and views of the varied landscape of the rather uncharted territory that this special course has aimed to explore. The journey has offered a far from complete overview; there are more legal facets and some caveats. For example, no separate chapters have been devoted to analyse such important areas of international organizations law as membership, decision-making, financing, privileges and immunities, and responsibility issues. A major caveat is the absence of systematic overviews of relevant practice. While there is a wealth of practice of the hundreds of existing international organizations, this practice has hardly been documented. It is the exception rather than the rule for international organizations to have publications such as the UN's *Repertory of Practice of United Nations Organs* and its *Juridical Yearbook*. Nevertheless, the five different legal facets discussed in this special course cover important aspects of the topic and give an impression of its scope, nature and complexities.

Legal facet one: Practice as a rule

This first legal facet is the ultimate evidence of the legal relevance that the practice of international organizations can have. Over time, the qualifier "established" has to an important degree become recognized as the condition that a certain practice must fulfil before it is accepted as a rule of the organization, although it is not yet widely and *expressis verbis* used in the practice of many organizations.

The flexibility needs of international organizations are recognized in the two Vienna Conventions on the Law of Treaties. While the general rules laid down in these Conventions also apply to constituent instruments of international organizations, they also recognize that international organizations may need their own treaty law rules that depart from those in the two Vienna Conventions. Furthermore, the flexibility needs of international organizations are particularly respected in the definition of "rules of the organization", by including "established practice of the organization" and by not requiring that such practice is in accordance with the organization's constituent instrument.

This part of the rules of international organizations is their most dynamic component. It reflects certain needs originating from the ever-changing *milieu* in which international organizations perform their functions, but the resulting practices have not (or: not yet) been crystallized into written rules of the organization. It is this part of the rules of international organizations that is of growing importance due to the ageing of international organizations and the difficulties involved in amending their constituent instruments.

As was discussed at the end of Chapter 1, the notion of "established practice" has so far remained ill-defined. Nevertheless, it may be questioned whether it would be necessary or wise at all to fully define this notion or whether it would be better to leave its interpretation and implementation to the infinite variety of practices of international organizations for the benefit of flexibility and optimal performance of their functions. It is indeed necessary to proceed in this area with caution. At the same time, without defining this notion in detail, some further guidance or specifications could be helpful, to make it less arbitrary when the UN or any other international organization might claim that a certain practice is established, thereby improving the rule of law for international organizations and their members in the twilight zone between mere practice and law. Therefore, even though it is by now generally accepted, the notion of established practice should be given greater consideration, both in practice, at the level of each specific international organization, and more generally, at a conceptual level. While the emphasis should be on the specific way in which established practice is used by each individual organization, at the same time there is merit in further circumscribing it. Such further specification would meet the twin needs of stability and change. It would lay down certain minimum requirements that would need to be fulfilled before a certain practice – whatever it is – can be considered "established". For the purpose of drafting such specifications, it is obvious that existing practice must be taken into account. Chapter 1 gave some examples, mainly from the experience of the UN and the specialized agencies. The relevant practice of other international organizations is hardly documented. The examples mentioned are therefore only the tip of the iceberg, but they already show the great variety of practices that have become established. If a fuller overview of established practices of international organizations were available, this would provide an important source of information when preparing sufficiently solid minimum requirements.

Such minimum requirements would need to circumscribe the qualifier "established", which is not unlike the *opinio iuris* requirement for rules of customary international law. In developing criteria that must be fulfilled for practice to be established, inspiration could be drawn from how *opinio iuris* is interpreted and applied in practice. Moreover, in general, in developing criteria that the qualifier "established" must fulfil, the bar must be high. Other types of rules of international organizations are required to be in accordance with their constituent instruments and, therefore, there is a link with the consent that the member states have once expressed, even though this may have been a long time ago. Such a link is missing in the case of established practice, which is not required to be in accordance with the relevant constituent instrument. The support by the members of a certain organizational practice is therefore of special importance. This is particularly true for "treaty-modifying" (in contrast to "treaty-extending") established practice because such practice is different from what the members originally consented to and is difficult to consider as a further development of the inherently dynamic project in which they decided to participate. *Prima facie*, "established" seems to require the lapse of a certain period of time, during which a certain conduct has become regular so that those involved may hold a legitimate expectation that this is no longer a coincidence but rather the norm. However, on second thought, while the time factor is certainly relevant, it seems to be the requirement of general acceptance that is key for the development of a certain practice into a rule, as its "passport for normativity" (Cahin).

Therefore, this first facet demonstrates that the law and practice of international organizations are not two separate parts of their existence. They are not only closely related, but they may even overlap: established practices are part of the rules of international organizations. At the same time, however, the legal relevance of the practice of international organizations is much wider. Without being a rule of the organization, its practices may have different kinds of legal facets.

Legal facet two: Practice as a power

The second legal facet covers a major area of international organizations law: their legal powers. The examples in Chapter 2 have shown how powerful practice can be, what "power-generating capacity" the practice of an international organization may have. Even though the attribution principle is generally recognized as the key, overarching principle governing the legal basis and scope of powers of international organizations, in practice international organizations may sometimes exercise powers that have hardly, or not at all, been attributed to them. The Security Council has established *ad hoc* criminal tribunals, the OPCW is now identifying those who are involved in the use of chemical weapons, NATO is carrying out operations that are sometimes characterized by mentioning the provision in the NATO Treaty on which these operations are *not* based ("non-Article 5 operations"), rather than the provision on which they *are* based (in accordance with the attribution principle). As a final example, the CTBTO PrepCom is using its verification installations for a purpose that is entirely outside the scope of its constituent instrument.

In none of these cases has there been sufficiently strong opposition to prevent the organization from using such questionably attributed powers. Those who criticize this would consider (some of) such practices as opportunistic, *ultra vires*, legal nihilism, or perhaps, most generally, against the rule of law. Those who support this would consider the criticizers overly formalistic and would emphasize the need for the organization to be flexible and to give a broad interpretation of its mandate in order to continue to be relevant in circumstances that could not be foreseen at the organization's creation.

While it could be argued that theory in this field is "clean and convincing and comprehensible" and that practice is "messy and full of nonsense" (Barnes), it could equally be argued that practice is responding to real societal needs based on a broad reading of the organization's functions and purposes, and that theory in this field is no longer fully adequate. At the same time, given that implied powers are generally accepted as a source of powers of international organizations, considerable flexibility already exists for international organizations to meet unforeseen needs. Only a restrictive interpretation of implied powers could hamper their functioning in practice. Nevertheless, even a broad interpretation of implied powers may not always suffice. It may therefore be necessary to take a fresh look at the attribution principle and to recognize a further source of powers of international organizations, that is customary powers. Traces of support for this can sometimes be found in doctrine and in case law.

Legal facet three: Practice in interpretation

A third legal facet is "practice in interpretation", more precisely the role of practice of international organizations in the interpretation of their law. International organizations are not states. Nonetheless, the law of treaties concluded by international organizations is almost completely similar to the law of treaties concluded by states. The rules on treaty interpretation are even fully identical. In two different ways, these identical rules can take into account that international organizations are not states, that constituent instruments of international organizations are different from other treaties and that treaties concluded by international organizations are not the same as treaties concluded between states. First, the rules on treaty interpretation are sufficiently broad and flexible to take into account these differences. For example, as illustrated by the 1996 ICJ Advisory Opinion requested by the WHO, greater weight may be given to subsequent practice when interpreting the organization's constituent instrument. It is also generally recognized that particular attention must be given to the object and purpose of constituent instruments and the aims of the organization concerned when these instruments are interpreted. Second, the two Vienna Conventions explicitly state that they apply to constitutions of international organizations and to treaties adopted within an international organization "without prejudice to any relevant rules of the organization". Each international organization may therefore have its own rules and arrangements for the interpretation of its rules. Apart from constitutions, the Vienna rules on interpretation are also relevant for the interpretation of other rules of international organizations, although such rules are often not treaties but unilateral acts. For example, the Vienna rules "may provide guidance" for the interpretation of Security Council resolutions, as the ICJ stated in its 2010 Advisory Opinion on Kosovo's unilateral declaration of independence. But the Court also emphasized that other factors, including the relevant practice of the organ concerned, play an important role in the interpretation of unilateral decisions, such as Security Council resolutions.

Since the art of interpretation is not an automatic process, and since the Vienna rules on interpretation offer considerable flexibility, the outcome of interpretative work is determined by the interpreter to a considerable extent. When it comes to the interpretation of the law of international organizations, there are two main interpreters: the organization and its members. The relationship between an international organization and its members is fundamental for understanding the law and functioning of international organizations. This is also true for the role of an organization's practice in the interpretation of its rules. First and foremost, in their daily practice, it is for organs of the organization to interpret the latter's rules. But second, the requirement that members generally agree with such interpretations is an important check.

Having analysed the practice of international organizations as a rule and in two key areas of international organizations law, the next two chapters followed a different approach. These chapters examined how the two UN organs that are most relevant for the topic of this special course, the ICJ and the ILC, have viewed the practice of international organizations in their work.

Legal facet four: The ICJ and the practice
of international organizations

Chapter 4 analysed how the PCIJ and in particular the ICJ have dealt with the practice of international organizations in their decisions. Arguments derived from this practice are a common phenomenon in the advisory opinions of the ICJ, even though this has not been undisputed. Judge Spender has probably expressed the most critical views in this regard, in his Separate Opinion in *Certain Expenses*, by rejecting the legal relevance of practice of UN organs which has been determined by a majority against the will of a minority. However, his views have not been followed by the Court. In its subsequent advisory opinions (and earlier ones as well), it has extensively relied on the practice of international organizations in different ways. In several advisory opinions (for example, in *Reparation* and in *Kosovo*), the Court only referred to practice as such, without any further qualification. However, in other advisory opinions the Court added a qualifier: the practice was consistent (*Second Admission*, *Certain Expenses* (twice), *Namibia*, *Chagos*); the practice was uniform *(Namibia)*; "settled practice" *(Certain Expenses)*; "a body of practice" *(Judgments of the ILOAT in cases against UNESCO)*; "standard practice" *(Cumaraswamy)*; "constant practice" *(Wall)*; the practice of the Organization "throughout its history" *(Certain Expenses)* or "extending over a long period" *(Namibia)*; the practice "has been generally accepted by Members of the United Nations" *(Namibia)*; "a general practice of that Organization" *(Namibia)*; "accepted practice" *(Wall)*. In the *IMCO* Advisory Opinion, the ICJ referred to "actual practice", but that seems to be closer to a pleonasm than to a qualifier. The Court has not yet referred to the notion of established practice.

The ICJ's recourse to the practice of international organizations has fulfilled two main functions: a supportive and an independent function.

As to the former, the Court has referred to such practice in support of a preceding conclusion based on legal arguments (e.g. *Reparation for Injuries*, *Second Admission*, *IMCO*, *Certain Expenses*, *WHO Nuclear Weapons* (1996), *Chagos*). In some of these cases, the Court even considered the relevant practice after it had concluded that the text of the applicable rule was sufficiently clear and did not require any further exegesis (already in 1922 (PCIJ); for the ICJ, see for example its two *Admissions* advisory opinions (1948 and 1950)). These supportive references to organizational practice in the Court's advisory opinions perform the same function as "supplementary means of interpretation" mentioned in Article 32 of the 1969 and the 1986 Vienna Conventions. However, paradoxically, this recourse to practice is in fact far from "supplementary". It is core business when it comes to the interpretation of constituent instruments of international organizations (see in particular the Court's 1996 *WHO Nuclear Weapons* Advisory Opinion). As discussed in Chapter 4, the use of the "practice argument" in this supplementary, supportive way has the advantage of being a "reality check", but also the risk of being circular.

In some cases, the ICJ's recourse to the practice of international organizations has fulfilled another, independent function. Here, the Court relied mainly on a "practice argument" to arrive at its conclusion. The best and most well-known example is the Court's *Namibia* Advisory Opinion. This demonstrates the importance of the subsequent practice of the Security Council, to which the Court referred in general terms in its 2010 *Kosovo* Advisory Opinion. Apart from *Namibia*, the *Wall* Advisory Opinion is the other main example of a case in which the "practice argument" fulfilled this independent function.

In short, the Court's referencing to the practice of international organizations is rich, full of nuances, and is seeking confirmation that its legal conclusions are not too far removed from reality, so that the Peace Palace is not seen as an ivory tower, sometimes at the risk of circularity. Following this analysis of the Court's judicial work, Chapter 5 focused on the role of the ILC.

Legal facet five: The ILC and the practice of international organizations

The fifth and final legal facet of this special course is devoted to the ILC, in particular to its work on two topics: the identification of customary international law and subsequent agreements and subsequent practice in relation to the interpretation of treaties. The way in which the ILC has dealt with the practice of international organizations is fundamentally different from the approach of the ICJ. This may be explained mainly by the different nature of the work of these two main international law organs of the UN. A request for an advisory opinion of the Court almost always requires the Court to consider the relevant practice of the UN or another international organization. For the ILC, however, its lawmaking task (progressive development and codification) is first of all oriented towards states. Only a few of the topics on its agenda have concerned the law of international organizations, and that part of its work has not always been the most successful.

In its preparations for the Vienna Convention on the Law of Treaties (1969), it was difficult for the ILC to decide whether the future Convention should only cover treaties concluded by states, or also international organizations' treaties. In this respect, history repeated itself during the ILC's work on the SASP Conclusions. Originally the idea prevailed that these conclusions should also cover subsequent agreements and subsequent practice in relation to the treaties of international organizations, but over time this work was narrowed down to (subsequent agreements and subsequent practice in relation to) treaties concluded by states. As mentioned above, the exclusion of (subsequent agreements and) subsequent practice of international organizations is in line with the earlier practice of the ILC itself. In this earlier practice, after the ILC had completed its work on the law of treaties concluded by states and on the articles on state responsibility, it began working on the law of treaties concluded by international organizations and the ARIO. However, after the ILC completed its work that resulted in the SASP Conclusions, it did not take any initiatives for commencing work on subsequent agreements and subsequent practice in relation to the interpretation of treaties concluded by international organizations.

In this respect, the ILC's work on the identification of customary international law is different. From the outset, the ILC and its Special Rapporteur took a broader, more integral approach, not limiting this project to the role of states but also covering the role of international organizations and other non-state actors. At the same time, it appears that it has not been easy for the ILC to implement this broader approach. The ILC Conclusions on the identification of customary international law reveal a certain ambivalence. On the one hand, the practice of international organizations is considered as equivalent to state practice, as far as its contribution to the formation, or expression, of rules of customary international law is concerned (even though this is only "in certain cases"). On the other hand, the ILC conclusions are primarily "state oriented" and do not fully take international organizations and their practice into account.

Both in the ILC and in the General Assembly (when discussing the ILC's annual reports), views on the role and relevance of international organizations and their practice regarding the two topics discussed in this chapter varied quite considerably. Whereas some members of the ILC and some states in the (Sixth Committee of the) General Assembly were in favour of a stronger recognition of the role and relevance of international organizations and their practice, others were opposed to this.

*

From this overview of five legal facets, the overall impression emerges that law, more specifically the law of international organizations, performs a variety of functions in the practice of international organizations. Essentially, it provides international organizations and their members with a flexible framework for shared sovereignty.

The law always provides a framework for the practice of international organizations. Established by law, the hundreds of existing international organizations are a collection of frameworks for international cooperation. As early as in 1974, Mosler could already conclude in his lectures for the Hague Academy that international organizations "now form a kind of superstructure over and above the society of states" [754]. However, neither fifty years ago nor now has the "society of states" become an international order in which sovereign states no longer play a central role. Even though the activities of international organizations have multiplied over the years, and even though they operate more or less autonomously, it is still generally true what Abi-Saab observed in 1987, also in lectures for the Hague Academy: international organizations "restent dans le sillage ou l'órbite des Etats, même quand elles développent un dynamism propre et agissent de manière autonome par rapport aux Etats membres" [755]. In the wake or in the orbit of states, international organizations perform their functions within their given legal frameworks.

---

754. H. Mosler, "The International Society as a Legal Community", *Recueil des cours*, Vol. 140 (1974-IV), at p. 189.
755. G. Abi-Saab, "Cours général de droit international public", *Recueil des cours*, Vol. 207 (1987-VII), at p. 82.

These frameworks are shaped by and elaborated in the rules of the organization. These rules consist first of all of the constituent instrument of the organization. In addition, they include decisions, resolutions and other acts adopted in accordance with these constituent instruments. Finally, they also cover the established practice of the organization, the first legal facet of this special course. This is a recognition of the legal relevance of practice of international organizations. In order to qualify as a rule of the organization, such practice must be "established". On the one hand, this requirement gives certain practices the necessary rigour, bringing them within the legal domain. On the other hand, the necessary flexibility is given for the formation of "established practices" as they are not required to be in accordance with the organization's constituent instrument.

There are more elements of these frameworks that make them flexible, and some of them appeared in the context of the legal facets discussed in this special course. One of them is the power-generating capacity of the practice of international organizations. Chapter 2 demonstrated that powers may be exercised by international organizations that are difficult to reconcile with the general principle of attributed powers, in situations in which there were compelling needs in practice and such action of the organization was sufficiently backed by its members. Another legal facet, practice as a means of interpretation, also contributes to the flexibility of these frameworks for cooperation. This is illustrated in the case law of the ICJ. The Court has strongly relied on arguments derived from practice, not only to support a conclusion that an organization had acted lawfully *(Namibia)* but also to conclude that it had acted *ultra vires (WHO Nuclear Weapons)*. The future is uncertain, and therefore international organization frameworks need to be flexible. At the same time, these legal frameworks imbue them with a minimum structure and rigour so that they perform their functions not in a lawless limbo but within rule of law boundaries.

The purpose *(la finalité fonctionnelle)* of this flexible framework provided by the law of international organizations, including the legal facets discussed in this special course, is to share sovereignty. The notion of shared sovereignty is somewhat paradoxical. Sovereignty, in early writings in Latin referred to as *suprema potestas*, is a quality generally reserved for the state. However, the *potestas* of states has become less *suprema* over the years. While the state is still the highest form of political authority in the world, forces of globalization have increased interdependence and have diminished states' capacities to effectively govern their part of the globe in full independence, in isolation. There is no sovereignty in solitude, as Draghi said to the Italian Senate in 2021. To govern effectively, states need to cooperate. They do so partly within international organizations, where they "pool" or "share" sovereignty. Obviously, such "sharing of sovereignty" within international organization frameworks does not mean fully controlling the future, in the area of operation of the organization concerned. The uncertainties of the future are many; sovereign and sometimes very powerful states still take most decisions on how the challenges brought by these uncertainties must be met. At the same time, the purpose of these frameworks is to give members of the organization more control over their future in the field of operation of the organization than they would have if they had remained unorganized. The versatile practice of international organizations shows the results of the functioning of this "superstructure". The legal facets of this practice discussed in this special course demonstrate the role of law: to provide flexible frameworks for shared sovereignty.

BIBLIOGRAPHY

Abi-Saab, G., "Cours général de droit international public", *Recueil des cours*, Vol. 207 (1987-VII).

Ahlborn, C., "The Rules of International Organizations and the Law of International Responsibility", *International Organizations Law Review*, Vol. 8 (2011), pp. 397-482.

Allott, P., "The Concept of International Law", *European Journal of International Law*, Vol. 10 (1999), pp. 31-50.

Alter, K. J., *The New Terrain of International Law: Courts, Politics, Rights*, Princeton, NJ, Princeton University Press, 2014.

Alvarez, J. E., *International Organizations as Law-Makers*, Oxford, Oxford University Press, 2005.

Amerasinghe, C. F., *Principles of the Institutional Law of International Organizations*, 2nd ed., Cambridge, Cambridge University Press, 2005.

Amirfar, C., R. Zamour and D. Pickard, "Representation of Member States at the United Nations: Recent Challenges", *ASIL Insights*, Vol. 26, No. 6 (August), https://www.asil.org/insights/volume/26/issue/6.

Arangio-Ruiz, G., "The Normative Role of the General Assembly of the United Nations and the Declaration on Principles of Friendly Relations: With an Appendix on the Concept of International Law and the Theory of International Organization", *Recueil des cours*, Vol. 137 (1972-III), pp. 409-742.

Arditi, L., "The Role of Practice in International Organizations: The Case of Government Recognition by the International Monetary Fund", *International Organizations Law Review*, Vol. 17 (2017), pp. 531-585.

Aust, A., *Modern Treaty Law and Practice*, 3rd ed., Cambridge, Cambridge University Press, 2013.

Barber, R., "The Role of the General Assembly in Determining the Legitimacy of Governments", *International and Comparative Law Quarterly*, Vol. 71 (2022), pp. 627-656.

Barkholdt, J., "The Contribution of International Organizations to the Formation, Interpretation and Identification of International Law", *International Organizations Law Review*, Vol. 18 (2021), pp. 1-45.

Barnes, J., *The Noise of Time*, London, Jonathan Cape, 2016.

Bekker, P. H. F., "The Work of the International Law Commission on 'Relations between States and International Organizations' Discontinued: an Assessment", *Leiden Journal of International Law*, Vol. 6 (1993), pp. 3-16.

Bernal, P. A., "The Importance of PTS Data for Tsunami Warning Centres", *CTBTO Spectrum*, Vol. 9 (January 2007), pp. 20-21.

Blokker, N., "International Organizations and Customary International law: Is the International Law Commission taking International Organizations Seriously?", *International Organizations Law Review*, Vol. 14 (2017), pp. 1-12.

Blokker, N. M., *Saving Succeeding Generations from the Scourge of War*, Leiden, Brill Nijhoff, 2021.

Blokker N., and S. Muller, "NATO as the UN Security Council's Instrument: Question Marks From the Perspective of International Law?", *Leiden Journal of International Law*, Vol. 9 (1996), pp. 417-421.

Boisson de Chazournes, L., "Subsequent Practice, Practices, and 'Family-Resemblance': Towards Embedding Subsequent Practice in its Operative Milieu", in G. Nolte (ed.), *Treaties and Subsequent Practice*, Oxford, Oxford University Press, 2013, pp. 53-68.

Bonucci, N., G. Marceau, A.-P. Ouellet and R. Walker, "IGO's Initiatives as a Response to Crises and Unforeseen Needs", *International Organizations Law Review*, Vol. 19 (2022), pp. 423-482.

Brölmann, C., "A Flat Earth? International Organizations in the System of International Law", *Nordic Journal of International Law*, Vol. 70 (2001), pp. 319-340.
Brölmann, C., *The Institutional Veil in Public International Law: International Organisations and the Law of Treaties*, Oxford, Hart Publishing, 2007.
Buga, I., "Subsequent Practice and Treaty Modification", in M. J. Bowman and D. Kritsiotis (eds.), *Conceptual and Contextual Perspectives on the Modern Law of Treaties*, Cambridge, Cambridge University Press, 2018, pp. 363-391.
Cahin, G., *La coutume international et les organisations internationales – l'incidence de la dimension institutionnelle sur le processus coutumier*, Paris, Pedone, 2001.
Caminos, H., and R. Lavalle, "New Departures in the Exercise of Inherent Powers by the UN and OAS Secretaries-General: The Central American Situation", *American Journal of International Law*, Vol. 83 (1989), pp. 395-402.
Canal-Forgues, E., "Sur l'interprétation dans le droit de l'OMC", *Revue générale de droit international public*, Vol. 1 (2001), pp. 5-24.
Chaumont, C. M., "La signification du principe de spécialite des organisations internationales", in *Mélanges offerts à Henri Rolin. Problèmes de droit des gens*, Paris, Pedone, 1964, pp. 55-66.
Clark, T., "The Teleological Turn in the Law of International Organisations", *International and Comparative Law Quarterly*, Vol. 70 (2021), pp. 533-567.
Coicaud, J.-M., and V. Heiskanen (eds.), *The Legitimacy of International Organizations*, Tokyo/New York, UN University Press, 2001.
Conforti B., and C. Focarelli, *The Law and Practice of the United Nations*, 5th rev. ed., Leiden, Brill Nijhoff, 2016.
Constantinesco, L.-J., *Das Recht der Europäischen Gemeinschaften – Das institutionelle Recht*, Baden-Baden, Nomos, 1977.
Crawford, J., "A Consensualist Interpretation of Article 31(3) of the Vienna Convention on the Law of Treaties", in G. Nolte (ed.), *Treaties and Subsequent Practice*, Oxford, Oxford University Press, 2013, pp. 29-33.
Crawford, J., "Chance, Order, Change: The Course of International Law", *Recueil des cours*, Vol. 365 (2013).
Daugirdas, K., "How and Why International Law Binds International Organizations", *Harvard International Law Journal*, Vol. 57 (2016), pp. 325-381.
Dekker, I. F., and E. P. J. Myjer, "Air Strikes on Bosnian Positions: Is NATO Also Legally the Proper Instrument of the UN?", *Leiden Journal of International Law*, Vol. 9 (1996), pp. 411-416.
Dobbert, J. P., "Evolution of the Treaty-Making Capacity of International Organizations", in *The Law and the Sea: Essays in Memory of Jean Carroz*, Rome, FAO, 1987, pp. 22-42.
Dupuy, R.-J., *Le droit international*, 4th ed., Paris, Presses universitaires de France, 1972.
Engel, S., "Procedures for the De Facto Revision of the Charter", in *Proceedings of the American Society of International Law at Its Annual Meeting (1921-1969)*, Vol. 59 (1965), pp. 108-116.
Engel, S., "'Living' International Constitutions and the World Court (The Subsequent Practice of International Organs under their Constituent Instruments)", in *International and Comparative Law Quarterly*, Vol. 16 (1967), pp. 865-910.
Engström, V., "Reasoning on Powers of Organizations", in J. Klabbers and Å. Wallendahl (eds.), *Research Handbook on the Law of International Organizations*, Cheltenham, Elgar, 2011, pp. 56-83.
Fennessy, J. G., "The 1975 Vienna Convention on the Representation of States in their Relations with International Organizations of a Universal Character", *American Journal of International Law*, Vol. 70 (1976), pp. 62-72.
Fitzmaurice, G., *The Law and Procedure of the International Court of Justice*, Vol. 1, Cambridge, Grotius, 1986.

Frid, R., "The European Economic Community: A Member of a Specialized Agency of the United Nations", *European Journal of International Law*, Vol. 4 (1993), pp. 239-255.

Gaja, G., "A 'New' Vienna Convention on Treaties between States and International Organizations or Between International Organizations: A Critical Commentary", *British Yearbook of International Law*, Vol. 58 (1987), pp. 253-269.

Gardiner, R. K., *Treaty Interpretation*, 2nd ed., Oxford, Oxford University Press, 2015.

Gasbarri, L., "The Notion of Institutional Practice in United Nations Law", *Max Planck Yearbook of United Nations Law*, Vol. 24 (2021), pp. 1-35.

Gautier, P., in O. Corten and P. Klein (eds.), *The Vienna Conventions on the Law of Treaties: A Commentary*, Vol. 1, Oxford, Oxford University Press, 2011, pp. 57-65.

Gianviti, F., "Members' Rights and Obligations Under the IMF's Articles of Agreement: The Role of Practice in the Interpretation of an Organization's Charter", in R. C. Effros (ed.), *Current Legal Issues Affecting Central Banks*, Washington, IMF, 1995, pp. 1-13.

Gianviti, F., "The Third Amendment to the IMF's Articles of Agreement", in R. C. Effros (ed.), *Current Legal Issues Affecting Central Banks*, Washington, IMF, 1995, pp. 14-17.

Gold, J., "Legal Technique in the Creation of a New International Reserve Asset: Special Drawing Rights and the Amendment of the Articles of Agreement of the International Monetary Fund", *Case Western Reserve Journal of International Law*, Vol. 1 (1969), pp. 105-123. Reproduced in J. Gold, *Legal and Institutional Aspects of the International Monetary System: Selected Essays*, Washington, IMF, 1979, pp. 128-147.

Gold, J., *The Rule of Law in the International Monetary Fund*, Washington, IMF Pamphlet Series No. 32, 1980.

Gold, J., "The IMF Invents New Penalties", in N. Blokker and S. Muller (eds.), *Towards More Effective Supervision by International Organizations: Essays in Honour of Henry G. Schermers*, Vol. 1, Dordrecht, Nijhoff, 1994, pp. 127-147.

Goodrich, L. M., and E. Hambro, *Charter of the United Nations: Commentary and Documents*, 2nd rev. ed., Boston, World Peace Foundation, 1949.

Grossman, V., *Life and Fate*, trans. Robert Chandler, London, Harvill Press, 1985. First published in Russian as *Жизнь и судьба* in 1980 (completed in 1960).

Happold, M., "Julian Assange and the UN Working Group on Arbitrary Detention", *EJIL:Talk!*, 5 February 2016, https://www.ejiltalk.org/julian-assange-and-the-un-working-group-on-arbitrary-detention/.

Heywood Anderson, D., in O. Corten and P. Klein (eds.), *The Vienna Conventions on the Law of Treaties: A Commentary*, Vol. 1, Oxford, Oxford University Press, 2011, pp. 88-103.

Higgins, R., "The Development of International Law by the Political Organs of the United Nations", *Proceedings of the Annual Meeting (American Society of International Law)*, Vol. 59 (1965), pp. 116-124.

Higgins, R., *United Nations Peacekeeping 1946-1967: Documents and Commentary*, London, Oxford University Press, Vol. 1: *The Middle East* (1969); Vol. 2: *Asia* (1970); Vol. 3: *Europe and Africa* (1980).

Higgins, R., *Problems and Process: International Law and How We Use It*, Oxford, Oxford University Press, 1994.

Higgins, R., "The Legal Consequences for Member States of the Non-fulfilment by International Organizations of their Obligations Toward Third Parties", *Annuaire de l'Institut de Droit International*, Session de Lisbonne, Vol. 66-I (1995), https://www.idi-iil.org/app/uploads/2017/06/1995_lis_02_en.pdf.

Hooghe, L., T. Lenz and G. Marks, *A Theory of International Organization: A Postfunctionalist Theory of Governance*, Vol. 4, Oxford, Oxford University Press, 2019.

Kelsen, H., *The Law of the United Nations*, London, Stevens, 1951.

Klabbers, J., "Virtuous Interpretation", in Fitzmaurice *et al.* (eds.), *Treaty Interpretation and the Vienna Convention on the Law of Treaties: 30 Years On*, Leiden, Brill Nijhoff, 2010, pp. 17-37.
Klabbers, J., *An Introduction to International Organizations Law*, 4th ed., Cambridge, Cambridge University Press, 2022.
Klein, P., "Les compétences et pouvoirs de l'organisation internationale", in E. Lagrange and J.-M. Sorel (eds.), *Droit des organisations internationales*, Issy-les-Moulineaux Cedex, Librairie générale de droit et de jurisprudence, 2013, pp. 714-734.
Klein E., and S. Schmahl, "Die neue NATO-Strategie und ihre völkerrechtlichen und verfassungsrechtlichen Implikationen", *Recht und Politik*, Vol. 35 (1999), pp. 198-209.
Korontzis, G., "Making the Treaty", in D. B. Hollis (ed.), *The Oxford Guide to Treaties*, Oxford, Oxford University Press, 2012, pp. 177-207.
Kreuder-Sonnen, C., *Emergency Powers of International Organizations*, Oxford, Oxford University Press, 2019.
Lagrange, E., and J.-M. Sorel, *Droit des organisations internationales*, Issy-les-Moulineaux Cedex, Librairie générale de droit et de jurisprudence, 2013.
Lash, J. P., *Dag Hammarskjöld*, London, Cassell, 1961.
Lauterpacht, E., "The Development of the Law of International Organization by the Decisions of International Tribunals", *Recueil des cours*, Vol. 152 (1976), pp. 379-478.
Lawson, R. A., *Het EVRM en de Europese Gemeenschappen – Bouwstenen voor een aansprakelijkheidsregime voor het optreden van internationale organisaties*, Deventer, Kluwer, 1999.
Lazarus, L., "The United Nations Working Group on Arbitrary Detention Decision on Assange: 'Ridiculous' or 'Justifiable'?", *EJIL:Talk!*, 9 February 2016, https://www.ejiltalk.org/the-united-nations-working-group-on-arbitrary-detention-decision-on-assange-ridiculous-or-justifiable/.
Letsas, G., *A Theory of Interpretation of the European Convention on Human Rights*, Oxford, Oxford University Press, 2007.
Limburg, G., "The United Nations Conference on the Law of Treaties Between States and International Organizations or between International Organizations", *Netherlands International Law Review*, Vol. 33 (1986), pp. 195-203.
Malanczuk, P., *Akehurst's Modern Introduction to International Law*, 7th rev. ed., London, Routledge, 1997.
Manin, Ph., "The European Communities and the Vienna Convention on the Law of Treaties between States and International Organizations or between International Organizations", *Common Market Law Review*, Vol. 24 (1987), pp. 457-481.
Mathias, S., "The Work of the International Law Commission on Identification of Customary International Law: A View from the Perspective of the Office of Legal Affairs", *Chinese Journal of International Law*, Vol. 15 (2016), pp. 17-31.
Merkouris, P., "Introduction: Interpretation is a Science, is an Art, is a Science", in M. Fitzmaurice *et al.* (eds.), *Treaty Interpretation and the Vienna Convention on the Law of Treaties: 30 Years On*, Leiden, Brill Nijhoff, 2010, pp. 1-13.
Merkouris, P., "Debating Interpretation: On the Road to Ithaca", *Leiden Journal of International Law*, Vol. 35 (2022), pp. 461-468.
Monaco, R., "Le caractère constitutionnel des actes institutifs d'Organisations internationals", in *Mélanges offerts à Charles Rousseau – La communauté internationale*, Paris, Pedone, 1974, pp. 153-172.
Morgenstern, F., *Legal Problems of International Organizations*, Cambridge, Grotius, 1986.
Morgenstern, F., "The Convention on the Law of Treaties between States and International Organizations or between International Organizations", in Y. Dinstein (ed.), *International Law at a Time of Perplexity: Essays in Honour of Shabtai Rosenne*, Dordrecht, Nijhoff, 1989, pp. 435-447.

Mosler, H., "The International Society as a Legal Community", *Recueil des cours*, Vol. 140 (1974-IV).
Murphy, S. D., "Identification of Customary International Law and Other Topics: The Sixty-Seventh Session of the International Law Commission", *American Journal of International Law*, Vol. 109 (2015), pp. 822-844.
Nascimento e Silva, G. E. do, "The 1986 Vienna Convention and the Treaty-Making Power of International Organizations", *German Yearbook of International Law*, Vol. 29 (1986), pp. 68-85.
Nascimento e Silva, G. E. do, "The 1969 and the 1986 Conventions on the Law of Treaties: A Comparison", in Y. Dinstein (ed.), *International Law at a Time of Perplexity: Essays in Honour of Shabtai Rosenne*, Dordrecht, Nijhoff, 1989, pp. 461-487.
Neffe, J., *Einstein – Eine Biographie*, 3rd ed., Rowohlt, Reinbek, 2005.
Nolte, G. (ed.), *Treaties and Subsequent Practice*, Oxford, Oxford University Press, 2013.
Orakhelashvili, A., "The Attribution Decision Adopted by the OPCW's Conference of States Parties and Its Legality", *International Organizations Law Review*, Vol. 17 (2020), pp. 664-681.
Pellet, A., "Le droit international à la lumière de la pratique: l'introuvable théorie de la réalité", *Recueil des cours*, Vol. 414 (2021).
Pescatore, P., *Les objectifs de la Communauté européenne comme principes d'interprétation dans la jurisprudence de la Cour de Justice* (W. J. Miscellanea Ganshof van der Meersch, Vol. 2), Brussels, Bruylant, 1972.
Peters, C., "Subsequent Practice and Established Practice of International Organizations: Two Sides of the Same Coin", *Goettingen Journal of International Law*, Vol. 3 (2011), pp. 617-642.
Peters, C., *Praxis Internationaler Organisationen – Vertragswandel und völkerrechtlicher Ordnungsrahmen*, Berlin, Springer, 2016.
Pollux (E. Hambro), "The Interpretation of the Charter", *British Yearbook of International Law*, Vol. 23 (1946), pp. 54-82.
Reinisch, A., "Sources of International Organizations' Law: Why Custom and General Principles are Crucial", in S. Besson and J. d'Aspremont (eds.), *The Oxford Handbook on the Sources of International Law*, Oxford, Oxford University Press, 2017, pp. 1007-1024.
Reuter, P., *Institutions internationales*, 7th ed., Paris, Presses universitaires de France, 1972.
Reuter, P., "Quelques réflexions sur la notion de 'pratique internationale', spécialement en matière d'organisations internationales", in *Studi in onore di Giuseppe Sperduti*, Milan, Giuffrè, 1984, pp. 189-207.
Reuter, P., "La conférence de Vienne sur les traités des organisations internationales et la securité des engagements conventionnels", in F. Capotorti *et al.* (eds.), *Du droit international au droit de l'intégration : Liber Amicorum Pierre Pescatore*, Baden-Baden, Nomos, 1987, pp. 545-564.
Riphagen, W., "The Second Round of Treaty Law", in F. Capotorti *et al.* (eds.), *Du droit international au droit de l'intégration : Liber Amicorum Pierre Pescatore*, Baden-Baden, Nomos, 1987, pp. 565-581.
Rohde, C., "Organizational Practice as a Source of Law", in D. Petrović (ed.), *90 Years of Contribution of the Administrative Tribunal of the International Labour Organization to the Creation of International Civil Service Law*, Geneva, ILO, 2017, pp. 53-73.
Romano, C. P. R., K. J. Alter and Y. Shany (eds.), *The Oxford Handbook of International Adjudication*, Oxford, Oxford University Press, 2014.
Rosenne, S., *Developments in the Law of Treaties 1945-1986*, Cambridge, Cambridge University Press, 1989.
Roucounas, E., "Practice as a Relevant Factor for the Responsibility of International Organizations", in M. Ragazzi (ed.), *Responsibility of International Organizations*, Leiden, Nijhoff, 2013, pp. 159-171.

Ruffert, M., and C. Walter, *Institutionalised International Law*, Baden-Baden, C. H. Beck/Hart/Nomos, 2015.
Sands P., and P. Klein, *Bowett's Law of International Institutions*, 6th ed., London, Sweet & Maxwell, 2009.
Sauer, H., "Die NATO und das Verfassungsrecht: neues Konzept – alte Fragen", *Zeitschrift für ausländisches öffentliches Recht und Völkerrecht*, Vol. 62 (2002), pp. 317-346.
Schachter, O., "The Invisible College of International Lawyers", *Northwestern University School of Law Review*, Vol. 72 (1977), pp. 217-226.
Schermers, H. G., and N. M. Blokker, *International Institutional Law*, 6th ed., Leiden, Brill Nijhoff, 2018.
Schwob, J., "L'amendement de l'acte constitutif de la FAO visant à permettre l'admission en qualité de membre d'organisations d'intégration économique régionale et la Communauté économique européenne", *Revue trimestrielle de droit européen*, Vol. 29 (1993), pp. 1-16.
Seidl-Hohenveldern, I., and G. Loibl, *Das Recht der Internationalen Organisationen einschließlich der Supranationalen Gemeinschaften*, 7th rev. ed., Cologne, Carl Heymanns, 2000.
Seyersted, F., "Can the United Nations Establish Military Forces and Perform Other Acts Without Specific Basis in the Charter?", *Österreichische Zeitschrift für Öffentliches Recht*, Vol. 12 (1962), pp. 190-229.
Seyersted, F., *Common Law of International Organizations*, Leiden, Nijhoff, 2008.
Sievers, L., and S. Daws, *The Procedure of the UN Security Council*, 4th ed., Oxford, Oxford University Press, 2014.
Simma, B. (ed.), *The Charter of the United Nations: A Commentary*, 2nd ed., New York, Oxford University Press, 2002.
Simma, B. et al. (eds.), *The Charter of the United Nations: A Commentary*, 3rd ed., New York, Oxford University Press, 2012.
Simon, D., *L'interprétation judiciaire des traités d'organisations internationales*, Paris, Pedone, 1981.
Sinclair, I., *The Vienna Convention on the Law of Treaties*, 2nd ed., Manchester, Manchester University Press, 1984.
Skubiszewski, K., "Remarks on the Interpretation of the United Nations Charter", in R. Bernhardt et al. (eds.), *Völkerrecht als Rechtsordnung, Internationale Gerichtsbarkeit, Menschenrechte, Festschrift für Hermann Mosler*, Heidelberg, Springer, 1983, pp. 891-902.
Stavropoulos, C. A., "The Practice of Voluntary Abstentions by Permanent Members of the Security Council under Article 27, Paragraph 3, of the Charter of the United Nations", *American Journal of International Law*, Vol. 61 (1967), pp. 737-752.
Sur, S., *L'interprétation en droit international public*, Paris, Librairie générale de droit et de jurisprudence, 1974.
Tammes, A. J. P., "Decisions of International Organs as a Source of International Law", *Recueil des cours*, Vol. 94 (1958), pp. 265-363.
Trebilcock, A., "The International Labour Organization", in M. Bowman and D. Kritsiotis (eds.), *Conceptual and Contextual Perspectives on the Law of Treaties*, Cambridge, Cambridge University Press, 2018, pp. 848-880.
Urquhart, B., *Hammarskjold*, New York, W. W. Norton and Company, 1972.
Viterbo, A., *International Monetary Fund (IMF)*, 3rd ed., Alphen aan den Rijn, Wolters Kluwer, 2019.
Watson-Wright, W., "Buttressing the Global Tsunami Warning Network", *CTBTO Spectrum*, Vol. 18 (March 2012), pp. 33-35.
Webb, P., "Should the *2004 UN State Immunity Convention* Serve as a Model/ Starting point for a Future UN Convention on the Immunity of International Organizations?", *International Organizations Law Review*, Vol. 10 (2013), pp. 319-331.
Weiß, N., *Kompetenzlehre internationaler Organisationen*, Dordrecht, Springer, 2009.

Weller, M., "Is the ICJ at Risk of Providing Cover for the Alleged Genocide in Myanmar?", *EJIL:Talk!*, 11 February 2022, https://www.ejiltalk.org/is-the-icj-at-risk-of-providing-cover-for-the-alleged-genocide-in-myanmar/.

Werner, W. G., "Custom as Rewritten Law: The Text and Paratext of Restatement Reports", *ESIL Reflections*, Vol. 11, No. 3 (29 September 2022), https://esil-sedi.eu/esil-reflection-custom-as-rewritten-law-the-text-and-paratext-of-restatement-reports/.

Wessel, R. A., "Dissolution and Succession: The Transmigration of the Soul of International Organizations", in J. Klabbers and Å. Wallendahl (eds.), *Research Handbook on the Law of International Organizations*, Cheltenham, Elgar, 2011, pp. 342-362.

White, N. D., *The Law of International Organisations*, 3rd ed., Manchester, Manchester University Press, 2017.

Wickremasinghe, C., "Casenote: The Bustani Case before the ILOAT", *International Organizations Law Review*, Vol. 1 (2004), pp. 197-207.

Wood, M. C., "The Interpretation of Security Council Resolutions", *Max Planck Yearbook of United Nations Law*, Vol. 2 (1998), pp. 73-95.

Wood, M., "International Organizations and Customary International Law", *Vanderbilt Journal of Transnational Law*, Vol. 48 (2015), pp. 609-620.

Wood, M., "The Interpretation of Security Council Resolutions, Revisited", *Max Planck Yearbook of United Nations Law*, Vol. 20 (2016), pp. 3-35.

Wood, M., and E. Sthoeger, *The UN Security Council and International Law*, Cambridge, Cambridge University Press, 2022.

Wouters J., and P. De Man, "International Organizations as Law-Makers", in J. Klabbers and Å. Wallendahl (eds.), *Research Handbook on the Law of International Organizations*, Cheltenham, Elgar, 2011, pp. 190-224.

Zemanek, K., "The United Nations Conference on the Law of Treaties between States and International Organizations or between International Organizations: The Unrecorded History of its 'General Agreement'", in K.-H. Böckstiegel *et al.* (eds.), *Law of Nations, Law of International Organizations, World's Economic Law: Liber Amicorum Honouring Ignaz Seidl-Hohenveldern*, Dordrecht, Kluwer Law International, 1988, pp. 665-679.

Zwanenburg, M., "NATO, Its Member States, and the Security Council", in N. Blokker and N. Schrijver (eds.), *The Security Council and the Use of Force*, Leiden, Nijhoff, 2005, pp. 189-211.

PUBLICATIONS DE L'ACADÉMIE
DE DROIT INTERNATIONAL
DE LA HAYE

PUBLICATIONS OF THE
HAGUE ACADEMY OF INTERNATIONAL
LAW

RECUEIL DES COURS Depuis 1923, les plus grands noms du droit international ont professé à l'Académie de droit international de La Haye. Tous les tomes du *Recueil* qui ont été publiés depuis cette date sont disponibles, chaque tome étant, depuis les tout premiers, régulièrement réimprimé sous sa forme originale.

Depuis 2008, certains cours font l'objet d'une édition en livres de poche.

En outre, toute la collection existe en version électronique. Tous les ouvrages parus à ce jour ont été mis en ligne et peuvent être consultés moyennant un des abonnements proposés, qui offrent un éventail de tarifs et de possibilités.

INDEX A ce jour, il a paru sept index généraux. Ils couvrent les tomes suivants :

1 à 101	(1923-1960)	379 pages	ISBN 978-90-218-9948-0
102 à 125	(1961-1968)	204 pages	ISBN 978-90-286-0643-2
126 à 151	(1969-1976)	280 pages	ISBN 978-90-286-0630-2
152 à 178	(1976-1982)	416 pages	ISBN 978-0-7923-2955-8
179 à 200	(1983-1986)	260 pages	ISBN 978-90-411-0110-5
201 à 250	(1987-1994)	448 pages	ISBN 978-90-04-13700-4
251 à 300	(1995-2002)	580 pages	ISBN 978-90-04-15387-7

A partir du tome 210 il a été décidé de publier un index complet qui couvrira chaque fois dix tomes du *Recueil des cours*. Le dernier index paru couvre les tomes suivants :

311 à 320	(2004-2006)	392 pages	Tome 320A	ISBN 978-90-04-19695-7

COLLOQUES L'Académie organise également des colloques dont les débats sont publiés. Les derniers volumes parus de ces colloques portent les titres suivants : *Le règlement pacifique des différends internationaux en Europe : perspectives d'avenir* (1990) ; *Le développement du rôle du Conseil de sécurité* (1992) ; *La Convention sur l'interdiction et l'élimination des armes chimiques : une percée dans l'entreprise multilatérale du désarmement* (1994) ; *Actualité de la Conférence de La Haye de 1907, Deuxième Conférence de la Paix* (2007).

CENTRE D'ÉTUDE ET DE RECHERCHE Les travaux scientifiques du Centre d'étude et de recherche de droit international et de relations internationales de l'Académie de droit international de La Haye, dont les sujets sont choisis par le Curatorium de l'Académie, faisaient l'objet, depuis la session de 1985, d'une publication dans laquelle les directeurs d'études dressaient le bilan des recherches du Centre qu'ils avaient dirigé. Cette série a été arrêtée et la dernière brochure parue porte le titre suivant : *Les règles et les institutions du droit international humanitaire à l'épreuve des conflits armés récents*. Néanmoins, lorsque les travaux du Centre se révèlent particulièrement intéressants et originaux, les rapports des directeurs et les articles rédigés par les chercheurs font l'objet d'un ouvrage collectif.

Les demandes de renseignements ou de catalogues et les commandes doivent être adressées à

MARTINUS NIJHOFF PUBLISHERS

B.P. 9000, 2300 PA Leyde   Pays-Bas   http://www.brill.nl

COLLECTED COURSES

Since 1923 the top names in international law have taught at The Hague Academy of International Law. All the volumes of the *Collected Courses* which have been published since 1923 are available, as, since the very first volume, they are reprinted regularly in their original format.

Since 2008, certain courses have been the subject of a pocketbook edition.

In addition, the total collection now exists in electronic form. All works already published have been put "on line" and can be consulted under one of the proposed subscription methods, which offer a range of tariffs and possibilities.

INDEXES

Up till now seven General Indexes have been published. They cover the following volumes:

1 to 101	(1923-1960)	379 pages	ISBN 978-90-218-9948-0
102 to 125	(1961-1968)	204 pages	ISBN 978-90-286-0643-2
126 to 151	(1969-1976)	280 pages	ISBN 978-90-286-0630-2
152 to 178	(1976-1982)	416 pages	ISBN 978-0-7923-2955-8
179 to 200	(1983-1986)	260 pages	ISBN 978-90-411-0110-5
201 to 250	(1987-1994)	448 pages	ISBN 978-90-04-13700-4
251 to 300	(1995-2002)	580 pages	ISBN 978-90-04-15387-7

From Volume 210 onwards it has been decided to publish a full index covering, each time, ten volumes of the *Collected Courses*. The latest Index published covers the following volumes:
311 to 320   (2004-2006)   392 pages   Volume 320A   ISBN 978-90-04-19695-7

WORKSHOPS

The Academy publishes the discussions from the Workshops which it organises. The latest titles of the Workshops already published are as follows: *The Peaceful Settlement of International Disputes in Europe: Future Prospects* (1990) ; *The Development of the Role of the Security Council* (1992); *The Convention on the Prohibition and Elimination of Chemical Weapons: A Breakthrough in Multilateral Disarmament* (1994); *Topicality of the 1907 Hague Conference, the Second Peace Conference* (2007).

CENTRE FOR STUDIES AND RESEARCH

The scientific works of the Centre for Studies and Research in International Law and International Relations of The Hague Academy of International Law, the subjects of which are chosen by the Curatorium of the Academy, have been published, since the Centre's 1985 session, in a publication in which the Directors of Studies reported on the state of research of the Centre under their direction. This series has been discontinued and the title of the latest booklet published is as follows: *Rules and Institutions of International Humanitarian Law Put to the Test of Recent Armed Conflicts*. Nevertheless, when the work of the Centre has been of particular interest and originality, the reports of the Directors of Studies together with the articles by the researchers form the subject of a collection published by the Academy.

Requests for information, catalogues and orders for publications must be addressed to

MARTINUS NIJHOFF PUBLISHERS

P.O. Box 9000, 2300 PA Leiden   The Netherlands   **http://www.brill.nl**

TABLE PAR TOME DES COURS PUBLIÉS CES DERNIÈRES ANNÉES

INDEX BY VOLUME OF THE COURSES PUBLISHED THESE LAST YEARS

Tome/Volume 367 (2013)

Kolb, R. : L'article 103 de la Charte des Nations Unies, 9-252.
Nascimbene, B. : Le droit de la nationalité et le droit des organisations d'intégration régionales. Vers de nouveaux statuts de résidents?, 253-454.

(ISBN 978-90-04-26793-0)

Tome/Volume 368 (2013)

Caflisch, L: Frontières nationales, limites et délimitations. – Quelle importance aujourd'hui? (conférence inaugurale), 9-46.
Benvenisti, E. : The International Law of Global Governance, 47-280.
Park, K. G. : La protection des personnes en cas de catastrophes, 281-456.

(ISBN 978-90-04-26795-4)

Tome/Volume 369 (2013)

Kronke, H. : Transnational Commercial Law and Conflict of Laws: Institutional Co-operation and Substantive Complementarity (Opening Lecture), 9-42.
Ortiz Ahlf, L. : The Human Rights of Undocumented Migrants, 43-160.
Kono, T. : Efficiency in Private International Law, 161-360.
Yusuf, A. A. : Pan-Africanism and International Law, 361-512.

(ISBN 978-90-04-26797-8)

Tome/Volume 370 (2013)

Dominicé, Ch. : La société internationale à la recherche de son équilibre. Cours général de droit international public, 9-392.   (ISBN 978-90-04-26799-2)

Tome/Volume 371 (2014)

Lagarde, P. : La méthode de la reconnaissance est-elle l'avenir du droit international privé?, 9-42.
Charlesworth, H. : Democracy and International Law, 43-152.
de Vareilles-Sommières, P. : L'exception d'ordre public et la régularité substantielle internationale de la loi étrangère, 153-272.
Yanagihara, M. : Significance of the History of the Law of Nations in Europe and East Asia, 273-435.

(ISBN 978-90-04-28936-9)

Tome/Volume 372 (2014)

Bucher, A. : La compétence universelle civile, 9-128.
Cordero-Moss, G. : Limitations on Party Autonomy in International Commercial Arbitration, 129-326.

Sinjela, M. : Intellectual Property : Cross-Border Recognition of Rights and National Development, 327-394.
Dolzer, R. : International Co-operation in Energy Affairs, 395-504.

(ISBN 978-90-04-28937-6)

Tome/Volume 373 (2014)

Cachard, O. : Le transport international aérien de passagers, 9-216.
Audit, M. : Bioéthique et droit international privé, 217-447.

(ISBN 978-90-04-28938-3)

Tome/Volume 374 (2014)

Struycken, A. V. M. : Arbitration and State Contract, 9-52.
Corten, O., La rébellion et le droit international : le principe de neutralité en tension, 53-312.
Parra, A. : The Convention and Centre for Settlement of Investment Disputes, 313-410.

(ISBN 978-90-04-29764-7)

Tome/Volume 375 (2014)

Jayme, E. : Narrative Norms in Private International Law – The Example of Art Law, 9-52.
De Boer, Th. M. : Choice of Law in Arbitration Proceedings, 53-88.
Frigo, M. : Circulation des biens culturels, détermination de la loi applicable et méthodes de règlement des litiges, 89-474.

(ISBN 978-90-04-29766-1)

Tome/Volume 376 (2014)

Cançado Trindade, A. A. : The Contribution of Latin American Legal Doctrine to the Progressive Development of International Law, 9-92.
Gray, C. : The Limits of Force, 93-198.
Najurieta, M. S. : L'adoption internationale des mineurs et les droits de l'enfant, 199-494.

(ISBN 978-90-04-29768-5)

Tome/Volume 377 (2015)

Kassir, W. J. : Le renvoi en droit international privé – technique de dialogue entre les cultures juridiques, 9-120.
Noodt Taquela, M. B. : Applying the Most Favourable Treaty or Domestic Rules to Facilitate Private International Law Co-operation, 121-318.
Tuzmukhamedov, B. : Legal Dimensions of Arms Control Agreements, An Introductory Overview, 319-468.

(ISBN 978-90-04-29770-8)

Tome/Volume 378 (2015)

Iwasawa, Y. : Domestic Application of International Law, 9-262.
Carrascosa Gonzalez, J. : The Internet – Privacy and Rights relating to Personality, 263-486.

(ISBN 978-90-04-32125-0)

Tome/Volume 379 (2015)

Lowe, V.: The Limits of the Law.
Boele-Woelki, K.: Party Autonomy in Litigation and Arbitration in View of The Hague Principles on Choice of Law in International Commercial Contracts.
Fresnedo de Aguirre, C.: Public Policy: Common Principles in the American States.
Ben Achour, R.: Changements anticonstitutionnels de gouvernement et droit international.

(ISBN 978-90-04-32127-4)

Tome/Volume 380 (2015)

Van Loon, J. H. A.: The Global Horizon of Private International Law.
Pougoué, P.-G.: L'arbitrage dans l'espace OHADA.
Kruger, T.: The Quest for Legal Certainty in International Civil Cases.

(ISBN 978-90-04-32131-1)

Tome/Volume 381 (2015)

Jayme, E.: Les langues et le droit international privé, 11-39.
Bermann, G.: Arbitrage and Private International Law. General Course on Private International Law (2015), 41-484.

(ISBN 978-90-04-33828-9)

Tome/Volume 382 (2015)

Cooper, D., and C. Kuner: Data Protection Law and International Dispute Resolution, 9-174.
Jia, B. B.: International Case Law in the Development of International Law, 175-397.

(ISBN 978-90-04-33830-2)

Tome/Volume 383 (2016)

Bennouna, M.: Le droit international entre la lettre et l'esprit, 9-231.
Iovane, M.: L'influence de la multiplication des juridictions internationales sur l'application du droit international, 233-446.

(ISBN 978-90-04-34648-2)

Tome/Volume 384 (2016)

Symeonides, S. C.: Private International Law Idealism, Pragmatism, Eclecticism, 9-385. (ISBN 978-90-04-35131-8)

Tome/Volume 385 (2016)

Berman, Sir F.: Why Do we Need a Law of Treaties?, 9-31.
Marrella, F.: Protection internationale des droits de l'homme et activités des sociétés transnationales, 33-435.

(ISBN 978-90-04-35132-5)

Tome/Volume 386 (2016)

Murphy, S. D.: International Law relating to Islands, 9-266.
Cataldi, G.: La mise en œuvre des décisions des tribunaux internationaux dans l'ordre interne, 267-428.

(ISBN 978-90-04-35133-2)

Tome/Volume 387 (2016)

Lequette, Y. : Les mutations du droit international privé : vers un changement de paradigme ?, 9-644. (ISBN 978-90-04-36118-8)

Tome/Volume 388 (2016)

Bonell, M. J. : The Law Governing International Commercial Contracts : Hard Law versus Soft Law, 9-48.
Hess, B. : The Private-Public Divide in International Dispute Resolution, 49-266.
(ISBN 978-90-04-36120-1)

Tome/Volume 389 (2017)

Muir Watt, H. : Discours sur les méthodes du droit international privé (des formes juridiques de l'inter-altérité). Cours général de droit international privé, 9-410.
(ISBN 978-90-04-36122-5)

Tome/Volume 390 (2017)

Rau, A. S. : The Allocation of Power between Arbitral Tribunals and State Courts, 9-396. (ISBN 978-90-04-36475-2)

Tome/Volume 391 (2017)

Cançado Trindade, A. A. : Les tribunaux internationaux et leur mission commune de réalisation de la justice : développements, état actuel et perspectives, Conférence spéciale (2017), 9-101.
Mariño Menéndez, F. M. : The Prohibition of Torture in Public International Law, 103-185.
Swinarski, C. : Effets pour l'individu des régimes de protection de droit international, 187-369.
Cot, J.-P. : L'éthique du procès international (leçon inaugurale), 371-384.
(ISBN 978-90-04-37781-3)

Tome/Volume 392 (2017)

Novak, F. : The System of Reparations in the Jurisprudence of the Inter-American Court of Human Rights, 9-203.
Nolte, G. : Treaties and their Practice – Symptoms of their Rise or Decline, 205-397. (ISBN 978-90-04-39273-1)

Tome/Volume 393 (2017)

Tiburcio, C. : The Current Practice of International Co-Operation in Civil Matters, 9-310.
Ruiz De Santiago, J. : Aspects juridiques des mouvements forcés de personnes, 311-468.
(ISBN 978-90-04-39274-8)

Tome/Volume 394 (2017)

Kostin, A. A. : International Commercial Arbitration, with Special Focus on Russia, 9-86.
Cuniberti, G. : Le fondement de l'effet des jugements étrangers, 87-283.
(ISBN 978-90-04-39275-5)

Tome/Volume 395 (2018)

Salerno, F.: The Identity and Continuity of Personal Status in Contemporary Private International Law, 9-198.
Chinkin, C. M.: United Nations Accountability for Violations of International Human Rights Law, 199-320. (ISBN 978-90-04-40710-7)

Tome/Volume 396 (2018)

Jacquet, J.-M.: Droit international privé et arbitrage commercial international, 9-36.
Brown Weiss, E.: Establishing Norms in a Kaleidoscopic World. General Course on Public International Law, 37-415. (ISBN 978-90-04-41002-2)

Tome/Volume 397 (2018)

D'Avout, L.: L'entreprise et les conflits internationaux de lois, 9-612.
(ISBN 978-90-04-41221-7)

Tome/Volume 398 (2018)

Treves, T.: The Expansion of International Law, General Course on Public International Law (2015), 9-398.
(ISBN 978-90-04-41224-8)

Tome/Volume 399 (2018)

Kanehara, A.: Reassessment of the Acts of the State in the Law of State Responsibility, 9-266.
Buxbaum, H. L.: Public Regulation and Private Enforcement in a Global Economy: Strategies for Managing Conflict, 267-442.
(ISBN 978-90-04-41670-3)

Tome/Volume 400 (2018)

Chedly, L.: L'efficacité de l'arbitrage commercial international, 9-624.
(ISBN 978-90-04-42388-6)

Tome/Volume 401 (2019)

Wood, P.: Extraterritorial Enforcement of Regulatory Laws, 9-126.
Nishitani, Yuko: Identité culturelle en droit international privé de la famille, 127-450.
(ISBN 978-90-04-42389-3)

Tome/Volume 402 (2019)

Kinsch, P.: Le rôle du politique en droit international privé. Cours général de droit international privé, 9-384.
Dasser, F.: "Soft Law" in International Commercial Arbitration, 385-596.
(ISBN 978-90-04-42392-3)

Tome/Volume 403 (2019)

Daudet, Y.: 1919-2019, le flux du multilatéralisme, 9-48.
Kessedjian, C.: Le tiers impartial et indépendant en droit international, juge, arbitre, médiateur, conciliateur, 49-643. (ISBN 978-90-04-42468-5)

Tome/Volume 404 (2019)

Rajamani, L.: Innovation and Experimentation in the International Climate Change Regime, 9-234.
Sorel, J.-M.: Quelle normativité pour le droit des relations monétaires et financières internationales?, 235-403.
(ISBN 978-90-04-43142-3)

Tome/Volume 405 (2019)

Paulsson, J.: Issues arising from Findings of Denial of Justice, 9-74.
Brunée, J.: Procedure and Substance in International Environmental Law, 75-240. (ISBN 978-90-04-43300-7)

Tome/Volume 406 (2019)

Bundy, R.: The Practice of International Law, Inaugural Lecture, 9-26.
Gama, L.: Les principes d'UNIDROIT et la loi régissant les contrats de commerce, 27-343. (ISBN 978-90-04-43611-4)

Tome/Volume 407 (2020)

Wouters, J.: Le statut juridique des standards publics et privés dans les relations économiques internationales, 9-122.
Maljean-Dubois, S.: Le droit international de la biodiversité, 123-538.
(ISBN 978-90-04-43643-5)

Tome/Volume 408 (2020)

Cançado Trindade, A. A.: Reflections on the Realization of Justice in the Era of Contemporary International Tribunals, 9-88.
González, C.: Party Autonomy in International Family Law, 89-361.
(ISBN 978-90-04-44504-8)

Tome/Volume 409 (2020)

Shany, Y: The Extraterritorial Application of International Human Rights Law, 9-152.
Besson, S.: La *due diligence* en droit international, 153-398.
(ISBN 978-90-04-44505-5)

Tome/Volume 410 (2020)

Koh, H. H.: American Schools of International Law, 9-93.
Peters, A.: Animals in International Law, 95-544. (ISBN 978-90-04-44897-1)

Tome/Volume 411 (2020)

Cahin, G: Reconstrution et construction de l'Etat en droit international, 9-573.
(ISBN 978-90-04-44898-8)

Tome/Volume 412 (2020)

Momtaz, D: La hiérarchisation de l'ordre juridique international, cours général de droit international public, 9-252.
Grammaticaki-Alexiou, A.: Best Interests of the Child in Private International Law, 253-434. (ISBN 978-90-04-44899-5)

Tome/Volume 413 (2021)

Ferrari, F.: Forum Shopping Despite Unification of Law, 9-290.
(ISBN 978-90-04-46100-0)

Tome/Volume 414 (2021)

Pellet, A.: Le droit international à la lumière de la pratique: l'introuvable théorie de la réalité. Cours général de droit international public, 9-547.
(ISBN 978-90-04-46547-3)

Tome/Volume 415 (2021)

Trooboff, P. D.: Globalization, Personal Jurisdiction and the Internet. Responding to the Challenge of adapting settled Principles and Precedents. General Course of Private International Law, 9-321.
(ISBN 978-90-04-46730-9)

Tome/Volume 416 (2021)

Wolfrum, R: Solidarity and Community Interests: Driving Forces for the Interpretation and Development of International Law. General Course on Public International Law, 9-479.
(ISBN 978-90-04-46827-6)

Tome/Volume 417 (2021)

d'Argent, P.: Les obligations internationales, 9-210.
Schabas, W. A.: Relationships Between International Criminal Law and Other Branches of International Law, 211-392. (ISBN 978-90-04-47239-6)

Tome/Volume 418 (2021)

Bollée, S.: Les pouvoirs inhérents des arbitres internationaux, 9-224.
Tladi, D.: The Extraterritorial Use of Force against Non-State Actors, 225-360.
(ISBN 978-90-04-50380-9)

Tome/Volume 419 (2021)

Kolb, R.: Le droit international comme corps de «droit privé» et de «droit public». Cours général de droit international public, 9-668.
(ISBN 978-90-04-50381-6)

Tome/Volume 420 (2021)

Perrakis, S.: La protection internationale au profit des personnes vulnérables en droit international des droits de l'homme, 9-497.
(ISBN 978-90-04-50382-3)

Tome/Volume 421 (2021)

Estrella Faria, J. A.: La protection des biens culturels d'intérêt religieux en droit international public et en droit international privé, 9-333.
(ISBN 978-90-04-50829-3)

Tome/Volume 422 (2021)

Karayanni, M.: The Private International Law of Class Actions: A Functional approach, 9-248.
Mahmoudi, S.: Self-Defence and "Unwilling or Unable" States, 249-399.
(ISBN 978-90-04-50830-9)

Tome/Volume 423 (2022)

Kinnear, M.: The Growth, Challenges and Future Prospects for Investment Dispute Settlement, 9-36.
Weller, M.: "Mutual Trust": A Suitable Foundation for Private International Law in Regional Integration Communities and Beyond?, 37-378.
(ISBN 978-90-04-51411-9)

Tome/Volume 424 (2022)

Asada, M.: International Law of Nuclear Non-proliferation and Disarmament, 9-726. (ISBN 978-90-04-51769-1)

Tome/Volume 425 (2022)

Metou, B. M.: Le contrôle international des dérogations aux droits de l'homme, 9-294.
Silva Romero, E.: Legal Fictions in the Language of International Arbitration, 295-423. (ISBN 978-90-04-51770-7)

Tome/Volume 426 (2022)

Kuijper, P. J.: Delegation and International Organizations, 9-240.
McCaffrey, S. C.: The Evolution of the Law of International Watercourses, 241-384.
(ISBN 978-90-04-51771-4)

Tome/Volume 427 (2022)

Kaufmann-Kohler, G.: Indépendance et impartialité du juge et de l'arbitre dans le règlement des différends entre investisseurs et Etats (leçon inaugurale), 9-50.
Boyle, A.: International Lawmaking in an Environmental Context, 51-108.
Weller, M.-P.: La méthode tripartite du droit international privé: désignation, reconnaissance, considération, 109-210.
Mourre, A.: La légitimité de l'arbitrage, 211-288. (ISBN 978-90-04-52770-6)

Tome/Volume 428 (2023)

Laghmani, S.: Islam et droit international, 9-128.
Oyarzábal, M. J. A.: The Influence of Public International Law upon Private International Law in History and Theory and in the Formation and Application of the Law, 129-525.
(ISBN 978-90-04-54440-6)

Tome/Volume 429 (2023)

Moreno Rodríguez, J. A.: Private (And Public) International Law In Investment Arbitration, 9-702.
(ISBN 978-90-04-54462-8)

Tome/Volume 430 (2023)

Casella, P. B. : Droit international, histoire et culture, 9-610.

(ISBN 978-90-04-54463-5)

Tome/Volume 431 (2023)

Yeo, T. M. : Common Law, Equity and Statute. The Effect of Juridical Sources on Choice-of-Law Methodology, 9-88.

Frigessi Di Rattalma, M. : New Trends in Private International Law of Insurance Contracts, 89-200.

Roosevelt III, K. : The Third Restatement of Conflict of Laws, 201-284.

Sands, P. : Colonialism: A Short History of International Law in Five Acts, 285-410.

(ISBN 978-90-04-54464-2)

Tome/Volume 432 (2023)

Ruiz Fabri, H. : La justice procédurale en droit international, 9-44.

Shaw, M. : A House of Many Rooms: The Rise, Fall and Rise Again of Territorial Sovereignty?, 45-78.

Kovács, P. : L'individu et sa position devant la Cour pénale internationale, 79-421.

(ISBN 978-90-04-54465-9)

Tome/Volume 433 (2023)

Eyffinger, A. : The Hague Academy at 100: Its Rationale, Role and Record, 9-97.

Thorn, K. : The Protection of Small and Medium-Sized Enterprises in Private International Law, 99-205.

Moollan, S. : Parallel Proceedings in International Arbitration. Theoretical Analysis and the Search for Practical Solutions, 207-303.

(ISBN 978-90-04-54469-7)

Tome/Volume 434 (2023)

Stephan, Paul B. : Applying Municipal Law in International Disputes, 9-214

Casado Raigón, R. : La contribution des juridictions internationales au développement du droit de la mer, 215-511.

(ISBN 978-90-04-69182-7)